On-Premise Catering

On-Premise Catering

HOTELS, CONVENTION CENTERS, ARENAS, CLUBS, *AND* MORE

Second Edition

PATTI J. SHOCK, CPCE | CHERYL SGOVIO, CPCE |
JOHN M. STEFANELLI

WILEY

JOHN WILEY & SONS, INC.

Published by John Wiley & Sons, Inc., Hoboken, New Jersey
Published simultaneously in Canada

For general information on our other products and services or for technical support, please contact our Customer Care Department within the United States at (800) 762-2974, outside the United States at (317) 572-3993 or fax (317) 572-4002.

Wiley also publishes its books in a variety of electronic formats. Some content that appears in print may not be available in electronic books. For more information about Wiley products, visit our web site at www.wiley.com.

Library of Congress Cataloging-in-Publication Data:
Shock, Patti J.
   On-premise catering : hotels, convention centers, arenas, clubs, and more / Patti J. Shock, Cheryl Sgovio, John M. Stefanelli. — 2nd ed.
      p. cm.
   Includes bibliographical references and index.
   ISBN 978-0-470-55175-2 (cloth); ISBN 978-1-118-10887-1 (ebk); ISBN 978-1-118-10888-8 (ebk); ISBN 978-1-118-10889-5
   1. Caterers and catering—Handbooks, manuals, etc.   I. Sgovio, Cheryl.   II. Stefanelli, John M.   III. Title.
   TX921.S48 2011
   642'.4—dc22
                                                                                            2010037968

Printed in the United States of America
10 9 8 7 6 5 4 3 2 1

Contents

Foreword

Search online for the definition of the word *catering* and you will find more than 120,000 pages of results. Most of these definitions have merit. Yes, caterers do provide food, entertainment, and supplies at social gatherings. Caterers are attentive and solicitous. And yes, caterers take special pains in seeking to gratify others' needs. Turn on the television though, and you may get a different definition of what it is like to be in the catering profession. It is all about party planning, celebrity events, cooking, decor, entertainment, and showcasing over-the-top food and beverage. Being a caterer has to be the most exciting and fun job ever . . . right?

Perception, though, is not always reality. But with the right passion and dedication, a career in catering can be an amazing ride.

As a student attending the University of Nevada Las Vegas, I did not know where I would end up. I knew I loved working with people and wanting to make them happy. I knew I belonged someplace in the hospitality field. I was fortunate to have two of the authors of this book, Patti Shock and John Stefanelli, as professors. Imagine having the ability to get their first-hand knowledge in this exciting field. As many caterers have, I took an indirect route after college, working in other areas of hospitality. But fate brought me into the catering business. A stroke of luck would give me the opportunity to work with the third author, Cheryl Sgovio, during her tenure at the Rio All-Suite Hotel and Casino.

My time with Cheryl helped me develop into the person I am today. I was fortunate to get both academic learning and real-world experience from these three amazing people.

What makes a great catering executive? One critical skill is the ability to wear many different hats. A catering executive has to be a great salesperson, often selling him or herself along with the facility. You must be proficient in food and beverage knowledge, presentation styles, event types, religious practices, and dietary needs. You have to stay on top of trends. You need to be knowledgeable about the production and audio-visual components of an event. And, all the while, you have to be able to paint the picture in the clients' minds on how their events will meet their goals and expectations.

You must be able to clearly communicate clients' expectations to everyone involved. A catering executive has to be strong yet amenable to ensure that what has been promised is what is delivered. You are the producers of a sea of paperwork that gives the operating departments direction on every element of the event.

An effective catering executive also has to have thick skin and a warm heart and the ability to hold his or her ground yet be compassionate to the client's needs. Catering executives are given the charge to find balance between the business side and the human side of every event. Having the ability to be everything to everyone is not a skill that can be learned, but one that has to be earned. You are the orchestra leader, the captain, the glue that keeps it all together.

The catering industry provides you with the incredible opportunity to be involved in the most special days in people's lives, times of great celebration, and events that allow companies to grow their businesses. The catering business is like no other, demanding and rewarding all at the same time. For most, once you are in, you are hooked. There is no other feeling in the world that compares to getting that big contract signed, completing a really successful event, or receiving sincere gratitude from a client because the event would not have been the same without you. The euphoria is infectious, and it keeps you coming back for more.

Yet all of these things just scratch the surface of what being a catering executive really means.

The authors took on the enormous task of researching and funneling down what the real job of an on-premise caterer is. In this text, you will find a good foundation of learning on the organizational structures, day-to-day operations, and realities of the job. It is a comprehensive resource for students and will help them gain a better understanding of the various roles the catering executive may play in different types of catering operations. This book will give you insight into the infrastructure of the complex job of a catering professional.

As you set forth on your educational and professional journey, I hope you find this industry to be as exciting, inspiring, and satisfying as I have. Put on your seatbelts and get ready for the ride!

Michele Polci, CPCE, CMP
Director of Catering Sales / Las Vegas
Caesars Entertainment

Preface

Catering is one of the fastest-growing segments of the food and beverage industry. The objective of this book is to provide all levels of on-premise catering and banquet professionals with an in-depth, one-stop source of generally accepted catering principles and procedures.

This book includes several major topics. Readers wishing to gain a perspective of the on-premise catering business will be especially interested in Chapters 1 and 2. Those who want specific information that can be used to plan, develop, implement, supervise, and follow-up on a catering function should read and study the remaining chapters.

Chapters 3 through 11 contain an extensive discussion of on-premise catering procedures as well as a considerable amount of reference material. This book will assist the reader who needs to know, for example, how many servers to schedule for a particular function, how to price meal and beverage functions, how to develop a catering proposal, and how to set up function space.

No one book can claim to be the last word on any subject. Much of the material here is subject to opinion and interpretation. We believe the material presented in this book provides a thorough view of on-premise catering. However, because a book is a document subject to revision as our industry changes, we welcome your ideas and suggestions.

We want to thank the following reviewers of the manuscript for their important contributions.

Linwood Campbell, CPCE

The Westin Charlotte, Charlotte, North Carolina

Amy Dyke, CPCE, CMP

Caesars Entertainment, Las Vegas, Nevada

James Filtz, CPCE

Sheraton Hotel, New York, New York

Alisa Gaylon, CCP

The Cooking and Hospitality Institute of Chicago

Lisa Hopkins, CPCE, CMP

The Houstonian Hotel, Club and Spa, Houston, Texas

Michele Polci, CPCE, CMP

Caesars Entertainment, Las Vegas, Nevada

Chapter 1

OVERVIEW OF ON-PREMISE

CATERING

On-premise catering is considered to be any function—banquet, reception, or event—that is held on the physical premises of the venue or facility that is producing the function. On-premise catering differs from off-premise catering, where the function takes place in a remote or off-site location, such as a client's home, a park, an art gallery, a museum, or even a parking lot, and where the staff, food, and decor must be transported to that location.

While some on-premise caterers offer off-premise catering, most do not "cater out." A few of them, though, particularly hotels and restaurants, have entered the off-premise catering market and are capable of providing off-site production and service. Particularly during economic slowdowns, hotels, restaurants, and other catering venues have begun looking to capture additional revenues by expanding their off-site options. While exact statistics are not kept for these two segments, it is estimated that on-premise catering accounts for about two-thirds of all catering sales in the United States, with off-premise catering accounting for the remaining one-third.

Generally speaking, each catered event, on- or off-premise, has one host and one bill, although some events are paid for in cash by individual guests, either in part or in full.

Catering, both on-premise and off-premise, has enjoyed success and growth over the years. It is thought that catering and take-out will generate considerable growth in U.S. foodservice sales throughout the foreseeable future. This generally holds true even during recessions, as people still celebrate marriages, birthdays, anniversaries, and various corporate events, though they may be scaled back.

Every day thousands of business and social groups get together to hold meetings and enjoy other people's company and the variety of refreshments that are usually found at these gatherings. Groups generally prefer professionally prepared and served food and beverages. This allows hosts to concentrate solely on their personal, social, and business activities while simultaneously enjoying the events. And, as a bonus, they can leave the cleanup to someone else.

On-premise caterers—such as hotels, convention centers, conference centers, private city and country clubs, and restaurants with banquet rooms or event space—usually have the advantage of offering many services under one roof. They can also provide sufficient space to house the entire event and plenty of parking.

Many localities have other spaces where events can be held, such as independent banquet halls, civic auditoriums, stadiums, arenas, ethnic social clubs, fraternal organizations, women's clubs, athletic clubs, hospitals, universities, libraries, executive dining rooms in office buildings or corporate headquarters, churches, recreation rooms in large apartment or condominium complexes, retirement communities, parks, fairgrounds, museums, and aquariums. Some of these facilities are often very competitive, as they have more flexible price structures due to their lower overhead expenses. Some are public facilities and are tax-exempt. A number of these facilities provide their own catering in-house, while others are leased to and operated by contract foodservice companies that have exclusive contracts. Still others will rent their facilities to off-premise caterers and usually have a list of preferred or approved caterers.

Another competitor for catering business is the proliferation of take-out services. Many supermarkets, warehouse clubs, and department stores have developed gourmet take-out, deli, and bakery facilities and can produce beautiful, reasonably priced buffet platters and specialty items. More and more restaurants are heavily engaged in take-out business, particularly around the holidays. However, catering out may disrupt the normal workflow and efficiency of the operation, can damage morale, and can skew ordering and purchasing routines if not properly monitored.

Off-premise functions can be a significant source of additional sales revenue and profits for those catering organizations that have the necessary equipment and personnel to handle large off-site catered affairs. However, unless the company is set up to do this correctly, the work can be too distracting and the added expense could wipe out any incremental profits. For example, transporting perishable food requires a refrigerated truck or a lot of ice to maintain safe food temperatures.

Staffing is also an issue. Servers in on-premise facilities are accustomed to a division of labor and often are not pleased when they are asked to do tasks off-site that are not required when in the facility. In most facilities, servers do not set up tables, chairs, and equipment or do the cleaning, hauling, and other duties that are required at an off-premise site. There may also be union implications if job descriptions are violated.

TYPES OF CATERING

Catering can be classified as social catering or corporate (business) catering. Social catering includes such events as weddings, bar/bat mitzvahs, high school reunions, birthday parties, and charity events. In most markets, it is estimated that social catering accounts for about 25 percent of all catering sales.

Business catering includes such events as association conventions and meetings, civic meetings, corporate sales or stockholder meetings, recognition banquets, product launches, educational training sessions, seller-buyer entertaining, service awards banquets, or hospitality suites. It is estimated that business catering accounts for about 75 percent of all catering sales in most markets. This is due to the sheer volume of people served daily at meetings in hotels, arenas, and convention centers, where meals for thousands are produced regularly.

Some mobile caterers, with the proper equipment, provide complete meal production and service on location. For instance, a few companies specialize in feeding firefighters working in remote areas; disaster relief workers; concert, movie, and television production staff on location; people taking extended camping trips or on fishing/rafting excursions; construction workers on-site; and so on.

TYPES OF CATERERS

Hotel Catering

The hotel caterer often has an advantage in this competitive business because normally it can offer many services under one roof as well as sufficient space to house the entire event, including sleeping rooms, thereby enticing the customer with a one-stop shopping opportunity. In addition, if a client is able to book all or a large percentage of the sleeping rooms in the hotel, he or she may receive catering concessions because of the sleeping room revenue that comes with booking the group at the hotel.

Hotels can have anywhere from less than 5,000 square feet of meeting and event space to 1 million or more square feet. Some hotels are also able to do events in other areas of the hotel, such as the pool area, restaurants that may be closed for lunch, showrooms, and so on.

An upscale hotel can provide a more glamorous and exciting location, in addition to upgraded service and amenities. Resorts often have additional options to hold outdoor functions at remote locations on the property. For example, at one time, the Pointe Hilton at Tapatio Cliffs Resort in Phoenix, Arizona, had a special hayride party where guests were transported by horse-drawn wagon to a hill-top where they enjoyed a mountainside barbecue with all the trimmings.

Convention Center Catering

Most convention centers are public facilities and foodservice is contracted out to companies such as Aramark or Sodexo. Convention centers primarily attract business catering, as the facilities generally are built for trade shows, association meetings, and corporate events. Venues are typically classified as a convention center if they have at least 25,000 square feet of exhibit space in addition to other meeting and event rooms. While they may have some upscale rooms targeted at high-end social events, the main purpose of these facilities is to attract groups of people to the city to fill hotel sleeping rooms and bring revenue to the city's overall economy.

Conference Center Catering

Conference centers are similar to convention centers in that they have a variety of meeting and banquet rooms. They differ in that while they may be able to accommodate small exhibit setups, they do not have an exhibit hall.

Most conference center catering is done buffet-style in a common dining hall. Attendees are assigned sections of the dining hall and certain time ranges, so not all groups are hitting the buffet at one time. They usually have private dining rooms for special meals. Some even have restaurants.

Conference centers operate on a complete meeting package (CMP) plan, which means that guests pay one price for sleeping room, food, meeting space, and audiovisual and related services. There would be additional costs for alcoholic beverages or for dining in the restaurant.

Conference centers are also noted for the permanent refreshment break, which is available all day instead of only at predetermined times. This allows a group the flexibility to break when it is convenient.

Restaurant Catering

Some restaurants have attached banquet or private dining rooms that can be used for catered events. It is expensive to maintain a room that might be empty three or four nights per week, though, so the banquet room is often used as overflow restaurant dining space on busy nights. A restaurant may also be willing to close the entire restaurant for a private event if the group does a "buyout" of the entire facility. The restaurant or catering manager who books these events must be certain, though, that the revenue gained from the event is greater than the revenue that would be realized if the restaurant was open to the general public. Additionally, closing the restaurant to the public could potentially harm future sales, as guests may not be willing to go there on another night not knowing if the establishment will be open to the public or closed for a private event.

A restaurant can book many small functions if it takes the time to court this business. One type of business that a restaurant generally can pursue is regular, ongoing meetings. Examples of these events include meetings of Toastmasters, local associations, and fraternal organizations such as Rotary Club and Kiwanis. A hotel, though, often is not able to commit to these types of ongoing events, as they tie up space that may be needed for a large property-wide conference.

Private Club Catering

Private clubs do a great deal of catering for their members. Country clubs concentrate mainly on social events, such as weddings and dances, often because of their built-in amenities such as golf courses or lovely pools that make for attractive photograph locations. In-town clubs specialize in business catering, such as corporate meetings, board luncheons, and civic events.

An average club has less space and fewer staff than many hotels or large restaurants, so the catering director there likely will wear many hats.

Private clubs are limited in the amount of outside business they may accept. However, if the group has a participant who is a member of the club, the member can sponsor the event.

For more information on private membership clubs, visit the Club Managers Association of America website at www.cmaa.org.

Stadium and Arena Catering

Stadiums and arenas generally cater for a wide variety of events. This includes both publicly ticketed events (for example, meals served in dressing rooms, crew meals, pre- or post-event VIP parties) and events that are booked for private companies, organizations, and individuals. Their size and location often influence the type of events they attract. These venues may offer an appealing alternative to a hotel or convention center for large corporate events. They may also appeal to more budget-conscious groups, particularly if they are located on a college campus that is looking to fill dates between major events.

Many stadiums and arenas also offer catering in VIP and luxury suites along with other exclusive areas within the venue such as a club level or sky lounge.

These areas have restricted access and generally either are available through special-purchase tickets or are leased for a specified period of time by an individual or company. For example, a company may lease on an annual basis a private suite that it uses to host clients, potential clients, and other invited guests during events. The company will then work with the catering executive to have various high-end food and beverages available for its guests. The club level is generally a larger common area that guests purchase tickets for either on an event-by-event basis or for a specified period of time. These areas are usually in a preferred area and have higher-end seating, restrooms, and amenities than the general arena. In outdoor stadiums, both suites and club levels are most often indoors with additional outdoor seating, giving guests the option to remain indoors if the weather is not favorable during an event. Typically there is complimentary food available along with either complimentary or reduced-price beverages. With anywhere from twenty to more than a hundred suites and one or more club-level areas per stadium or arena, this can represent a significant amount of catering.

Casino Catering

In many regards, casino catering is similar to hotel catering, as most casinos with sizeable event space are located within a hotel.

One notable difference is the order in which events may be booked. In a non-gaming hotel, the sales department has the first opportunity to book event space to groups that require sleeping rooms, as those groups bring in more overall revenue to the hotel. Catering-only events (with ten or fewer sleeping rooms required per night) are then able to fill in within a given window of time, such as thirty, sixty, or ninety days prior to the date. In some markets, particularly those that do a lot of social business, catering-only events are permitted to book weekend events further out, while weekdays are still reserved for corporate business.

In gaming hotels, though, there is a third element to factor in: the needs of the casino marketing department. This is the department responsible for developing events that will attract high-stakes gamblers to the property. These events may range from a simple slot tournament to an elaborate New Year's Eve gala. The catering department will then work with casino marketing to develop and implement the theme for each of these events. In casinos where gaming revenue is the hotel's largest revenue source, these events are given first priority when booking space, followed by business events with large sleeping room needs, and last by catering-only events.

Other Types of Catering Operations

For-profit hospitals do a good amount of catering business for medical meetings and staff functions. In most cases, they compete directly with hotels or high-end restaurants for these functions.

There are several types of tax-exempt organizations that offer catering services to anyone willing to pay for them. For instance, universities, colleges, hospitals, libraries, churches, museums, and military clubs vigorously compete for these events, which help subsidize their primary, nonprofit activities. Many taxpaying catering businesses are especially unhappy with these nonprofit competitors; however, nonprofit groups consistently fight any type of government restraints on these activities.

Contract foodservice companies operate many facilities that are capable of supporting catering events. For instance, many of these firms operate foodservice in large office buildings, where executive dining rooms can be used for special parties and meetings. Some contract foodservice companies also are capable of handling off-premise catering functions.

Take-out and delivery business accounts for an ever-increasing proportion of total U.S. foodservice sales. While it has been very successful for restaurants, it is unlikely that most hotel caterers would want to compete heavily in these business segments. However, in some cases hotel properties have done so quite successfully. For example, at Marriott's Camelback Inn in Scottsdale, Arizona, residents living next to its golf courses can dial the hotel's room service department. A room service server hops on a golf cart and delivers the finished products. The hotel also takes orders for box lunches.

Off-premise catering is done at an off-site location where everything must be transported to that location. Often, off-premise catering involves producing food at a central kitchen with delivery to and service provided at a client's location.

Part or all of the production of food can be executed or finished at the event location. Often off-premise caterers must rely on generators for electricity, truck in potable water, devise a trash system, and otherwise "rough it." Off-premise caterers work in a different environment for virtually every event and have available only what they bring with them.

Usually the biggest barrier facing the on-premise caterer who wants to get involved with off-premise catering is the lack of adequate vehicles. One way for hotels, stadiums, arenas, or convention centers to get around this stumbling block is to borrow another department's truck or van. Another method used is to rent old UPS vans, milk trucks, or laundry trucks; they work well because they back up readily to loading docks and equipment can be rolled in very easily. The only problem with these strategies, though, is unless the vehicles meet local health district codes, you cannot use them to transport food.

If a regular client requests off-premise catering, it is not smart to refuse the request. If you cannot handle the request, it is best to refer the client to a reputable off-premise caterer whose standards and reputation parallel yours. It is a mistake to refer the client to an unknown off-premise caterer who does not share your standards.

Even though off-premise projects may be minimally profitable for some catering organizations, a few may be willing to get involved with them in order to satisfy good clients. These caterers may decide to maintain vending machines, prepare box lunches, cater an off-site picnic, stock the sleeping rooms' in-room bar cabinets, and so forth, rather than divert this business to competitors.

One form of off-premise catering provided by many on-premise caterers is the box lunch option. For instance, a group may request individual box lunches for a day when they will be taking a bus tour. Alternatively, a catering and/or kitchen employee could pack foods and beverages, ride with the group, and set up a small picnic-style buffet at a rest stop location.

It would appear that sooner or later, the on-premise caterer will get involved with some type of off-premise catering function. As the costs of business increase every year, so too does the need to seek out other forms of business. At the very least, you must be prepared to handle the occasional request or else risk losing current and future business.

CATERING DEPARTMENT MANAGEMENT FUNCTIONS

The person in charge of the catering department must perform the normal management functions. Whether a one-person department in a restaurant or a convention center with a staff of thirty, the catering department manager(s) must engage in the following:

1. *Selling.* The catering department must first book events by obtaining new clients and/or working with previous clients. This is accomplished through various forms of advertising, attending industry-related and networking events, prospecting for new clients, cultivating relationships with existing clients, and so on. Once a potential event is identified, the catering manager will do site visits as needed, prepare contracts, and work with the client on all aspects of the event.

2. *Planning.* The catering department must accomplish its financial and non-financial objectives. To do so, it must develop appropriate marketing, production, and service procedures. It also must ensure that the department's operating budgets and other action plans are consistent with the facility's overall company objectives.

3. *Organizing.* The catering department must organize the human and other resources needed to follow the plan. Staff members must be recruited and trained, work schedules must be prepared, and performance evaluations must be administered.

4. *Directing.* Employee supervision is an integral part of every supervisor's job. Supervisory style will emanate from top management. The catering department's supervisory procedures must be consistent with company policies.

5. *Controlling.* The catering department manager must make certain that actual performance corresponds with planned performance. Effective financial controls ensure that actual profit and loss statements are consistent with pro forma budgets. And effective quality controls mean that production and service will meet company standards.

CATERING DEPARTMENT OBJECTIVES

Catering departments have a variety of objectives. The weight given to each one will depend on company policy. Some of the most common objectives are:

1. *Earn a fair profit on assets invested in the catering business.* Assets include both hard cost items, such as furniture, fixtures, equipment, and small wares, that are needed before any events may take place, and soft cost items, such as supplies, linens, and food and beverages, that are needed for specific events.

2. *Generate sufficient catering sales volume, enough to defray all expenses and leave a fair profit.* Caterers must be careful not to generate a lot of business that will not pay for itself. They must practice selective sales strategies in order to maximize profits. Usually the only time a catering executive should consider booking a marginally profitable event is if it is a party designed to show off the catering facilities, such as a charity event. It may also be contemplated if the property wants to host VIPs who may indirectly generate future catering revenues, or if the event occurs during the slow season and will keep part-time staff employed.

3. *Deliver customer satisfaction.* This will lead to repeat patronage as well as positive referrals. Any foodservice operation thrives on repeat patronage; the same holds true for the catering segment.

4. *Provide consistent quality and service.* Customers are happy when the actual quality and service received parallel those that were promised. Punctuality and consistency are hallmarks of the well-run catering department.

5. *Convey a particular image.* Caterers often want to be known as specialists in certain types of products and services, such as weddings or unusual themed events. They strive to be unique because they want customers to think of them whenever a specific atmosphere or ambience is required. Catering is often a facility's most visible characteristic on the local and national levels. It alone has the most potential to become a facility's "signature," that is, its major claim to fame.

6. *Develop a reputation for dependability.* Regardless of the pressure that any event places on the staff, catering departments want clients to have confidence that their needs will be met. The catering department must serve as an effective liaison between clients and all of the company's services.

7. *Develop a reputation for flexibility.* To be dependable, the typical caterer must be flexible. The catering department must be able to react on a moment's notice. Clients will remember fondly a company that bailed them out at the last minute.

8. *Deliver what was promised.* It is important to stay within the budget that was discussed with the client by not adding unexpected charges. If clients request an item or service on-site that will increase the bill, it is imperative to let them know of the charge at the time of request and have them approve the increase on the banquet check. Delivering what was promised, at the price agreed upon, is essential for developing and maintaining good client relationships and ensuring repeat business.

CATERING DEPARTMENT ORGANIZATION

Catering departments are organized according to the needs and size of the particular organization. With a hotel, often the primary profit center is its sleeping rooms, with the catering department usually being the second most profitable department. Consequently, all hotel departments generally are organized and administered to maximize the sales and profits of sleeping rooms and catered functions. The exception to this would be a gaming hotel, notably those in Las Vegas and Atlantic City, where often gaming revenues bring in the most profit, as discussed previously.

There are two general types of hotel catering department organizations. In one form, the department is organized in such a way that all catering personnel are under the supervision of the hotel's food and beverage director. (See Figures 1.1 and 1.2.) Most non-hotel-based catering facilities also use this structure. In this method, the food and beverage director is responsible for the hotel's kitchens, restaurant outlets, and banquet operations as well as for client solicitation and service. Under this structure, catering must secure the right to sell function space from the sales department, which controls meeting space. However, meetings are often booked years in advance, and savvy meeting planners, not knowing all of their space needs that far in advance, will institute a "hold all space" clause in their contracts; sales managers are often reluctant to call their clients and ask

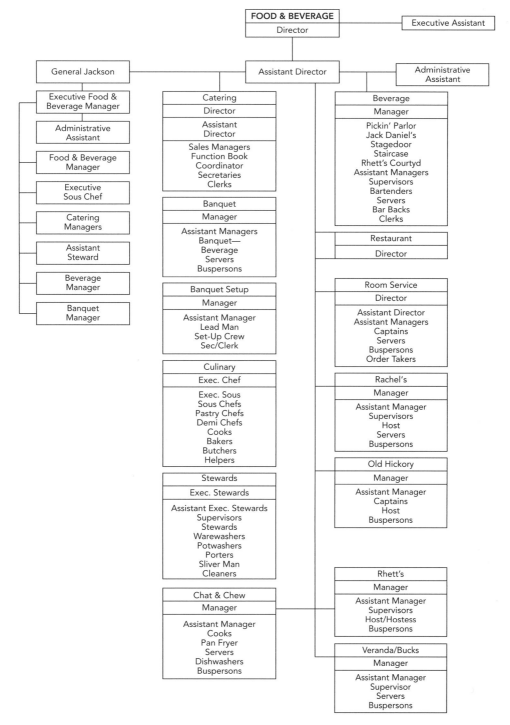

FIGURE 1.1 Food and beverage department organization chart. (Courtesy Opryland Hotel, Nashville, Tennessee.)

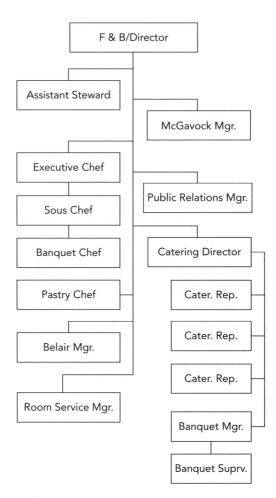

FIGURE 1.2 Food and beverage department organization chart. (Courtesy Music City Sheraton Corporation.)

them to release space that they are holding for a meeting they have booked. In this organization structure, convention services managers are primarily responsible for room setup, not food or beverage.

Alternatively, the catering department may be organized so that catering sales personnel are under the supervision of the sales and marketing director, while other employees, especially the banquet servers, may or may not report to the food and beverage director (see Figure 1.3, pages 16–17). In this situation, there is generally a director of catering and convention services, who must work closely with the director of sales and marketing as well as with the food and beverage director.

Catering managers and convention services managers would be in the same department, both taking care of the food, beverage, and room setup needs of the clients. Convention service managers don't sell the event but take over client business booked by sales and marketing. They handle the planning and logistics of any meals or receptions and develop the appropriate service procedures needed to plan and implement successful and profitable catered events. In this scenario, the only type of selling the convention services managers would do would be "upselling," such as trying to get the client to purchase a more expensive meal, wine, or service. Catering managers sell food and beverage events to the local market or to functions without sleeping rooms, such as weddings, local banquets, and so on. With the revenue of catering being the responsibility of the sales and marketing director, rather than food and beverage, sales managers are more likely to call clients to get rooms released for local events.

In the second type of organizational pattern, the sales and marketing and food and beverage directors split the workload and oversee catering sales and service. In some hotels, convention services personnel handle room setup and any food function that uses more than twenty sleeping rooms, while the catering department handles all local functions. In other hotels, the catering department handles all food and beverage service, while convention services personnel take care of all non-food-related logistics, such as function room setups and teardowns, sleeping room arrangements, and so forth.

There are advantages and disadvantages to each organizational form.

The major advantages associated with the organizational forms depicted in Figures 1.1 and 1.2 are:

1. *Increased efficiency.* Clients work with one designated person who has the authority to oversee the event from inception to completion. Last-minute requests and changes can be implemented quickly.

2. *Isolated responsibility.* Responsibility is assigned to one person. Management and clients know exactly whom to contact if questions arise. It is a very critical

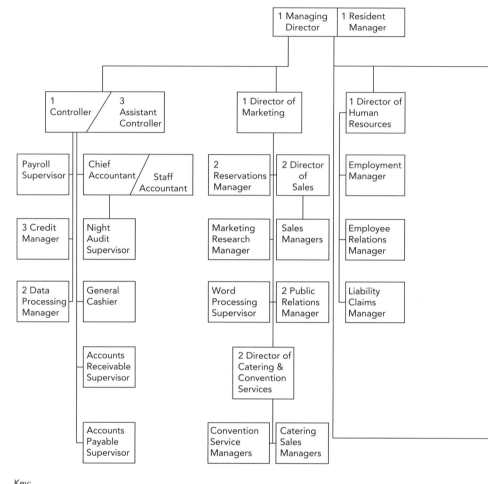

Key:
1 - Executive Committee/Operations Committee and Department Head
2 - Operations Committee and Department Head
3 - Department Head

FIGURE 1.3 Hotel organization chart. (Courtesy Westin Peachtree Plaza Hotel, Atlanta, Georgia.)

position in that the contact person is responsible for translating a client's needs and wishes into reality.

3. *Job enrichment.* A person in charge of all aspects of an event enjoys more variety than does the person involved with only one or two aspects.

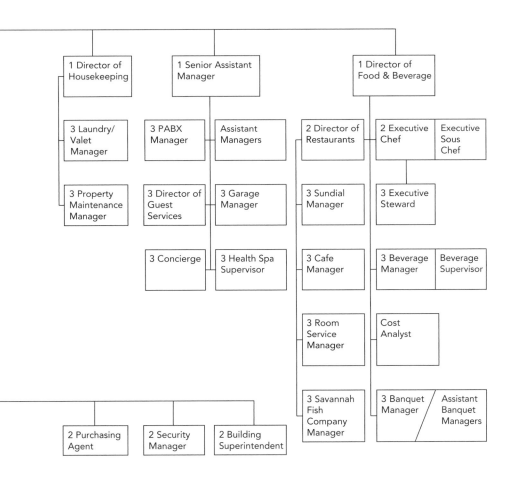

FIGURE 1.3 (Continued).

4. *Repeat patronage.* When clients deal with one person, there are additional opportunities to solicit repeat patronage and referrals.

5. *Improved communications.* Since there are fewer people in the communications chain, ambiguities and misinterpretations should be minimal.

6. *Focus.* Each manager will have fewer groups he or she is working with, and so will have more time to focus on each group, rather than dividing his or her attention among more clients.

The major disadvantages of the organizational forms depicted in Figures 1.1 and 1.2 are:

1. *Excessive workload.* One person may not have enough hours in the day to perform all the necessary tasks, particularly with large, complex groups.

2. *Too many bosses.* The food and beverage department cannot be totally isolated; it must interact to some degree with the sales and marketing department. Unfortunately, this overlap may violate established chain-of-command policies unless the relationships are spelled out clearly.

3. *Lack of specialization.* Some industry experts feel that it is difficult to train one person to be an expert in many areas.

4. *Excessive delegation.* If one person is not expert in all areas, the odds are that he or she will delegate responsibility freely. This can defeat the positive aspects of including all tasks under one person's direction. It also can confuse catering support staff members.

The advantages and disadvantages associated with the organizational form depicted in Figure 1.3 are the opposite of those associated with the organizational form depicted in Figures 1.1 and 1.2.

Which organizational form is appropriate? As a general rule, catering department organization will be influenced by the support of upper management and by the size of the facility, the types of functions catered, corporate policy, and the overall level of service offered by the facility.

While there is no one single organizational form suitable for all properties, and it is possible to adapt elements of each to create a hybrid that works best for the individual property, it would appear that the most traditional organizational pattern is the one depicted in Figure 1.4. In this case, the catering and convention services staffs work together, each handling specific activities. Catering typically handles all food and beverage requirements, while convention services handles all non-food-related arrangements.

In recent years, though, the industry has seen a shift in this division of labor. It is becoming increasingly more common to see a combined position, such as

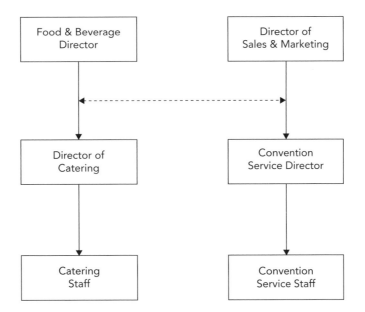

FIGURE 1.4   Typical catering organizational pattern.

catering/convention services or meeting/events manager, that handles all of a group's needs.

Catering Staff Positions

All types of catering organizations require a variety of staff positions in order to operate effectively and efficiently. Depending on the type of catered event, they may also rely on other departments' employees to handle food and beverage functions. In a large facility, the typical positions needed to service clients are:

1. Director of catering (DOC) or director of catering and convention services (DOC/CS)
2. Assistant (or associate) director of catering (ADOC)
3. Senior catering manager
4. Catering (or catering sales) manager
5. Catering sales representative (or coordinator)
6. Director of convention (or conference) services

7. Convention (or conference) service manager
8. Banquet manager
9. Banquet setup manager
10. Assistant banquet manager
11. Captain
12. Server
13. Busperson (or buser)
14. Food runner (or food steward)
15. Bartender
16. Bar back
17. Cashier
18. Sommelier
19. Houseman (or porter)
20. Attendant (or ticket taker, or usher)
21. Administrative assistant
22. Engineer
23. Audiovisual technician
24. Steward
25. Security
26. Room service manager

Job Descriptions

A job description contains a list of duties an employee must perform. It also may include the job candidate's manager, job performance evaluation criteria, job objectives, and a career path.

Sample abbreviated job descriptions for the staff positions involved directly or indirectly with catering are:

1. *Director of catering (DOC), or director of catering and convention services (DOC/CS).* Assigns and oversees all functions; oversees all marketing and sales efforts; interacts with clients and catering managers; coordinates with sales staff; creates menus (in cooperation with the chef and the food and beverage director).

2. *Assistant (or associate) director of catering (ADOC).* Services accounts; helps with marketing and sales. In larger catering operations, may fulfill some of the responsibilities of the DOC.

3. *Senior catering manager.* Seasoned catering manager; handles large or special groups.

4. *Catering (or catering sales) manager.* Maintains client contacts; services accounts.

5. *Catering sales representative (or coordinator).* May be involved only in selling; handles outside sales and/or inside sales. In larger properties, this may be an entry-level, junior position that services only smaller events, whereas in some smaller facilities, jobs 3, 4, and 5 are one and the same. The rule of thumb in these smaller properties seems to be "If you book it, you work it."

6. *Director of convention (or conference) services.* Generally a position in larger hotels; assigns and oversees all convention functions; interacts with clients and convention (or conference) service managers.

7. *Convention (or conference) service manager.* Handles room setup in hotels, conference centers, and/or convention centers; sometimes handles catering for meetings and conventions.

8. *Banquet manager.* Implements the DOC's requests; oversees captains; supervises all functions in progress; staffs and schedules servers and bartenders; coordinates all support departments. He or she is the operations director, as opposed to catering sales executives, who handle primarily the selling and planning chores.

9. *Banquet setup manager.* Supervises the banquet setup crew (housemen); orders tables, chairs, and other room equipment from storage; supervises teardown of event.

10. *Assistant banquet manager.* Reports to banquet manager; supervises table settings and decor. There may be two (or more) assistants, one for the day shift and one for the evening shift.

11. *Captain.* In charge of service at meal functions; typically oversees all activity in the entire function room or a portion of it during a meal; supervises servers.

12. *Server.* There are two types: food servers and cocktail servers. Food servers deliver food, wine, nonalcoholic beverages, and utensils to tables; clear tables; and attend to guest needs. Cocktail servers perform similar duties but concentrate on serving alcoholic beverages, usually at receptions.

13. *Busperson (or buser).* Provides backup to servers; the primary responsibilities are to clear tables, restock side stands, empty waste receptacles, and serve iced water, rolls, butter, and condiments.

14. *Food runner (or food steward).* Prepares finished food products noted on banquet event orders (BEOs). Responsible for having them ready and in place according to schedule.

15. *Bartender.* Concentrates on alcoholic beverage production and service.

16. *Bar back.* Provides backup and assistance to bartenders; the primary responsibilities are to stock initially and replenish the bars with liquor, ice, glassware, and other supplies, and to empty waste receptacles.

17. *Cashier.* Collects cash at cash bars; sells drink tickets; may also sell meal tickets.

18. *Sommelier.* A trained wine steward who specializes in all aspects of wine service, including food and wine pairing. Usually used only at upscale events.

19. *Houseman (or porter).* Physically sets up rooms with risers, tables, chairs, and other necessary equipment; reports to assistant banquet manager.

20. *Attendant.* Refreshes meeting rooms, that is, does spot cleaning and trash removal during break periods and replenishes supplies such as notepads, pencils, and iced water; responds to requests for service by meeting function hosts. Some catered functions may require restroom attendants. And some events may require coat check personnel, ticket takers, ushers, or parking attendants.

21. *Administrative assistant.* Handles routine correspondence; types contracts; types BEOs; handles and routes telephone messages; distributes documents to relevant staff members and other departments.

22. *Engineer.* Provides necessary utility services, such as setting up electrical panels for major exhibits; hangs banners; prepares special platforms and displays; sets up exhibits; maintains catering furniture, fixtures, and equipment (FFE).

23. *Audiovisual technician.* Handles audiovisual (AV) and lighting installation, teardown, and service.

24. *Steward.* Delivers requisitioned china, glass, flatware, salt and pepper shakers, and other similar items to function rooms, kitchens, and bar areas. May also be responsible for putting away these items after each event and performing routine maintenance on the equipment.

25. *Security.* Primarily responsible for crowd control and the safety of guests and employees. May also provide additional services, such as personal bodyguards for an event's high-profile speaker.

26. *Room service manager.* In large hotels, room service typically handles hospitality suites, which are held in a hotel suite on a sleeping room floor. Clients work with the room service manager to plan the service for this type of function. Generally the catering department is involved only when selling the event and/or the hospitality suite is held in a public area.

CATERING DEPARTMENT POLICIES

The facility must establish policies to guide the catering department's relations with clients. The typical policies include:

1. *Food and beverage prices.* These must be clearly listed. It is a good idea to note that any listed prices are subject to change; in other words, the caterer should not assume responsibility if potential clients are viewing outdated menus. Usually caterers note that published menu prices are subject to change unless firm price guarantees are negotiated and noted on a catering contract. All printed menus should be dated to ensure that the client is not looking at an outdated version.

2. *Taxes.* Clients must be informed that all relevant state and local consumption taxes, such as sales tax and entertainment tax, will be added to the catering prices. It is helpful to the client when applicable taxes are stated on the menu. Tax-exempt clients usually must furnish an exemption certificate to the caterer prior to the event.

3. *Gratuities or service charges.* These are automatic charges added to the catering (and in some locations to the audiovisual) prices. Most organizations

add an 18 to 23 percent gratuity to the bill. You cannot assume that all clients are aware of these traditional charges; inform them up front. Most gratuities go directly to the service staff (though sometimes a portion goes to middle management personnel, such as a catering or banquet manager).

4. *Tips.* These are voluntary gifts over and above the required gratuity. Some clients will want to tip some or all employees if they receive exceptional service. If you have a no-tipping policy, though, clients must know about it. Most government-owned facilities do not allow tipping.

5. *Deposits.* The deposit procedures must be spelled out clearly. Clients must be informed of the amount(s) that must be paid, when they must be tendered, what forms of payment you accept, and how the deposit will be applied to the final billing.

6. *Cancellations and refunds.* While no one likes to broach a negative subject, it is important to detail your policies and procedures in advance.

7. *Guarantees.* Usually a client must give a firm guarantee (guest count) three or more business days in advance of the event. The facility will prepare food, set the room, and assign staff for that number of guests plus a stipulated percentage over the guarantee to handle any guests who decide to attend at the last minute. For instance, most facilities will agree to handle the guaranteed number of guests and to overset about 3 to 5 percent up to a maximum number—for example, 5 percent over, or up to fifty maximum. Requests for any other overset arrangements should be evaluated on a case-by-case basis. Negotiating guarantees is a very tricky undertaking. The wise catering executive ensures that clients clearly understand the facility's position. As with deposits, refunds, miscellaneous charges, menu prices, and so forth, policies regarding guarantees should always be spelled out very clearly in the catering contract. Some caterers require a client to initial each page of the contract to indicate understanding.

8. *Setup and labor charges.* If these are not included in the food and beverage menu prices, clients must be told in advance about these charges. Often labor charges are incurred for bartenders and for in-room chefs (such as at carving stations and live-action cooking stations). Usually a large function will not incur additional setup charges; however, small groups may be subject to them, as there may not be enough food and/or beverage revenue to adequately cover labor expenses. Extra charges can also accrue if a room needs a fast turnover and extra labor must be called in to accomplish the job.

9. *Room rental rates.* Most facilities will charge clients rent for the use of function rooms if they are used for meetings and other events that do not include significant food and beverage sales. For instance, there may be a charge for the room if the event does not generate a specified food and/or beverage minimum. The rental rate is usually calculated to cover the fixed overhead, pay for the labor utilized to prepare and clean up the room, and provide a fair profit for the caterer. Some facilities have a sliding scale for room rental, and the charge depends on the total dollar amount generated by the event.

10. *Other charges.* Depending on the size and revenue generation of the function, a facility may add on charges for cashiers, valet parking, coat-checking services, stages, dance floors, and directional displays. If clients require additional labor because their functions are scheduled to last longer than normal, they usually will be assessed a service charge to cover the extra payroll cost (sometimes calculated as man-hour overtime).

11. *Credit terms.* Business clients who have established credit ratings will usually be allowed to put down a minimum deposit and pay the remaining balance within an allotted time, generally thirty days. Clients without credit approval and generally all social events usually must put down a large deposit and pay the remaining balance two weeks prior to the event.

12. *Outside food and beverage.* Most, if not all, facilities will not allow clients to bring in their own food or beverages. In most situations, the facility's liquor license, liability insurance, health permit, and/or business license forbids the use of outside products.

13. *Corkage fees.* If the law and the facility allow clients to bring in their own products, there usually will be a charge for setup service. For instance, if clients are allowed to bring in their own liquor, there may be a standard, one-time corkage fee for the service, or the facility might charge a standard fee for each drink prepared and served. A gratuity is also generally charged, in addition to the corkage fee, and is distributed to the staff who worked the event. While it is very uncommon for a facility to allow food items to be brought in, the one exception that is often made is for a wedding cake, if they are not made on the property. Typically a cake-cutting fee is charged for this. This fee covers setup, use and washing of the facility's plates and forks, and labor for the cutting and service. Anytime this is allowed, the facility should require, and ensure, that the cake is prepared in a facility that is licensed by the local health department.

14. *Underage or visibly intoxicated guests.* The facility must ensure that clients realize that the pertinent liquor laws will not be suspended during their catered events. For instance, wedding hosts may not see anything wrong with serving wine to an underage guest at a private party. However, the law does not make this distinction. The same thing is true for service to visibly intoxicated guests: they cannot legally be served by the banquet staff. If a client requests self-service bars, some caterers will require the client to sign a waiver of liquor liability so that they are not held responsible for guest actions. This type of waiver is necessary because in the case of self-service, the facility does not have bartenders and cocktail servers on-site to prevent underage drinking and service to visibly intoxicated guests. Because of this potential liability, many caterers will not permit self-service bars.

15. *Display restrictions.* Many clients wish to use their own signs, displays, decorations, and/or demonstrations at booked events. Usually the facility will reserve the right to approve these and to control their placement and location. If clients are allowed to have displays, the facility usually expects the clients to be responsible for any damage done and any extraordinary cleanup that may result. For example, confetti (especially Mylar confetti), rice, and birdseed can pose a challenge to remove. Similar restrictions may apply to other materials, such as paper products, decorations, and equipment. Tape and tacks can damage walls, and some items can be fire hazards.

16. *Responsibility for loss or damage.* Personal property brought into the facility by guests usually will not be covered by the facility's insurance policies. In addition, it is the client's responsibility to cover any damage that is done to the venue by any guest during the event or in connection with it. Consequently, clients need to be informed of these policies, and agree to them, in advance.

17. *Insurance.* Based on the nature of the event, many facilities require clients to obtain, at their own expense, an insurance policy naming the facility as an additional insured. It is also common that an outside service contractor be required to have current similar insurance on file with the venue prior to being allowed to perform services on-site.

18. *Indemnification.* Facilities usually expect clients to agree to indemnify the facility against any claims, losses, or damages, except those due solely to the negligence or willful misconduct of the facility staff. The facility also wants protection from claims made by outside service contractors, such as florists, entertainers, or audiovisual firms engaged by clients. Furthermore, clients are expected to stipulate that, by paying the final bill, they agree that there are no disputes regarding the products and services received.

19. *Uncontrollable acts (force majeure).* There are times when the facility will be unable to perform through no fault of its own. For instance, bad weather, strikes, labor disputes, and so forth could hamper the facility's ability to service its clients. Consequently, clients must agree to hold harmless the facility under these types of uncontrollable conditions.

20. *Substitutions.* This is similar to the uncontrollable acts policy mentioned above. Occasionally supply problems may force the caterer to substitute menu products. Or it may be necessary to move a function from one meeting area to another. For instance, an outside event may have to be moved indoors at the last minute because of inclement weather. Or a contractor's strike could force the facility to substitute other space of comparable size and quality. While few of us want to think about these potential problems, the clients must be advised in advance that they could happen. Always provide proper advance communication with clients so that surprises do not anger them.

21. *Security.* A facility may require clients to provide additional security for certain events. For instance, a meeting of diamond dealers would be expected to schedule a great deal of personal security that is provided by or approved by the facility. Alternatively, the facility may reserve the right to hire additional security guards and bill the event host. If you outsource valet parking, always check references to ensure the security of your patrons' automobiles.

22. *Licenses and permits.* Some functions may need to be approved and/or licensed by the local government licensing agency. For instance, a function that has a cover charge may need a temporary admission license. The facility should reserve the right to refuse service to any client who does not obtain the appropriate licenses and permits prior to the event.

23. *Live entertainment taxes.* Publicly ticketed events may be subject to federal, state, and local taxes relating to admission or merchandise receipts. The venue will want to be assured that the client shall indemnify it against all liability, claims, loss, or payment of any kind by reason of the client's failure or omission to comply with any such law or regulation and/or to pay all of any such taxes or charges.

24. *Act or show contract.* When working with a client that is selling tickets to an event that advertises a particular act or show, the venue needs to ensure that the client has a valid, properly executed, and compatible contract with the performers whose services form the basis for the event. While the venue may not require it for every booking, clients must be advised that they should be prepared to submit to the venue, upon demand, a copy of the contract.

Most of these policies will be included in the catering contract. See Chapter 10 for information on contracts.

MAJOR CHALLENGES FACED BY THE CATERING DEPARTMENT

The catering department may encounter several challenges while working to attain its objectives. Some of the major ones are:

1. *Marketing the catering department's services.* A great deal of time must be spent in this effort to distinguish your property in the minds of potential clients. Too many caterers can seem exactly alike. Clients tend to perceive caterers as being as interchangeable as buses: there is always another one available that can handle their needs. You will constantly need to battle this perception.

2. *Excessive time spent with clients.* Unfortunately, only a small number of individuals and groups contacted will end up purchasing catered events. Moreover, once business is booked, a great deal of time must be spent planning and coordinating the events. While some clients need more hand-holding than others, the wise catering executive expects to devote a lot of time to these tasks.

To maximize available catering sales time, savvy caterers learn to determine how much time is necessary and/or appropriate to spend with a prospective client, and will learn ways to determine who may be a serious buyer and who is merely a casual catering shopper. Additionally, they will develop ways to ask for the sale at the appropriate time and in a way that does not make clients feel like they are being rushed.

3. *Unique demands.* For instance, clients may not adhere to the schedule for refreshment breaks, instead wanting to visit the refreshment area when time permits. This is especially true in conference centers, where attendees can break at will. Consequently, setups need to be freshened periodically, which requires an employee to be constantly alert to fluctuating needs.

4. *Difficulty of costing out and pricing certain functions.* Special requests and last-minute needs will cost more because of the specialized circumstances. The refreshment breaks noted above fall into this category. Since the demands these events present cannot always be predicted, function hosts usually must wait until a final accounting is made by the catering department. This can cause ill will among clients, especially those who are on a tight budget and would appreciate price guarantees. In these situations, it is advisable to sell food and beverages at either a per-person price or with a maximum number of items available so that the client will not go over an established budget.

5. *Ethical traps.* Sometimes the catering organization may encounter conflict-of-interest dilemmas. For example, clients who need outside contractors, such as tour buses, entertainers, and decorators, may ask the caterer for a recommendation. The facility, always mindful of its image and reputation, will tend to recommend only a few outside contractors that can fill the bill adequately. Vendors that have been thoroughly checked out and determined to be reputable and of high quality often are placed on the property's preferred vendor list. To ensure high levels of quality and alleviate feelings of undue favoritism, it is the director of catering's job to confirm these vendors and negotiate either a percentage of sales or a flat amount that is given to the facility as a referral fee, not as an individual kickback, which can be unethical. Catering managers can then use the preferred vendor list as an opportunity to upsell services and bring in additional revenue for the organization.

6. *Division of responsibility.* It is very important to determine in advance who is responsible for each part of the event. For instance, a convention may want to hire its own band but simultaneously expect the facility to coordinate the details. This can easily lead to misunderstanding, uncompensated work by the catering executive, and unhappy clients unless everything is spelled out clearly.

7. *Time pressures.* The catering department is a pressure cooker. It seems as if everything must be ready yesterday. Catering personnel must learn to work well under time constraints.

8. *Working with and coordinating with other departments and outside agencies.* Proper advance planning is necessary to avoid service glitches that could cause guest dissatisfaction. Caterers must cultivate the ability to communicate effectively.

9. *Maintaining qualified staff members.* Many catering organizations experience severe volume swings. For instance, convention centers pose a unique challenge in terms of volume and staffing. One day you might have a breakfast for five thousand, which requires a lot of labor. You may not have another similar function for two weeks; as a result, it is very difficult to keep qualified employees, many of whom prefer more predictable work schedules.

In addition to full-time management and hourly employees, many facilities maintain two or more lists of service staff (i.e., banquet staff): an A-list, a B-list, a C-list, and so on. The A-list personnel are the steady extras; they are the first ones called by the manager when help is needed. If not enough people are available from the A-list, the manager will call those on the B-list before moving on to the C-list.

The B-list and beyond personnel are casual labor, used to fill in the gaps. They present more problems than do A-list people because the typical B-list worker is probably on the B-list of two or more catering facilities in town. As a result, major functions can go begging for adequate staff. The catering executive must be a creative personnel recruiter and a superb planner in order to overcome these obstacles.

A unionized facility usually will be required to go through the local union hiring hall for its steady and casual servers. The union generally keeps lists of steadies and extras similar to the A-list and B-list kept by non-unionized properties. If the union has enough advance notice of all of your labor requirements, chances are it can plan for them and satisfy the catering department's needs. The Christmas season and New Year's Eve are a challenge everywhere. To ensure staff are available during these busy times, caterers must have their labor call done far in advance and will often offer an increased gratuity and/or higher wage to staff who commit to working these events.

10. *The lack of technical foodservice skills.* Many caterers today have less food knowledge than ever before. They are more and more reliant on chefs and food and beverage directors for advice. This would not be a major problem if standardized menus were used consistently; however, things are trendier these days, there is more competition, and many clients want custom menus and something special. This can make it difficult to respond quickly to unusual customer requests.

A potential client may become restless with the catering executive who needs to confer constantly with other food and beverage people in the organization. However, confidence and poise can make a difference here. Instead of being dismayed, a potential client may be quite pleased with the executive who may not have the answer at that very moment but who promises to, and does, get it quickly.

In this day and age, no one is expected to know everything. Catering professionals do, however, need to know where to get the expertise and information to handle client needs. In a well-run facility, there is a tremendous network of specialized professionals available as well as a sophisticated communications system that can be used to tap into this bundle of resources. The Web is an excellent source of information. Food blogs provide valuable information. The Food Blog Blog (www.foodblogblog.com) has an extensive amount of information. Organizations such as the National Association of Catering Executives (NACE, www.nace.net) provide education on a national level through conferences and through more than forty local chapters that hold monthly meetings. There are excellent trade journals with online searchable archives, such as *Event Solutions (www.event-solutions.com), Special Events (www.specialevents.com), Catersource (www.catersource.com), BizBash (www.bizbash.com), Food Arts (www.foodarts. com),* and *Food & Wine (www.foodandwine.com),* that provide excellent articles to educate the neophyte or aspiring caterer. As catering clients become more sophisticated (or jaded), the caterer cannot remain competitive without knowing how to draw upon these resources.

Many clients travel extensively and eat out frequently. The Food Network and the design and decor shows on HGTV have elevated the food and design knowledge of the average consumer. Their life experiences shape their menu, room setup, and decor choices when planning events. They expect the catering executive to keep pace with trends in menu planning, event planning, and design. These challenges must be met by any catering executive who strives to be successful in either the off-premise or on-premise arena.

SUMMARY

On-premise catering takes place on the physical premises of a hotel, club, convention center, conference center, stadium, and so on, where the food is prepared and served at the location. Catering can be classified as social or business.

KEY TERMS

On-premise catering	Off-premise catering	Venue
Cater out	CMP	Hold all space
Upselling	DOC	CSM
Houseman	Steward	Sommelier
Gratuities	Corkage fee	

REVIEW QUESTIONS

1. What is corporate catering?
2. Which type of caterer usually has an advantage in the on-premise catering market?

3. What is unique about conference center catering?
4. Which type of facility is limited in the amount of outside business they can accept?
5. Which is the best organizational structure for catering departments?
6. What are a banquet manager's primary duties?
7. What is the difference between social catering and business catering?
8. Are gratuities the same as service charges?
9. What is the difference between a gratuity and a tip?
10. What does cater-out mean?
11. What is unique about convention center catering?
12. What is the hotel room service department's typical role in on-premise catering?
13. List one type of consumption tax clients would have to pay.
14. What is the typical type of catering a country club offers to its members?
15. What is the biggest barrier on-premise caterers face when they want to get involved in off-premise catering?

Chapter 2

SALES AND MARKETING

Catering is a consumer-driven industry that is stimulated by clients who demand exceptional quality and excellent value for a reasonable price. Value is determined by the buyer, not the seller. A buyer's perceptions are a seller's realities. This means that the impression a potential client has of the catering ability of your facility—whether positive or negative—is what is real for the client and will influence his or her buying decision. Most of your potential clients will comparison-shop when they are considering the location of their event. Your facility must be perceived as the best choice because you are reliable, consistent, and creative, and because you can execute the best-quality event.

The number and types of potential catering clients are unlimited. New markets are emerging constantly. On-premise caterers service all types of events, from the smallest business meeting to the largest industry convention and exposition.

The hotel often has an advantage over other types of caterers because it can handle several types of events simultaneously and in the same location where most guests are staying. Convention centers, stadiums, and arenas also have a wide selection of available space to service very large groups; however, they do not have any sleeping rooms on-site. Restaurants and smaller clubs, on the other hand, often have only one banquet room on the premises.

Catering clients are everywhere. Our society has a never-ending love affair with parties, meetings, conventions, celebrations, ceremonies, and various other special events.

Some of the largest catering markets include associations, businesses, and organizations/groups known as the SMERF (social, military, educational, religious, fraternal) market. Each catering salesperson will handle one or more of these markets, depending on the volume. If a facility specializes in one particular type of event, it may have a catering manager who handles only those events. For example, a country club may have a catering manager who handles only weddings and is the property's expert on those events.

ASSOCIATION MARKET

For many catering organizations, the largest market segment is associations, followed by business. An association is a group of people who share a common interest. Association members participate in local chapter meetings, educational events, charitable works, and regional, national, and international conventions. Most have conventions or meetings at least once each year.

Trade associations represent people employed in a particular trade. Membership usually is sponsored and paid by the member's employer. As an example, the American Culinary Federation (ACF) is a trade association, with membership dues generally paid by the chef's employer.

Professional associations represent people who practice a particular professional activity. Membership usually is sponsored and paid by the individual member. For instance, the American Medical Association (AMA) is a professional association, with each doctor paying his or her own membership dues.

There is an association for almost every vocation or avocation in existence. According to the American Society of Association Executives (ASAE), about 70 percent of Americans belong to one association, about 50 percent belong to two, and about 25 percent belong to four or more. There are more than 20,000 national associations based in the United States. In addition to their membership rosters, they employ approximately 500,000 people to manage their affairs.

While there is great potential for generating revenue, large national association business can be challenging for some hotels, as it generally requires a large amount of meeting space that is disproportionate to the number of sleeping rooms a group books. However, as many association attendees are bona fide business or community leaders, their exposure to your property may convince them to use your facility instead of a competing property for other catered functions.

BUSINESS MARKET

The association and corporate business market represents approximately 75 percent of total catering sales in the United States. Companies and corporations may have a variety of catering needs. Business functions range from small meetings to lavish conventions. Some of the typical business events are:

1. *Meetings and conventions.* These events represent the bulk of the business market. Some, such as sales meetings, can be rather routine affairs that are easily serviced. Others, though, such as an annual stockholders meeting, can severely test the catering executive's skill and ingenuity.

Probably the biggest advantage of working with the corporate meetings segment is that this type of client can usually give you relatively precise predictions about the number of attendees. For instance, if a company plans a meeting for 100 people, it usually will have 100. If a person cancels, normally he or she will be replaced at the function by the company. Corporations don't have to market and sell registrations the way associations do. A corporate group also tends to allocate more money per attendee than do other types of markets. As a general rule, corporate events are usually attended by businesspeople accustomed to judging overall value without concentrating solely on price.

The corporate meeting market is also considered to be a more stable market group than others. There are many events, such as training meetings, that must be held periodically.

2. *Incentive events.* The purpose of these events is to encourage company employees to meet or exceed sales or production goals. When the goals are met, a celebration is planned to honor those who contributed to their successful achievement.

Usually a company's marketing department plans these types of events. They typically are used to motivate salespeople. In addition to a special celebration, high achievers can also be rewarded with a free trip (incentive travel) or some other prize.

Incentive events are very profitable business for catering. Companies usually reward their star performers with lavish functions, as maximum reward leads to maximum effort and results. Economy is not in the vocabulary for this type of event, but companies do not want to waste their money either, particularly after the bad press following the federal government bailout of banks and automakers in 2008 and 2009.

3. *New product introductions.* These types of events range from film premieres to new software releases. These are usually very elaborate, expensive events. First-class food, beverage, entertainment, and decorations are standard fare—all designed to attract maximum media coverage.

4. *Building openings.* Most companies celebrate groundbreakings, topping-offs, and grand openings with gala parties. Many of these are off-premise functions; however, there are a number of pre-opening functions that could be held in a facility. For example, a building developer's leasing department may host a party to promote interest among potential tenants.

5. *Recognition events.* These are similar to incentive events. Generally, though, they are less elaborate. Typically they involve awards dinners and other types of ceremonies intended to recognize several employees at many levels of performance. For instance, many companies and associations will hold an annual recognition luncheon to recognize long-term employees and to honor the employee of the year or someone who is retiring.

Some recognition events are actually a form of public relations. A company or association may hold a function that is designed to honor someone but also is used to generate publicity. As one example, the National Academy of Motion Picture Arts and Sciences holds Oscar parties and other similar events that honor industry members as well as generate interest among the movie-watching public. There is a major banquet for Academy Award nominees and movie business insiders before the awards ceremony. Other parties are spawned from this event, with movie studios, agents, and other entities producing after-event parties with exclusive guest lists.

6. *Training sessions and seminars.* If an educational event is expected to last a half day or more, the company usually will want to hold it at a place where food and beverages are readily available.

7. *Anniversaries.* Most companies will celebrate decade anniversaries as well as silver, golden, diamond, centennial, sesquicentennial, bicentennial, and tercen-tennial anniversaries. Coca-Cola's 100th birthday celebration, held in Atlanta, was an incredible event. Coca-Cola executives and other guests from around the world were feted at parties over a period of several days. The celebration encompassed events at all the major hotels and culminated in a reception for 16,000 people at the city's convention center.

8. *"In conjunction with" (ICW) or "affiliate" events.* Many smaller events "piggyback" on larger events. They are ancillary to the main event. Trade show exhibitors often host events during conventions. For example, during the Consumer Electronics Show (CES) in Las Vegas, IBM or Microsoft may throw a party for potential clients or host a dinner for their best clients. This business is not from CES per se, but it is generated because of CES. For shows that meet in the same location each year, it is quite easy to go to the convention center and pick up an exhibitor directory that you can use during the year to solicit ICW business for the upcoming show. You can also go to the trade show website and obtain a listing of exhibitors.

Usually all participating hotels as well as restaurants, clubs, and arenas try to book this segment, as it is among the highest revenue producers for catering. The smart caterer researches this segment at least one year in advance, often by paying a site visit to the current year's meeting location to find those customers, meet them, and establish a relationship. While each convention has many rules as to how these affiliates may book at the hotels, generally speaking, these efforts always pay off and generate extensive revenues.

9. *Traveling exhibitions.* There are many traveling events, such as music or entertainment extravaganzas or sports events. Sports teams may be a particularly good market segment. Whether major league, college, or high school, when they are on the road they tend to have healthy appetites. While at times they may be difficult to service because of their time constraints, generally speaking, their catered functions involve very specific types and quantities of foods and beverages and relatively simple service procedures. The one item to be careful of, though, when working with sports teams is pricing, particularly for teams of hearty eaters (think football players). As these individuals generally consume larger quantities than an average person, that must be taken into account when costing out the menu.

In addition to the customary catered events that come with traveling events, (dressing room hospitality, crew meals, etc.), a savvy catering executive can generate additional revenue by soliciting VIP events, pre- or post-event receptions, alumni events, and so on.

10. *Customer appreciation parties.* This is another type of corporate special event. They are quite common in some industries. And they are occasionally based on some sort of theme. For instance, a company may throw a party for current clients as a way of showing its appreciation for their patronage. Oftentimes customer appreciation parties can be used by a company to solicit future business. As one example, an equipment manufacturer can host a party that might also include a brief display of its collection of equipment prototypes. This can encourage its current and potential customers to pre-order this merchandise. It is also a good bet that these customers will provide profitable referral business for the client and the caterer.

Even though many large business events are booked years in advance, the caterer who specializes in the business market must be prepared to service a client at a moment's notice. The loyal client expects this and is willing to pay for it. This has become increasingly true as the trend in the industry has been shorter-notice bookings, even for large events. With travel and economic uncertainties, clients are not willing to commit as far in advance as they once were.

SMERF MARKET

Most events in the social, military, educational, religious, and fraternal market are considered special events by the client. To some extent, though, almost any catered event could be considered a special event, at least for clients and their guests. For instance, a convention could book several "refueling" functions, such as breakfasts and luncheons, but also schedule one special event, such as a surprise birthday party for the company president.

Special events differ from daily, ordinary events in at least three ways. A daily event generally occurs spontaneously, while a special event is always planned in advance. A daily event does not necessarily arouse expectations, but a special event always does. And while a daily event usually occurs for no particular reason, some type of celebration is the motivating force behind a special event.

While high-end social events can be lavish affairs, other SMERF events often have low budgets. For example, the government market limits per diems (per day limits). While the budgets can be low, these markets can still represent sizeable income for a catering facility if booked properly.

Social Events

Many social events are life-cycle events. Birthdays, anniversaries, reunions, and so forth mark time in our lives. They are usually celebrated with specific ceremonies and rituals. Many are celebrations catered by off-premise social caterers at clients' homes or other locations. Some use restaurants, clubs, and other small to midsize facilities. Others are larger affairs that would be of interest to the typical hotel or convention center catering department.

1. *Weddings.* Today's wedding is longer and often more expensive than ever before. Many couples are marrying later in life, have more money to devote to this special day, and have more input in the planning. Facilities that can provide a one-stop or specialized service are apt to have a competitive edge among today's active brides and grooms, who have many demands on their time.

Many weddings have specific religious requirements. For instance, the Jewish wedding requires a chuppah (canopy) and the breaking of a glass, while the reception requires special service of the challah (ceremonial bread). The caterer will need to be aware of these types of traditions or else it might disappoint (or even insult) guests. Ethnic weddings, such as Italian, Indian and Greek weddings, are quite often very extravagant affairs.

Increasingly brides and grooms are looking for a caterer that meets requirements that are important to them, such as being able to provide a destination or themed wedding or a "green" event.

The wedding is the ultimate theme party, and is discussed further in Chapter 3.

2. *Wedding anniversaries.* These are often surprise celebrations hosted by adult children in milestone years. The silver (twenty-fifth) wedding anniversary is especially popular. The children planning the party generally need a good deal of advice when putting together their celebrations. The caterer could consider advising them to choose a theme based on what was going on in the world at the time the parents were married. This is usually a very popular choice, especially with guests who are contemporaries of the anniversary couple. The Web or the local library has plenty of information about what was happening during the wedding year, as well as on the specific wedding date.

3. *Reunions.* The reunion market encompasses many areas, including high schools, colleges, families, military units, or former work groups. High school reunions are especially popular these days because of private reunion planners who specialize in locating alumni and planning memorable events, tasks that well-intentioned alumni usually are unable to perform well.

Reunions require a lot of pre-planning. A successful event usually needs a one-year lead time. Usually there are a few faithful alumni who shoulder the bulk of the planning, or they will engage a professional reunion planner. The caterer, though, oftentimes will be part of the overall planning process.

4. *Bar and bat mitzvahs.* A bar mitzvah is the traditional Jewish ceremony celebrated on a Jewish boy's thirteenth birthday. It marks the coming of age in the Jewish faith. During the ceremony, the young man publicly recites passages from the Torah (the Jewish scripture) and accepts personal responsibility for observing the commandments set down in the Torah. The bat mitzvah, for Jewish girls, is similar to the bar mitzvah.

The celebrations of these events traditionally were very serious and glamorous, similar in scale to large wedding receptions, though more and more a themed event is requested, generally following the honoree's likes, such as soccer, dance, or another favorite hobby or interest. Important elements include the blessing of the bread and wine and the lighting of candles. Menus and food preparation and service may follow the kosher dietary restrictions, or be kosher-style.

Bar and bat mitzvahs are discussed in more detail in Chapter 3.

5. *Baptisms and confirmations.* A baptism is the Christian rite that results in the acceptance of the baptized person into the faith. The post-ceremony celebration is most often held at the parents' home, though larger functions would need to be held at a hotel, restaurant, or similar location.

A confirmation is the Christian rite confirming a child's infant baptism into the faith. The ceremony allows the young person to confirm that he or she knows right from wrong and that Christ is the chosen savior. Receptions usually are very popular, with the confirmed receiving several gifts and a considerable amount of attention.

Depending on the facility, bar/bat mitzvahs and baptisms and confirmations may be classified under either the social or religious segment of the SMERF market.

6. *Birthdays.* Sweet sixteen and quinceañera celebrations can be a large market for caterers, particularly with the popularity of TV shows such as MTV's *My Super Sweet 16.* Often large, expensive birthday celebrations tend to be surprise parties. When this is the case, the caterer must be involved in a considerable amount of pre-planning and subterfuge. A trend of having a party upon turning forty (or fifty, or sixty, etc.) has remained strong, with special themes and menus, as baby boomers in our society are aging.

7. *Gourmet clubs.* Groups such as the Chaîne des Rôtisseurs and the American Institute of Wine and Food host extremely upscale, high-priced meals. When evaluating a caterer, the members will give priority to those establishments that are fellow members and hold menu design and execution in high esteem. Consequently, the facility seeking this type of business must see to it that the chef, director of catering, and food and beverage director hold active memberships in these organizations.

8. *Fund-raising events.* Fund-raisers and other types of charity events continue to be popular. Oftentimes the facility is a partner in these events, in that it contributes all or part of the products or services needed to hold them. These events create a showcase opportunity for the caterer. Some of these functions are multifaceted events. For instance, a fund-raiser may include a reception, dinner, silent auction, and dance.

9. *Quinceañera.* The quinceañara is a celebration of the fifteenth birthday of a girl in the Latin culture. It signifies the young lady's transition into adulthood. This is usually a lavish affair where young ladies wear elaborate gowns. The celebration includes a banquet and dancing.

Military Events

The military segment can represent a good source of catering business, particularly in cities that house major military bases. There are many awards functions, Armed Forces Day, and birthday events. For instance, every November 8, or the closest weekend, the Marine Corps holds its Marine Birthday Ball. While it is true that most military bases have club facilities capable of providing catering services, local catering facilities can expect to attract some of this business by providing a welcome change of pace.

Educational Events

The education segment can also generate a respectable amount of revenue and profit. There are many continuing-education seminars, symposiums, graduation parties, alumni events, donor recognition events, fund-raising events, and fraternity and sorority events.

There are also many high school functions. For instance, proms can represent sizeable revenue in April and May. However, underage students, coupled with tight budgets, do not always result in profitable, successful affairs, and security at these types of events is essential. Still, many companies are specializing in marketing prom packages or after-prom party packages to generate additional revenue.

Graduations can be a very attractive market segment these days, especially given the fact that many older people are graduating from college. They have fulfilled lifelong dreams and usually are very anxious to celebrate.

Religious Events

The religious segment includes events such as Passover dinners, church fundraisers, and the like. While many churches and synagogues have their own buildings, not all of them have kitchen and event space that is suitable for events, and therefore these events can offer opportunities for local catering organizations.

Fraternal Events

Another portion of the SMERF market is the fraternal group. Fraternal organizations abound. Most areas of the country have Rotary, Kiwanis, Lions, Soroptimist, and other similar service organizations. They can represent a good source of steady business because of their desire to meet at the same location each month. They like it when their members know that, for example, the meeting is always held on the third Tuesday of the month at a local restaurant.

MARKET CLASSIFICATIONS

Catering organizations will divide markets in different ways. While most companies assign one or more of the above markets to each catering manager, some companies divide their markets by geographic regions (for example, northeastern states, southeastern states, midwestern states, and so on). Each catering salesperson is given one of the geographic regions and handles all business that comes from that region regardless of the type of event. This sort of differentiation is more common in large hotels that do the majority of their business with companies and individuals from outside their city.

Within each market there are ranges of budgets for each group or event. Budgets are generally divided into three classifications: low-end (shallow), mid-level, and high-end (deep). Caterers must be aware of unique characteristics relevant to each level.

Low-End

These groups have limited resources and are very cost-conscious. These types of events often involve a short lead time for the caterer. Clients in this segment usually shop around for the best price, often requesting the least expensive selection on the menu. This does not mean that they ignore quality and service; however, they are on a limited budget and cannot afford the very best.

Caterers can use low-end groups to fill in slow periods (the "shoulders") between more lucrative events.

The low-end customer of today can very easily be the corporate meeting planner of tomorrow. As a result, the caterer who does a good job with these groups is apt to win repeat patronage as well as gain an inside track on securing potentially more profitable functions in the future.

However, a caterer should not undertake any event that could damage its reputation or create a loss in revenue due to a low budget. If you can't show yourself in the best way possible or finish without any profit within the budget, don't book the event. (The exception would be an event, such as a charity function, that incurs a planned loss but which has potential for future high-profile business.)

Midlevel

The midlevel function can quickly lead to repeat business. For instance, the executive business luncheon can easily become a monthly affair. The caterer who provides excellent value will more than likely become the favored provider for these clients. Businesspeople are trained to shop around for the best value; however, when it comes to their personal pleasures, they are no different from the rest of us in that they will not switch loyalties on the spur of the moment. Furthermore, these small functions can lead to bigger and more profitable events in the future.

High-End

The high-end segment typically involves especially fancy, upscale business meal functions. These are expensive events where cost takes a back seat. The incentive travel market would fit here. These types of functions oftentimes represent repeat business. While many large conventions and other similar events tend to move around the country, some tend to patronize the same locations or geographical areas on a regular basis.

Caterers in casino hotels work very often on high-end events and are at times asked to produce such a party with a few hours' notice. It is not unusual for a casino catering department to be asked to produce an elaborate wedding or birthday celebration for a high-end player who has just come into town. As casinos always try to accommodate any requests from their best players, short-notice catering events are no exception.

Other high-end events in casinos often include Asian New Year and New Year's Eve celebrations. Often casinos in Las Vegas try to outdo each other in order to attract very lucrative high rollers to their property. These elaborate events often include the most innovative decor and entertainment and the best in food and beverages. The casino's marketing department works closely with the catering team to pull all the elements of the event together to dazzle these important guests.

CLIENT DECISION MAKERS

Who makes the purchase decision? This is one of the first things to find out when soliciting catering business. In some instances it could be a company administrative assistant or executive assistant. In other cases, the chief executive officer (CEO) may be the decision maker.

Usually the type of function dictates who will make the purchase decision. An assistant may plan the office Christmas party, whereas the CEO might plan the annual board of directors meeting.

Some companies employ a meeting planner. Meeting planners, depending on the size of the company and the amount of meeting, training, or convention activity, may or may not have other job responsibilities. The meeting planner who concentrates exclusively on this activity is easier to work with because the planner with other company responsibilities often has less time to concentrate on planning meetings.

Some very large companies employ a corporate meeting planner to plan and organize functions for all company-owned satellite locations. The corporate meeting planner is normally based at the corporate headquarters; for instance, Coca-Cola's corporate meeting planner is based in Atlanta. However, even though the planner resides in Atlanta, this person has the responsibility for planning and organizing events for all regional Coca-Cola bottlers.

Many associations have professional meeting planners on staff. Some associations are too small to afford this type of support, however, and so they tend to hire independent (third-party) or contract meeting planners to help them. If the association cannot afford to support an office and an office staff, it may use an independent contractor to handle all of its affairs, including its meeting and convention needs. There are also companies that manage several associations.

Association meeting planners on the national level are concentrated in a few cities. Most national associations are based in Washington, D.C., because lobbying Congress is often one of their main activities. New York, Chicago, Atlanta, and San Francisco also have high concentrations of associations' headquarters staffs.

The American Society of Association Executives, an association for association executives, publishes a membership directory at www.asaenet.org. Gale Research publishes an annual *Encyclopedia of Associations*, and usually the reference section of the local public library will have this directory. Another online source for association information is at www.marketingsource.com.

The regional, state, and local chapters of national associations also have catering needs. Regional and state chapters usually have one or two functions per year. The meeting planner at the national level oftentimes will help the regional and state chapters plan and organize their events.

Local chapters usually have monthly meetings where association business is discussed. These functions usually include a meal or reception as well as a guest speaker. For instance, the National Association of Catering Executives (NACE; www.nace.net) has more than forty chapters that plan and organize these types of monthly events.

Local chapter meeting planners are usually volunteers. Caterers will experience a great deal of variety with the local chapters; some volunteers are well versed in planning and organizing events, whereas many are willing to work but require considerable care and attention.

Travel agencies are planning more catered events today. Some corporations and associations feel that it is good business practice to use travel agents to plan meetings, since, theoretically, it is much more efficient to deal with one person for travel, catering, and sleeping room needs. Unfortunately, some travel agents do not understand the catering piece of the overall meeting. For instance, the typical travel agent may be unaware of the difference between meal couponing and meal guarantees. With meal couponing, when a travel agent books a meal function, he or she will pre-sell event tickets to the guests and reimburse the caterer for each ticket redeemed. If some guests do not use their tickets, the travel agent keeps the "breakage" (the money paid by guests to the travel agent but not given to the caterer). With meal guarantees, though, there is no breakage. The caterer must be paid based on the number of guests the agent guaranteed, regardless of the number who attend. This is troublesome for a travel agent accustomed to earning considerable breakage income, and it can be especially disturbing to the travel agent who books a great deal of breakfast business, as there can be a very large no-show factor for this meal.

Another challenge with travel agents is their concept of professional compensation for their services. They have a commission orientation, whereas meeting planners do not. For instance, a travel agent usually receives as much as a 10 percent commission for sleeping rooms business booked for a hotel. If a travel agent books a meal function or two, he or she may expect a commission for each function. If your company agrees to pay a commission, it needs to be agreed to in writing in advance, so there are no surprises for either side after the event.

Administrative assistants in just about any field are often called on to plan events. These events could include employee picnics or holiday parties, retirement dinners, recognition events, shareholder or advisory board meetings, and so on.

The client decision maker in the social and special-events markets is not always easy to identify. For instance, just because a bridal coordinator may be the first one to make contact with the caterer, it does not necessarily follow that he or she is empowered to make the decision. The caterer must qualify each caller to avoid wasting valuable time with the wrong person.

Some special-events market segments employ event managers or event coordinators. For instance, sports leagues usually have hospitality and special-events coordinators; some are employed full-time at league headquarters, while local independent coordinators are hired to handle temporary assignments on location.

Sports leagues represent profitable catering opportunities. For example, the hospitality coordinator for the U.S. Open Championship arranges about a hundred parties during each tournament. The director of special events for Major League Baseball plans several banquets throughout the year, some as large as 3,500 people. The Super Bowl generates a legion of parties in the host city.

Many clients do not simply purchase a meal; they buy an experience. They buy fantasy. They buy fun, service, ambience, entertainment, and memories. The food and beverage are only two components of the fun and fantasy. Much of what a caterer sells is intangible. The client cannot touch or feel an event beforehand, so the caterer is selling something that has yet to be produced and delivered. Because clients purchase what they think will happen, it is a gamble for them. They are understandably nervous and need to be reassured that they made the correct decision. The caterer must create a sense of trust with his or her clients.

THE MARKETING BUDGET

Marketing expenses usually represent a significant percentage of expected sales revenue. For instance, the average U.S. foodservice operation will spend about 2 to 5 percent of sales revenue for direct marketing expenses such as advertising, promotion, public relations, franchising fees, royalties, and other fees and commissions.

Some hospitality operations allocate a set percentage of expected annual sales revenue for marketing at the beginning of the year. The catering executive, then, is expected to use these funds to accomplish the stated objectives. Sometimes there is some flexibility with these funds, whereby monies can be shifted from one marketing expense to another. Other companies, though, assign a line-item budget, meaning the department head has no flexibility (for example, the director of catering cannot spend less money for brochures and shift the savings to radio advertising).

Some catering organizations are allocated a specific dollar amount for marketing expenses, not a set percentage of expected sales revenue. Prior to the beginning of a fiscal year, the director of catering, in conjunction with top management, will prepare an annual budget for the catering department. This budget will include all anticipated departmental incomes and expenses.

As a general rule, the sales forecast is based on tangible factors, such as business already booked, and expenses, such as food, beverage, and payroll costs, that are expected to be a certain percentage of these projected sales. If estimated sales increase or decrease, most expenses (except those that are completely fixed) must follow the curve and stay within their allocated percentage. If there are any variances, you usually do not change the budget. You document them, pay the extra costs (if necessary), and learn from them so that the next budget does not suffer the same fate.

When allocating the marketing budget, management generally will consider historical trends as well as new business opportunities. Usually, past performance is the key variable influencing the budget. An analysis of previous revenues and expenses will reveal expected future trends.

The marketing budget's accuracy depends primarily on effective sales analyses. A thorough sales analysis will include:

1. *Total revenue.* Monthly revenue totals should be evaluated with an eye toward establishing trends. This helps ensure that marketing dollars are directed to the seasons with the most sales potential, based upon market conditions and any changes or trends noted.

2. *Average revenue per function.* This statistic will reveal average productivity per function. If there is a consistent shortfall between the actual average revenue and the potential average revenue, marketing dollars can be devoted to reconciling this inequity.

3. *Average revenue per type of function.* This figure will indicate which functions carry the greatest sales potential. Marketing funds can therefore be allocated appropriately.

4. *Average guest count per function.* Some functions have few guests. Unless they are paying a large amount per guest, it may be more profitable to forgo them and concentrate on larger groups. More guests mean more exposure.

5. *Average check.* The per-person price for different types of functions is a good measure of labor productivity. It also can reveal opportunities where marketing dollars can be spent in an effort to increase the average revenue per guest.

6. *Average contribution margin.* This is similar to the average check. The difference is that it is the amount of money available from the average check after you pay the cost of food and beverage used to serve a guest. Most foodservice experts feel that the average contribution margin per guest is more important than the average check because it represents the amount of money left to cover all other expenses and a fair profit.

7. *Number of functions.* A monthly analysis can indicate how well the facility manages and sells its available space. Trends will reveal where marketing dollars should be deployed. For instance, if February is a slow month, perhaps a slight change in the marketing plan can improve sales and profits significantly during this time period.

8. *Space utilization percentages.* This analysis can indicate periods of time where certain function space is underutilized. For example, if a particular meeting room is vacant almost every Wednesday and Thursday, some change in the marketing plan should be considered in order to increase business on those days.

9. *Popularity of different types of functions.* These statistics can indicate the catering department's strengths and weaknesses. If, for instance, weddings are the most popular function, it is obvious that clients view your facility as a good place to hold these events. This can be a mixed blessing. On one hand, it can give you a competitive edge for this type of business. But on the other hand, it may eliminate you from consideration by other types of potential clients.

10. *Percentage of repeat business.* It takes more time, money, and effort to create a new customer than it does to retain an old one. Turning a customer into a repeat patron can be a major challenge, but the rewards are substantial.

11. *Percentage of business that comes from referrals.* You know a product is good when you can recommend it to your friends. The caterer who receives a considerable percentage of business as referrals is obviously doing something right.

The primary purpose of performing this type of sales analysis is to determine the success rate of the current marketing plan. If the results of the analysis suggest that changes should be made, then future marketing efforts will need to be altered to reflect a new direction.

If the marketing plan requires significant alterations, the director of catering should ensure that a thorough market and competition analysis is performed before taking any steps to change it. The analysis will reveal potential opportunities and suggest profitable changes that should be considered.

A market and competition analysis involves a thorough evaluation of (1) the facility's capabilities, (2) the types of markets available, (3) potential sales trends in these markets, (4) number and types of competitors, (5) the facility's strengths and weaknesses, as compared to its competitors, and (6) trends in sales solicitation efforts.

MARKETING RESEARCH

Marketing research should be an ongoing activity. It involves a continuing analysis of the potential clients and competitors that reside in the facility's market area. The catering department's trading area is not easy to define. Theoretically, it could be the world; realistically, it is a lot closer to home.

What products and services should your catering organization offer? A critical first step is to review previous bookings to identify which menus, services, and types of functions were most frequently booked. These historical data serve as the primary basis for determining product and service selection.

Which products and services does your facility do best in terms of quality, cost, and presentation? Remember that it is better to offer a limited number of items that are done well than to offer many items without the ability to guarantee that the facility will provide quality preparation, presentation, and service.

A major consideration when determining the menu items to be offered depends on the skill level in the kitchen as well as the available equipment. What items can the kitchen staff prepare well and what are the equipment limitations? Many restaurants do not stray from their regular menus, so banquets are restricted to what the kitchen already produces and what they do best. Other facilities have separate catering menus or are willing to create custom menus for their clients.

Restaurants also tend to segregate their trading areas into meal segments, such as lunch market areas and dinner market areas. It is thought that lunch customers will not travel more than ten minutes to a preferred restaurant, whereas dinner guests generally will travel up to thirty minutes.

Caterers do not have such neat rules of thumb to guide their marketing research efforts. However, they usually maintain adequate records that will help them determine as accurately as possible the sales revenues and profits they can expect to earn in the future. The major records are (1) group history, (2) lost business, (3) tracer file, and (4) market and competition surveys.

Group History

Usually a catering organization (unless very small) uses a software program, such as Delphi or Daylite, to record client information and events. For instance, when a potential client calls the caterer for price quotations and space availability, the important details are recorded. If the initial inquiry results in a booked event, the appropriate entries are made in the function diary of the software program and a hard copy group file is started.

A group history record should be created whenever initial contact is made with a prospective client. Eventually this record will include all facets of the business relationship with the client. The record involves a synopsis of all relevant aspects of the catered event, from initial inquiry to final disposition.

A group history record is also created when a sales representative solicits catering business from a prospective client. In some instances, there may be tentative group history files created for potential clients; sales representatives may develop open files of potential clients whose names and group affiliations are obtained from mailing lists, directories, or referrals.

The group history record should contain all relevant information, such as dates and details of correspondence, the name and contact information of the client decision maker, attendance figures, contracts, potential for future business, credit history, business referrals, testimonial letters, and other similar data. Group history records help the sales and marketing effort because they reveal consumer desires, trends, and price sensitivity. They usually contain information that, when analyzed carefully, can indicate future business opportunities. The information noted in them can lead directly to additional catering business.

Group history records represent the caterer's major source of repeat patronage. The wise director of catering will ensure that the client decision makers noted in these files are not forgotten. He or she will personally maintain some sort of communication link with them, or assign this responsibility to another member of the catering staff. For instance, birthday cards, direct mail flyers, or holiday greeting cards might be sent to these individuals. Since clients are from a variety of faiths, always opt for "Season's Greetings" instead of "Merry Christmas." Thanksgiving cards or New Year cards should be considered in lieu of, or in addition to, holiday cards, as these cards stand out instead of being lost in the jumble.

This is called relationship marketing—in other words, you develop professional friendships and a positive rapport with your clients. Clients should feel that they have a "friend in the catering business," because then they will tell others about you.

Lost Business

If client inquiries or sales solicitations do not lead to booked business, the group history record should be transformed into a lost business record. These records must be evaluated periodically in order to determine why potential business did not materialize. If certain patterns—such as space unavailability, high prices, or inadequate menu offerings—are discovered, perhaps the facility can do something to improve the underlying problems. For instance, if there is a consistent problem with space availability, the facility could use this information to support a proposal to construct additional function rooms, erect a permanent tent, or create a poolside or roof patio area for outdoor events. Future sales and marketing plans, highlighting the additional space, thereby could lead to a significant increase in business.

Some lost business records will be created after the catering event is booked. These are considered canceled events. For instance, the event could be scheduled, but the client may cancel at the last minute. The director of catering would want to know why the client had a change of heart. It is inappropriate merely to retain the client's deposit; some further contact with the client must be made to determine why the cancellation occurred.

Tracer File

Tracer files (sometimes referred to as tickler files) are similar to a manager's personal list of "things to do today." For instance, if a current client books catering business on a fairly regular basis, the manager's tracer file will include this information. These files are typically kept on a computer using one of the excellent software packages available. The file will note when the client should be contacted, how he or she should be approached, any special considerations that must be offered, and so forth. A tracer file should be established for tentative bookings so that space is not held more than, say, one week without a deposit or definite option. Similarly, a tracer file can be developed that will trace the number of bookings per market segment.

A market segment that provides 5 percent or more of total catering business should be monitored closely for trends and other indicators of future business. Furthermore, if the facility has, say, eighteen separate market segments, it should consider developing a specific marketing plan for each one.

Lost business records should be part of the facility's tracer filing system. Lost business should be coded according to the reason why it was lost. Individual lost business events should be put onto a calendar so that a catering sales representative will be prompted to go back to the record the same time next year and attempt to solicit the client's future business.

Catering sales representatives should update the tracer files daily. They will add information to them as it is obtained. They also will use a system whereby the group history records will be traced and reviewed a few days before client decision makers are contacted.

Market and Competition Surveys

Market and competition surveys consist of detailed descriptions of potential clients and current and potential competitors.

Sales representatives are expected to canvass for new clients. That is, they are responsible for sourcing new clients by studying consumer trends, client desires, and other similar data. One of the best ways to obtain these data is to conduct a market and competition survey. A market survey can be a simple questionnaire sent to potential clients asking them about their catering needs and the amount of money they would be willing to pay for these services. More elaborate, professionally conducted surveys are very costly, but they do reveal considerably more information. Often a local college can provide assistance at a nominal cost if it has a hospitality program. Many times a marketing class will do this as a class project.

Food and beverage trade associations, such as the National Restaurant Association, usually conduct market surveys that may be useful to the director of catering.

A competition survey should include the following information for each competitor, whether hotel, club, restaurant, or other type of venue:

1. Competitor name and address
2. Amount and type of function space available
3. Guest capacity
4. Major markets serviced
5. Franchise or chain affiliation, if any
6. Number of catering employees (service level)
7. Average check or similar data
8. Main products and services offered (menus, package plans, etc.)
9. Daily analysis of any reader boards in the facility lobby or foyer
10. Style of ambience (rustic, elegant, trendy, traditional, etc.)

When gathering data on competitors, you must not violate federal, state, and local antitrust laws. You cannot get together with a competitor and discuss your pricing strategies. Nor can you agree to charge the same prices that a competitor charges.

The competition survey will reveal any unmet market niches. For instance, if the director of catering learns that no one seems to be specializing in the civic events market segments or the after-theater dinner crowd, he or she may decide to explore the possibility of targeting this pool of potential business.

The competition survey also lets the catering executive know what he or she is up against. It is important to differentiate yourself from your competitors. Differentiation involves being the best by comparison to your competition on the criteria valued by your customers. It is like branding. Today's consumer looks to brands, such as Coca-Cola, Wagyu Kobe beef, or Provimi veal, for products they trust when making purchasing decisions. Consumers are loyal to brands that stand for something, such as quality and reliability. In the competitive hospitality business, it is necessary to carve out a unique reputation, image, or specialty. However, any attempts to do this should be initiated only after analyzing the competitive environment.

OPTIONS FOR DETERMINING PRICES FOR CATERING EVENTS

Price is perhaps one of the most important and troublesome parts of the sales and marketing effort. It is a major concern to clients, although generally not the primary or sole determining factor of where to book their events. And it can present several problems for caterers, particularly because it is risky to quote prices too far in advance.

Every business must grapple with the question "How much do I charge?" Pricing is not an easy task. There are many variables to the decision-making process. There is a delicate balance between client demand and the price level. Pricing methods should account for inflation, fixed and variable costs, waste, profits, and changing markets. No matter how prices are calculated, they should be reviewed for competitive factors, reasonableness, potential acceptance, and profitability before adding them to menus and other promotional materials.

Sometimes caterers use more than one pricing method when calculating menu prices, labor charges, rentals, and so forth. The prices that clients will tend to focus on will be the menu prices for food and beverage events. Let's examine some of the ways caterers may decide to price them.

Management Experience

Sometimes prices are a function of management experience. Some of these pricing procedures are:

1. *Reasonable price method.* This is setting a price to represent a value to the client based on the question "If I were a customer, what would I be willing to pay for this meal?" This method often involves developing a pricing structure that is just a bit higher or lower than the ones used by competitors who offer similar types of products and services.

2. *Highest price method.* Another possibility is to set the highest price a caterer thinks the customer will pay. This method does not consider profit requirements, food cost, or labor cost, but rather relies on the principles of supply and demand (whatever the market will bear).

3. *Loss leader price method.* This method involves marking the price of one or more items unusually low with the rationale that clients will be attracted by the low price and will subsequently purchase other items at regular or inflated prices. Prices calculated this way may generate a little profit or none at all; if the price is so low that it doesn't even cover all of the variable expenses, the caterer may wind up losing money.

Pricing so low as to lose money is not a recommended strategy, especially if it includes discount coupons or other similar forms of promotional material; things such as coupons tend to place caterers' facilities in the same category as dry cleaners. However, there are times when a caterer may intentionally price goods and services to break even or to incur a loss. For instance, catered events for charities may be provided free of charge, or they may be priced to cover only the prime cost (food, beverage, and labor expenses). This strategy may be a good choice whenever customers are solicited for other types of profitable business in the future, or for the public relations value.

4. *Trial-and-error method.* Sometimes a caterer will take a guess, and if that price doesn't work, he or she will try another price. This method does not consider profit requirements. Caterers should avoid using the trial-and-error pricing method. They don't really have to; since events are booked in advance, they are reasonably predictable. Besides, it may create a negative impression if prices fluctuate too frequently. Trial and error may be considered when a client asks a restaurant to close its regular business one night so that a party can be booked that will take over the entire operation. In this case, the owner/operator who wants this business will propose a very high price, much higher than the amount of total sales revenue that could be earned with the regular restaurant business.

Thirds Method

The thirds method is normally used to calculate a total price for a function that is planned from scratch; the client does not order off standardized menus but expects something unique. This pricing method is used primarily by properties that have only a few parties a year. For instance, it is commonly used by restaurants that have small private party rooms. The main focus of their business is the regular restaurant, with private parties adding a little extra profit.

The thirds method involves calculating a per-person price that covers three things equally:

1. Cost of food, beverage, and other supplies (such as linens and florals)
2. Cost of payroll to handle the function, plus overhead expenses needed to open the room (such as turning on the air-conditioning units)
3. Profit

For instance, with a $30.00 price per person, the caterer will have approximately $20.00 to cover expenses, leaving a $10.00 profit from each guest. The caterer will also add taxes and gratuities (or service charges) to this price. In Las Vegas, for example, the final price quoted to the meeting planner would be approximately $38.43 ($30.00 + $2.43 sales tax [8.10%] + $6.00 gratuity [20%]). Another way to phrase it is that the price quoted would be "$30.00 plus plus"—that is, $30.00 plus tax and gratuity.

Contribution Margin Method

The contribution margin (CM) method is a typical pricing method used by large caterers. It is based on the belief that everything must make a profit.

It is too difficult for large caterers to build each party from scratch, so they must standardize quite a few things. In these cases, the CM method often is a good choice.

If a caterer offers pre-priced, standardized catering options, he or she must be willing to place limits on what the client can and cannot have. This may cause the caterer to refuse some business. Furthermore, the caterer must enforce other stipulations, such as the minimum number of attendees needed; in most cases, it is not cost-effective for a caterer to open a room for a small number of people unless the client is willing to pay a separate room rental charge.

A caterer cannot have any surprises when pre-pricing everything offered because the profit structure can take a big hit if he or she strays too far from the standard. The CM method works well only in a very predictable environment where the caterer has a great deal of control over what the clients can have. He or she can adjust prices a little bit if they are very high to start with, although potential clients may avoid that caterer if they think the initial prices are out of line.

To use this method for, say, pricing individual menu items, the caterer must know as precisely as possible all the expenses associated with opening the room, apart from the types of menu items that will be ordered. Salaries and wages, utilities, and marketing are essentially fixed catering expenses. It is a good idea for caterers to calculate these types of expenses for a full year. It is also critical for them to keep these numbers up-to-date because the menu prices will be based on them, and caterers must keep in mind that once they set these prices, they may have to live with them for a while.

Then the caterer divides these total fixed expenses by the number of guests expected for a year. This will provide a reasonable estimate of the amount of fixed expense per attendee. To this number, it is necessary to add the per-person cost for the food, beverage, and other variable costs (such as specialty linen) that come with a particular catering menu option.

Once the caterer knows how much the total variable and fixed expense is per person, he or she then adds the desired profit margin to each menu option. This markup is usually pretty substantial, as much as 75 percent. Although this may seem like a high markup, caterers who do a considerable amount of catering business have more unanticipated overhead. This markup also allows the caterer negotiating room; for instance, he or she can throw in a few extra party platters at no charge for a reception without taking a big hit to the bottom line. The markup also covers any last-minute surprises. Given the larger catering volume, there will be more complaints, and caterers may need to reduce part of the bill or include additional items to resolve them. Caterers cannot do this if the profit margin is too low, but they can be more gracious if the profit margin is high enough to begin with.

Let's assume that a caterer determines that all fixed expenses average $15.00 per attendee to put on a party. Also assume that the variable cost of food and beverage associated with a particular menu option is $10.00 per person. The out-of-pocket costs are, therefore, $25.00 per attendee. Add a 75 percent markup for profit, and the menu price becomes $43.75 ($25.00 × 1.75). This can be rounded up to, say, $45.00 plus plus per person. If clients have additional unique requests (e.g., decor that is not part of the caterer's in-house inventory), the costs for these must be added in separately or included with the other variable costs before calculating the menu price.

Multiplier Method

This method is a version of the contribution margin method. Generally speaking, when pricing menu items, some caterers calculate the variable cost (i.e., the cost of the food or beverage) needed to sell one of them. This variable cost is the basis for calculating the selling price. Once it is established, caterers then multiply it by a factor that usually varies from about 3 to 7 but can go higher.

For the typical caterer, the factor is related to the type of services, ambience, and so forth provided to guests; the more expensive they are, the higher the factor will be. But the factor can also be independent of these variables; for instance, during the high season, even the most modest catering facility can command a high price. In the end, the factor, and hence the price, is influenced by the competition and what the market will bear. In all cases, it will be as high as possible. It will be especially expensive during the high seasons. During those periods, the typical caterer practices what is sometimes referred to as "congestion pricing," that is, price based on demand. High demand equals high price. As far as the caterer is concerned, there is no such thing as a price that is too high.

This method is also used by some caterers to price labor and offerings other than food or beverage. For instance, assume that the variable cost for a bartender is $45.00 for a four-hour shift. If the caterer multiplies it by a factor of 3, the price quoted to the client will be $135.00.

This method can be used to price everything the caterer offers. It is very similar to à la carte menu pricing in a restaurant. Some "value meals" will include a few offerings for one price, but most of the upgrades a client wants to purchase will be individually priced.

Level Pricing Method

This pricing method involves creating prices that allow clients to comparison shop. For instance, the caterer may show a client a chart like the one on the following page with many price options. Catering clients can choose one of the three options for each line item in this example. It also may be possible for them to select something from more than one column, thereby creating a fourth option for themselves. However, since the three options are typically priced assuming there will be no substitutions allowed, the caterer may not allow this without an additional cost.

	Popular	Upscale	Value-Based
Chicken, per person	Piccata $24.00	Oscar $32.00	Dijon $22.00
Staff	B team $500.00	A team $700.00	C team $400.00
Linen	Color	Overlays	White
Chair rental	Stacking $850.00	Ballroom $1,400.00	Padded $600.00
Floral	Roses $400.00	Orchids $600.00	Carnations $300.00
Music	Duo $550.00	Trio $750.00	Solo $375.00

Range Pricing Method

This is a pricing method used by caterers when clients have a wide range of expected guests. For instance, this chart gives you an idea of the impact fluctuating guest counts can have on the total bill:

Prime Rib Dinner	Number of Guests	Price per Guest
	235 or fewer	$39.75
	236–265	$37.45
	266 and up	$34.25

If the caterer uses a traditional restaurant pricing method, a client might be quoted the same per-person price for the banquet whether 200 or 300 attendees are expected. This method works well for the caterer with the higher count but not as well if the count drops, because fixed costs are allocated over a smaller number of guests. So if a price of $34.25 per person was quoted based on 200 to 300 guests and the final count came in at 208 guests, the caterer's revenue would be $7,124.00 (208 × $34.25). Using range pricing, the caterer's revenues would be $8,268.00 (208 × $39.75), permitting the caterer to pick up an additional $1,144.00. This extra revenue will allow the caterer to absorb extra overhead costs associated with a higher guest count and add a bit more profit to the bottom line.

Consumption Method

Another way to price a meal function is to charge one price for the food and beverage items, one for labor, one for room rental, one for utilities, and so forth. The client therefore pays only for what is consumed or ordered, such as per gallon, per dozen, and so on. However, more and more caterers seem to be moving toward an all-or-nothing posture for some things that at one time were easier to purchase on an as-consumed basis. For instance, while it is still possible for clients to pay for alcohol by the bottle, charging per drink is the norm these days. Caterers have found that it is easier to sell a drink for, say, $8.75 than it is to sell a bottle for $175.00.

This type of pricing is more common with off-premise caterers than it is with on-premise facilities, especially those who "drop and go" (that is, those who just deliver what a client orders and then take off). As a general rule, on-premise facilities do not use this pricing strategy, primarily because it is too cumbersome. The typical on-premise client does not want to be burdened with an itemized list of charges even though it tends to be less expensive to negotiate for each charge separately. He or she prefers a per-person price. It is more convenient, and it makes it easier to compare price quotations from several caterers. Off-premise caterers, who must rent tables, chairs, china, flatware, and other items, are more likely to quote charges separately.

Market Method

This method is used to price certain items whose food cost can vary unpredictably from day to day. It is a common practice in high-end restaurants that offer fresh seafood items and other similar items that are subject to supply and demand costs throughout the supply chain. It is much easier to make these kinds of price revisions today than in the past, as there are several good computer applications, such as Adaco, that can be used to make the work easier and the results more accurate.

Caterers should not commit to prices for the long term for these types of menu items; if food costs increase, it is not easy to revise menu prices because some events are planned far into the future. Caterers might state in the contract, "If this meal were purchased today, the price would be $35.00 plus plus. At the time of your event, the price may be lower or higher depending on the Consumer Price Index (CPI) at that time, with a maximum of $40.00." This contract clause will give the client at least some idea of what to expect.

Other Pricing Considerations

Pricing is a little bit of science blended with a whole lot of art. There are a lot of moving parts in the food and beverage business, lots of ways to make mistakes. And every detail is critical. While catering may be a little more predictable than regular restaurant business, it is never easy. Here are some specific things that can impact the menu-pricing process.

1. Clients generally want good-quality products and services at the lowest possible price. A person who would not think of haggling over price at a restaurant will nickel-and-dime you over a catering menu. Prices established by management must strike a fine balance between the client's need for value and the facility's need for maximum return on investment. Value is very important to clients. Value is defined as the perception that quality and service are on a par with price. If quality and service are deemed too low, then the price will always be perceived by clients as being too high.

2. Consider what the competition is charging. Caterers need to be consistently aware of what the competition is charging and either try to meet it or distinguish themselves in such a way that they can demand higher prices. Clients can easily surf the Internet to find this information, so it is doubly important for caterers to know the competition, especially if they are using the Internet to display their prices. But they also need to recognize that price alone is not the only gauge clients use when making a decision. Overall value and experience are also very important.

One way to address competitors' prices is to use the price quotation as the competitive bid subject to modifications. For instance, a caterer could give potential clients several price/quality options and let them mix and match according to their needs.

3. Consider the total income from the event. If applicable, caterers should look at the total income from the event and not concentrate solely on the food and beverage portions.

4. Caterers should develop websites, brochures, and other promotional materials that include basic menus and accompaniments. This strategy lends itself to enhancements and upselling opportunities.

5. The pricing strategy should include built-in provisions for complimentary upgrades (added value to the client). In New Orleans, they use the term *lagniappe*, which means "a little bit extra." Caterers should try to add lagniappes to their pricing. The goodwill stemming from such unexpected, pleasant surprises can help produce client satisfaction and result in repeat business. For instance, a caterer could include a glass of wine, increased portion sizes, or upgraded breads at no extra charge.

6. The profit margins for catered events generally are much greater than those in the typical restaurant operation. However, the catering organization has many more slow days—even days when there is no business—with which to contend. As a result, even though the director of catering may sympathize with clients' budgetary constraints, the fact remains that there is only so much he or she can do to accommodate them. The key to remember for all pricing methods is to give clients as many pricing options as possible and do what the competition is not doing.

7. If applicable, the director of catering must determine room rental rates and other similar charges. The basic pricing format is the same as those used for setting menu prices. The total price is a compilation of variable costs, fixed costs, and profit. For instance, when setting room rental rates, one would consider the variable costs (such as utilities, setup, cleaning, and security) and the fixed costs (such as insurance, depreciation, and taxes). A profit margin then would be added.

8. Deposits, guarantees, cancellation fees, gratuities, tips, and refund policies also need to be detailed by the director of catering and reviewed by senior management. Usually these rates are influenced by the season, opportunity costs associated with last-minute cancellations, employee union contract provisions, and the facility's credit policies.

9. Menu options will need to be revised periodically. Some may be underperforming and will need to be dropped or changed somewhat in an attempt to increase their sales potential. Typically, any major revision will include a long, hard look at the current pricing structure.

Before embarking on a revision, a director of catering should perform a sales analysis to determine how well the current list of offerings is selling. The director needs to consider the popularity of various packages and individual menu items as well as the current variable costs needed to produce and serve them. A thorough sales analysis will also examine the contribution margin (CM) generated by current offerings. These data will be very helpful to those who are employed to market the catering experience.

Let's assume that a director of catering has analyzed the previous quarter's catering business and computed the data noted in the following table:

Menu Package	Number Sold	Popularity Index	Package Cost	Package Price	Total Cost	Total Sales Revenue	Total CM
A	125	17%	$11.75	$ 58.75	$1,468.75	$7,343.75	$5,875.00
B	90	12%	$12.63	$ 63.15	$1,136.70	$5,683.50	$4,546.80
C	80	11%	$22.50	$112.50	$1,800.00	$9,000.00	$7,200.00
D	27	4%	$14.35	$ 71.75	$ 387.45	$1,937.25	$1,549.80
E	91	12%	$14.95	$ 74.75	$1,360.45	$6,802.25	$5,441.80
F	45	6%	$18.85	$ 94.25	$ 848.25	$4,241.25	$3,393.00
G	65	9%	$21.35	$106.75	$1,387.75	$6,938.75	$5,551.00
H	40	5%	$11.65	$ 58.25	$ 466.00	$2,330.00	$1,864.00
I	20	3%	$52.00	$260.00	$1,040.00	$5,200.00	$4,160.00
J	90	12%	$12.29	$ 61.45	$1,106.10	$5,530.50	$4,424.40
K	30	4%	$22.47	$112.35	$ 674.10	$3,370.50	$2,696.40
L	48	6%	$17.55	$ 87.75	$ 842.40	$4,212.00	$3,369.60
Totals	751	100%			$12,517.95	$ 62,589.75	$50,071.80

In this example, the caterer is currently offering twelve meal packages. In the past quarter, a total of 751 packages were sold. Each package's cost of the food and beverage and perhaps a few other variable expenses (such as upgraded centerpieces instead of the standard ones used) are listed along with the prices charged to clients. The total cost over the past quarter was $12,517.95 and the total sales revenue was $62,589.75. The difference between these two figures is the total contribution margin (CM) earned during the quarter.

These data give us a good idea of the profitability of individual packages, but they also tell us something about each package's popularity. The popularity index column shows that package A was most popular. Its popularity index was 17 percent—that is, of the total number of packages sold during the quarter (751), 125 of them were package A. (The popularity index of a package is computed by taking its number of sales and dividing it by the total number of packages sold, then multiplying by 100; for package A, the formula is 125 ÷ 751 × 100 = 17%.)

Further analysis reveals that while package A was most popular, package I was least popular. Considering only popularity, one could conclude that package I should be dropped from the list of offerings, or at least given a complete makeover. Or maybe it should have its price changed.

But before doing that, we need to evaluate how much CM package I contributed last quarter. It seems that this figure ($4,160.00) is higher than five other packages, all of which were more popular.

The lesson learned here is that there are two things we should evaluate very closely when viewing these data: a package's popularity and its CM. The two go hand in hand and can help us make a better decision about revising some of these packages.

What can we do with package I in order to increase its popularity and CM? For one thing, maybe a slight price reduction might increase both of these things dramatically. If, say, we reduced the price to $240 and doubled the package's sales from 20 to 40, its popularity index would increase slightly, but its total CM will increase dramatically. It would now be $7,520 ((40 × $240) − (40 × $52.00)). To make this happen we might have to increase our promotion of package I, spending a little more money to give it a push. But even so, the new CM surely will be much higher than it was last quarter.

The same concept can work in reverse. For instance, package A is very popular. Given this level of popularity, maybe clients wouldn't mind paying another $5.00 or $10.00 per person. If we bump up its price from $58.75 to, say, $63.75, and if there is no drop-off in the number sold, we will enjoy an additional CM of $625.00 ($5.00 × 125 = $625.00).

Calculating the food and beverage cost of a package is extremely difficult. The main problem is that few foodservice people have access to up-to-date standard recipe costs. The typical caterer doesn't have time to constantly update these costs. Even with the computer software packages available, it is still an onerous task. Consequently, the caterer may be working with inaccurate figures.

If the caterer is part of a huge restaurant or hotel company, the standard recipe cost calculations can more readily be performed at corporate headquarters. At that level of management, there are financial analysts who can stay on top of the frequently changing food and beverage costs and use them to update the standard recipe costs.

Value

Recall that value is a function of price, quality, and service. There has been a gradual shift from value pricing to service. This involves the enhancement of service so that it will be perceived as a greater component of overall value. It is less expensive to improve service and amenities than it is to discount prices. Sell service first. Assure the potential client that you will provide dependable, knowledgeable, experienced personnel to make certain that their event will be successful.

When your price is too high, customers will tell you—and not buy. When your price is too low, customers buy—and never tell you they would have paid more.

The perception of value is greater when something extra is offered, as opposed to merely discounting prices. If a client asks for a reduced price, offer complimentary centerpieces, decor, microphones, and the like instead. Value-added menus can include specialty items that are environmentally conscious, such as serving free-range chicken and organic vegetables, not using plastic or foam disposables, using napkins made from recycled paper, donating excess food to a shelter, and so on.

PROMOTION

As you know, a satisfied guest is the best advertisement for your catering operation, but you cannot rely only upon word of mouth to increase your catering business. You should also regularly promote your business to generate additional awareness and sales.

Promotion includes the cost of developing and maintaining a website; advertising in newspapers, magazines, telephone directories, and trade media; outdoor billboards and other signage; radio and television advertising; fees paid to advertising and promotional agencies; entertaining business clients (such as hosting a customer appreciation party for meeting planners); memberships in professional associations, civic groups, and business groups; and promotional materials such as sales brochures, menus, photographs, DVDs, direct mail pieces, social media, and written solicitations for catering business.

If the facility is a franchise or part of a chain or referral group, the franchising fees, referral fees, and royalty payments that must be paid to the parent company are part of promotion expenses.

Public relations and publicity fees are another type of promotional effort. The cost of preparing press releases that will be sent to food editors; writing books, columns, and articles about the catering industry; and hosting charity and media events is considered part of promotion expenses.

Salespeople's salaries and commissions may be included in the promotional budget. In some cases, the catering salesperson earns no salary, or a minimal salary, and commissions make up the bulk of his or her paycheck. Under this income arrangement, the facility usually expects the salesperson to concentrate solely on selling directly to one or more market segments.

Salespeople may also be paid commissions for developing leads. They may be hired to generate interest among potential corporate clients. Once a lead is established, it would be turned over to a catering manager, who would handle proposals, planning, contracts, and so forth.

In our opinion, the most effective and efficient type of promotional plan a catering organization can use should include (1) an effective, up-to-date website, (2) well-designed, creative menus and brochures, (3) creative proposals, (4) DVDs and photos, (5) word-of-mouth advertising, and (6) soliciting future business at a current event. Additionally, depending on the property, blogs and social networking may be important tools in promoting the facility.

These types of promotions are not listed in order of importance. For instance, you cannot say that a brochure is always more important than word-of-mouth advertising. It would be if you were using a mass-mailer campaign, but it would be much less effective than word-of-mouth advertising if you wanted to solicit specific local civic events.

Online

An effective, up-to-date website is invaluable. A website is a living brochure that should contain photos, video clips, menus, contact information, and descriptive information. Too many websites are merely bulletin boards on the information highway. If your site doesn't provide your customers with the information they are looking for, it is useless. If the content isn't kept fresh and up-to-date, it reflects poorly on your operation. Websites are easy to create and maintain, as long as you keep the format simple. Stay away from flash intros, expensive frames, Java, and the bells and whistles that the professional webmasters promote. Search engines do not "crawl" sites with frames, which will keep your site out of many search engines. Many computers cannot access all of the deluxe capabilities without downloading a plug-in, and the novelty soon wears off. And with the move to handheld mobile units, text-based websites will become simpler by necessity. Provide an email address, phone number and answer messages in a timely manner.

Be sure the website diagrams of your function space show columns, doors, electrical outlets, and any other obstructions or features. Additional information should include parking information, maps, and directions from the airport.

When planning a website, consider whether you want to build it yourself or hire someone to do it for you. If you don't have the interest or skill, you are better off hiring someone. However, most colleges and many private companies offer classes that can teach you the basics, using software such as Adobe PageMaker. There is no need to learn HTML.

If you are part of a much larger entity, see if upper management will give you permission to create a separate website or blog just for the catering department. When you create your own website or blog, you have more control and can keep information timely and relevant to avoid a static site. Your site can be linked to the main site for the facility. It is important to register your own domain name, so your Web address would read www.myfacility.com, not www.internetprovider .com/myfacility. The latter makes it appear that your facility isn't willing to pay $35 per year to register its own domain name. You can go to http://internic.net to register your name. If your facility name is no longer available, try a variation, such as www.mynamemycity.com. You can also choose a .net or other extension.

You would then select an Internet provider. This is where your site will reside. Depending on the size of your site, this should cost from $25 to $50 per month.

Your website should be consistent with other marketing efforts, including colors, logos, and fonts. Provide content that is useful, informative, and entertaining. Include interior and exterior photos, plate presentations, theme parties, your menu, and contact information.

Target your market. Remember market segmentation. You can create additional pages for different markets and use them as alternative ways to draw users to your site. Each individual page on your site can be submitted to the search engines. You can create a separate page for weddings, one for meeting business, and so on, and link them all through your main page.

Avoid garish colors and backgrounds that clash with the text or make reading difficult. Avoid backgrounds with the .bmp extension, as they take an inordinate amount of time to load and people have no patience for slow-loading sites. Look at other sites to see what you like and don't like. Just go to any search engine and type in "catering" and you will get thousands of sites to view. Type in "catering" and the name of your city and you will be able to do a competition analysis online. Many sites include their prices, but we do not recommend this practice.

Don't participate in banner ads, as they cheapen a site. Don't submit your site to the search engines until it is finished; a half-ready site creates a negative image. You can submit it for free by going to www.addme.com.

In addition to a website, with online services (e.g., Craigslist) caterers can easily advertise their services, sometimes without paying a fee to the hosting service. As with all types of marketing, be sure that the text is well written, include high-quality photos as appropriate, and be sure to provide several methods of contact (such as phone, fax, and email).

Brochures

Sales brochures generally include a considerable amount of information that potential clients can evaluate when they are in the market for catering services, and they can be one of your best marketing tools. The brochure should note the facility's logo, slogan, address, phone number, website, catering policies, available rooms, suggested menus, prices, credit information, and service procedures.

Since the brochure might be the potential client's first contact with the catering department, it must be professionally prepared. It is an invitation to potential clients that will create a lasting impression. It should be complete and attractive. If it is mailed, it absolutely must be sent to a specific person, not to "manager." A great brochure isn't an expense; it is an investment that pays off.

The brochure is an integral part of any successful marketing strategy and must convey a stimulating message that will be understood by the market you are addressing. The copy should be both tasty and tasteful—the words should convey mouth-watering images. It is important to create and maintain an image in the client's mind. Descriptions of menu items should generate both interest and sales. The copy must talk to the consumer in his or her own words. Avoid clichés such as "the best-kept secret," "chef's special," "as you like it," and so forth. Clients must be able to understand the names of food items, or a descriptor should be included, such as "Kartoffel Kloesse/*Savory Potato Croquettes*."

Brochures and menus include the following elements:
- Cover
- Design format

- Layout
- Typeface (font)
- Paper stock
- Colors
- Illustrations/graphics
- Copy

The brochure should be printed on a good-quality, durable paper stock. Few things bring a better return on investment than a high-quality design printed on high-quality paper. There is a fine line here, however. While you want your brochures to be elegant, they should not convey the image that you are too expensive or that you are spending too much money on fancy brochures.

Be sure you see the colors you have chosen on the actual paper you will be using, as colored ink looks different on different types of paper. Colors are important. Choose classic colors. For the covers, deep royal purples, rich dusky blues, dark greens, and chocolate to mahogany browns are elegant and convey reliability and a sense of permanence. Trendy colors, such as lime green or hot pink, create a faddish look. Menu pages on a rich cream paper stock are more cultured than a stark white finish. Pantone has an excellent website on color: www.pantone.com.

Brochures must be easy to read. The smallest font used should be 12 point. Avoid the Courier and Times New Roman fonts, which look typewritten and not as professional. Script type can be difficult to read; all capitals can be difficult to read as well. You should use clean fonts such as **Tahoma,** Calibri, **Verdana, Arial,** or **Garamond.**

Be sure the print jumps off the page. There should be a contrast between the page and the print. Red print on a dark pink background would be impossible for a color-blind client to read.

Leave adequate spacing between items. Brochures that are difficult to read may be discarded quickly.

Pages and brochures should incorporate graphics and color photographs. Photographs can help stretch the imagination. Clients should be able to picture themselves in the setting. Photographs of activities are more effective than photographs of just the facilities. If you plan to include food in the photographs, use close-up photos of finished products, not just the ingredients. Avoid the overdone, common photos, such as the smiling chef standing next to the buffet table. Strive for a fresh approach. Bad photographs are worse than no photographs. Be sure, though, that the food the client actually receives looks like the representation in the photographs.

The brochure should not appear crowded or cluttered. We recommend leaving at least 50 percent of the page blank, including wide margins and space between menu items. This is known as "white space" and gives the eye a place to rest, making the overall page easier to read.

Be concise in your verbiage, but make your points. Be consistent in your style of writing. Mixing casual phrases with dignified-sounding statements can confuse the client.

Tell potential clients about the benefits of holding their events in your facility. Give them the information that will sell the event. You must maintain credibility. Mention any awards or favorable reviews. Include testimonials. Tell them the background of your chef, awards you have won, and other important information.

The cover can be a designed as a folder, and the letter of agreement, correspondence, flyers, and other paperwork can be placed into the pockets. The two-panel 9-by-12-inch cover is a popular size, and it easily accommodates standard 8½-by-11-inch stationery. This size will also fit into a standard mailing envelope. Before having odd-size brochures printed, check with the post office to see what the mailing costs will be. Sometimes a fraction of an inch can greatly increase postage costs.

Many facilities use direct mail efforts to solicit catering business. Specific names, titles, and addresses can be obtained from several database sources and used to construct mailing lists of potential catering clients.

Mailing lists are the key to an effective direct mail campaign. Facility executives are often active in many local associations and fraternal organizations; their membership rolls can be excellent, fruitful mailing lists. You can obtain mailing lists from tradeshows, i.e., a bridal show would be a good source for wedding business.

Lists also are available from the local chamber of commerce, economic development authorities, and local charitable groups and foundations. Local department stores also have mailing lists; for instance, some of them have bridal registries that they might be willing to share.

Mailing lists also can be obtained from companies that specialize in developing them. For instance, American Business Lists, a division of American Business Information, prepares and sells business mailing lists and mailing labels encompassing just about any type of group, industry, or profession the catering executive may wish to solicit.

Direct mail is an effective marketing tool. It can be personalized, a specific audience can be targeted, and the results of a direct mail campaign are readily measurable. However, it can be an expensive marketing tactic; the cost of the brochure, other inserts (such as a cover letter, response card, or promotional flyer), envelope, postage, labor, and other ancillary expenses can be quite high.

Menus

Standardized banquet menus usually are included in the sales brochures and on the website. They should always be well written and attractively presented. The smart catering executive will resist the temptation to create a laundry list of menu items; he or she will note one or more examples of menu formats that clients can select for their functions.

The menus should also include mention of the facility's ability and willingness to create a custom menu. In our experience, the successful, competitive caterer is one who can accommodate specific client needs.

A facility's restaurant menus can also be used as an effective marketing tool. For instance, a creative menu in a club or hotel's gourmet room or restaurant's dining room can impress meeting planners who are visiting the facility on a fact-finding mission. Restaurant menus also can carry discreet notations that advertise catering services.

The menu portion of the brochure is vitally important. Menus should be centered symmetrically for aesthetic appeal. Symmetry is pleasing to the eye, and this style leaves blank spacing, which is easier on the eye than a page filled with print.

Course headings should be in a larger or bolder type than the rest of the menu. Course headings serve to divide the menu into areas such as appetizer, salad, entree, and dessert. Menu item names should stand out. Descriptive wording identifying the menu ingredients, method of preparation, or other applicable information should follow. Do not overestimate the knowledge of your customers—explain items they may not understand, such as Beef Wellington or Veal Oscar. Any nutritional claims included on the menu must be verifiable.

With restaurant menus, selection is usually an impulse decision. Catering decisions are usually given much more thought and deliberation, and often more than one person is involved with the decision. Guidelines to keep in mind when developing a menu include:

- Do not use the word *starch* with a client or on menus (starch is for shirts).
- Do not use abbreviations such as *w/* for "with" or *&* for "and."
- Never give a client a duplicated copy on standard copy paper. If menus are printed on-site, use a high-quality paper or letterhead.
- Do not use documents with typographical errors, misspellings, or grammatical errors.
- Be consistent with capitalization.
- Do not list prices in ascending order from least to most expensive. This will encourage your clients to shop by price instead of for specific menu items.
- Use appropriate descriptors for menu items. Be specific. The second example below is much better than the first:

Assorted Cheeses

or

An Array of Creamy Brie, Tangy Muenster, and Sharp Cheddar Cheeses

Descriptive wording (*crisp, hot, flaky*, etc.) evokes an image. Be careful about using words that will worry the weight-conscious, such as *rich, heavy*, and *thick*. Only use words that actually describe an item. What is a Surprise Omelet? What is a delicate sauce? Examples of good descriptive wording include:

Exquisite Lean Chateaubriand with a Velvety Rich Flavor
Melt-in-Your-Mouth Maple-Cured Smoked Ham

- Printed menus incorporated into a brochure should include only your normal offerings. If your chef can prepare off-menu specialty items, insert a discrete message on the printed menus noting this possibility for clients who are looking for something different.
- À la carte menus price each food on an individual basis. The client may choose from a variety of different options for appetizers, soups, salads, entrees, vegetables, and desserts.
- Custom-printed menus may be developed especially for a particular client for a particular event. The customized menu is primarily designed for those clients who want something different. Guests often prefer to incorporate their personal preferences into the menu. For instance, a client may want to assemble a unique set of menu items and print a souvenir or commemorative menu. This is typical with awards dinners, anniversaries, and weddings. Customizing menus also allows the caterer to work within a client's specific budgetary or dietary constraints, or to fit within the designated theme.
- A client may want to develop a specialized printed menu to include a certain logo, advertising, or style. For instance, a computer convention may want menus printed in the shape of a personal computer. If you are asked to print a customized menu, you should have menu items printed symmetrically in the center of the page, not on one side or the other like a laundry list. It is important to create an attractive visual presentation.
- Convention clients who book several meals may want to communicate the menus to attendees ahead of time. A professional association convention may last several days. The convention program could list each day's menus so that attendees will know in advance what to expect. Attendees with special dietary needs then have enough time to order a special meal or make alternative plans.
- We recommend that every page with a price on it also be dated. Clients often have old menus in their files. When you talk to a client, be sure he or she has a menu with current prices.

Proposals

A proposal is an offer to provide specified goods and services, explaining the terms, the costs, and how the goods and services satisfy the client's needs. The proposal is an attempt, in writing, to persuade the potential client to give you his or her business. It is a written sales presentation! A proposal is the first serious written understanding of a client's desires.

If the client accepts the offer and signs an agreement, the proposal ceases to be a proposal and becomes a contract for specified services.

Proposals typically include one or more options that the client can consider. For instance, if a qualified client is in the market for a company holiday party, the caterer may prepare one or more competitive bids for his or her perusal. If the client selects one of the options, there usually is a confirmation notice included in the proposal that can be signed by the client and returned to the caterer.

Proposals usually are prepared only when there is serious client interest. Normally a sales representative will not prepare and send one to a client until both parties have met once or twice to explore possibilities.

Since the proposal is the first major step toward a signed catering agreement (contract), it must include all relevant information. Nothing should be left to chance or assumption. And, of course, there should be no verbal side agreements; if it is worth negotiating, it is worth writing down. This will prevent misunderstandings that can result in unhappy clients and a cloud on the facility's reputation.

If proposals are part of the sales solicitation efforts, they should include sales brochures, menus and, photos. A DVD or audio CD might also be included, which could include sales presentations, previous or suggested plate presentations, function room setups, and so forth.

Generally, though, a proposal is a direct response to a client inquiry by a serious shopper. Beware of potential clients who are merely trolling for new ideas or shopping for the cheapest caterer. Sales brochures and other similar materials normally are sent to people who represent potential business but have not actively sought to use your facility for their catered events.

CDs, DVDs, and Photos

CDs, DVDs, and photos are excellent promotional materials that should be part of all sales representatives' sales kits. Though they may be expensive to produce, they can be exceptionally useful marketing tools. They could also be used in direct mail campaigns.

Most people have CD players in their cars. With the average commute lasting between thirty-five and sixty minutes each way, you would have a potential client's undivided attention during that time. You can describe the event in detail, without interruption. But always include a written proposal and a brochure along with the CD. Identify what you want to talk about and script an outline with key points to describe the highlights of different aspects of your catering program. Upsell the features you wish to promote, such as flowers or decorations. You could develop one CD for weddings and others for various theme party options. The content should not exceed twenty minutes in length. Practice voice modulation so that you do not speak in a monotone.

Video recording is very popular. Many catering clients are willing to spend a considerable amount of money to record their functions; this is especially true for weddings, bridal showers, and similar events. The caterer should consider recording some of these functions and using them to impress potential clients. For instance, if a video recording company is hired to record a wedding, the catering executive could make some arrangement with the bride and groom and the videographer to prepare a short version of the final recording for the facility's marketing purposes, such as uploading to YouTube (www.youtube.com). You can even create a channel on YouTube, and people can subscribe to be notified when you upload a new video.

The facility also should consider developing a video sales presentation. For example, a video walk-through of the facility can be a very persuasive part of the marketing plan. Successful videos are usually no longer than three minutes in length, as most people today have a short attention span. Alternatively, a short full-motion video presentation could be included on your website or uploaded to YouTube.

Beautiful color photos are another very effective marketing tool. Today's digital cameras make photos easy, inexpensive, and readily available to email to clients. Available photos should include some food items, especially the facility's specialty products. They should also highlight the property's function space and other amenities.

The director of catering should see to it that a binder is maintained for sales use that includes photos of suggested plate presentations, lavish parties that were previously produced, and similar pictorial materials. The binder also should include testimonial letters. A copy of this binder should always be on display in the catering sales office waiting room or conference room.

Local Newspapers

A well-written text accompanied by an eye-catching illustration or photo-graph is an excellent reminder about your facility's catering program. Send press releases to media regularly, featuring menus, creative themes, awards won or other similar accomplishments, and even a popular recipe. If you or your chef has some writing skill, offer to provide a weekly or monthly food column to the editor. Whenever you pay for an advertisement, the copy and illustrations should be professionally prepared if you do not have desktop publishing capabilities on your computer. Be sure the copy is eye-catching and appropriate for your target audience. When considering the cost, remember that your ad is competing for attention with other professionally prepared ads.

In-House Opportunities

If your facility uses an answering machine or voice mail for messages, a brief, friendly invitation can be extended to callers suggesting they consider holding their next special event in the facility.

Professionally designed posters and flyers placed in high-traffic areas such as the elevator or lobby will heighten awareness of your catering operation.

Attractive inserts can be prepared for enclosure with monthly statements, dues notices, or your calendar of activities.

Sunday brunches, live entertainment, or catering services can be promoted with table tents and high-quality flyers.

Employee recommendations can result in additional bookings. Make sure your employees know about your catering program, and offer them an incentive (e.g., a $50 reward) if an event is held based on their recommendation.

Word-of-Mouth Advertising

This is by far the most effective form of advertising. Many foodservice operations, especially table service restaurants, rely exclusively on this type of notoriety. Word-of-mouth advertising is the prelude to referral business. Most catering clients put a great deal of stock in current and previous customers' recommendations. This is especially true if the client knows the customer and trusts his or her opinion. No other marketing efforts will carry as much weight as will the opinions and recommendations of a trusted colleague or friend.

Social Media

In recent years, social media have provided a new way of marketing. Included in social media is any communication format where users publish the content. It allows for mass two-way communication, allowing many people to talk to many people. It is transforming the way humans interact using technology.

While most of the social media services are free, there is a cost in time, especially when you are getting started. Once you have them running smoothly, it only involves about thirty minutes a day to check in and update. And that thirty minutes doesn't have to be all at once. Just as you check your email in between other tasks, you can get in the habit of checking Twitter and other social media resources too. Before starting any social media outreach, it is helpful to identify the goals you want to achieve, so you can choose the tools that best match your objectives. Possible goals for a social media program might include:

1. Being seen as an expert in your niche
2. Driving traffic to your sites
3. Promoting blog postings
4. Documenting your passions (for example, wine or food)
5. Communicating with clients and potential clients
6. Finding others with similar interests
7. Learning new ways to do things

A personal online brand is made up of the many strands of online presence you have:

1. *Twitter.* Twitter (http://twitter.com) is a micro-blog—an exchange of quick short messages. You are allowed only 140 characters per post, including spaces and your user name. You can see an example of Patti's Twitter account at http://twitter.com/pattishock.

Twitter becomes more beneficial to you when you give value to others. The more you put in and the more helpful you are, the more value you bring, and the more comes back to you.

Most people on Twitter want cool links to click on, something worth replying to or retweeting, and the feeling of being closer to others. The rule of thumb is that 85 percent of your tweets should be interesting, informative, or educational, and 10 percent of your tweets should be humorous; then 5 percent of your tweets can be marketing. If you only market, you may lose your followers.

The best way to get followers is to follow. It is etiquette to follow back those who follow you. Twellow (www.twellow.com) is like the yellow pages for Twitter. You can look for people to follow by category or location. Twellow makes it easy to find relevant people or organizations to follow, such as food experts, wine experts, industry publications, and other caterers. Tweetdeck (www.tweetdeck .com) is a desktop download that allows you to manage your tweets by dividing incoming tweets by categories you create.

Twitter limits how fast the number of your followers can grow. The rules are vague, but if you get the notice that you can't add any more followers, that means you have met your daily quota and have to wait until the next day to add more. It also limits how many more people you can be following than are following you. Tweepi (www.tweepi.com) is a great tool for reciprocating those who are following you, flushing those you are following who are not following you back, and growing your followers. You may have to purge people who are not following you so you can grow.

You can leverage your Twitter account further with a blog.

2. *Blogs.* A blog, short for "Web log," is a website where entries are displayed in reverse chronological order. You can post menus, specials, and other relevant information on your blog. Then you can tweet the blog post's URL on Twitter. It is a good way to circumvent the 140-character limit on Twitter. And once you have readers on your blog, you can promote other features and benefits of your catering service.

Blogs are free and easy to set up. You can use Blogger (which is owned by Google; www.blogger.com), WordPress (www.wordpress.com), or TypePad (www.typepad.com).

3. *Facebook.* Create a fan page on Facebook (www.facebook.com). Facebook is a place to connect with current clients. A person subscribing to your fan page is usually already a fan. This is where you can promote loyalty programs and discounts for frequent clients.

4. *LinkedIn.* Create a profile on LinkedIn (www.linkedin.com). LinkedIn is only for people you know, but it is important to have a presence. There are many discussion groups you can join on LinkedIn, including BizBash.

5. *Listserv.* Receive discussions in your email from groups such as MeCo (www.meetingscommunity.com) and MiForum (http://groups.google.com/group/MiForum). List subscribers include meeting planners as well as suppliers. Marketing is not allowed on the lists, but you can answer questions and develop name recognition with the group. The lists are great places to ask questions.

6. *YouTube.* On YouTube (www.youtube.com) you can create an account and upload videos of your events and facility. Here is Patti's YouTube page, with videos she has taken of plate presentations, tablescapes, and so on: www.youtube.com/profile?user=pattishock1&view=videos.

SALES PROCEDURES

One of the nice things about the restaurant business is that once a guest enters the establishment, he or she most likely will buy something. Other retailers would love to be in this enviable position. Unfortunately, many of them, especially department stores, must put up with a great number of casual shoppers who are just browsing and are not interested in buying anything.

Many potential catering clients are also casual shoppers. This is understandable—you cannot assume a person is apt to purchase a catered event just because he or she called or walked in the door seeking information. Unlike the restaurant patron who is willing to risk a bit of money to try out a new foodservice operation, the potential catering client cannot afford to do this. A potential client feels obligated to perform a bit of research, since there is no second chance to do the event again next week if something goes wrong. So before the final agreement can be signed, he or she must be "sold."

Client Inquiry

Potential clients will often visit your website, call, or stop by, seeking information about the catering department's products and services. Most of these clients will be categorized as walk-in business, while the remainder usually will be referral business.

The director of catering should develop a standardized procedure for catering staff members to follow when handling these inquiries. This procedure should be based on the assumption that a booked event will be the obvious result.

Sometimes potential clients inquire about dates, meals, and other services the facility is unable to accommodate. The word *no* is probably the hardest one to utter when dealing with potential clients. You do not want to lose any type of business. The skillful catering executive should be able to negotiate with the potential client to the satisfaction of all parties.

There are six ways a potential client can contact a caterer: letter, phone, fax, email, social media sites such as Facebook, or in person.

While not common, if a potential client inquires with a letter or fax, the caterer should always respond with a phone call. If other caterers have also been contacted by this client, you would want to respond as soon as possible in order to avoid being upstaged by a competitor. A phone call follow-up also is necessary because additional information most likely will be needed in order to prepare a proper proposal. For instance, the client's objective, budgetary constraints, dietary restrictions, and so forth must be considered before advancing to the proposal stage.

A phone call follow-up also allows the catering executive the opportunity to invite the potential client to visit the facility. You should make every effort to get the potential client to make a site visit. Experience shows that your selling task is much, much easier if you have potential clients on-site, where you can control the presentation and eliminate interruptions. While there, they can be treated to lunch, given a facility tour, and allowed to visit with other catering staff members. If you visit potential clients in their homes or places of business, you do not enjoy this "home court" advantage.

If a potential client inquires by phone, ideally the receptionist or catering salesperson will answer it before the third ring. The voice should be pleasant, modulated, and unhurried. "Good morning/afternoon, this is Mary Smith in the Catering Department. How may I help you?" When you are away from the office, call and see how many times the phone rings before it is answered. What does the staff say? What is their tone of voice? Are you placed on hold? For how long? Ask a question; do they know the answer? If not, do they find out for you? Whoever answers the phone must be able to answer questions. At the very least, the receptionist must be able to route the call to the right person as quickly as possible. There should always be someone in the office who can handle these calls adequately. A knowledgeable person should always be present. Too often the lowest-paid, least knowledgeable people answer the phone. They may be unable to answer questions because they have not been trained to do so. Many times the caller is not even asked to leave a message or number when the person he or she is trying to reach is unavailable. Consequently, a considerable amount of business is lost.

For times when no one from catering is available, develop a form for the receptionist or hostess to fill out during the conversation to obtain initial information, such as date, type of function, number of guests, and so on. This can then be given to the sales manager, who can check on availability prior to returning the call. However, the director of catering should ensure that a manager is assigned to each shift who is able to process these inquiries properly.

Voice mail is a blessing and a curse. You must learn how to use it effectively to avoid playing phone tag. For incoming voice mail, (1) change your message when you are out of the office so clients will know why you aren't returning their call; (2) in your message, leave a time they can reach you; and (3) provide alternative ways to contact you if necessary, such as your email address, your cell phone number, or your assistant's phone number.

When you are leaving a voice mail message, (1) state the purpose of your call, so that if the person needs to find information for you it will save an extra call; (2) let the person know when he or she can reach you; and (3) leave your phone number, for even if the person has it, he or she may have to hunt for it.

Computer-based "phone" calls, using applications such as Skype or Google Voice, are becoming more popular, as there are no fees or long-distance charges when the call is from computer to computer. All you need is a headset, or a microphone and earbud.

The fax machine, once an essential business tool, is nearly obsolete with advancements in email and other computer technologies. When used, faxes should not be scribbled notes—they should be typed as professionally as anything you send out via regular mail.

When the inquiry is by email, respond by email. This type of client generally loves technology. The advantages of email are numerous: (1) you can print a hard copy of all information exchanged; (2) you can provide an immediate reply; (3) you can forward and copy messages to others; (4) you can archive information in folders; (5) it is less expensive than long-distance phone calls; (6) you don't have to worry about time zones; and (7) you can retrieve messages at your convenience without interruptions.

If a potential client inquires in person, it is imperative that someone sees this person as soon as possible. The inquirer should be made to feel comfortable. He or she should be offered coffee, soda, or other refreshment. An accurate estimate of waiting time should be indicated. The receptionist or hostess should be instructed to take some preliminary information on a form from the inquirer, such as name, company, type of function, date needed, and number of guests. This activity gets the client involved—a positive step toward consummating a sale.

To be able to sell effectively, you must present a well-organized catering office. Sales staff must be trained and goals must be set. You never get a second chance to make a first impression. The appearance of your office is a reflection of your personality and job performance. A messy, cluttered office does not instill confidence in prospective clients. Clients' initial impression of the office affects their impressions of how well the facility will handle their event.

Your office should serve as a marketing tool. The pictures on the walls should be of events you have produced, to show unique or interesting room setups. The top of a credenza should have a sample place setting. Also, empty bottles of quality champagnes and wines that you offer make a nice display and assist you in upselling the event.

The office environment should be tastefully furnished and decorated. The office projects an image. An office that is too elegant or too plain may not be suitable in your environment. Offer the client a comfortable chair with a convenient place to take notes. If you have a waiting area, a testimonial book should be strategically placed on the coffee table for the potential client to peruse while waiting, along with samples of linen, china, stemware, and other items. Testimonial books should contain not only positive letters from satisfied clients but photos taken at events, suggested menus, catering policies, and so forth. Photo binders should be displayed in a creative, elegant, or eclectic manner, depending on the image of the facility. The binder should always be in good condition and free of dust and fingerprints. It is important that you project a competent and professional image to your client.

Whenever possible, it is preferable to meet prospective clients by appointment. This allows the catering staff time to prepare and to give their full attention to the client. It also provides adequate time to discuss arrangements and answer questions. Be ready to meet with the client when he or she arrives. Be familiar with the client's file. Avoid interruptions. Have coffee, tea, and water available.

Have necessary information at hand so you don't have to hunt it down while the client is waiting. This information may include:

- Color samples for linens, both in-house and rentals
- Types and quantities of china patterns and colors available
- Rental brochures for props, dance floors, risers, and so on, including cost for all options
- Referral lists of recommended suppliers, such as florists and photographers
- Audiovisual information
- Precise floor plans, along with sample configurations

All materials mailed from the office must be on good-quality paper in pristine condition. The professional appearance of a letter reflects on the professionalism of the writer. This means that misspelled words, incorrect punctuation, type-overs, or visible corrections are not acceptable.

When using a spell-checker on the computer, always proofread, as spell-checkers do not differentiate between words such as *their* and *there* or *here* and *hear*. Spell-checkers also do not catch mistakes in tenses or plural words.

The punctuation mark that follows the salutation is a colon, not a comma ("Dear Major Smith:"). However, a comma follows the closing ("Cordially,").

Letters should never start with "I" or "we." Psychologically, it is preferable to bring the client into the letter before presenting yourself. "Thank you for the opportunity to create the enclosed proposal" is better than "I am pleased to have the opportunity to submit the enclosed proposal," and "Your wedding will be in good hands with us" is better than "We look forward to your wedding reception."

Client Solicitation

Some caterers may have all the incoming business they can handle, and so they do not need to solicit business. Most catering executives, though, cannot wait for business to walk in off the street. Nor, for that matter, should the facility that currently has all the business it can handle rest on its laurels. It should always plan ahead and have a system ready to use for those times when its business cycle bottoms out. Furthermore, the type of current incoming business may not be the best business for maximizing profits.

There will always be a certain amount of off-the-street, referral, and repeat business. However, in order to maximize the catering department's profit potential, client solicitation is usually needed. It is especially necessary if you want to book business during the shoulder (i.e., slow) periods.

Many facilities assign their sales representatives quotas that cannot be satisfied only with walk-in business. If sales representatives are unable to meet these quotas on an ongoing basis, they may quickly find themselves out of a job. Generally speaking, there should always be a certain amount of prospecting and solicited business because this ensures that you continue to get the business you want, not just the groups that walk in the door.

Client solicitation takes many forms. Sales representatives canvass for new business with telephone solicitation, direct mail, cold calling, networking, and sales blitz techniques.

A national sales survey discovered that 80 percent of all new sales are made after the fifth call on the same prospect. On the other hand, 48 percent of all salespeople make one call and then cross the prospect off their list if they get a negative response, while 35 percent quit after the second call. Only 10 percent keep calling. Result: on the average, 10 percent of the salespeople make 80 percent of new sales. Persistence and patience pay off!

Direct mail with telephone follow-up, sales blitzes (where the catering staff works the phones once or twice a year in marathon solicitation efforts), and cold calling (where a sales representative personally calls on potential clients unannounced) are the most common forms of client solicitation efforts.

Direct mail involves sending out a stock information kit (such as a sales brochure with menus, prices, photos, and so forth) to potential clients whose names were gleaned from a mailing list. The most effective type of mailing is personalized. A sales representative should not send out the information kit until he or she finds out something about the potential client, so the mailing can be personalized. This tends to generate more positive responses. It also enhances the caterer's image and reputation, which is certain to pay huge dividends in the future.

The direct mail piece should have some unique physical characteristics to distinguish it from those sent by competing facilities. Printed material could be inserted in an attractive, uniquely colored folder that will stand out in a potential client's files.

Some direct mail efforts are aimed at previous clients who have not visited the facility lately. For instance, a tracer file might be kept that shows customers who have not held an event at your facility for over a year. An information kit with telephone follow-up can be sent as a courtesy so that these old friends do not forget that the facility remains ready to satisfy their needs.

Some repeat customers should receive an occasional telephone solicitation. For instance, if the facility is in the process of booking next year's Christmas party business, it can call previous customers to let them know that space is filling up fast and that the catering staff looks forward to booking space for them and servicing their events.

Telephone marketing can be an excellent source of new business. First, you need a plan that includes whom you wish to target, what information you wish to convey, and the results you expect to achieve. You only have a brief opportunity to state the reason for your call, describe the catering services you offer, and create enough interest to gain a positive response from the potential client. To improve opportunities for successful selling, prepare a script containing the key points that you wish to convey. Rehearse what you plan to say until it sounds natural and not as though you were reading from a script. Be clear, concise, and gracious. Use the following guidelines:

- Ask permission to discuss your services at this time. (If they do not grant it, ask to schedule a more convenient time for them.)
- Prepare a list of items you wish to discuss or points you wish to make.
- Be as specific as possible.
- Complete each area before moving on to the next subject.
- Be sure to take notes and date them.
- Follow up immediately.
- Log every telephone call for future reference.

A sample script might consist of the following:

Good morning, Mrs. Benson. This is Carl Whitman from the catering department of the Bountiful Hotel. I noticed the announcement of your daughter's engagement in the newspaper, and I would like to extend our best wishes to the family. May I have just a few moments of your time? [Wait for a response, and then proceed if appropriate.] We are proud of our catering department and would like to offer our catering services for the reception. As you may know, we specialize in wedding receptions and we are very competitive. Our mission is to make every reception a memorable one. I'd like to extend an invitation for you to visit our catering office so that we can show you the many attractive services that we offer. It would be our pleasure to cater your daughter's reception.

This type of telephone marketing can be applied to almost any situation, person, or group. For example, suppose the call was to a person whose name just appeared in the newspaper. The following sample may be appropriate:

Good afternoon, Ms. Duffy. Congratulations on your company's upcoming 50th anniversary. This is Mary Forest, from the catering department of the Bella

Napoli Restaurant. I'd like to offer our catering services for your anniversary party if you haven't made other arrangements already. I would like to extend a personal invitation for you to visit our facility so that we may show you our full range of party services.

The ideal success from this type of inquiry would be a tentative reservation or a firm appointment to discuss the special event further. Your minimum goal should be to obtain the prospective client's approval to send a copy of the catering brochure.

Always follow up if a potential client needs to talk to a spouse or family prior to making any decisions.

Sales blitzes and cold calls can yield considerable catering business if they are handled correctly. The most important aspect of these sales techniques is to use a process whereby you can quickly identify potential business. You do not want to waste anyone's time, but to be successful, you need to ask the right questions. For instance, you need to know: (1) Who is the decision maker? (2) How often are events planned? (3) Is your type of facility ever booked? (4) What are the size, type, and budget of the typical event? (5) How are events planned? (6) How far in advance do they start planning their events? This information will help streamline selling efforts and make them more productive.

Once qualified, the sales representative should set an appointment to meet with the potential client. Ideally, the appointment would be at the facility so that the client can tour the function rooms, visit a restaurant, if appropriate, and personally witness the facility's capabilities to handle the proposed event.

After the initial appointment, the sales representative may have enough information to prepare a formal proposal. If necessary, one or more additional meetings or conversations can be scheduled before a competitive bid is submitted to the potential client.

Once the proposal is presented, the usual next step is to commence negotiations. If all goes well, a formal agreement that is mutually acceptable to all parties will be signed.

Client Contact

Serious contact with potential clients usually begins with a general discussion of the event. Specific details are then discussed, such as prices, times, room availability, and other customer requirements. Eventually there will be a meeting of the minds and a signed contract or letter of agreement will be prepared. (*Agreement* is a more palatable word than *contract* to many catering clients.)

For this process to become reality, sales representatives must be knowledgeable. They must be able to answer clients' questions. They cannot afford to lose face. A stumbling, bumbling answer leaves a terrible impression.

Sales representatives must be very familiar with food and beverage production, presentation, and service. They also must know and understand the property's limitations, especially those restricting the types of functions that can be hosted properly.

Sales representatives also must be enthusiastic and likable. They must be polite and friendly. And they should exude the proper amount of sophistication consistent with the facility's competitive position.

Clients want to know that they are being handled correctly and professionally. They want to trust someone to do a quality job and make them look good in the eyes of their guests. They expect to pay a reasonable price for the catered event, but they must be satisfied with the results. Consequently, an effective sales representative will ensure that he or she knows exactly what the client wants.

A checklist of things to ask the client is an essential part of the sales representative's sales kit. The list should contain the obvious questions, such as the number of guests, the event's starting and ending times, and the required room setup. It also should contain unique questions, such as dietary and religious restrictions, entertainment needs, and the profile of the attendees. Ask why they are holding the event; what is it they hope to accomplish? Are they seeking to raise money? Are they looking to provide a networking opportunity? Do they have a website you can check out for more information on their organization?

A sales representative must find out as much as possible about the potential client before advancing to the negotiating and proposal stages. This information will indicate the potential for upselling, how many other competing caterers the client is considering, and any unusual service needs that must be provided.

Meeting With Prospective Clients

Be friendly. Smile. Be enthusiastic and outgoing. People want to do business with people who seem to enjoy what they do for a living. Address clients by name. This shows your personal interest in them. Be helpful. Go out of your way to offer service and tell clients about products and services. Be flexible. Do it the client's way. Put the client first. Be patient. Show good posture, make direct eye contact, open doors for others. Say "please," "thank you," and "you're welcome." Never argue. Speak clearly, use appropriate language, and avoid bad habits.

Determine the client's needs and objectives before you begin promoting your food, beverages, and services. It is important to know what the client is trying to achieve with the function. The client wants to be assured that the event will be done right. Concerns may include:

- Does the catering manager understand my needs?
- Does he or she show a willingness to ease my concerns?
- Will the food be good?
- Will the servers be courteous and attentive?
- How much is this going to cost?
- Are there any hidden costs?
- What happens if something needs to be changed?
- Will this person be there during my event?

Face-to-face contact is the most effective method of selling. It is more personal and communication is visual as well as verbal. Body language can communicate a person's mood or interest. Rapport is developed through in-person contact.

When calling upon a potential client without an appointment (cold calling):

- Introduce yourself and ask permission for a few minutes of the person's time.
- Inform the potential client immediately of the purpose of your visit.
- Explain the variety of special events you can cater (e.g., picnics, themed events).
- Listen carefully to what a client says.
- Keep your presentation brief and to the point unless the prospective client asks for additional information.

- Thank the person for his or her time.
- Leave brochures and menus before you leave.

When meeting with prospective clients, try to obtain the following information:
- What type of functions they plan
- Minimum/maximum number of guests at each
- Date(s)
- Time(s)
- Where they have held previous events

While cold calls are done primarily to inform and to gather information, appointments are made to sell. When scheduling appointments, it is preferable to meet at your facility. Extend a warm welcome. Phrase your initial questions to obtain a clear understanding of what the client is seeking. A sales presentation is not complete without a tour of the facilities. Describe the full scope of the facility's catering products and services. Provide the client with a copy of your catering brochure. You can also introduce the client to the chef, the banquet manager, and perhaps the food and beverage director.

Potential clients who have made an appointment with you already have an interest in your facility's offerings. It is up to you to provide the information and reassurance that will nudge the prospective client from undecided to committed.

Begin with the menu suggestions and selection process. In addition to the regular catering menus, extend the opportunity to the client to custom-design a menu. Designing custom menus makes clients feel special and pampered. You can also take advantage of seasonal foods that may be at their peak of freshness and at their lowest price point.

Always accept (or offer) a beverage during a meeting. It buys you time with the client. Courtesy requires that you (or the client) be allowed to finish a drink that is provided.

Be sure the rooms you are going to show the prospective client are in good order, clean, and with the lights on. The client needs to envision how the room will look during his or her event. Stacked furniture or dirty rugs will not convey a positive image.

Shop the competition. How can you compete effectively if you don't know your competition?

- What menu items do they offer?
- What are their specialties?
- What are their prices?
- What types of services are available?
- How do they respond to inquiries?
- What policies do they have that make you more (or less) competitive?
- How do their facilities compare to yours?
- How do their brochures and other materials compare to yours?

If you are serving the same menu item as your competitors, yours should look better, taste better, and be served better. Add unique touches to your menu. Try to place yourself in the position of the client. Does the competition's presentation paint a better picture than yours? What are the differences that you need to address in your own presentation?

Clients expect quality, value, and attention. Knowing your facility's strengths and your competitor's weaknesses will give you an advantage. Distinguish your catering operation by offering more and better service and personalized assistance.

Avoid bad-mouthing your competition. This is unprofessional and will be perceived negatively by the prospective client. You could also leave yourself open to charges of slander. Instead, emphasize your positive benefits in areas in which the competition cannot compete.

Don't miss out on important details that will help you close more sales. Listen more and talk less. We were given two ears and one mouth. If you listen to people, they will tell you what to sell. Say, "I would like to hear what your ideas and needs are before I propose any ideas." Wait for their response, then be creative!

There are many places in which communication can break down. Factors that can influence and cloud communication include:

- Being very busy
- Being preoccupied with personal or business matters

- Not feeling well
- Being biased, or holding preconceived notions
- Being in an emotional state
- Not understanding the information
- Environmental factors such as noise, temperature, etc.
- Having a high degree of sensitivity

To prevent these factors from diminishing your communication with a client, watch for body language that indicates the potential client is not listening. Be aware of positive and negative signals. When you meet someone, the first few seconds are critical in projecting a positive first impression. Body language communicates attitude much more powerfully than the sound of the voice or the words that are used.

You must project confidence. Direct eye contact communicates confidence. Leaning forward slightly communicates that you are listening intently. A friendly smile can make you seem attractive and open. Nodding when a client is expressing their needs conveys understanding.

Complaints are opportunities. The client is saying, "Will you help me?" Every successfully resolved complaint increases customer satisfaction. Never allow the client to make you upset. Listen to the complaint and make sure you understand what the client wants. Accept responsibility on behalf of the organization, even if you are not at fault, and take immediate action. Always thank the client for bringing the matter to your attention.

Selling

Service is frequently defined as the manner in which the client is treated. Good service is often felt, rather than seen. Making the sale is the ultimate goal, and serving the customer is the means to achieving that goal. Service is something you do that results in a sale or a rebooking.

Selling is both an art and a skill. Not everyone excels at selling; however, with practice, you can develop a sales presentation to accomplish the task successfully. The average catering manager spends approximately 60 percent of his or her time selling and 40 percent servicing catered events.

Focusing on Benefits

It is important to focus on benefits rather than features. Features are information about your facility, menu, and service. Benefits explain why the features are important to the client. Never sell what your catering is; instead, sell what your catering does for the client. When you are focused on features, you would say things like:

"We have a great chef and a great service team."
"We have a great view."

But when you focus on benefits, you would instead say:

"Our chef will prepare a wonderful meal that will please your guests, and our staff will make them feel like VIPs."
"The view of the mountains and the water will be the perfect romantic backdrop for your wedding reception. Just think about your wedding photos in this setting."

Remember, clients purchase a happy bride, not a wedding.
You must know everything about your facility, including:

- Room sizes and capacities
- A variety of setup alternatives
- Ingredients, preparation method, presentation, and price of every menu item
- Electrical capacity and number and location of outlets
- Audiovisual availability and capability
- Floor load capacity
- Sizes of doors
- Skill level of the kitchen staff
- Skill level of the servers
- Availability of equipment
- How long it takes to turn a room (e.g., from a classroom set to a banquet set)—many caterers do not know what their facility can do during a crunch, so they often do not leave enough time between events

The sales manager should without hesitation be able to say, "Mrs. Nelson, this room will seat 160 banquet style and accommodate 200 at a reception."

If the desired booking date is unavailable, you may be able to offer prospective clients a discount, complimentary food items, or other incentives if the client is willing to hold the event on another date.

Overcoming Objections

Objections are based on fear of non-delivery. If you don't overcome client objections, you won't get their business! Ask potential clients partway through the sales presentation if they have any concerns or objections. This way you'll be able to adjust your presentation based on their feedback. The concerns that most frequently cause client hesitation are:

- Availability of dates
- Adequacy of space
- Price
- Menu suggestions
- Lack of confidence that the event will be done right

Techniques for Overcoming Client Objections

First, listen for the objection. It may not be immediately obvious. Ask questions and address the objection. Change the objection to client acceptance by:

- Reviewing features and benefits with the client
- Reviewing how you plan to meet the client's needs
- Guaranteeing satisfaction
- Building trust
- Referring to testimonials
- Referring to visual presentations
- Supplying a referral list for client use
- Closing the sale by asking direct questions

Solutions to Objections

If the objection is based on price:

1. Determine the prospective client's budget. If it is reasonable, build a menu that fits the budget.

2. Be specific. Ask what it is that the client feels is too expensive.
3. Ask how the client would propose to lower the cost.
4. Offer suggestions, and read the person's reactions.
5. Explain and show value for items under consideration.

If the objection is based on space:
1. Offer an alternative date when more space is available.
2. Suggest a different type of service (e.g., buffet stations with cocktail tables instead of a sit-down meal).
3. Change the time of event so that another room may be used.
4. Adjust the layout.
5. Look for alternative locations, such as poolside or in a tent.

If the objection is based on the menu:
1. Ask if the client has any suggestions. Does the client have favorites or items he or she prefers to yours? Can the client supply you with pictures or recipes?
2. Discuss and resolve any dietary concerns.
3. Know your competitions' product, presentation, and pricing. If possible, meet or beat it. If not, offer value alternatives.
4. Involve the chef if customized menus are under consideration.

Closing Statements

Close the sale by asking, "Now that we agree on the menu, the timing, the room arrangements and the entertainment, are you ready to sign the agreement?"

Offer provisional choices:

"If I provide x, y, and z, will this satisfy your budget [taste, concern, etc.]?"
"If we change the balsamic vinaigrette to raspberry vinaigrette, will the salad be to your liking?"

If the client answers yes, close the sale.

It is important to restate any objections and counter the objection with positive action.

"Mrs. Hamilton, I understand your concern about backup space for the ceremony. If we can make arrangements for a tent and include the string ensemble as well, will you commit to having Kimberly's ceremony and reception here at our club?"

"Mr. Tuttle, if we can get white chair covers and pink satin bows for the ceremony and make it within your budget, may I consider your date with us firm?"

"Ms. Reed, I understand your concern about having hot food served to 150 guests within twenty minutes. I will guarantee it can be done, and you are welcome to call upon other satisfied customers. If I give you a 100 percent guarantee that all 150 guests will be served hot food in twenty minutes, will you confirm your event here at our restaurant?"

You are ready to close the sale when:

- Client needs and wants are met.
- Menu and beverage arrangements are satisfactory.
- The price is right.
- The atmosphere and decor are acceptable.
- The date, time, and agenda are confirmed.
- Trust and confidence have been established.
- Value and anticipated satisfaction are perceived.

Closing the Sale

For many, closing the deal is the most difficult part of sales. You must ask for the business and get the commitment. After all details have been noted and all questions answered to the satisfaction of the client, the last steps before presenting the agreement for signature include:

- Verbally recapping the specifics of the function and what has been agreed upon. At this point, review the arrangements and the sequence of events that will occur during the function. To avoid possible misunderstandings, ensure that the agreement spells out the arrangements and the sequencing and timing of events.
- Confirming things that you will check on and agreeing when you will get back to the client.

- Recapping the information the client will provide to you.
- Asking for his or her business.
- Getting a commitment.

Upselling

Once the event has been booked, the next crucial element in the sales process is possessing the ability to upsell. Upselling is painting a mental picture of enhancements that convince the client that spending a little more money on extra service or elaborate presentations will increase guest satisfaction.

Upselling is suggestive selling to upgrade the menu, arrangements, decorations, and so on by recommending specific extras or enhancements. It could be changing the entree from chicken to prime rib, adding a specialty dessert, or serving a better-quality wine. Upselling also includes adding extra courses, such as an intermezzo, cheese cart, cordial service, hot hors d'oeuvres, petit fours on the table, ice carvings, flavored coffees, and similar items. Upselling pertains to anything associated with the event; it may include extra staffing, a separate service station, specialty linen, special serving equipment, or a live action station, for example. Instead of asking "Do you want to serve wine?" ask, "Which type of wine will you be serving?" or "Do you prefer a red or a white wine with that course?"

Upselling increases the per-person selling price. There are several methods that can be used to achieve this goal. While each is effective individually, combining methods will help you retain more revenue for your bottom line and deliver a more complete service to your client and his or her group. Some methods are:

1. *Upgrading individual items.* Client budgets are often focused more toward the chicken price range than the filet mignon range. Some clients want to feel more involved in their menu planning than simply ordering from the standard menu. To facilitate upgrading, it is important to have the appropriate sales tools. Each manager should have lists of prices and be prepared to upgrade appetizers, suggest showy dessert presentations, add specialty salads such as Caesar salad prepared tableside, and so forth.

2. *Upgrading entree items.* Have choices available, including a variety of fresh seafood and fish items and a number of beef and poultry preparations

using different stuffings, sauces, or accompaniments. Top-end upselling would be things such as veal, prime rib, Kobe beef, pork loin, Peking duck, or venison. Another example would be to add two jumbo butterflied shrimp to a filet mignon.

3. *Upgrading refreshment breaks.* Offer specialty beverages, such as lattes, cappuccinos, fresh fruit smoothies, juices, or flavored bottled waters. Suggest food items to go with the beverages at a per-person price; $10.00 per person coffee/refreshment breaks can contribute more to your end-of-month statement than an upgraded appetizer. Themed refreshment breaks are discussed in Chapter 3.

4. *Upgrading ambience.* Special china, glassware, linen, and props are potential (and often reusable) moneymakers. These items should be of special interest because they can greatly increase menu price without any additional food cost. Usually the cost of the special item can be recovered after its first use and whenever it's sold after that, the increase in menu price can be considered pure profit.

5. *Custom proposals.* All catering operations have standard menus. Flatter your client with the attention and creativity of custom proposals. Always seek to custom-design at least one or two items on the menu. It removes the pressure of dealing with printed lists and pre-suggested prices. Ask the client for his or her budget within the first few conversations. This question will save you time and effort and allow you to creatively exceed your client's expectations.

6. *Early involvement.* Offer to assist the client in making arrangements for flowers, audiovisual equipment, photographers, and other services, and create a budget including these items. By working with preferred vendors, you can negotiate a price that will be attractive to the client and include a profit for the facility. By doing this, you are providing a service—one-stop shopping and added convenience for the client.

7. *Pre-packaged theme parties.* A package eliminates the client's need to handle details such as decor, entertainment, and menus. Many of your clients may be unaware that you offer such complete services and will be impressed by and more confident about your range of services, as well as your ideas and proposals. Theme parties are discussed in Chapter 3.

CLIENT RELATIONS

Retain records of comments concerning the event, as well as any personal information, in a client file. Always refer to these files prior to contacting clients. Clients appreciate being asked how their golf game is going or how their daughter is doing in college. This is what is meant by relationship marketing.

Establishing a personal link with your client is important for repeat business. You should strive to establish rapport with clients and potential clients as well as their spouses. Find a common interest to discuss. Establish a professional friendship.

Networking is part of the selling process. It is relationship building. It allows the opportunity to establish rapport, find a common interest, and establish a business friendship.

In catering sales, you will be attending many lunches, dinners, and receptions. You need to be sure you know the rules of etiquette. Letitia Baldrige's *New Complete Guide to Executive Manners* is an excellent resource. A reception may look like a party, sound like a party, feel like a party, and taste like a party—but it is *not* a party. It is a social business environment. It is a vehicle to relax attendees so they can meet in a casual manner instead of over a desk in an office. Remember, your good or bad manners are always with you. Do not drink too much, station yourself in front of the food, or otherwise make a spectacle of yourself. People have long memories. You need to make people feel at ease. People gravitate to other people who make them feel comfortable. No one wants to feel ill at ease. Know when to say "please." Know how to say "I'm sorry." Know how to say "thank you." Know how to give and receive a compliment.

The catering manager should develop relationships within the community and become a central part of the social and professional fabric of the people with whom he or she does business. Positive community relations pay off. A potential sale often begins with a casual inquiry.

There are many alternatives from which clients may choose for their event. Most of your clients will comparison-shop. They want assurance that your catering team has the professional skills to make their event enjoyable, memorable, and hassle-free.

As soon as one event is completed, you should be trying to book the client's next function. Providing customer service is an art. Providing customer service profitably is a science. We cannot talk about sales and marketing without discussing service. The best sales and marketing plans in the world will fall short if high-quality service is not part of the equation. High-quality service is your invisible asset. Good service adds value to the purchase and brings the customer back.

A marketing definition of customer service is giving your clients what they want, when they want it, where they want it, at a price they are willing to pay. The purposes of customer service are:

- Customer satisfaction (how you did)
- Customer retention (striving to secure repeat business)
- New customer development (word of mouth, firsthand observance of the facility's performance)

Quality service is not tangible and cannot be stored. Your "product" is the service you offer your guests. Service is effort expended to provide a memorable experience for our guests. Every effort should be made to meet and exceed the client's needs and expectations.

Poor service just happens; good service is an ongoing effort. Training service personnel is a continuing process. The more you expect from your staff, the greater the requirement to provide ongoing training, feedback, and two-way communication. It is your staff that determines whether or not you retain your clients for future events.

SUMMARY

Catering markets can be divided in a number of ways. One type of division is low-end (shallow), midlevel, and high-end (deep). Another type of division is association, business, and SMERF (the last including weddings and other life-cycle events). Whatever the market you wish to target, it is essential to develop a marketing budget and a cohesive marketing strategy, using market research as a guide. Determining appropriate pricing is an essential part of marketing, and there are a range of methods you can consider to develop a pricing strategy. Marketing activities such as direct mail, social media, and websites are also essential to generating business.

KEY TERMS

ICW	Life-cycle events	Bar mitzvah
Bat mitzvah	Meal couponing	Group history record
Relationship marketing	Lost business record	Tracer file
Thirds method	Contribution margin	Upgrades
Direct mail	Features versus benefits	Cold calls
Upselling		

REVIEW QUESTIONS

1. Who determines value, the buyer or the seller?
2. Is the SMERF market shallow, midlevel, or deep?
3. Which types of meetings are most accurate in predicting the number of attendees?
4. How do special events differ from daily or ordinary events?
5. What is included in a market and competition analysis?
6. Describe the thirds method of pricing.
7. How do catering profit margins compare with restaurant profit margins?
8. What is the difference between a feature and a benefit?
9. What is upselling?
10. What does "space utilization percentages" refer to?
11. What is an incentive event?
12. What is a recognition event?
13. What is the difference between a trade association and a professional association?
14. What is a shoulder period?

15. Describe the level-pricing method.
16. Describe range pricing.
17. What is an affiliate event?
18. What is the primary difference between the loss leader and the lost leader pricing methods?
19. Should a caterer's web site participate in banner ads?
20. What does social media refer to?

Chapter 3

THEME PARTIES, WEDDINGS, OUTDOOR PARTIES, AND SPECIAL EVENTS

Catered events—from cocktail receptions to seated dinners—need excitement and drama in addition to delicious food. For this reason, themed events are very popular. A theme party transports the attendees to another dimension, another place and time, away from the mundane and ordinary world. Themed events create a magical space of fantasy and fun. Caterers have the opportunity to show their creativity and expertise by developing one-of-a-kind themed events for their clients.

Before developing a proposal or planning a function, it is necessary to know the reason for the event and who will be attending the party. The demographics (age, gender, income, ethnicity, etc.) will influence what would be appropriate.

Every function or party should be treated as a special event. According to Dr. Joe Goldblatt, author of several books on special events, "A special event recognizes a unique moment in time with ceremony and ritual to satisfy specific needs." A caterer may create 200 parties a year, but for the client, it is truly a special occasion. The bride wants a perfect wedding to remember; the association meeting planner wants a spectacular closing event to wow the convention attendees; the corporation wants to impress current and potential clients.

Some attendees may not be able to tell you what they had to eat the day before. What they do remember, though, sometimes for years to come, is creative themes, unique presentations, and outstanding entertainment. Themed events create memories.

Theme parties are events that tie in:
• Creativity
• Food
• Beverage
• Entertainment
• Decor
• Activities

Event elements include:
• Fun
• Flavor
• Excitement
• Action
• Color
• Sound
• Entertainment
• Showmanship
• Surprise

A caterer should strive to involve all of the five senses: sight, sound, taste, touch, and smell.

Whenever possible, create something out of the ordinary for each event. It can be a visual object, something as simple as a mashed potato "duck" the authors were served on a plate at the Contemporary Hotel at Disney World.

The key is to involve and excite. It also provides an opportunity to upsell by adding additional components to the event. Guests like interactive events.

John Steinmetz, a caterer from Southern California, once produced a party using bubble wrap as an overlay on a tablecloth, then topped the tables with Lucite cut to fit the entire tabletop. The centerpiece consisted of an assortment of soap bubbles, Silly String, water pistols, and other fun toys. As the evening progressed, one could hear the bubble wrap being popped all around, making the room sound like a giant popcorn popper. Guests soon got into the mood and were blowing bubbles, shooting Silly String, laughing, and having a great time.

As themes are limited only by your imagination (and sometimes by the client's budget), these types of events provide great opportunities to showcase your creativity and style. Recently there has been a trend of producing themed events that focus on regional foods and seasonal approaches. Much of this stems from the green movement of utilizing local foods and sustainable practices.

Below are additional theme party ideas that can be adapted and modified in countless ways to fit the event and the client's goals.

TV CLASSICS. Any television show can be a theme: *The Untouchables*, *I Love Lucy* (Cuban music and servers in red wigs and poodle skirts), *Saturday Night Live*, *Miami Vice*, *The Streets of San Francisco*, *The Wonder Years*, *Little House on the Prairie*, *The X-Files*, *America's Funniest Home Videos*, etc.

GAME SHOWS. *Jeopardy*, *Wheel of Fortune*, *The Price Is Right*, *Hollywood Squares*, *Who Wants to Be a Millionaire*, etc.

REALITY SHOWS. *Survivor*, *American Idol*, *Dancing with the Stars*, *The Amazing Race*, etc.

MOVIE CLASSICS. Any movie can be a theme: *Twilight*, *The Matrix*, *The Wizard of Oz*, *The Godfather*, *Gunfight at the O.K. Corral*, *Alice in Wonderland*, the Rambo movies, the Indiana Jones movies, *Titanic*, or *Star Wars*.

Be careful about possible copyright infringement if trademarked images are used. Companies such as Disney have aggressively protected their images and characters. When in doubt, contact the marketing department of the studio that produced the show. Information about studios is available at the Internet

Movie Database (www.imdb.com), which is also a great place to look for ideas.

Additional theme ideas include:

MUSIC THEMES. Try an Elvis tribute, the Beatles, "Fly Me to the Moon" (1960s, with Sinatra).

WESTERN THEMES. Try rodeo, hoedown, frontier days, or "on the trail" themes. These are great for barbecues.

ROARING TWENTIES. Flappers, Betty Boop, *The Great Gatsby.*

LAS VEGAS NIGHT. Casinos, *Viva Las Vegas*, a Vegas vacation, *Ocean's Eleven* (or its sequels).

GREAT ROMANCES. Antony and Cleopatra, Elizabeth Taylor and Richard Burton, Romeo and Juliet, Brad Pitt and Angelina Jolie.

SCIENCE FICTION. "Beam me up, Scotty" (*Star Trek*), Flash Gordon.

FAMOUS FADS. Hula Hoops, Pet Rocks, Cabbage Patch Kids dolls.

FAMOUS HIGHWAYS. You can take any highway, historical route, or coastline and create a theme; use your imagination. Highway 101, for instance, runs down the California coast. You could have food and beverage stations representing stops along the way: At the Napa Valley station, you could serve wine, cheeses, and breads. At the San Francisco stop, serve Chinese stir-fry to eat right out of a takeout container, and sourdough bread or cracked Dungeness crab cocktails. At the Santa Barbara station, you could serve fajitas and tacos. End up in Hollywood with a salad bar and yogurt.

Route 66, the legendary old highway immortalized in song, wound its way from Chicago to Los Angeles. The Chicago station could serve Chicago deep dish pizza, ribs, etc. The Oklahoma City station could be a carved steamship round, and in Albuquerque would be Mexican food. California pizza could be at the last stop in Los Angeles.

Caterers on the East Coast could do an I-95 theme, starting in Boston with seafood. One stop could be Baltimore for crab cakes, and you could end up in Miami with Joe's stone crabs.

Another variation could include the Orient Express—an elegant train ride with food stations based on the stops along the route, perhaps including murder-mystery-themed interactive entertainment and decor. This theme would also work internationally, with Marco Polo's trade route, circling the Mediterranean, or all of the islands in the Caribbean. The possibilities are limited only by the imagination and the budget.

PUTTING ON THE RITZ. Think big bands, art deco, mirror balls, tap dancing, trains, tuxedos, top hats, nightclubs, long slinky dresses (à la Erté), nightclubs, champagne, veal Oscar, prime rib, cherries jubilee, Caesar salad, shrimp cocktail, lobster.

SOUTH BEACH STYLE. Lounges have become extremely popular, and guests tend to gravitate to lounge seating, with leather furniture, ottomans, end tables, faux fire pit, and so on.

DREAMSCAPES. These might feature nightmares, sexy dreams, youthful dreams, and the like.

THEMING WITH COLOR. Coordinate linens, candles, menu, flowers, lights, and decor on a color-based theme: "Rhapsody in Blue," in the pink, black-and-white ball, "Silver Threads Among the Gold," paint the town red, *How Green Was My Valley*, Green Berets, red herrings, *Blue Velvet*, red-hot mama, deep blue sea, "Blue Danube," "Yellow Rose of Texas."

LOCATION THEMES. Paris, Rome, London, Hong Kong, Singapore, New York, New Orleans, midnight in Moscow, MacArthur Park, Panama Canal.

THEMES-WITHIN-LOCATION THEMES. At a convention for the National Association of Catering Executives (NACE) held in Seattle, several Seattle themes were presented, including a "Purple Haze Lunch" (Jimi Hendrix was from Seattle) and a "Rain Breakfast" satirizing the famous Seattle climate, with upside-down umbrellas as centerpieces with water and rubber duckies inside. New Orleans caterers are well versed in the Mardi Gras theme, as Atlanta caterers are with the *Gone with the Wind* theme.

TIME THEMES. Popular periods include the 1890s, the 1920s, the 1950s, or a futuristic slant.

TIME AND LOCATION. San Francisco in the 1960s, New York in the 1930s, Hollywood in the 1940s, Paris in the 1700s, New Orleans in the 1920s, Berlin in the 1930s.

HISTORICAL THEMES. Stanley and Livingstone, Genghis Khan, Attila the Hun, the Renaissance, Marco Polo, *Pirates of the Caribbean.*

CULTURAL THEMES. Among the choices might be the Bolshoi Ballet, the opera, French Impressionist painters, Picasso, Salvador Dalí, or *Swan Lake*.

SPORTS THEMES. *Monday Night Football*, the Super Bowl, the America's Cup, Wimbledon, the Masters golf tournament, soccer madness.

With the above theme ideas as a starting point, think about what you could use to create the decor and ambience. Let your imagination run wild. The more creative, the better.

BUDGET CONSIDERATIONS

In recent decades, the mood was "eat, drink, and be merry." Now, however, budgets are tighter, and the average budget per person has dropped by about 25 percent—while costs have escalated by about 25 percent. However, expectations are just as high as they were before. Clients want freshness, quality, service, and creativity. Theming allows creativity to make up the difference. "Where we used to use 12/16 jumbo shrimp, we now offer 26/30 blackened shrimp for New Orleans Night—or coconut-breaded shrimp for Tropical Night," notes caterer Ricky Eisen.

LIGHTS ARE MAGIC

Whether tiny Italian Tivoli lights, pin spots, strobes, black lights, beacons, rope lights, fiber-optic lights, neon, or lasers, lights attract and dazzle the eye. Lights are truly eye candy. The caterer should explain to the client, and demonstrate whenever possible, how lighting impacts an event. For example, point out that the client is spending so much money on beautiful centerpieces that he or she should highlight them to maximize their impact in the room.

Gobo lights are portable spotlights that can create colors or focused pattern projections on the ceiling, wall, or floor, depending on the metal or glass templates affixed to the lens. The images can be trees, cityscapes, the client's company name, the event logo, or any image relating to the theme of the event. They are also available in versions that rotate slowly back and forth, creating changing patterns that can pulsate in tempo with the music. A gobo with a company logo is a great way to provide branding and decor. You can uplight the room in company colors or match the theme of the event with fantastic ambience and decor elements that aren't overly expensive.

A portable light tree contains a base with two pipes forming a T and lights hanging off the crossbar. PAR lights are used for short throws and create a wide beam of light. A Leko light is used for a longer throw distance and creates a narrow beam of light. Gels are heat-resistant, transparent-colored polyester or polycarbonate materials placed in front of a lens to bathe an area in a particular color. The Star Light and Magic website (www.starmgc.com) provides many photos and valuable information on a variety of lighting options.

SOUNDSCAPES

Soundscapes are a way of "decorating" with sound. Sound can envelop and create a mood. Commercially prepared tapes are available with the sounds of foghorns, rainstorms, ocean waves, cooing seagulls, tropical birds, clopping horses, the clickety-clack of a train rolling down a track, and a variety of other background elements. Music playing in a room upon entry reinforces the theme, such as Dixieland jazz for a New Orleans theme, the theme from *The Godfather* for an Italian-flavored event, or "Tara's Theme" for a *Gone with the Wind*–style affair.

MOVING DECOR

Placing people in costumes is known as "moving decor." This can be simply the servers and bartenders in costume, or it can involve actors hired to roam around and entertain. They are part of the decor and add life to the theme. Walking tables, used for serving, are popular, as are walking opera singers, jugglers, and the like.

Some planners request the attendees to dress in costume as well. An example would be the "Denim and Diamonds" theme that is popular in Dallas. Attendees are asked to dress in Western chic. A male attendee might wear jeans and a tuxedo jacket. A female might wear a sequined dress with boots and a cowboy hat.

ENTRANCE

The entrance to an event sets the mood. If the client's budget allows, a few props relating to the theme could be placed in proximity to the doors. Entering a room through a prop of a plane fuselage set the tone for an *Indiana Jones and the Temple of Doom*–themed event that was held at the Sheraton Boston. Be sure the height is appropriate and does not interfere with any existing hotel signage or the egress path. Ask to see a rendering to be sure it meets the standards of the venue.

PROPS

Facilities with sufficient storage space can develop a prop collection for signature themed events. Most major cities also have one or more prop houses, which maintain warehouses full of every imaginable type of prop, from rickshaws to Grecian columns or trellises. For a western theme, corral fencing may be used to separate the reception area from the seating area. You should take a tour of a prop house to get an idea of what is available. This is an excellent vehicle for upselling. Remember, the client pays separately for the props, or you build it into the cost of the event.

When renting props, it is important to place them correctly and highlight them with good lighting, not just stick them up against the wall. With decor, always remember to stay within the planned budget. It is very easy to add "just one more thing" and overspend the budget. The most common error when costing these types of events is underestimating labor.

With any decor, be mindful of safety and flow issues. Do not create a hazard where guests may trip on cords or otherwise injure themselves. Likewise, do not place props in a location that will deter a nice flow within the room. For example, do not place decor in an area that will cause a backup at the entrance or make it difficult for guests to access food and beverage stations.

When designing an event and selecting props, remember that guests eat more food in brightly lit, colorfully decorated surroundings. Vibrant colors (red, hot pink, bright yellow) stimulate the appetite, whereas dark tones (deep green, dark blue, brown, gray, black) dull the appetite.

If you want to keep your own props in-house for often-used themes and you have the storage space, look for bargains at party centers, ethnic food stores, arts and crafts stores, sports clubs, second-hand shops, antique shops, Goodwill, military surplus stores, auto supply stores, import shops, toy stores, garden centers, garage sales, travel agencies (destination posters), flea markets, pawn shops, eBay, and Craigslist, among other places. Remember, whatever clients do not have to spend out of their budget with a prop house can be spent with the caterer.

You can pick up fabric remnants for about $1.00 per yard to decorate buffet or refreshment break tables and add a special touch to the visual display. Fabric is available in an amazingly wide variety of prints that fit various themes. Always be sure the fabric meets the fire code. Ample fabric creates the look you are after; skimpy attempts with fabrics will harm the overall effect. Typically, a 6-foot buffet table will need 10 yards of fabric to achieve an ample look.

FUN FOOD

Guests like to be surprised. Fun food makes your guests say "Wow!" There are many things you can do to add visual interest to the shape of the food for plate presentations: noodle cages for deep-fried shrimp, julienne of carrots in scallion-tied crepe pouches, chocolate pianos (available ready-made from specialty food suppliers) filled with fruit and chocolate sauce, and more. Fun food often requires guest participation; sloppy ribs, build-your-own ice cream sundae stations, and taco bars all change the context of social eating. This usually works best when guests will be in casual dress.

Signature Items

Providing something people cannot get elsewhere can give your facility a reputation for doing unique things. This is an example of niche marketing. There is a dairy in Atlanta that makes signature ice cream for clubs and restaurants in the area, including muscadine ice cream exclusively for Callaway Gardens. Lawry's Seasoned Salt started out as a specialty blend of spices at a Los Angeles restaurant; it became so popular the company produced it for the mass market. Every chef should be encouraged to develop two or three items he or she is particularly proud of, and these should be featured on the menu. They can be fresh signature breads, a pâté, special house salad dressing, or a specialty dessert, such as the bourbon bread pudding at Atlanta's Omni Hotel.

Themed Refreshment Breaks

Coffee breaks can add significantly to total revenue and therefore should be considered an integral portion of food income. Turning them into unique refreshment breaks can be a strong selling point in obtaining and improving business. The traditional coffee break, including Danish or doughnuts, is often expected or required. However, the same items presented over and over again can become boring. The purpose of the break is to provide refreshment between periods of work in order to improve concentration and boost energy. Offer the client a selection of refreshing ideas for breaks to add variety to the standard fare. It makes a professional impression to offer a choice of refreshment breaks instead of the usual service. Below are food, beverage, and decor examples of creative themed refreshment breaks:

- *Greek:* grape juice, feta cheese, spanakopita, baklava, mounds of grapes, melons, Greek coffee, music from *Zorba the Greek*, Greek columns, blue and white checked linen
- *Southwestern United States:* tacos, cacti, pottery, Indian baskets
- *German (Oktoberfest):* apple juice, beer steins, strudel, Bavarian soft pretzels, cheese, cold cuts, polka music, white and blue linen
- *New York deli:* V8 juice, bagels and lox, pound cake, hanging sausages, hanging cheese balls, checked linen
- *French:* freshly squeezed juices, crepes, warm Brie cheese, croissants, French bread, café au lait, white porcelain china, wicker baskets, accordion music, fresh flowers
- *Mexican:* papaya juice, churros, exotic fruits, sopapillas (fried dough), sombreros, serapes, piñatas
- *English:* fruitcake, tea, plum pudding, fruit compote, crumpets, scones, spicy iced tea, tin boxes, teapots
- *Circus:* caramel apples, popcorn, peanut butter cookies, fruit punch, balloons, clowns

- *Flower Drum Song:* Chinese fortune and almond cookies, Chinese green tea, Chinese calligraphers, lacquer umbrellas
- *101 Dalmations:* nuts, candy, and puppy chow mix served in dog food bowls; churros and cinnamon bowties cut to simulate dog chews
- *Biker Break:* biker food, such as doughnuts, beef jerky, Twinkies, coffee from a thermos; props such as a motorcycle; music such as Steppenwolf's "Born to Be Wild" and Bruce Springsteen's "Born in the USA"
- *Other creative food ideas:* fresh Belgian waffle station with assorted toppings; fresh strawberries infused with flavorings or liqueurs; selection of nuts, dried fruits, and chocolate chips or candies for guests to make their own trail mix; s'mores station; root beer floats; make-your-own ice cream sandwich station; barista cart for flavored coffees, espresso, cappuccino, or Irish coffee; nuts in the shell with nutcrackers; peanut butter and jelly finger sandwiches; hot cider, hot chocolate with marshmallows, caramel apples, Cracker Jack, peanut brittle; flavored popcorns; pomegranate or açai berry juice

In addition to creative food items, the decorative setting should be a selling point. Creative break settings should include flowers, linen, unusual food containers, and anything else that creates a "wow" impression and will enhance the presentation.

Michele Polci, CPCE, CMP, director of catering sales for Caesars Entertainment in Las Vegas, did a "Bet on Red" refreshment break for a NACE Leadership Conference. This was a play on both a casino theme and the color red. All the linens and decor were in shades of red, as were the food and beverage items:

Red Twizzlers and Red M&Ms
Chocolate Strawberry Tree
Raspberry Tarts
Freshly Baked Strawberry Bread
Cranberry Trail Mix
Red Tortilla Chips with Fire-Roasted Salsa
Cranberry Juice, Strawberry Soda, and Red Zinger Iced Tea

For a separate break at the same conference, Michele did a "Stick It to Me" break, where every food item was on a stick:

Antipasto on a Stick
Fresh Fruit Kabobs with Honey Yogurt Dressing
Almond Bar Pops
Rice Cereal Pops Drizzled in Chocolate
Cheesecake Pops
Frozen Bananas, Ice Cream Bars, and Frozen Fruit Bars

WEDDINGS

The wedding is the ultimate theme party. Wedding receptions are excellent revenue generators. The average spent on wedding receptions in the United States in 1990 was $15,208; in 1999 it was $19,104; and in 2007 it was $28,704. It is interesting to note that the price of a typical wedding often equals the price of an average car. Even though the amount spent on the average wedding was expected to be lower in 2010 than it was in 2007, wedding ceremonies and receptions are still big business.

Since the occasion is so special to the bride and groom, their families, and their friends, the importance of quality often takes precedence over cost. Memorable weddings don't just happen. They are created as the result of careful attention to detail.

When first meeting with the couple, ask them questions such as how they met, what their favorite restaurant is, what their favorite type of music is, and so on—anything that will help in knowing what to suggest. Get to know them as a couple. Ask if they anticipate children at the wedding; if they do, have kids' meals available. Offer to coordinate the invitation with the menu cards, place cards, and cocktail napkins for a great look and upsell opportunity.

In the beginning stages of planning:
- Build trust and confidence in your initial conversations.
- Listen and take lots of notes.
- Touch their lives—get excited and share the client's enthusiasm for the wedding.

- Involve their senses—use visuals such as photos, table settings, and sample decorated cakes.
- Describe the benefits of using your facility versus the competition's.

A wedding is one of the most important events in a person's life. The choice of a caterer and location for the wedding reception is a major decision. A wedding reception requires the utmost skill, attention to detail, and careful coordination with the bride and groom and their respective families. Some couples prefer an informal, relaxed reception, while others will request a more formal affair. Each couple's tastes will be different. Many couples pay for their own wedding expenses today, and grooms are becoming more involved in wedding planning.

Many couples are opting to hold the ceremony as well as the reception at a hotel, club, or other facility. Do you have an area that would be particularly well suited for a ceremony—perhaps a gazebo, or an area with a spectacular view? Gazebos and other decor can be rented from prop houses, professional floral houses, or decorators if you don't have them on-site. Outdoor receptions can be beautiful, especially in the spring or fall.

Many venues and arenas have ventured more and more into the wedding market as themed and unique weddings become increasingly popular. For example, a bride and groom may have their reception as a tailgate party prior to their favorite football team's game, or the couple who are die-hard rodeo fans may throw a western-themed reception prior to one of the National Finals Rodeo events. Catering executives who work at these types of venues need to find ways to let prospective brides and grooms know that these services are available to them in order to capture this business.

Advantages to the client for holding the ceremony at the same place as the reception include:
- One-stop shopping
- Everything under one roof
- Guests do not have to travel from the ceremony to the location
- No or reduced limousine costs
- Saves time and travel arrangements

Advantages for the catering organization include additional revenues and the ability to be creative and imaginative with tents, canopies, fabric-lined ceilings, rental of foliage, the bridal runner, and other elements.

Saturday evenings and Sundays are the most popular times for weddings. Saturday afternoons and those held on other days of the week, may be sold at a lower price.

According to Atlanta caterer Shelley Pedersen, CPCE, the five basic elements of all wedding receptions are:

1. **MENU**
   - Start with your menu. Be accommodating by offering custom menus.
   - Listen to the client—what should the menu accomplish for the client?
   - What does the client want the guests to say about the event?
   - Involve the senses: sight, sound, taste, touch, smell.
   - Be aware of trends in the marketplace and the popularity of certain foods, as well as innovative preparation methods.
   - Keep traditional menu approaches in mind, as some clients will prefer an "old-fashioned wedding."
   - Upsell.

2. **BEVERAGES**
   - Be aware of beverage trends in your market.
   - Describe the special features you offer.
   - Learn your client's preferences.
   - Discuss wedding traditions with your client, such as toasts.
   - Upsell.

3. **DISPOSABLES**
   - Describe options (personalized menu cards, napkins, etc.).
   - Present samples to your client.
   - Be familiar with trendy items in the marketplace.
   - Draw upon popular traditional wedding items (e.g., Jordan almond favors).
   - Upsell.

4. **EQUIPMENT**
   - Make the most of your facility's equipment strengths (e.g., silver service, outdoor grill, etc.).

- Be aware of trends in the wedding market (cupcake trees, monogrammed cookies, etc.).
- Upsell.

5. SERVICE

- Know how the service you propose and the menu will work together.
- Be knowledgeable about different styles of service and offer choices.
- Train your staff in different service styles.
- Suggest new trends in styles of service (e.g., action stations).
- Offer traditional styles of service (e.g., French, Russian).
- Upsell.

Consider:

- Enhancements for each element. These provide opportunities to upsell.
- Trends and traditions (especially with ethnic weddings).
- Processions, recessions, blessings, candle lighting, communion, gift tables, toasting table, guest book table, and so forth.
- Client needs—what will make a reception perfect in the eyes of your client, and what you can do to make it happen.
- Event management. A representative from the catering office or management should be present from the moment the first guests arrive until all guests leave. The single most important role of the catering staff should be the sincere assurance that the wedding reception is in the capable hands of an experienced staff and that it will be done right.
- The finale. Create a lasting impression of the event and make it a "wow" moment by creating a memorable finale (e.g., live butterfly release, indoor fireworks).

Develop a checklist that covers virtually every facet of planning and execution of a wedding reception. This helps avoid last-minute problems and reduces the chances of major omissions in the planning and arrangements. Is there to be a head table? What service style is preferred? When is the limo arriving? Is there scripting for the first dance? When is the champagne toast? Will there be a groom's cake?

Wedding Checklist

Day, Time, and Date of the Wedding: _____

Bride's Name: _____

Bride's Address: _____

PHONE NUMBERS:

Home:_____ Cell: _____

Fax: _____ E-mail: _____

Phone at Work: _____ Fax: _____

Name of Groom: _____

Future Name of Bride:_____

Contact, (if other than Bride), Address: _____

Phone Number: _____

Location of the Wedding Reception: _____

Minimum - Maximum Number of Guests Expected: _____

   Location of the Ceremony: _____

   Ceremony Start Time: _____

End Time: _____

Transportation: _____

   Type:_____

   Company: _____

   Driver's Name: _____ Phone Number: _____

Reception Start Time: _____ End Time: _____

LOCATION PLANNING

Receiving Line/Introductions Time:_____

Gift Table: _____

Guest Book Table: _____

Escort Card Table: _____

Head Table: _____

_____ Guest Tables: _____

_____ # and Location of Reserved Tables _____

Type of Chairs: _____

Chair Covers:_____

Napkins: _____ Color: _____

Size: _____ Quantity: _____

Tablecloths: _____ Color: _____

Size: _____ Quantity: _____

Overlays: _____ Color: _____

Size: _____ Quantity: _____

Skirting: _____ Color: _____

Total Footage:_____

China Color and Pattern: _____

Glassware Type: _____

Flatware: _____

STAFF:

Bartenders: _____

Number:_____ Location: _____

Specialty Staff, (Cocktail Servers, Coat Check, Valet, etc.):_____

MUSIC:

Company Name & Contact Person: _____

    Cell Phone: _____

    Start Time: _____ End Time: _____

    Hourly Play Time: _____

Type of Bar: _____

Champagne Toast: _____ Time: _____

Cake Cutting: _____ Time: _____

MEAL:

Buffet: _____ Served: _____

Cocktail Reception: _____

Proposed Food Items: _____

Hors d'Oeuvres: _____

    Passed: _____

    Stationary: _____

Appetizer: _____

Soup: _____

Salad: _____

Intermezzo: _____

Main Course: _____

Dessert: _____

Wines: _____

FLORAL REQUIREMENTS

CENTERPIECES:

Tables: _____ Number: _____

Size: _____ Type: _____

Buffets: _____ Number: _____

Type: _____

Bridal Bouquet: _____

Groom's Boutonniere: _____

Boutonnieres for Father: _____ Grandfather: _____

Best Man, Groomsmen: _____

Bridesmaids' Corsages: _____

Bouquets: _____

Bouquet to Toss: _____

Corsages for Mother and Grandmother: _____

Flower Girl Petals: _____

Photographer   Name: _____ Phone: _____

Time of Attendance: _____

Videographer   Name: _____ Phone: _____

Time of Taping: _____

Wedding Cake   Bakery: _____ Phone: _____

Type: _____ Spec. Requirements: _____

Cake Floral Design: _____

Delivery Time: _____ Refrigerate: Yes   No

Number of Anticipated Servings: _____

Groom's Cake   Bakery: _____ Phone: _____

Type: _____ Spec. Requirements: _____

Delivery Time: _____ Refrigerate: Yes   No

Number of Anticipated Servings: _____

Cake Knife and Server: _____

Bride and Groom Glasses: _____

Cocktail Napkins   Color: _____ Quantity: _____

                               Inscription: _____

                               Printer: _____ Phone: _____

                               Fax: _____ E-mail: _____

                               Date Promised: _____

Floor Plan: _____

After the Event: _____

Who Is in Charge of Gifts? _____

Cake Top to be Saved? _____

OTHER:

_____

_____

_____

_____

_____

_____

_____

_____

_____

_____

_____

Developing a Wedding Brochure

It is wise to develop a separate wedding brochure and page on your website. By doing this, your facility conveys the importance it places on weddings. The needs and desires of this client segment differ greatly from those of a corporate client, and your wedding marketing pieces should reflect the fact that you, the catering professional, recognize and acknowledge these critical differences and stand ready to address them.

In your wedding literature, use descriptive language that evokes warm emotions and visual images, such as:

- "Reminiscent of a Victorian garden"
- "Crackling fire in our fireplace"
- "Soft sunlight"
- "Sparkling moonlight"
- "Panoramic view"
- "Grand staircase"
- "Attentive staff"
- "Knowledgeable, experienced service"
- "Let us custom-tailor a wedding as individual as you are"
- "Offers intimacy and charm"
- "We are at your service"
- "Let us take care of all your needs"
- "A wedding of style and grace"
- "A romantic setting"
- "The wedding your love deserves"
- "Weddings of sophisticated simplicity"
- "An event of perfection"
- "Romantic weddings"
- "Something old, something new"
- "The room is aglow in a festive fashion"
- "Be the center of attention, surrounded by friends and family"
- "Our elegant ballroom provides the perfect ambience"
- "Fairy-tale wedding"

- "Cathedral ceilings"
- "Crystal chandeliers"
- "White-gloved waiters"
- "Award-winning chef"
- "A dream come true"
- "A custom-made package just for you"
- "With more than twenty-five years of experience, weddings are our specialty"
- "Complimentary personalized wedding planning"
- "Affordable elegance"
- "Custom-tailored menus for your special day"
- "Memories destined to last a lifetime"

Wedding Package Plans

Facilities should offer a minimum of three complete plans for each of the following wedding functions:

- Hors d'oeuvres receptions: tray-passed only or a combination of tray-passed and buffet stations
- Buffet brunch, lunch, or dinner
- Combination buffet and served brunch, lunch, or dinner
- Served brunch, lunch, or dinner

Complete plans should include everything; food, beverages, entertainment, champagne toast, wedding guest book, color-coordinated linen, embossed napkins, wedding cake, groom's cake, floral arrangements, photography, and so on.

Promote your personalized wedding planning services and your willingness to custom design the event while discussing all of the enhancements (upselling) that you can provide.

One-stop Shopping

Position yourself as a wedding expert who will handle all of the wedding details and take the care and worry away from the bride. Develop a list of preferred vendors who will grant the facility discounts for providing services, including:

- Entertainment
- Wedding and formal attire
- Videography and photography
- Limo, horse and carriage ride from the ceremony, and other unique methods of transportation
- Baker for wedding cake, groom's cake, petit fours, guest favors
- Decorations
- Floral designer
- Wedding invitations and social stationery
- Calligraphy for invitations, menu cards, and place cards
- Embossed napkins
- Favors, keepsakes, mini bubble bottles for guests to blow bubbles as the bride and groom depart
- Upgraded china, flatware, glasses
- Specialty linens (overlays, runners, swagging)
- Red carpet in entryway
- Upgraded chairs (chiavari, chair covers with tie)
- Candelabra (silver, brass, gold)
- Fireworks display
- Skywriting message
- Hot-air balloon send-off
- Luminarias to line the footpath after dark

Independent wedding consultants typically charge 15 to 20 percent of gross wedding costs. When you provide this service and earn the discounts from vendors, you and the client both benefit.

Entertainment

Music sets the mood. When suggesting entertainment, think not only of the reception but of the ceremony as well. Music should start about half an hour prior to the ceremony, while guests are arriving. Most churches use organists, but organs are not portable, so a harpist or chamber music ensemble is ideal when the wedding ceremony is being held at the facility. A lively band can play at the reception, but calming, soothing tones are best for the ceremony, during the receiving line, and while guests are dining. The music can be religious, contemporary, romantic, or classical; song lists should be discussed in advance with the bride and groom.

Types of music available for ceremonies and receptions include:

Classical ensembles
Chamber music ensembles
Harpists
Strolling strings
Herald trumpets
Jazz combos
Vocalists
Various types of bands, including Top 40, country and western, classic rock, bluegrass, Dixieland, etc.
Dance orchestras
Disc jockeys
Pianists
Guitarists
Mariachi bands
Bagpipers

Floral Decor

There are many opportunities for selling various floral arrangements for wedding ceremonies and receptions. Some of the most common arrangements include:

Bride's bouquet and bouquet to throw
Maid of honor's and bridesmaids' bouquets
Corsages for mother of the bride and groom and other special female guests
Boutonnieres for the groom, best man, groomsmen, ushers, fathers of the bride and groom, and other special male guests

Loose petals for the flower girl(s)

Flowers for the bride's and flower girl's hair

Flowers for the church aisles and altar

Flowers for a chuppah

Flowers for an outdoor gazebo where the ceremony will be held and/or photographs will be taken

Roses to present to mothers during the ceremony

Table centerpieces for the reception

Flowers for the cake and/or cake table

Arrangements for the buffet, bar, guest book table

Arrangement for the ladies' restroom

While it is not necessary for the catering salesperson to be an expert in flowers when outsourcing to a vendor, he or she will need to be well versed in the types of customary arrangements as well as colors, types of flowers, and pricing. For larger or more complicated floral orders it is advisable to have the bride and groom speak directly with the florist to finalize those details.

Other Opportunities and Ideas

Don't forget that there are usually a variety of other functions surrounding a wedding that your catering organization can book. Examples of these include the engagement party, showers, bachelor and bachelorette parties, and rehearsal dinner.

The book *How to Manage a Successful Catering Business* contains an excellent wedding chapter that gives specific instructions and diagrams for how to set up weddings for Christian and Jewish ceremonies. It also includes detailed instructions on cutting the wedding cake and the tossing of the bridal bouquet and the garter.

Sample Wedding Package Plan

You are about to begin planning one of the most important days in your life—your wedding! We at [*name of your facility*] want to assure you that our attention to detail will make your wedding reception one of the most cherished memories of your life.

We offer several complete, all-inclusive plans to accommodate any budget. You may also custom-design your arrangements or use a combination of your choosing. We offer served dinners, buffet dinners, and stand-up receptions. In each category, there are various menus and options that enable you to tailor your reception as you would like. Trust us to make your arrangements and planning smooth, stylish and worry-free.

ROOM SELECTION & SETUP: We will work with you to ensure the setup is as you like it. This will include size and shape of head table, number and location of guest seats, dance floor placement, flow of the room, etc. A detailed diagram will be provided to you in advance for your approval.

Room capacities vary according to the table, bar, and entertainment requirements. For your planning purposes, room capacities are listed below:

Room	Served Dinner	Buffet Dinner	Stand-Up Reception
Azalea	350	320	500
Dahlia	75	65	110
Rose	110	80	150

Wedding receptions are booked for four hours for served or buffet meal functions and two and one-half hours for stand-up receptions.

RESERVATIONS/DEPOSITS: Reservations and arrangements are provided on a first-come, first-served basis. Reservations for a particular room are determined by availability, number of guests, and the arrangements and services to be provided. A tentative reservation may be made by phone, by email, or in person. The reservation for a particular room or date is tentative, and the room or date may be offered to another party until a deposit of [*dollar amount or percentage*] is made and the host signs a catering agreement. The agreement should be signed at least [*number*] days prior to the wedding date.

MENUS AND PRICING: Pricing for the all-inclusive plans is based on the menu and type of reception selected. The menus available for served dinners, buffet dinners, and stand-up receptions follow this section.

BEVERAGE/BAR SERVICE: An open bar is included in the package price. The bars are open for the entire two-and-one-half-hour period for stand-up receptions. For served and buffet dinners, the bars are open for three hours. During the meal period, two bottles of wine are provided for each table of ten guests. A champagne toast is also included with the plans.

LIVE ENTERTAINMENT: All plans include live entertainment. When there is a final count [*guarantee*] of 100 or more guests, a trio is provided; if your plan is for fewer than 100 guests, it includes a pianist.

FLOWERS: Floral decorations are provided for the head table and cake table for served and buffet dinners. For stand-up receptions, the buffet centerpiece is provided in place of the head table centerpiece. The remaining guest tables are furnished with candles.

LINEN: Napkins are available in a variety of colors for seated functions. We offer traditional white tablecloths, and tables that require skirting (cake, gift, book, etc.) are skirted in white. Additional selections and decorations are available, if desired, for a nominal charge.

From start to finish your wedding reception will be supervised by a trained, professional catering sales representative. Each plan includes the wedding guest book and all service charges and setup fees [*except those related to package plan modifications*].

ADDITIONAL TOUCHES: Listed below are suggested enhancements that are available upon request for a nominal charge.

- Additional appetizers and hot hors d'oeuvres
- Ice sculptures
- Silver candelabra
- Champagne fountain
- Specialty linen and overlays for the bridal, guest, and cake tables
- Take-home deli tray for the family
- Premium champagne (Moët et Chandon or Veuve Clicquot)
- Additional or specialty desserts

PAYMENT: Full prepayment of all estimated charges, less the deposit, is due a minimum of two weeks prior to the wedding. The final guarantee is due a minimum of three days prior. Any credit or debit will be reconciled after the event.

Checks may be used for the initial deposit. However, for final prepayment and additional charges on the day of the event, we accept cash, Visa, MasterCard, American Express, and Discover.

BAR AND BAT MITZVAHS

A bar mitzvah is a Jewish rite-of-passage celebration of a thirteen-year-old boy becoming a man within the faith. A bat mitzvah is for girls. The religious service is often celebrated with an elaborate event, sometimes rivaling the pomp and ceremony of a wedding.

The bar/bat mitzvah usually commences with a Friday evening, Saturday morning, or Saturday afternoon service. It could also be on a Monday morning or Thursday morning—anytime the Torah is read. The celebration that follows is often a breakfast, luncheon, or dinner with entertainment of a grand variety. Many bar/bat mitzvahs serve kosher or kosher-style food, depending on whether the family observes the rules of kashruth (that is, keeps kosher).

True kosher food must follow stringent rules and pass the approval of a *mashgiach*, who does not have to be a rabbi but must be recognized in the community as a person authorized to give certification for kashruth. Kosher-style food may use traditional Jewish recipes but does not necessarily follow the kosher rules. Kosher food conforms to strict biblical laws regarding the type of food that may be eaten. Pork, shellfish, rabbit, and parts of the hind-quarter cuts of beef and lamb are not allowed. Visit www.cyber-kitchen.com/rfcj for an archive of Jewish recipes. In addition to the kinds of animals considered kosher, the laws also state that animals be fed organically grown food and killed in the specified manner. Also, there are rules governing the kinds of food that can be combined during a meal. For example, in kosher service, meat products must not be served on any plate that has ever had dairy products on it (with the exception of glass and some china, which can undergo purification).

While there is no requirement to have a theme at one of these parties, it is very common and popular. The theme is often selected to reflect the child's special interests. Some of the more popular themes include:

- Sports
- Celebrities
- Tropical or luau
- Locations
- Movies
- Music
- Theater

As with all theme parties, you should offer to coordinate the menu selections, decorations, entertainment, centerpieces, room decor, cake, and party favors to fit the theme—all of which present multiple upsell opportunities.

Unlike a traditional wedding reception or many other theme parties, at a bar/bat mitzvah there is guaranteed to be a diverse age range of guests. When selecting menus and entertainment, therefore, you need to be sure that what is selected is suitable for the different ages of the guests.

Many bar/bat mitzvah clients will request two separate menus, one for the adults and one for the kids. Often the kids' meal is a buffet, while the adults' may be either a buffet or a served meal. While preparing and serving separate meals is more challenging for the kitchen and service staff, the catering organization must be willing to accommodate this request in order to attract these often lucrative events.

Selecting entertainment may be a challenge also, as you don't want all of the entertainment geared toward the kids or, conversely, to entertain only the adults, leaving the kids bored and looking for something to do.

To ensure all guests are entertained, you may need to look at more than one type of entertainment or having some kind of entertainment that can be targeted at multiple audiences. For example, during the adult cocktail hour you may have a DJ doing interactive games or leading dances that are appropriate for the children.

Arts-and-crafts tables or video game stations are also a popular activity during the event. With all the new technology (which kids particularly enjoy), you could set up screens around the room with either a live video feed of the party or live "tweets" and text messages being displayed from both attendees in the room as well as those unable to attend. If you do this, though, be sure you have an adult monitoring the content of the posts.

Other activities such as arcade-style games, karaoke, and photo booths can be fun for both kids and adults alike.

QUINCEAÑERA

The fifteenth birthday marks the transition from childhood to womanhood and is a significant rite of passage for girls in the Latin culture. It's like a cross between a Sweet Sixteen and a debutante's coming out party. The birthday girl arrives in a fancy full-length gown often with a wide skirt, frills, and other décor. She will have up to seven damas (maids of honor) in similar dresses, and an equal number of chambelanes (chamberlains), selected from friends and family. There is a religious ceremony, followed by a fiesta with music, dancing, and lots of food. Highlights include the cutting of a multi-tiered birthday cake. The celebration varies among the different Latin cultures. Visit http://en.wikipedia.org/wiki/Quineanera for more information.

OUTDOOR PARTIES

Outdoor parties can be held on a patio or balcony or by a swimming pool, golf course, beach, or other featured spot. They may also be at an off-site location.

When going off-premise, advance preparation is essential. Plan travel time by driving to the site on a day and time that matches that of the event. Take a sketchpad and/or a camera. Draw the area, including where you plan to place food, bars, work space, etc. If it is a wedding, be sure neither the bridal couple nor the guests will be squinting into the sun. Plot the traffic flow.

At times, the smartest thing may be to plan the party partly indoors and partly outdoors.

Whenever an outdoor event is booked you need to be sure there is a backup space reserved in the event of rain, high winds, or extremely high heat. This could be a room in your facility or a tent with transparent vinyl siding that can be raised or lowered as needed. Tents are discussed further in Chapter 6.

There is generally an additional charge for this backup plan, as holding indoor rooms prohibits you from booking another event in the room, and the rental cost of the tent must be covered. If there is no backup space available, you will need to make that very clear to the client and have him or her acknowledge that in writing in the contract.

When planning outdoor events, you should discuss with the client when to make the call to move inside due to inclement weather (usually at least four hours prior to the start of the event). That allows enough time to set the backup space and notify guests of the change in location.

Be sure to advise the client of any potential noise or other activity going on in the outdoor setting. You can have a lovely ceremony on a golf course, but if planes are flying by every five minutes, your guests may not be able to hear. If the event is by a pool, especially at hotels, lifeguards are required at a cost to the client. Inform the clients in advance of all applicable guidelines and associated costs. For example, they may love the idea of lights strung over the pool and the elegance of fine china and crystal, but having electrical wiring near the water may not be safe, and glass is not allowed at most pools. Offer alternatives, such as battery-operated lighting and upgraded single-use (disposable) china and plastic drinkware.

Prior to quoting prices and confirming availability, make sure that you have all required licenses and equipment in place. Most on-premise facilities do not have off-premise liquor licenses, and thus their on-sale licenses would not be valid for events held off the property. Be sure to obtain either a one-time-only or annual license for any off-premise event where you will be serving alcoholic beverages, as your municipality may dictate.

Facilities doing "cater-outs" may need to rent tables and chairs and build the cost into the price, instead of transporting these items from their properties.

Transporting involves labor costs and the potential for damage and loss. And since you will most likely need the equipment simultaneously for events inside your facility, there may not be enough available to accommodate the off-site event.

If the event is in the evening, outdoor lighting will likely be necessary. Visit the site one to two weeks prior, at the time of day of the party, to determine if auxiliary lighting is required. (If you go too far in advance, the sun may be setting at a different time and you will not be able to get an accurate assessment of lighting needs.) You can use strategically placed spotlights, tiki torches (which can also be insect repellants), strings of tiny Tivoli lights in trees, or other styles of lighting. Many times outdoor lighting is controlled by an automatic timer, and you may have to arrange to have them turned on earlier or left on later.

Don't forget to provide an adequate number of portable lavatories for outdoor and off-site events if permanent ones do not exist. Attendees can get rather uncomfortable without proper facilities. A rule of thumb is to provide one portable lavatory for every 100 attendees. Be sure there are directional signs that make them easy to locate, and that they can be removed when full without creating any site damage by the truck. You can also rent hand-washing sinks with portable water tanks, which in many areas are required by the local health department.

Be sure your clients are aware that they should specify a dress code and let their attendees know what types of shoes to avoid or if they should bring a light sweater. A woman in high heels would sink right into a grassy area. If it is likely that some women will be in high heels, arrange the area so that part of it covers a solid area, such as a sidewalk or parking lot. An alternative would be to lay out a portable dance floor, just to be sure the ladies have something solid to stand on.

Be sure any automated sprinkler systems are turned off to avoid drenching guests. It's also a good idea to avoid excessive watering for a few days prior to the event, so guests don't sink into squishy ground. Request that the lawn be mowed rather short so that tables are level, linens hang properly, and mosquitoes do not hide in the grass.

An added benefit with outdoor parties is that the site is often the decoration, especially in a garden in full bloom.

If you are using cut flowers in very hot weather, avoid very delicate blooms, as well as camellias, gardenias, and similar varieties that do not draw water.

If insects could be a problem, have the area sprayed six hours before the event. If this is not feasible, ask the host to advise the guests not to wear perfume, which attracts insects including bees and wasps. Bright colors also attract bees. Likewise, while it may be nice to hold the event in the middle of a flower garden, remember that bugs also find flowers attractive. Plan your party so the guests can see and enjoy the flowers without being close enough to upset stinging or biting creatures.

Mosquitoes love warm, moist, moving bodies. They also love carbon dioxide (produced by breathing) and favor dark, non-reflective clothing. Pyrethroid insecticides are deadly to mosquitoes. For an environmentally safe pesticide, there is a fogger available that vaporizes an insecticide called resmethrin (a synthetic pyrethroid). It is a low-toxicity pesticide that's people-friendly and has a less severe impact on the environment. Or you can suggest that clients incorporate crushed leaves of the citrosa plant into centerpieces and floral arrangements. The citrosa plant emits a substance (citronellal) that repels mosquitoes, but because of the odor, it should be used some distance from food.

Bees and yellowjackets are attracted to food, especially sweet items, and will sting the hand that shoos them away. People have been known to take a drink from a can of soda and get stung. At buffet tables and close to each dining table, place a saucer filled with equal parts of honey and beer. This will draw the insects away from guests' plates, and they will circle woozily around the saucer and eventually fall in. These saucers must be changed constantly, as a saucer full of dead insects would be an unappetizing sight on a buffet. Meat, especially if it is raw, attracts yellowjackets, so if you are cooking steaks, keep them covered until they are tossed on the grill.

Water attracts children, and at times can present a hazard to adults, so at all times watch areas such as reflecting pools, swimming pools, or golf course water hazards.

When planning menus for outdoor events, be careful not to serve a hot, heavy meal on a muggy day. Likewise, on a hot day avoid foods that spoil quickly, such as raw shellfish, mayonnaise-based items, or cream pies and cakes. Humidity also quickly wilts pretzels, potato chips, and cut cheeses.

To be sure food is served fresh and hot at sit-down off-premise events, pre-plate the appetizer and dessert, but you may wish to serve the other courses with French service. Pre-plated food that sits in a hot cart loses presentation value.

No matter how you spell it, barbecue (barbeque, bar-b-q, or just BBQ) is a popular item for outdoor events. Barbecue can be loosely defined as meat plus fire plus a sauce. The meat can be a variety of cuts and types, such as pork ribs, a side of beef, half chickens, or shrimp kabobs, depending on where you are and what your mood is. The meat should be precooked, either by oven baking or boiling. This will keep the outside from becoming overly charred before the inside is tenderized.

There are two basic types of barbecue. One style is to cook the food by direct heat and flame over a grill. The other way is with indirect heat and smoke, usually inside a cylinder-style smoker.

Barbecue experts abound, each with their own closely guarded secret sauce. Many of these recipes have been handed down through generations. Vinegar-based sauces tend to absorb more readily into the meat than tomato-based sauces, and act as a tenderizer when used as a marinade. Red meats also marinate well in red wine and olive oil with garlic and other spices. Rosemary goes well with lamb. Poultry and seafood marinate well in white wine, olive oil, and spices.

International versions of barbecue include tandoori cooking from India (the food is marinated overnight in a yogurt-based sauce and then either baked in a clay oven or grilled) and Greek-style barbecue (such as lamb kabobs).

SUMMARY

Caterers can let their creativity shine when planning themed events, including weddings and bar/bat mitzvahs. Ideas for innovative themes are included in this chapter to spark your creativity. Lighting, sound, decor, props, and food can all be used to set the tone for a themed event.

Outdoor events present unique challenges but can provide a unique experience for guests.

KEY TERMS

Budget considerations	Lighting	Soundscapes
Moving decor	Event entrance	Colors
Cater-out	Fun food	Signature items
Props	Wedding checklist	Wedding brochure
Wedding package plans		

REVIEW QUESTIONS

1. What are some advantages to holding the wedding ceremony in the same place as the reception?
2. What are the two methods of barbecue?
3. Do guests eat more in brightly colored rooms or with darker tones?
4. What are the five senses that should be considered when planning an event?
5. What key things should you know before preparing a proposal?
6. What are Gobo lights?
7. What does soundscape refer to?
8. What should a caterer be careful of doing when using trademark images as part of a proposal document?
9. What is moving décor?
10. What is a signature menu item?
11. Where should a caterer shop for bargain-priced props?
12. What are the five basic elements of all wedding receptions?

Chapter 4

MEAL FUNCTIONS

Providing outstanding food and exceptional service is a major marketing advantage in today's competitive catering environment. While all aspects of a catered function are important, it is reasonable to assume that the quality of food and guest service makes the deepest and most-lasting impression on attendees.

The caterer who strives for a competitive advantage would do well to emphasize consistent-quality food because this consistency is something some caterers cannot offer. While it may be easy for most facilities to offer clients similar function space or meeting times, such is not the case with food.

Other factors may initially attract clients, but food and service are the key variables influencing return patronage.

PURPOSE OF THE MEAL FUNCTION

One of the first things to consider when planning a meal function is the client's reason for hosting it. Does the client want a meal function primarily to satisfy hunger? Create an image? Provide an opportunity for social interaction and networking? Showcase a person, product, or idea? Present awards? Honor dignitaries? Refresh convention attendees and resharpen their attention? Provide a receptive audience to program speakers? Keep people interested in other non-food activities? Increase attendance at conventions?

The list of reasons is endless. The catering executive, though, should query the client about his or her particular reasons so that the appropriate menu and production and service plans can be created. If the catering executive knows about these considerations and concerns, he or she will tailor the function around them.

MENU PLANNING

The director of catering is often responsible for developing standardized menus (in cooperation with the chef and possibly the food and beverage director), as well as unique menus customized for particular clients. He or she also must see to it that the standardized menus are revised periodically, such as twice a year, in order to keep them current with changing consumer trends. Many upscale hotels and other caterers are abandoning printed menus and use only custom proposals for each client.

It also is a good idea to get input from other department heads, such as the purchasing agent, food and beverage director, and facility sales director. You can also run computer reports to see which items are popular and sell well and which don't.

The types of menu items a facility can offer its guests depend on several factors. Before adding a menu item to a standardized menu, or before offering to accommodate a client's particular menu request, the menu planner needs to evaluate all relevant considerations that will affect the facility's ability to offer it and the guest's desire to eat it.

Food Cost

Ideally, the catering department will offer a variety of menu prices to suit its target markets. However, these prices must also be consistent with the target market's needs and desires. Many clients appreciate the opportunity to work with several price options when allocating their meal budgets. These clients tend to shuffle their budgetary dollars back and forth among events; this routine is easier to accomplish if the catering department cooperates by offering several price variations. Caterers should be aware of ways to modify their standard menu, such as offering a less expensive entree or removing a course. Food cost margins affect profitability. Pricing is discussed in detail in Chapter 2.

Guest Background

A menu planner should consider the demographics of the group ordering the meal function. Average age, gender, ethnic backgrounds, socioeconomic levels, diet restrictions, where the guests come from, employment and fraternal affiliations, and political leanings can indicate the types of menu items that might be most acceptable to the group. Psychographics (the study of guests' lifestyles and the way in which they perceive themselves) can also be a useful indicator.

Age is often an excellent clue. For example, senior citizens usually do not want exotic foods or heavy, spicy foods. In this case, you should try to avoid excessive use of garlic, hot spices, and onions. You should plan to avoid other distress-causing foods, such as monosodium glutamate (MSG), vegetables in the cabbage family, and beans and legumes.

Guests with special diets will influence the types of foods served. Some people cannot tolerate MSG (allergic reactions), onions and garlic (digestive problems), certain spices or peanuts (allergic reactions), sugar (diabetes), salt (high blood pressure, heart problems), fat (weight problems, high cholesterol), wheat, rye, or barley (celiac disease), or milk products (allergic reactions, lactose intolerance).

An acute allergic reaction to a food may manifest as swelling of the eyelids, face, lips, tongue, larynx, or trachea. Other reactions can include difficulty breathing, hives, nausea, vomiting, diarrhea, stomach cramps, or abdominal pain. Anaphylactic shock is a severe whole-body reaction that can result in death.

The eight most common food allergies are:

1. Dairy allergy
2. Egg allergy
3. Peanut allergy
4. Tree nut allergy

5. Seafood allergy
6. Soy allergy
7. Wheat allergy
8. Carmine allergy

Some guests consume special diets for religious or lifestyle reasons. For example, some Jews require kosher foods; others may not keep kosher but will not eat pork or shellfish. Some devout Muslims may only eat halal (approved) foods. Some people will not eat red meat but will eat poultry and seafood. Many vegetarians (often called lacto-ovo vegetarians) will not eat animal flesh but will eat animal by-products such as eggs and dairy products, but vegans will not eat anything from any animal source, including cream, eggs, butter, and honey. Accommodating some ethnic or religious requirements may create added expenses because of a need to hire outside specialized personnel (such as a rabbi to supervise kosher preparations) or to acquire special food items.

If a group is coming from a previous function where heavy, filling hors d'oeuvres were served, the meal should be lighter. If guests are coming from a liquor-only reception, then the meal could be heavier. If a group will be going to a business meeting immediately after the meal, you need to serve foods that will help keep attendees awake. Protein foods, such as seafood, lean beef, and skinless chicken, will keep guests alert. Carbohydrates, such as rice, bread, and pasta, tend to relax guests and put them to sleep. Fats, such as butter, whipped cream, and heavy salad dressings, also tend to make guests sleepy, sluggish, and inattentive.

Politics can play an important role in menu planning. Serving veal to animal-rights organizations, for example, can anger guests because these groups believe that most veal is raised under inhumane conditions. Politically active groups may insist that the facility purchase and serve politically correct products. You may be prohibited from purchasing beef raised on recently deforested tropical rain forest land. You may be asked not to purchase tuna from countries that use drift nets that trap and kill dolphins and other sea life indiscriminately. And for your clients with "green" concerns, you may be prohibited from packaging finished food products in disposable containers. You may need to use reusable containers instead, and must incorporate the cost of this in the menu for this service.

Nutrition Concerns

Nutrition is a consideration for all caterers, but especially for groups that will be at a hotel or conference/convention center for several days during a convention. Since virtually all meals during their stay will be consumed on the premises, special attention must be paid to nutritional requirements when planning menus.

Because there are many different types of diets, customers will appreciate it if the facility provides alternatives, including some low-fat, low-calorie, sugar-free, or high-protein meal options as well as a variety of low-carbohydrate foods. Some caterers list calories, fat, carbohydrates, and sodium information on menu items.

Many people are avoiding trans fats, high-fructose corn syrup, sodium benzoate, and other unhealthy additives.

Whenever possible, serve sauces and dressings on the side so that guests can control their own portion sizes. Use fresh ingredients instead of processed foods that contain preservatives and other additives.

Caterers notice, though, that many guests are reluctant to give up their dessert course. Ironically, when people are "good" in terms of what they eat, they often like to reward themselves with a rich dessert. In spite of the fact that people are becoming more health-conscious, fancy desserts are expected at a catered meal. The typical guest feels cheated if the meal ends without a dessert, or if the dessert offered is viewed as mediocre.

The dessert creates the last impression of the meal and should be spectacular. A small portion of a rich dessert is sufficient if the presentation is very artistic. For instance, desserts can be very impressive if served atop a decorative coulis on an oversized decorated plate, or perhaps prepared tableside.

Special service presentations can be very effective. For instance, a baked Alaska parade, where the lights are dimmed and the servers carry in the flaming dishes, is a dazzling sight.

Dessert action stations (performance or exhibition cooking) are certain crowd pleasers that are guaranteed to have a favorable impact on guests. Chefs working at these stations can prepare hot crepes with different fruit sauces. Or they can prepare bananas Foster, fruit beignets, or cherries jubilee to order.

Always consult with the fire marshal when planning to use an open flame in food preparation. Open flames are not permitted in many jurisdictions. Know what is allowed in your area. Be sure that the station is not set up directly under a sprinkler head or smoke detector and that it is a safe distance from guests.

Dessert buffets are also a nice touch, especially when served with champagne, flavored coffees and teas, liqueurs, or brandies. This type of service allows the guests an opportunity to move around, a good idea if you expect the meal function to be more than one and one-half to two hours.

If you provide dessert buffets or dessert action stations, you should prepare bite-sized "taster" dessert items. Guests will appreciate this because many of them will have a hard time choosing just one. You do not want them to take two or three full desserts because this will increase waste and food costs.

When stocking a dessert buffet, a good idea is to display full-sized desserts on an upper tier of the table, then on the lower tier place duplicate miniature versions of the showcased ones. This type of presentation is especially effective if the dessert tasters are placed on mirrored or decorative platters. Experience shows that cheesecake, tarts, tortes, cakes, baklava, cannoli, gourmet cookies, chocolate leaves, and fresh fruit are especially attractive and inviting when presented like this.

Hard-to-Produce Foods

Certain delicate items cannot be produced and served in quantity without sacrificing culinary quality. For example, lobster, soufflé, rare roast beef, medium-rare tuna or salmon steak, and rare duck breast are almost impossible to prepare and serve satisfactorily for more than a handful of guests.

If a client insists on having these types of items, the facility may need to implement a creative and possibly costly procedure to accommodate the request. For instance, flaming desserts do not lend themselves easily to quantity production. However, a caterer could install an action station on an elevated platform safely away from tableside but not near sprinkler heads. Guests can view the flaming displays without worrying about getting burned. And servers can retrieve the finished desserts when the chefs are done. If necessary, to ensure timeliness, additional desserts could be prepared in the kitchen to supplement the number prepared by the action station chef(s).

Standardized Menu Offerings

If the facility has a restaurant, the catering sales representative should encourage clients to order menu items offered in the restaurant outlets. This will keep food costs under control since banquet leftovers can be utilized elsewhere, and you will have extra inventory on hand if needed.

Usually the chef will prepare enough food to serve more than the guaranteed guest count. This overproduction is necessary to avoid running out. Unfortunately, if the menu includes unusual foods that cannot be used in other areas or events, a client will need to pay a higher price to defray the extra food costs. With a standardized menu, clients may not have to worry about paying for overproduction. Chefs usually prepare for 3–5 percent over the guarantee. That is important for the client to understand.

Some hotels (the Wynn in Las Vegas, for example) offer a discount if you order standardized menus. The menu price may be more economical if clients order X standardized menu on Monday, Y standardized menu on Tuesday, and so on. The catering operation may wish to do this as having one standardized menu on a given day makes the kitchen more efficient. It is much easier to make larger quantities of the same items rather than producing an entire menu and then starting all over on another menu. In addition, food, (that has not yet been put out for guest consumption), can be reallocated from one event to the other if one group is consuming more than anticipated and the other is consuming less than anticipated. This can be a win-win situation, in that it is perceived value for clients because they receive a discount on the menu price, and it also helps the caterer with food and labor cost and product ordering.

Variety

The most important rule: if guests will be with your organization for several days and will be eating mostly catered meals, you must be careful not to repeat food items from meal to meal and from day to day. For instance, you would not want to serve carrot cake for dessert if you served a carrot and raisin salad or glazed carrots last night, serve chicken for dinner if you served it yesterday for lunch, or serve beef two nights in a row.

Similarly, you should not use the same ingredients in more than one course unless the meal is specifically designed for this. For instance, a convention group visiting Atlanta may be pleased if some courses include Georgia peaches. Likewise with a group visiting Seattle, where the creative director of catering might be able to include Pacific salmon in two or three courses. These instances should be marketed as such, so attendees understand the reason for the repetition.

The most important consideration is to provide variety and nutritious options. The longer the meeting, the more critical these factors become.

Meeting attendees often do not eat every meal in the facility. Whether you are the on- or off-site facility hosting the group for one or more meals, you should try to find out what they are scheduled to eat at any other meal locations before they come to your function. This will prevent your using too many of the same ingredients. For example, when Prince Charles once visited the United States, he was taken to several places for meals. Each facility served him a veal dish, which caused the prince to wonder aloud if veal was the only meat that Americans ate.

Seasonality and Market Availability

A catering sales representative should always try to recommend seasonal foods. The quality of food items is greatly enhanced when they are in season. In-season foods also are less expensive. Lower food costs will increase profitability. Moreover, the lower food costs will allow you to pass on some of the savings to the client in the form of lower prices, thereby possibly capturing catering clients who would not purchase standard-priced meal functions. The client who wants strawberry shortcake in January must pay a premium because the strawberries will have to be shipped from South America.

Before committing to a specific menu item, the catering executive must ensure that the food is available. Some fish, such as halibut, is not available during certain months of the year. It is especially imperative to check the availability of any ethnic products needed before preparing a client proposal.

At times there may be seasonal restrictions, product shortages, or distribution shortcomings that interfere with acquiring some products. For instance, while vine-ripened tomatoes may be in season, there may be a temporary shortage and local purveyors may be unable to satisfy your needs.

Local and Sustainable Foods

The growing locavore movement espouses locally grown and produced food. Locally grown food is generally in season and fresher, the financial and environmental costs of transportation are lower, and local food is considered to be part of the sustainability movement. According to the United Nations World Commission on Environment and Development, sustainability is defined as "forms of progress that meet the needs of the present without compromising the ability of future generations to meet their needs." Additional information on practicing sustainable catering can be found at http://web.mit.edu/workinggreen/docs/sustainable_catering_giuide.pdf or www.sustainabletable.com.

Caterers who practice sustainable methods are able to use this as a marketing tool, as more and more companies and individuals are aware of and asking for these services.

Easy-to-Produce Foods

The director of catering should resist the temptation to emphasize only easy-to-prepare foods. Clients may think that these menus lack creativity and flair and may have doubts about the caterer's capabilities.

Chicken is a very common item served on banquet menus primarily because it is easy to cook and can be prepared and served in so many ways. It is also the most widely accepted form of protein used as a center-plate item.

Beef is another very common menu offering for at least three reasons. One, it is usually a safe choice for clients; most people will eat beef at least once in a while. Two, a tremendous variety of cuts is consistently available. And three, it can be prepared and served in many ways.

In general, catering executives tend to favor poultry, beef, and other similar items that lend themselves to assembly-line production and service. If nothing else, the menu offers no disastrous surprises, and usually it can be prepared and served very efficiently.

Some clients will be satisfied with these tried-and-true menu options. For instance, a survey conducted by the Marriott Corporation revealed that association meeting planners tend to prefer familiar products. However, this same survey indicated that corporate meeting planners are likely to be more adventurous when they develop menus for meal functions and are more receptive to unique cuisine. It is risky to offer items such as fish or lamb to a large group, as these items are not universally appreciated. If you want to be a bit adventurous, you might try a split entree (or dual entree), which would still provide something "safe" for the meat-and-potatoes diner. An example would be surf and turf, perhaps a small filet mignon with three grilled jumbo shrimp. Avoid wacky or unusual entree duets such as sea scallops with buffalo medallions or lamb with ahi tuna. Usually you will simply increase the number of requests for an alternative or vegetarian meal, which can throw the kitchen into a tailspin.

Some venues may offer the client's guests a choice of entree. Most caterers who provide this option require a count in advance. In addition, the servers will need a way to know who is to get which entree. This is most often done with color-coded meal tickets or place cards. If the client wishes for the guests to make their selections tableside on the evening of the event, the cost will be greater, as the kitchen will need to prep more. This may be more expensive in terms of food cost, but it is also a good opportunity to upsell this style menu. To ensure success, a choice of menus during the event needs to be limited—for example, 200 people maximum.

Product Shelf Life

Since catered events do not always run on time, it pays to have foods that will hold up well prior to and during service. This is also an important consideration whenever a banquet is scheduled for a large group and you anticipate a few minor logistical problems.

Large pieces of food hold heat or cold longer than small pieces. Solid meats hold temperature better than sliced meats. Lettuce wedges stay fresher and colder than tossed salad. Whole fruit and muffins stay fresher longer than sliced fruits or sliced cake. Whole vegetables hold better than julienne cuts.

Generally speaking, cold foods stay cold longer than hot foods hold heat. In addition, cold foods will stay cold longer if they are served on cold plates, and hot foods will stay hot longer if they are served on warm plates.

Sauces tend to extend a hot food product's holding capacity and keep foods from drying out. Sauce can also add color to a finished dish. However, if not planned properly, a sauce could run all over the plate, skin over, or pick up flavors and odors from other foods or heating fuels. Topping the main course with a hot sauce just before serving can bring the dish back to life, as well as raise the temperature. Sauce is not always poured on the meat by the kitchen. Often the food servers pour the sauce onto the meat from a small press pot at the table. This provides better service and presentation.

Menu Balance

The menu planner should try to balance flavors, textures, shapes, colors, temperatures, and so forth. Appetites are stimulated by all of the senses. You should not plan meals that tend to overpower one of them. Color is pleasing to the eye. How appetizing would it be if you prepared a plate of sliced white-meat turkey, mashed potatoes, and cauliflower? Guests will be turned off by the lack of color contrast.

Be cautious of clashing strong flavors. For instance, you would not want to serve broccoli, cabbage, cauliflower, and Brussels sprouts at the same meal. They are all strong-flavored vegetables and are in the same vegetable family. You would need more variety and contrast to create a successful menu.

You should strive to have something mild, something sweet, something salty, something bitter, and something sour on the menu. Textures also are very important. Ideally you would have a pleasing combination of crisp, firm, smooth, and soft foods.

Product forms, shapes, and sizes should be mixed and matched. You should offer as much variety as possible. For instance, a menu could include a combination of flat, round, long, chopped, shredded, heaped, tubular, and square foods. A temperature contrast will also appeal to most guests. A menu should offer both hot and cold food options.

The type of preparation offers an opportunity to provide several pleasing contrasts. For instance, an appropriate combination of sautéed, broiled, baked, roasted, steamed, sauced, and smoked foods will be more pleasing to customers than foods prepared only one or two ways.

The menu planner also should offer several types and varieties of food courses. A client should be able to select an appropriate combination of appetizer, soup, salad, main course, starch, vegetable, bread, dessert, and beverage from the standardized menu offerings. Ideally, the catering sales representative would be able to offer more than one combination.

Avoid the common mistake of serving two or more starches, such as potatoes and rice, pasta and stuffing, or corn and potatoes. (And remember that the word *starch* should only be used in-house, never with clients and their guests.)

Equipment Limitations

Certain foods require special equipment in order to be prepared or served properly. For instance, a standing rib roast dinner for 2,500 people usually requires a battery of cook-and-hold ovens. Buffets cannot be set up properly unless sufficient steam table space or chafing dishes are on hand. And a large banquet that requires several hundred deep-fried appetizers cannot be serviced adequately unless you have sufficient deep fryer capacity or automated deep fryers.

The size of your food and beverage production and service facilities and their layout and design also impact menu-planning decisions. For instance, while you may have a sufficient number of cook-and-hold ovens, if they are not located correctly, your ability to serve large numbers of guests could be severely limited.

Experience suggests that if there is any question about equipment capacity, an equipment specialist can usually provide the correct answer. An equipment manufacturer, dealer, designer, sales representative, or leasing company usually is able to help you estimate your facility's capacity and recommend minor, inexpensive changes that can increase it significantly. The chef may also be able to offer useful suggestions. If your facility is large enough to have an engineer, he or she may also be helpful.

Labor

Some menu items are very labor-intensive, especially those made from scratch in the facility's kitchens. It is not unusual for labor costs to be as much as one-third or more of a meal function's total price.

Labor is expensive in the foodservice industry. There are many hidden labor costs that are not readily apparent. To say the least, there is a great deal of pressure in our industry to hold the line on labor costs. Unfortunately, this puts you in a very awkward position when planning the menu. To control labor, you may need to purchase more convenience foods, reduce menu options, eliminate menu items that require a great deal of expertise to prepare and serve, or charge the client more. It is not an option to schedule fewer servers or compromise on other services.

The director of catering must stay within the labor budget, but it is equally important to avoid alienating guests. Instead of cutting labor to the bone and possibly incurring the customer's wrath, it is much better to charge the client a modest labor surcharge or adjust the menu price so that the meal can be prepared and served professionally. If you feel that a labor surcharge is a client's best option, you should suggest it and plan for it in advance; it should not be a last-minute consideration.

Matching Food and Wine

Generally speaking, delicate, less flavorful foods should be served with white wines. Red meats, pastas with meat and tomato sauce, and other strong-flavored foods should be served with red wines.

Some wine lists are not based on the color of the wine. A list could note wines according to their degree of sweetness, lightness, alcoholic strength, point of origin (region) or other relevant factors. In fact, it is a good idea to have many wine options available for client selection.

The catering sales representative should be prepared to suggest food and wine combinations to clients. Since many clients are unsure of these selections, it is important to help them make the right choices. Some wine companies provide assistance to foodservice professionals whereby a company representative will come to your establishment and help you pair all of your wines and foods. These purveyors usually will pair all wines, not just those you purchased from them.

Some clients have personal preferences that could interfere with selecting appropriate wines for the meal. For instance, a client may want to serve red wine with fish. If so, the catering executive should convince him or her to have alternative wines available so that guests who may not embrace this unconventional pairing will not think that the caterer is incompetent. Furthermore, some guests cannot tolerate or do not enjoy red wine and will appreciate having a choice.

Entertainment Value

Some menu items lend themselves to entertaining displays in the dining room. For instance, action stations are very popular. Seafood bars and other similar food stations are attractive and tend to generate enthusiasm among guests. And flaming dishes, when prepared safely, are always well received by the dining public.

Any form of entertainment is bound to be expensive. For instance, the examples just noted can be very costly. There is considerable setup and teardown work, labor hours, and labor expertise involved that can strain a client's budget.

On the other hand, though, special touches may promote attendance. For example, the association meeting planner who wants to attract the maximum number of attendees and their spouses must be willing to provide an extra incentive. Special foods, prepared and served in an entertaining, exciting way, are sure to enhance attendance. Furthermore, this form of entertainment may be the least expensive way to motivate guests to attend the event.

Menu Trends

It is important to keep up with trends, but it is equally important to be able to differentiate between a trend and a fad. Trends seem to be more permanent. They are like roads, providing direction—a way to go. Fads or crazes, on the other hand, are like highway rest stops, which come and go along the way.

The move to a healthier diet is a trend. Significant numbers of people want less fat, salt, and sugar in their diets.

Sliders (mini burgers) are a trend, and can be beef, chicken, seafood, or vegetarian. Chocolate is a trend, especially with all the recently published health benefits it offers. Even without the health benefits, many people who eat healthy all week reward themselves on the weekend with rich, gooey chocolate desserts.

Nouvelle, Cajun, southwestern, and spa cuisine were fads. Although grilled food is a trend that is still with us and thriving, mesquite and cedar plank grilling was a fad. Complicating matters is the possibility that a trend or fad can be popular in one part of the country and disdained in others. It may take a fad or trend started in California a long time to catch on in the Midwest. The menu planner can assume the risk by trying to lead the pack. For instance, someone had to get on the cutting edge and introduce goat cheese pizza with sun-dried tomatoes. At the other extreme, if you are risk-averse, you could be classified as a laggard or someone woefully behind the times. Some chefs, trying to make a name for themselves, come up with outlandish combinations such as lamb chops dipped in Japanese tempura batter and fried, then set afloat on Italian-style tomato sauce with Moroccan spices. This is an example of good ingredients being manipulated to create unnatural combinations. Is molecular gastronomy a fad or a trend? Only time will tell. It would appear that most caterers take the middle ground by staying close behind the leader.

Style of Service

Oftentimes the style of service clients want will influence the types and varieties of foods the menu planner can offer. For instance, foods that will be passed on trays by servers during an afternoon reception must be easy to handle. They also must be able to hold up well. In this case, sauced items, which could drip, should not be served, but easy-to-eat finger foods would be appropriate.

The service styles that can be used for a catered meal function are:

Reception service. Light foods are served displayed buffet-style on a table. Guests usually stand and serve themselves. They normally do not sit down to eat. This type of event is sometimes referred to as a "walk and talk." Food is finger food or fork food. It is inappropriate to serve food that requires a knife or is difficult to eat while standing.

Butlered hors d'oeuvres service. Food is put on trays in the kitchen and passed by servers. Guests serve themselves, using cocktail napkins provided by the server. This is a typical style of service used for upscale receptions. This style of service is only appropriate for finger food.

Buffet service. Foods are arranged on tables. Guests usually move along the buffet line and serve themselves. When their plates are filled, guests take them to a dining table to eat. Servers usually provide beverage service at tableside. A very elegant buffet would have servers carry guests' plates to their tables for them.

Action station service. Similar to a buffet. Chefs prepare and serve foods at the buffet (rather than in the kitchen). Foods that lend themselves well to action station service include wok stations, mashed potato bars, fajitas, pastas, grilled meats, omelets, crepes, sushi, flaming desserts, and spinning salad bowls. These stations are sometimes called performance stations or exhibition cooking.

Cafeteria service. Similar to a buffet. Guests stand in line but do not help themselves. They are served by chefs or servers from behind the buffet line. This is a way to control portion sizes. Sometimes the inexpensive items, such as salads, will be self-service, and the expensive meat items will be served by an attendant.

Plated buffet service. Selection of pre-plated foods, such as entrees, sandwich plates, and salad plates, set on a buffet table. They may also be placed on a roll-in (a rolling cart or table) and then moved into the function room at the designated time. Because of individual plates, trays are usually used. This is a particularly good idea for groups who want to continue working while they eat.

Plated (American) service. Guests are seated. Foods are pre-portioned in the kitchen, arranged on plates, and served by servers from the left. Beverages are served from the right. Used dishes and glasses are removed from the right. This is the most functional, common, economical, controllable, and efficient type of service. However, if foods are plated too far in advance, they could run together, discolor, or otherwise lose culinary quality.

Family-style (English) service. Guests are seated. Large serving platters and bowls are filled with foods in the kitchen and set on the dining tables by servers. Guests help themselves from a lazy Susan or they pass the foods to each other. Occasionally a host would carve the meat.

Pre-set service. Food is already on the dining tables when guests are seated. Since pre-set foods will be on the tables for a few minutes before they are consumed, you must pre-set only those that will retain sanitary and culinary qualities at room temperature. Most common are bread and butter, but often the appetizer will be pre-set as well. For lunches with a limited time frame, occasionally salad and dessert will be pre-set.

Butlered service. Foods are presented on trays by servers with utensils available for seated guests to serve themselves. (Often confused with Russian service.)

Russian (silver) service. Guests are seated. Foods are cooked tableside on a rechaud (portable cooking stove) that is on a gueridon (tableside cart with wheels). Servers put the foods on platters and then pass the platters at tableside. Guests help themselves to the foods and assemble their own plates. Service is from the left. (Often confused with French service.)

Banquet French service. Guests are seated. Platters of foods are assembled in the kitchen. Servers take the platters to the table. Guests select foods, and the server, using two large silver forks in his or her serving hand (or silver salad tongs if the forks cannot be coordinated with one hand), places them on the guests' plates. Each food item is served by the server from platters to individual plates. Guests are served from the left.

French cart service. The type of French service that is used in fine-dining restaurants. Guests are seated. Foods are prepared tableside. Hot foods are cooked on a rechaud that is on a gueridon. Cold foods are assembled on the gueridon. Servers plate the finished foods and serve them to guests. This is the only style of service where food is served from the right. Some foods, such as desserts, are already prepared. They are displayed on a cart, the cart is rolled to tableside, and guests are served after making their selections.

Synchronized service. Guests are seated. There is one server for every two guests and all guests at a table are served at precisely the same time. Servers wear white gloves. Foods are pre-plated and the plates are fitted with dome covers. Each server carries two servings from the kitchen and stands behind the two guests assigned to him or her. At the direction of the captain or maître d'hôtel, all servings are set in front of all guests, and the dome covers are removed, at precisely the same time. This procedure may be followed for all courses. This is a very elegant style of service that is sometimes used for small gourmet meal functions. This style is sometimes called "service in concert" or "hand service."

The wave. This is a method of serving where all servers start at one end of the function room and work straight across to the other end. Servers are not assigned workstations. In effect, all servers are on one team and the entire function room is the team's workstation. The wave is typically used in conjunction with plated and pre-set service styles. Large numbers of guests can be served very quickly.

As noted, there is a good deal of confusion between butlered, Russian, and French service, with even many professionals disagreeing over the exact interpretation. The key is that you and your client have the same understanding so that there will not be any surprises. If clients are not knowledgeable about service styles, the catering sales representative may wish to explain some of them so that they can make informed choices. Of course, you should describe only those service styles your staff is equipped and trained to comfortably execute properly. Moreover, when you are pointing out service options, clients must be made aware of any extra labor charges associated with them.

Service styles play an important role in the success of a catered event. Clients can choose those that may be less expensive (such as pre-set) or can splurge with French or Russian service. Furthermore, some service styles (such as action stations) are very entertaining and can contribute significantly to guest satisfaction.

For variety, you can mix service styles during a single meal function. For instance, you might begin with reception service for appetizers, move into the banquet room where the tables are pre-set with salads, rolls, and butter, use French service for the soup course, use Russian service for the entree, and end the meal with a dessert buffet.

TRUTH-IN-MENU GUIDELINES

The menu planner must ensure that he or she does not inadvertently misrepresent menu items. Printed menus, photos, illustrations, signage, verbal descriptions, and other media presentations must not deceive or mislead clients.

The National Restaurant Association (NRA) recognized the problem of menu misrepresentation in 1923. At that time it issued a report entitled *Standards of Business Practices*. In 1977 it published the *Accuracy in Menus* report, which reaffirmed its position decrying menu misrepresentation.

In some parts of the country, local governments have enacted truth-in-menu legislation. For instance, in Southern California, health district sanitarians are empowered to inspect a restaurant's menu items and determine if customers are receiving the advertised value.

The NRA identifies eleven potential menu misrepresentations. The menu planner must see to it that menus do not misrepresent in any of these ways.

By doing so, ambiguity will be eliminated and guests will not be unpleasantly surprised.

1. Misrepresentation of quantity

   If portion sizes are listed on the menu, they must also be noted on the standardized recipes. The sizes noted must be as-served sizes. Alternatively, a size can be noted with a qualifier, such as "weight before cooking."

   Sometimes you may get into trouble if you misuse terms that are recognized sizes. For instance, you cannot use the term "large egg" if in fact you are serving the medium size. According to federal government guidelines, large eggs must weigh 24 ounces per dozen, while medium eggs must weigh 21 ounces per dozen. Anyone using the description "large egg" must serve a 2-ounce egg.

   Some terminology, such as "jumbo tossed salad," can be misleading. There is no established government standard for types of marketing qualifiers such as "jumbo," so you must be careful when using such language.

   Some terms have implied meanings. For instance, when a customer notices that you offer a cup of soup and a bowl of soup, he or she has the right to assume that the bowl contains the larger portion. Likewise, when you list the terms "small," "medium," and "large" to describe soft drinks, guests should be able to assume that the volume of liquid increases from small to large.

   Qualifiers such as "mile-high" for a pie or "world-famous giant" for a strawberry shortcake usually do not mislead consumers because they tend to view these terms as a permissible form of trade puffery. However, the menu planner may want to avoid even the appearance of impropriety and not use any term that cannot be supported.

2. Misrepresentation of quality

   The federal government, through the United States Department of Agriculture (USDA) and the Food and Drug Administration (FDA), has established quality-grading procedures for many foods. For instance, meats, poultry, and fresh produce have standardized quality grades that can be noted on the menu only if you purchase products that have received these grade designations from a government inspector. You cannot, for example, note that you serve U.S. Grade AA butter unless you can prove you are purchasing this type of item.

3. Misrepresentation of price
   You will run into problems if you do not disclose all relevant charges. For instance, if there will be an extra charge for each cook at an action station, all white-meat chicken entrees, and so forth, the client must know about it before he or she signs the catering contract.

4. Misrepresentation of brand name
   You cannot advertise that you serve a particular brand if in fact you do not offer it. For instance, you cannot say that you offer Starbucks coffee if you serve another brand of coffee.

   Sometimes we are guilty of using brand names as generic terms. For example, we tend to use casually the terms "Coke," "Tabasco," and "Jell-O," not realizing they are proprietary brand names. One major foodservice company was sued and eventually had to pay considerable monetary damages because guests were not informed when generic cola was served instead of the Coke product advertised or requested.

5. Misrepresentation of product identification
   The standard of identity defines what a food product is. The federal government has established standards of identity for more than 300 foods. For example, maple syrup is not the same as maple-flavored syrup, beef liver differs from calf liver, and a butter substitute cannot be served if butter is noted on the menu.

6. Misrepresentation of point of origin
   Some menu items traditionally note specific points of origin—areas of the world where the foods were harvested or produced. For instance, Idaho potatoes, Florida oranges, Maine lobster, Alaska crab, and Colorado trout are mainstays on many restaurant menus. You cannot make these claims, though, unless you can prove you are purchasing them from appropriate suppliers.

   Sometimes a misunderstanding can arise if you use a geographic term that describes a method of preparation. For instance, Manhattan-style clam chowder indicates that the chowder is tomato-based, not milk-based or cream-based. A naive client, though, could misinterpret this designation; it is up to the menu planner to foresee problems of this type and, if necessary, explain the situation to the client beforehand.

Obviously, french fries do not come from France, Russian dressing does not come from Russia, and Swiss steak does not come from Switzerland. The typical consumer realizes that these terms reflect a method of production or service. However, some qualifiers are too close to call and could confuse some guests. For instance, some customers may wonder about the origin of "imported cheddar cheese," while others will not give it a second thought. The astute caterer should not flirt with these types of potential problems.

7. Misrepresentation of merchandising terms
Sometimes you can get into trouble if you use too much trade puffery when describing menu items. For instance, saying that you serve "only the best-quality meat" implies that you serve the highest government quality grades. You should avoid using terms such as "fresh daily," "homemade," "center-cut portions," and so forth unless you can substantiate these claims.

8. Misrepresentation of means of preservation
This is when you say something is fresh when in reality it is frozen, canned, bottled, or dried. "Fresh" is probably the most overworked and incorrect term noted on the typical menu.

It is easy to fall into the freshness trap. You cannot indicate "fresh" on the menu if the foods you purchase and use to make these menu items are pre-prepared, processed products. To say one item is fresh and not others implies that the others are not fresh.

9. Misrepresentation of means of preparation
Guests consider several things when selecting items from a menu, but the way a dish is prepared is one of the most important determinants in the selection process. When a guest orders a broiled food, he or she will not be happy with oven-fried, pan-fried, or baked food. Likewise, if the customer orders deep-fried food, roasted, barbecued, or sautéed are unacceptable.

Sometimes a caterer encounters difficulty when booking a party of 2,000 broiled steaks, which necessitates browning them on a broiler and then finishing them in a convection oven. Some customers will be able to identify the browned, baked steaks and may be unhappy with the result.

Food preparation terms can also be used indiscriminately. For instance, it is tempting to use on the menu the phrase "made from scratch." However, the prudent caterer will avoid this description because it may be impossible to obtain raw food ingredients consistently. If a processed substitute must be used once in a while, some guests may notice it and be disappointed.

10. Verbal or visual misrepresentation of menu items

A catering sales representative must be careful when describing menu offerings to clients. If there is any doubt, he or she should contact the chef. At no time should a company representative promise something that cannot be delivered.

Photos should be a major part of the caterer's sales effort. But since they always display items at their very best, the difference between a picture and the real thing can sometimes be significant. Even when you try to live up to a pictorial representation, there may be times when it is impossible. For instance, a picture may show seven different vegetables in an Asian dish. But if one of them is temporarily unavailable, a few guests may notice it and cause you an embarrassing moment or two.

You must also be careful when doing menu tastings. The caterer and chef will of course want to showcase their menu items in the best possible light for the potential client. However, if the items tasted and then selected are not prepared in the same manner as they will be the day of the event, problems can certainly arise. It is wise in these cases to make detailed notes of the tasting as well as take photos of the food prepared. As tastings are often done many weeks or months in advance, this will assist the culinary team in the actual event preparations.

11. Misrepresentation of dietary or nutritional claims

No dietary or nutritional claim can be made unless you can prove the menu item meets the prescribed standards. In addition to being deceptive, false claims can be dangerous for your guests. For instance, if you note "salt-free" on the menu, people on a low-sodium diet can be harmed if they consume an item that does not live up to expectations.

MENU PRICING

A menu price must cover the cost of food, labor, and other variable and fixed costs, plus a fair profit for the caterer. As a general rule, though, the price charged for a particular menu item is based primarily on its food cost.

Generally speaking, if the food cost for a catered event is estimated to be $9.00 per person, the menu price for this function will range between $27.00 per person (a 33 percent food cost) to $36.00 per person (a 25 percent food cost), plus applicable consumption taxes, gratuities, and service charges. In some markets, as well as for some menu items, it is not uncommon for caterers to run an even lower food cost, ranging from 14 to 24 percent.

There are other menu pricing procedures that can be used. Pricing is a marketing function and is fully discussed in Chapter 2.

TAXES, GRATUITIES, SERVICE CHARGES, AND TIPS

It is important to note the required amount of applicable consumption taxes, gratuities, and service charges when quoting menu prices to potential clients.

Consumption taxes usually include local and state sales taxes. Some parts of the country also levy an entertainment tax, cabaret tax, or luxury tax on commercial foodservice meals. These taxes are usually equal to a set percentage of a catered function's net price (which does not include consumption taxes or gratuities), though there are some states and municipalities that require you to charge taxes on the net price plus the gratuity.

Generally speaking, if a gratuity is noted separately on the final bill, and if it is dispensed entirely to employees, you will not have to charge consumption taxes on it. But if you note a service charge on the bill and use this money to pay all employees a flat rate of compensation, then chances are you will need to charge consumption taxes on the function's net price plus the service charge.

In most states, if a commercial foodservice operation extracts a service charge from each guest in lieu of a voluntary tip, the caterer must charge consumption taxes on it. In effect, the service charge becomes part of the net price, whereas the tip or gratuity does not.

To say the least, the variations in taxing procedures between states and local municipalities can cause a great deal of confusion for clients, especially those who book events in several parts of the country.

It is conceivable that a specific meal might include both flat-rate employees and gratuity-earning employees. For instance, employees on the A-list usually receive gratuities, whereas B-list employees often work for a flat rate. In this situation, the client may be paying a bit more in consumption taxes than he or she would have to pay if the event was booked at another facility in another state or municipality.

The terms *tip* and *gratuity* are often used interchangeably. However, gratuities are mandatory charges, whereas tips are discretionary.

Gratuities are usually 18 to 22 percent of the catered function's net price. The gratuity is divided among various facility employees. Internal politics and traditions often dictate who receives a share and what the value of the shares will be. In some facilities, catering sales and operational managers as well as chefs receive a share, while in other properties managerial personnel are excluded. Servers and sometimes setup staff usually are the primary beneficiaries. Caterers should have clear policies regarding the method used to split gratuities/service charges and tips. Usually the gratuities/service charges are distributed among the servers, banquet crew, and bartenders, and sometimes the catering managers. Tips are usually pooled and distributed among the servers only. However, some properties include management in the pool. In fact, a recent decision by the Nevada Supreme Court upheld the Reno Hilton's policy of including all staff and managers in the tip pool.

Generally, at government-owned convention centers, tipping is not allowed in any form. In some parts of the United States, state laws govern the distribution of gratuities. For instance, in California, gratuities are "owned" by the service staff. Hotels and restaurants can keep service charges but cannot retain any portion of gratuities. You should check with the local state restaurant association to determine the pertinent regulations in effect in your area.

A client may wish to voluntarily award a tip to one or more catering employees because some additional service, or exceptionally good service, was provided. Some clients may also wish to reward employees who are not associated with the catering staff because of their help in making the function an especially memorable one.

Professional meeting planners recommend that convention clients consider tipping the "unseen" employees who do not participate in the gratuity pool, yet whose services can sometimes make or break a function.

Generally speaking, convention clients are advised to budget 1 to 3 percent of their master bill (i.e., total bill) for voluntary tips. For example, if the convention costs $100,000, a client should expect to award at least $1,000 to other employees, especially the "heart-of-the-house" employees (front desk staff, room reservationists, porters, AV techs, and so forth), if their services were particularly timely and beneficial.

Of the total tip, a suggested distribution (though each area will vary depending on the size of the meeting and complexity of responsibilities) is:

20 to 25 percent of the tip: convention coordinator

20 to 25 percent of the tip: sales or catering manager (if active during the meeting)

10 to 15 percent of the tip: house setup crew

5 to 10 percent of the tip: AV technician

5 to 10 percent of the tip: housekeeping (for VIP suites, staff rooms, and public areas)

3 to 5 percent of the tip: receiving department

2 to 5 percent of the tip: for storeroom employees who see to it that a client's convention materials, shipments, and so forth are handled correctly and quickly

20 percent of the tip: miscellaneous to additional staff deemed most helpful.

Convention clients are encouraged to distribute these tips after the function ends, not before. This is the traditional procedure. Once the tip is given, there may be less incentive for employees to provide above-average service.

A client may give money, gifts, or both. For example, he or she can see to it that when tip money is distributed, employees also receive a small memento.

In addition to tips, the client should write a letter to the general manager praising the employees' special efforts. In most cases, these types of letters can be the most valuable "tips" employees receive.

Some facilities require tips to be pooled and then distributed to members of the pool, while other properties allow the individual recipient to keep the entire amount. All tips received must be declared by staff members so that management can withhold the appropriate amount of income tax and social security tax from the tip earners' paychecks.

In catering operations service charges are neither gratuities nor tips. They represent a separate charge for labor and typically are part of an itemized price quotation. For instance, a service charge for extra servers would be added to a client's bill if he or she requested special or additional service for some VIP guests. And, as noted above, the appropriate consumption taxes must be charged on them.

Usually when a catering sales representative quotes a price, he or she will note a "price plus plus." The price is the menu price per person, while the "plus plus" represents the taxes and gratuity. For instance, a price quotation of "$30.00 + +" in Las Vegas tells the client that the total price per person will be $38.73 ($30.00 menu price, plus 8.1 percent sales tax [$2.43], plus 21 percent gratuity [$6.30]).

Most receptions are priced à la carte—that is, clients select the types and amounts of foods they want, and pay only for what they choose. For instance, a client may want to order coffee by the gallon, hors d'oeuvres by the piece, deli meats by the platter, and salads by the bowl, and pay accordingly.

The prices charged for typical food functions usually include all the necessary labor and other overhead charges. About the only time extras are added is when the function is very small (in which case a room charge may be added) or when it requires extra-special service (in which case a labor surcharge will be added).

Regardless of the type of pricing procedure used, you need to remember that your prices must be in line with your competitors' prices. You can charge more, but only if you give more. Clients seek overall value. They are willing to pay more if the quality and service justify a higher price. Conversely, they expect to pay less if the quality and service are marginal.

Usually a catering executive, under the guidance of senior management, will develop menu prices based on his or her costs of doing business. Once these are computed, though, the manager will compare them to competitors' prices. He or she must "shop" the competition and determine if the calculated prices are competitive. If they are overly high, they may be revised or, if that is impossible, the recipes, quality, or service must be adjusted to allow for lower menu prices.

TYPES OF MEAL FUNCTIONS

Each type of meal presents a unique set of challenges and opportunities. When planning a meal, the catering sales representative must know and understand the client's objectives so that the appropriate menu, room setup, service, and timing can be provided.

Breakfast

Speed and efficiency are extremely important to most breakfast-meal planners. This is especially true if the attendees are conventioneers who will be going to business meetings, seminars, or other events immediately after the meal. The last thing a client wants is to start the day's activities late and throw off the whole day's schedule. Everything must be ready at the appointed time in order to avoid this problem.

Many attendees will skip the breakfast meal. Some of them traditionally do not eat breakfast. A few may be in the habit of engaging in early morning exercise workouts and cannot make the scheduled breakfast time. And others may have been out late the night before and would rather sleep than eat.

Breakfast is a functional meal. Guests need to energize their brain cells. If they skip breakfast, chances are their attention span will decrease and they will become irritable by ten o'clock.

The breakfast menu should contain energizer foods, such as fresh fruits, whole-grain cereals, whole-grain breads, and yogurt. As a general rule, a person should try to start the day with these types of foods because, in addition to providing a bit of energy, they are much easier to digest than fatty foods. This will keep attendees awake and ready to tackle the morning's business needs.

There is a trend away from sweet rolls and toward whole-grain, blueberry, and oat bran muffins and fruit breads such as banana or date. Sugary and fatty sweets, such as Danish, doughnuts, and pecan rolls, give only a temporary lift.

There must be some variety, though, at breakfast. While many people will not make a whole meal of sugary, fatty foods, they may want to have at least a little taste of one. As much as possible, the menu should accommodate all guest preferences. For instance, you can offer bite-sized portions of several types of foods on a breakfast buffet table.

A buffet is the best type of service to have for breakfast functions because it can accommodate very easily the early riser and the latecomer. In some cases it may cost less than sit-down service. And it can be just the thing for guests who are in a hurry, because if there are enough food and beverage stations, a breakfast buffet can be over in less than one hour.

The traditional breakfast buffet includes one or two types of breakfast meats, three to six varieties of pastries, two styles of eggs, one potato dish, and several selections of cereals, yogurts, fresh fruits, cold beverages, hot beverages, and condiments.

An English-style breakfast buffet usually includes the traditional offerings along with one or more action stations. For instance, an action station where chefs are preparing omelets, Belgian waffles, or crepes is very popular with guests. This type of service can significantly increase the amount of time needed to complete the meal as well as food and labor costs, though, so it can only be offered if time permits and clients are willing to pay an extra charge.

For the cost-conscious client, the more economical continental breakfast buffet is appropriate. The traditional continental breakfast includes coffee, teas, fruit juice, and some type of bread. A deluxe version may offer more varieties of juices, a breakfast sandwich, breads, and pastries, as well as exotic fruits, yogurt, cereals, and cappuccino or espresso.

If a breakfast buffet is planned, you should separate the food and beverage stations so that people who want their coffee quickly or who do not want a full meal will not have to stand in line behind those who are deciding which omelet to order. You also should separate condiments, such as cream, sugar, and lemons, as well as flatware from the coffee urn areas. Since it usually takes a guest about twice as long to add cream and sugar as it does to draw a cup of coffee, this type of layout will prevent traffic congestion. If separate beverage stations are not feasible, you should have food servers serve beverages to guests at the dining tables.

Conventional sit-down breakfast service usually includes a combination of pre-set and plated services. This is an appropriate procedure if the guests have more time and want to savor the meal a little longer. Served breakfasts, though, make greater demands on the catering and kitchen staffs. More servers are needed and more food handlers are required to dish up the food in the kitchen. However, unlike buffet service, food costs are more controllable because you, not the guest, control portion sizes.

Many clients, especially incentive clients, want some added luxury touches at breakfast. For instance, they often appreciate things such as mimosa cocktails, virgin Marys, exotic flavored coffees, puff pastries, and exotic fruits and berries in season.

Many people are not very sociable at breakfast. Also, if the guests trickle in a few at a time, they might spread out in the banquet room so that they can be alone with their thoughts or with their last-minute work. The catering department might want to make available newspapers, such as *The Wall Street Journal* and *USA Today* as well as the local favorite, to those who do not wish to fraternize so early in the day.

Refreshment Break

A refreshment break is an energy break. It is intended to refresh and resharpen attention. It also helps alleviate the boredom that tends to develop when guests are engaged in tedious business activities during the day.

Refreshment breaks are typically scheduled at midmorning and midafternoon. They are usually located near the meeting and conference rooms. And they usually offer various types of "mood" foods—foods that increase guests' enthusiasm to tackle the rest of the day's work schedule.

Ideally, the refreshment break station would include hot and cold beverages, yogurt, muffins, and other types of breads and pastries that will hold up well and not dry out. Chewy foods, such as peanuts, dried fruits, and sunflower seeds, should also be available because these types of products are thought to relieve boredom.

Apples, pears, and bananas are good choices, and plums, grapes, and cherries sometimes are a nice change. Grab-and-go items are very important, as guests often have limited time at a break and may want to take their snack with them.

Many guests prefer cold beverages throughout the day. Bottled water has become a very important amenity. Most of those who drink soda prefer diet beverages. In fact, experience shows that 50 to 75 percent of guests selecting cold beverages will choose a sugarless drink, such as diet soda, bottled water, or club soda.

The caterer should strongly suggest to the client that water, soft drinks, and other cold beverages be available for each refreshment break, no matter what time of day the break is scheduled. There is a trend toward less individual bottled water as companies are being greener now. The alternative is to sell 5-gallon water crocks with a potential discount for refills. Some clients are interested in flavored waters, such as cucumber and melon, lemon or orange, strawberry with mint, and so on. This is an upsell opportunity that assists in recouping some of the revenue that was previously realized with individual bottled waters while being more environmentally friendly.

Some refreshment breaks include only beverages. This is especially true with the midmorning coffee break. A beverage-only break does not distract convention attendees as much as one where several foods are available. Guests get a beverage and are apt to return to business quickly, whereas foods take longer to select and consume, thereby possibly throwing off the rest of the day's schedule.

Speed is a major consideration for some refreshment breaks. If so, the menu should not offer any foods that will slow down service and cause attendees to arrive late at their next business activity. For instance, when you have a short break, you would not want to offer sliced fruit on a tray. Instead, you should offer fruit kabobs or whole fruits, which can be picked up quickly and easily as "walk-away" snacks.

Be cautious with the break location. When a refreshment break is set outside the meeting room, groups may encounter passers-by taking a beverage or snack off their break table. Depending on the break location, it may be necessary to have a sign on the table indicating the group the break is for, or even to have an attendant at the table.

Another major consideration is to locate the refreshment break station so that it serves the client's needs. Ideally, it should be placed in a separate room or in the pre-function space. It should not be located at the back of a meeting room. If it is, a speaker will have a hard time getting started if attendees are lingering too long around the food and beverage stations. The speaker also cannot compete easily with the food and beverage stations; guests are liable to sneak a quick trip to the back of the room and disrupt the proceedings. Furthermore, there may be a lot of noise pollution when tables are replenished.

Remember to have chimes available for breaks. A staff person will sound them at the conclusion of the break, indicating to attendees that it is time to move back into their sessions.

Be sure to provide trash receptacles for waste and trays for used tableware. A server should check the refreshment setup periodically and replenish foods and beverages as needed. He or she should remove trash and soiled tableware and not let them stack up. Someone also needs to be responsible for tidying up the break area regularly. Few things are as unattractive as finding a half-eaten pastry on a pastry tray next to whole, untouched ones.

Many clients, especially corporate meeting planners, want refreshment breaks available all day, so they can break at will instead of a predetermined time. In effect, they want permanent refreshment centers. Meeting planners who are accustomed to conference centers expect permanent refreshment centers. If other facilities want to compete favorably with conference centers, they must offer similar amenities. Of course, the client must be willing to pay the added cost.

Clients reap many advantages with permanent refreshment centers. For one thing, clients feel this will keep attendees around all day. If attendees go off to a restaurant for a beverage, they may never return for the business activities. A permanent refreshment center usually stocks coffee, tea, water, and cold soft drinks all day, with foods being offered only at certain times, say at 10:00 AM and 3:00 PM. All-day nonalcoholic beverage service provides an attractive, comfortable social atmosphere for attendees to congregate and discuss the day's activities.

Some clients want the traditional refreshment breaks, but they also want them to be preceded by exercise periods. For instance, just before the midmorning refreshment break, a corporate client may schedule an exercise leader to come in and lead attendees in a few stretching exercises.

Theme refreshment breaks are popular and provide an opportunity to upsell. Theme breaks are discussed in Chapter 3.

Luncheon

Oftentimes luncheons are very similar to breakfasts in that they are intended to provide a convenience to convention attendees and to ensure that they will not roam away and neglect the afternoon's business activities.

If a luncheon is intended solely to provide a refueling stop for attendees, the menu should not include an overabundance of "sink-to-the-bottom" foods—greasy, fatty foods (such as fried chicken) and complex carbohydrate foods (such as rice or pasta dishes). Fats can take a long time to digest, sitting in the stomach for as much as twelve hours, while complex carbohydrates take somewhat less time to digest. If attendees eat too many heavy foods, they most likely will become drowsy and inattentive later in the day. By contrast, fruit, vegetables, and lean proteins are digested more quickly.

Working luncheons, where attendees continue meeting during the meal, usually rely quite a bit on deli sandwiches and salad greens. Breads, pastas, heavy sauces, and so forth are usually deemphasized. If provided, they usually are served on the side so guests can take a small taste. Serving these products on the side will tend to discourage guests from consuming too much.

You should have some fatty foods on the menu. Some guests will be disappointed if, for example, they cannot have a few french fries or butter pats. The wise director of catering will see to it that alternatives are available to satisfy everyone. A crowd pleaser is the deli buffet. It serves the dieter, the big eater, and everyone else in between.

Whatever strategy is followed for a working luncheon, it is important to remember that attendees may be eating several luncheons during their stay at the facility. In this situation, variety is mandatory.

While most guests are satisfied with the few traditional breakfast selections, they normally seek greater variety when selecting luncheon menu items. If they do not get it from you, they will go to a restaurant or bar for lunch and be late getting back to the afternoon's business sessions. This also throws off the meal guarantees. In some cases, attendees may get sidetracked and not come back at all.

For luncheons where the participants do not continue to meet during the meal (sometimes referred to as nonworking luncheons), refueling and keeping attendees on the property are the major objectives. This type of luncheon frequently involves some sort of ceremony. For instance, many luncheons have speakers, audiovisual displays, fashion shows, awards, announcements, and so forth.

When you have a ceremonial type of luncheon booked in your facility, the logistics are more complicated. For instance, you must ensure that head tables and reserved tables are noted correctly, name badges prepared, AV equipment installed and ready to go, all lighting synchronized properly, and printed materials, if any, set at each guest's place. You also need to ensure that sufficient labor is scheduled to handle the food and non-food service demands adequately.

Buffet, pre-set, and plated services are the typical service styles used for luncheon meals. In most cases, luncheon service is similar to breakfast service. Speed is usually a major concern. Consequently, menus and service styles are usually selected with quickness and efficiency in mind.

Reception

Receptions are often pre-dinner functions designed primarily to encourage people to get to know one another. For instance, most conventions schedule an opening reception that serves as an icebreaker or welcome party, allowing attendees to make new friends and renew old acquaintances. If an opening reception is not scheduled, an attendee usually will meet only the handful of people sitting at his or her dining table.

Some receptions are not pre-dinner functions. For instance, many conventions have hospitality suites that are open late in the evening. Hospitality suites are similar to receptions in that they encourage participants to mingle. They also can be hosted by sponsors to introduce new products or build goodwill. For example, a book publisher at a booksellers' convention may sponsor a hospitality suite to introduce new authors or to allow guests to meet established authors. This is a type of business that restaurants can seek out if they are conveniently located in relation to the convention. In Las Vegas, many independent restaurants with banquet facilities are located right inside the hotels and are able to market successfully to these events.

One of the biggest complaints heard at convention opening receptions is that the music is too loud. Many attendees haven't seen each other for a year and want to talk, and there are generally a lot of introductions going on. Usually the reception is a networking event, and attendees end up having to shout over the music to be heard. If loud music is desired, save it until later in the evening, or for the final night's banquet.

Some receptions, referred to as networking events, are usually held during standard dinner hours and are intended to precede or take the place of dinner. A reception allows guests to have a drink, eat a little, and get to know one another.

One thing most receptions have in common is that they usually include alcoholic beverage service in addition to food. Another common trait is the fact that rarely are they scheduled during business hours; normally a reception never begins before 5:00 PM.

When planning a reception, it is best to locate several food buffet stations around the room, each with a different type of food. This encourages guests to move around and socialize. If possible, you should include one or two action stations. You also should have a server at each station to replenish foods, bus soiled tableware, remove trash, and be a psychological deterrent to curb guests' tendencies to heap their plates or return several times.

If beverages are served, the bars and nonalcoholic beverage stations should also be spaced around the room. You should place them a sufficient distance from the food stations so that there is ample room to move around each station and so people have to change locations in order to get a drink. This further increases guest participation and mingling.

If the reception is intended to take the place of dinner, you should offer a complete balance of food types, colors, temperatures, preparation methods, and so forth, to suit every taste. And since this type of reception normally extends for a longer period of time than the pre-dinner one, and people will in effect be consuming the equivalent of dinner, sufficient backup food and beverage supplies must be available to prevent running out.

The selection of foods offered should have broad appeal. You should be careful when serving exotic foods some guests may not recognize. For instance, if you are serving unusual fish items on a buffet table, you might want to identify them with name cards in a font large enough to be read in subdued party lighting. Servers should be able to answer any questions posed by guests for foods passed.

Menu items should be bite-sized. This allows guests to sample a wide variety of foods without wasting too much of it. It also ensures that the foods will be easy to consume. Ease of consumption is very important, since most guests must balance plates, glassware, handbags, and business cards while moving around.

Menu items must be easy for guests to hold and to eat. For instance, while kabobs are popular items served at receptions, if they are not prepared and assembled properly, guests will have a frustrating experience trying to eat them. If you serve kabobs, you should put the food ingredients on only the front half of the skewer. Otherwise, guests will be unable to get all the food off the skewer without making a mess.

Foods also should not be messy or greasy. Nor should they leave stains on clothes or teeth. For instance, you should be careful not to oversauce foods, such as barbecued chicken wings, that might drip when guests are eating them. Instead, offer boneless chicken tenders that are lightly coated or served with a stiff sauce on the side.

Using large plates can add as much as one-third to your food cost. Be certain not to use dinner-sized plates for receptions without the client's knowledge. Large plates encourage overeating and excessive waste because a guest may fill the plate, eat some of the food, set the plate down somewhere, forget it, and then go back for another plate of food. Guests with plates full of food will tend to sit down to eat and will not mingle and network very much, if at all. Caterer Gayle Skelton notes, "A caterer's dilemma is not what quantity people eat, it's how much they put on their plate!"

If you use plates, you could serve fork food—food that you need a fork to eat. Rarely would you serve food at a reception that requires a knife, as guests are generally eating while standing up and often balancing a drink while trying to exchange business cards.

Seating should be minimized at receptions. You do not want to encourage guests to sit and eat; remember, you want to promote mingling and networking. Seating should be provided for 25 to 30 percent of the guest count. Cabaret-style seating lounge furniture, or park benches, which have little or no table space, are suitable.

To encourage mingling and to control food costs, you should suggest having servers pass foods in addition to, or instead of, placing food buffet stations throughout the room. With passed foods it is easier to retain control of food quantities by pacing quantities, alternating expensive items with low-priced items, and avoiding the food excesses that buffets require. Guests tend to eat less if the foods are passed. Generally speaking, if the foods are displayed on a buffet table where guests can help themselves, they will eat twice as much as they would if all foods were passed butler-style by servers.

However, never hand-pass kabobs, baby lamb chops, shrimp with the shell on, or other foods with bones, skewers, and the like. Once the food has been eaten, the guest is left holding a skewer, greasy rib bone, or annoying shell that now must be disposed of. They create slip-and-fall issues, create litter, and can later be found tucked down into potted plants, seat cushions, and other unusual places.

Usually you would not have all foods passed. Generally, at least one or two food stations or action stations will enhance the visual appearance of the function room. To save the client money, expensive items should be passed, and less expensive food (such as cheeses, vegetable trays, and dry snacks) should be available on tables. A client without budgetary concerns, though, would probably prefer that his or her guests have access to a mountain of shrimp on ice and a sliced tenderloin action station.

If you offer butler-passed foods, you should place only one type of food on a tray, otherwise guests will take too long to make their selections. If they cannot decide easily what to take, they may take one of each. This will slow down service because the servers will not be able to work the room quickly and efficiently. It also might encourage overconsumption and food waste. Butlered food should always be finger food—food that can be consumed without utensils. The server should always carry a small stack of napkins.

With butlered service, the client's labor charge will be a bit higher. However, this should be offset by a lower food cost. As noted above, guests will consume less if foods are passed. You also can control the pace of service. For instance, you can stagger service by sending out servers with trays every fifteen minutes instead of taking all the food out at one time. Furthermore, the catering sales representative should remind clients that passed foods lend an air of elegance to the reception that many guests will appreciate. Be sure servers are assigned areas of the room to cover, or one side of the room may get all of the food.

Receptions can be tailored to any budget. Unlike other meal functions, the clients have more flexibility. There are many opportunities to be extravagant or frugal. For example, clients can control the time allocated for the reception; they can offer a seafood bar with a few shrimp and a lot of inexpensive mussels arranged on crushed ice; they can start with expensive hors d'oeuvres and back them up with cheeses and dry snacks. The breakfast, luncheon, and dinner planner does not always enjoy such a wide array of options.

Generally speaking, if you are charging clients according to the amount of food consumed, you would opt for buffet tables, dinner-sized plates, and self-service. On the other extreme, passed foods are appropriate if the client is paying a per-person charge for unlimited consumption. Since most clients prefer paying a per-person charge for foods, your service strategies will tend toward passed foods. However, usually you and your clients can find several mutually agreeable positions between these two extremes to satisfy everyone's quality and cost requirements.

Dinner

Dinner is the most typical catered meal. While it shares many similarities with breakfast and luncheon, usually it is a longer, more elaborate affair.

Unlike breakfast or luncheon, a client will be more adventurous when booking a dinner function because he or she usually has more money and time to work with. For example, Russian and French service styles are more common at dinner than at other meals. Even the buffet, pre-set, and pre-plated service styles are enhanced. Furthermore, entertainment and dancing are more common at dinner.

Many dinners are part of a theme, ceremony, or other type of major production where foodservice is only one part of the event. Rarely are dinners scheduled merely for refueling purposes.

Dinner guests are not usually on a tight time schedule. They normally do not have to be at a business meeting or any other sort of activity later on in the evening. As a result, some tend to wander in late, while others tend to linger well after the function ends. Catering staff must be aware of these tendencies and plan accordingly.

The catering sales representative should be prepared to work closely with the client in developing the dinner event. Many clients do not have sufficient background or expertise to plan a major function. Nor do they have the creative talents necessary to plan an unforgettable experience.

For instance, most conventions reserve one night for an awards banquet. Clients and catering executives need to find ways to take the boredom out of awards presentations without sacrificing the recognition that winners deserve.

An awards banquet is often part of a grand banquet given on the convention's last night. Unfortunately, this approach has several drawbacks. For one thing, attendees have just survived an intense few days of meetings and other business activities and are ready to party. Most of them have probably been to one or more receptions earlier in the day and have consumed a few alcoholic beverages. And if wine is served with the meal, the group may become boisterous.

The catering sales representative should suggest ways to avoid these problems. For example, there is a trend in the industry to present awards early in the convention, say on the first day. This ensures rapt attention from attendees. It also allows the recipients to bask in the limelight throughout the convention.

Awards can also be given at breakfasts or luncheons. Guests are a bit more alert during these times. Furthermore, they then can have the last night free to have fun and unwind.

If there are several awards to be given, another tactic is to spread the presentations throughout the convention. You should begin with the minor awards and save the most important, prestigious one(s) for the last night.

If a client insists on the traditional final-night awards banquet, you should suggest that the presentations be staggered between courses instead of scheduling them at the end of the meal. Since dinner meals tend to run overtime, if all awards are presented at the end, chances are the program will have to begin before or during dessert. Some guests may not be paying attention and conversation may continue throughout the program.

The catering sales representative also must be aware of the protocols, seating arrangements, and other similar considerations associated with various ceremonies so that the client can be advised correctly. The catering sales representative also should be prepared to suggest themes that can be used by clients to increase interest in their dinner functions.

Theme parties will promote dinner attendance. For instance, some convention attendees may be motivated to register because one or two theme parties are being offered. Furthermore, convention attendees' spouses are also more anxious to go to the convention if this type of entertainment is offered.

Theme parties are always in vogue. They add interest and provide a good deal of fun for the guests. While some themes are elaborate and pricey, you do not need to spend a great deal of money to throw a theme party. Some clients want to design themes that will enhance the image of the group booking the dinner. For example, a dairy convention may want to hold an ice cream social to introduce new frozen dairy products. The catering executive will need to work closely with the client to ensure that this party runs smoothly. Chapter 3 focuses on themed events.

A dinner usually is much more than just a meal. Food and beverage are only two parts of it. The catering executive must be able to juggle many attractions when helping clients plan these major events.

REMAINING FOOD

Clients may at times request to take away any remaining food. This is not recommended for sanitation and quality reasons. Protein-rich, moist foods may have been contaminated during service. These foods present excellent growing conditions for harmful bacteria. For instance, roast beef, cream-based soups, custards, and protein-rich salads made with mayonnaise or other similar dressings should not be saved unless you are certain they are safe to eat. If there are any doubts, they should be discarded immediately before they have a chance to come into contact with wholesome foods and contaminate them.

Leftovers

Once the food leaves your facility with a client, you have no control over whether it is properly stored. For example, if a client takes perishable items and leaves them unrefrigerated for several hours, this can present a health hazard to anyone who subsequently eats the items. In addition to being a potential liability issue, it is a poor representation of your product and presentations.

Food Donation

Some clients may ask you to donate leftover foods they have paid for to a homeless shelter or other similar charitable organization. This is certainly a socially redeeming activity we can all support. However, many caterers might worry that, just as with sending leftover foods back with the client, they may be liable if someone contracts a food-borne illness from the food. It is best to work with the client in advance on donating any remaining food to a local homeless shelter.

The Bill Emerson Good Samaritan Food Donation Act protects donors from liability when donating to a nonprofit organization as long as you used reasonable care when preparing, collecting, and delivering the leftover foods. It protects donors from civil and criminal liability should the product donated in good faith later cause harm to the needy recipient. It standardizes donor liability exposure so donors and their legal counsel no longer have to investigate liability laws in all 50 states. If you were not negligent in handling these products, and if you sincerely believe they are safe to eat, you can donate them and not worry about being sued. However, if there is any question about the wholesomeness of the foods, you should discard them. Not only do you risk a lawsuit, you do no one a favor by distributing foods that could make people sick. For more information on food donation, visit Washington State's Charity Food Donation Guidelines at http://www.doh.wa.gov/ehp/food/guide-charitydonations.pdf.

While it is a wonderful community service benefit to donate leftover foods, a lot of planning must be done in advance, and it is not always an easy task. Typically the client will need to agree to pay for disposable containers to put the food in, as pans and containers are generally not returned. In addition, transportation must be prearranged. As you will incur additional costs to prepare the food for delivery and transport the food (labor, gas, vehicle, etc.), this cost will also need to be covered by the client or by the charitable organization, unless your organization absorbs these costs as a policy. Also, some charities may not be open when the event has concluded, so storage must be arranged, which could interfere with upcoming events your kitchen is preparing for. Additionally, a charity may have an influx of unexpected donations at one time and may not have the facilities to store or distribute the items, so they will need advance notice as well. With careful planning, though, many of these issues can be overcome.

There are some volunteer organizations that will assist with these donations. In the stadium and arena business it is common for groups such as Rock and Wrap It Up! to collect all edible leftover food and distribute it to a local shelter. Their volunteers arrange for pickup and delivery of the food from the caterer.

Alternatively, should clients not meet the contracted minimum food and beverage purchase requirement, they may wish to purchase food from the caterer in the amount of the unused food and beverage minimum and donate it to a local charity. Clients can then take any applicable tax deduction.

SUMMARY

Caterers handle a wide variety of different meal functions, including breakfasts, refreshment breaks, luncheons, receptions, and dinners. When planning for any of these meal functions, there are a number of important factors to consider. The purpose of the meal function can affect menu development and selection, as can food cost, guests' backgrounds, nutrition concerns, and the availability of certain ingredients. The equipment, labor, and service styles that will be used are also important considerations. And when planning a menu, it is essential to pay attention to truth-in-menu guidelines so that the final product meets your customers' expectations.

KEY TERMS

Menu balance	Gratuity	Sustainable food
Product shelf life	Truth-in-menu guidelines	French cart service
Banquet French service	Butlered service	Russian service
American service	Food donation	

REVIEW QUESTIONS

1. Briefly explain how a group's demographics can influence the type of menu selected for its function.
2. What are the eight most common types of food allergies?
3. What is the difference between a vegan and a lacto-ovo vegetarian?
4. Why might it be more economical to order a meal function that contains standardized menu items as opposed to one with a specialized, custom menu?
5. Why do lettuce wedges stay fresher and colder longer than chopped lettuce?
6. What is the difference between a menu trend and a menu fad?
7. Why should you avoid ordering unusual foods for an event?
8. What is the difference between a buffet and a plated buffet?
9. What is the difference between banquet French service and French cart service?
10. Why might a meeting planner want to mix service styles for an awards banquet?
11. Why are speed and efficiency very important for the breakfast meal?
12. What is the difference between a working luncheon and a nonworking luncheon?
13. What is another name for an opening reception?
14. What is the most typical catered meal purchased by clients?
15. What is the most functional, common, economical, controllable, and efficient type of service?

Chapter 5

BEVERAGE FUNCTIONS

Beverage functions today almost always include food. Other than at nightclubs, it is very unusual for a beverage function to offer only alcoholic and nonalcoholic drinks. At the very least, clients want to include a few hors d'oeuvres or dry snacks.

In view of increasing host and host-property liability, the wise catering executive will not book events that offer only alcoholic beverages. For instance, all-evening drinking parties, such as fraternity bashes and bachelor parties, are inappropriate and ripe for liability lawsuits.

Alcohol consumption has been declining for decades in the United States. The National Institute on Alcohol Abuse and Alcoholism reports that the per-capita consumption of alcohol by Americans age fourteen and older has dropped over time.

PURPOSE OF THE BEVERAGE FUNCTION

Understanding the purpose of the beverage function will give the catering sales representative an insight into the client's wishes. This information is invaluable when working with the client to create an exciting, memorable event.

There are many reasons why clients schedule beverage functions. However, unlike meal functions, there tends to be at least one common thread appearing in all of them: these events usually serve as a way for guests to socialize and engage in networking.

An alcoholic beverage function is not a refueling stop. It is not scheduled primarily to give guests the opportunity to recharge their batteries. After all, no one needs to consume alcoholic beverages to survive.

Rather, beverage functions offer guests a chance to visit with other guests in a relaxed, leisurely setting. New acquaintances are made and old ones rekindled. Job openings are circulated. Hot tips are exchanged. And the seeds of many successful business dealings are planted.

Another common thread that most beverage functions share is the time of day they are offered. Usually they are scheduled after 5:00 PM. Every once in a while you will be asked to offer poured-wine service or specialty drinks such as mimosas or Bloody Marys at a brunch or luncheon meal function. However, it is less common today for a client to request liquor service before the end of the normal business day.

Still another common thread among beverage functions is that many of them are scheduled before a meal. Pre-meal cocktail functions, such as receptions, allow strangers the opportunity to get acquainted. For instance, if a guest is invited to a meal function where he or she knows very few of the other guests, it is much easier to meet them while strolling through a reception area than it is by sitting at one dining table for the whole evening.

Some receptions are intended to take the place of a meal. For instance, a cocktail reception scheduled from 5:00 PM to 8:00 PM usually must offer a reasonable variety and quantity of foods so that guests can select enough of them to satisfy their appetite and create a meal. Even if most guests expect to go out to dinner later, the host usually must see to it that sufficient foods are offered to suit those guests who will not make other dining plans.

A host may schedule a short reception in order to provide some sort of transition period from a long workday to an enjoyable meal function. For instance, the convention planner realizes that some attendees who were working very hard during the day may not stick around for a dinner function scheduled to begin at 8:30 PM.

Even though there are several commonalties found in each beverage function, the catering sales representative still must query clients regarding their primary objectives for scheduling them. By knowing as much as possible about clients' needs, desires, and objectives, the catering executive can suggest the types of functions that will satisfy them adequately.

MENU PLANNING

It is relatively easy to develop a drink menu. Generally speaking, if the client wants a particular type of drink, you can provide it. If you have sufficient production and service equipment to handle a standard drink menu, you essentially have enough equipment to prepare and serve just about any type of drink clients and guests might request. If you do not have the necessary ingredients in stock, you usually can get them before the date booked for the function. The exception to this would be if you have existing contracts with soft drink or liquor purveyors that limit the items you are permitted to offer. For example, many companies have a soft drink agreement with either Coca-Cola or Pepsi. Purchasing the competitive soft drink to have at an event may be in violation of your agreement.

Current alcoholic beverage trends to consider are:
- Declining hard liquor sales
- Flat to increased wine sales (depending on the market) and higher awareness of and more interest in varietal wines
- Increase in light beer, imports, and microbrews
- Increase in specialty drinks
- Quality (finer vintages) instead of quantity
- More nonalcoholic (neutral) beverages

Spirits

The category of spirits (another term for hard liquor) includes distilled beverages, such as bourbon, scotch, gin, vodka, brandy, rum, tequila, and a variety of blends. The most popular spirit today is vodka.

Spirits can be taken straight (neat), on the rocks (over ice), or as highballs or cocktails, mixed with a variety of ingredients.

Spirits consumption trends suggest that overall consumption will average three drinks per person during a normal two-hour reception period. Assuming that 50 percent of the people will order spirits, you should order the following quantities for every 100 guests:

# of Bottles	Type	# of Bottles	Type
2	Bourbon	1	Rum
2	Scotch	1	Brandy or cognac
3	Vodka	1	Tequila
1	Gin	1	Blended or Canadian whiskey

Take demographics and the group's history into account as well. Remember that these figures are averages and will not apply to every group. Whenever possible, try to obtain the history of the group for a more accurate estimate. A group of mainly women would tend to drink more wine than spirits.

There are also geographic differences in spirits consumption. Following is a list of the number of drinks consumed on average per person at a black-tie gala affair with a reception and dinner in various local markets:

Market	# of Drinks
Las Vegas	5.5
Chicago	5
Washington, D.C.	4.5
Orlando	3.5
San Diego	3
Honolulu	3
San Francisco	2.5

Wine

Wine consumption trends show that overall consumption will average three glasses per person during a normal two-hour reception period. Assuming that

50 percent of the people will order wine, you should order thirty 750 ml bottles for every 100 guests.

Wine consumption trends also suggest 30 to 40 percent of people will drink red wine, with the remainder preferring white. According to a *Meetings and Conventions* survey of meeting planners, the most popular white wine, by far, is chardonnay. The most popular red wine is cabernet sauvignon, followed by merlot.

Wine-savvy people are looking for wines that are terroir-driven. *Terroir* is a French term used for wine, coffee, and tea and refers to a sense of place or the sum of effects that a particular geographical place or environment has on a particular product. Those in the know are no longer just looking for a glass of chardonnay—they are looking for an expression of chardonnay from a particular place. For example, chardonnay from Chablis in France has a particular minerality and flavor of the sea that comes from its unique soils and the fossilized sea creatures they include. And terroir is important not just with imported wines. Chardonnay from the Central Coast of California displays an intense citrus and fruit character that announces its origin.

Varietal wines are named for the grape variety that is used to make the wine. U.S. regulations require that at least 75 percent of the grape variety must be used in making the wine. Examples of white varietal wines would be chardonnay or Riesling. Red varietal wines include pinot noir, merlot, and cabernet sauvignon. Blush wines would include white zinfandel and rosé.

Offer wines with good value for the client. Present a choice of several price/ quality levels of wine. Include simple taste descriptors on your wine list.

Beer

Beer is classed as domestic or imported. Domestic beers would include Budweiser, Coors, and Michelob. Don't forget to add light beers, such as Bud Light, Miller Lite, or Coors Light, as they are very often more popular than the higher-calorie versions. Imported beers would include Heineken, Corona, and Stella Artois.

There are also specialty beers from microbreweries that you may be asked to order. While these products were previously available only in the regions in which they are brewed, for many medium to large microbreweries this is no longer the case. However, it may still be difficult to get small-production varieties, in which case it is not advisable to have them on your menu due to availability fluctuations. Catering managers should know what is available in their area and be prepared to discuss these options with clients.

Beer is no longer considered unsophisticated, and more and more women are drinking this beverage. The varieties and subtleties of beer can be as complex as those of wine. It can be pale and sparkly or dark and coppery.

A subcategory of beers would be malt beverages. This subcategory has also been termed "malternative." These beverages are made from malted grains and flavored to taste similar to wines, ciders, or other beverages. Brands such as Doc's Hard Lemonade, Smirnoff Ice, and Jack Daniel's Country Cocktails have all been successful in this market. Besides being popular, malt beverages are an alternative to beer or wine if the client does not want to have a full bar available. In addition, they are easy to manage, as they are already packaged and ready to serve, just like a traditional bottle of beer.

Beer and food pairings are becoming more common as an alternative to wine and food pairings.

Kegs, or the smaller pony kegs, of beer would be appropriate for an outdoor tailgate, barbecue, or picnic, or where low price is a key factor. It is important to be sure, though, that you have the proper serving equipment and are experienced with kegs so you do not wind up serving warm or foamy beer.

Nonalcoholic Beverages

This category includes sparkling or still mineral waters; citrus-flavored, carbonated beverages without added sugar; herbal and decaffeinated teas; nonalcoholic wines or beers; juices; and sodas. The trends driving the nonalcoholic sector are healthfulness, natural foods, and single-serving containers. The use of juices from "superfruits" such as açai, pomegranate, cranberry, and bilberry, with their naturally high antioxidant content, fits in very well with the concept of healthfulness.[1] Many attendees are spurning soft drinks that contain high-fructose corn syrup and sodium benzoate, opting for water instead. Today, too, companies are developing less-sweet sodas that appeal more to adults. Most of these carbonated drinks have no artificial sweeteners, preservatives, or caffeine and are made with real fruit juices and extracts; some are also kosher. Refreshing flavors include grapefruit, dry orange, extra-dry ginger ale, and dry lemon.[2]

The Drink Menu

Most clients are satisfied with the standard drink menu. This menu usually includes a red wine and a white wine, a domestic light beer and a domestic regular beer, a few soft drink brands, bottled water, drink mixers, and at least one brand each of scotch, gin, vodka, bourbon, rum, tequila, and Canadian whiskey.

A more elaborate drink menu usually includes the standard offerings plus one brand each of blended whiskey, rye, brandy, champagne, and imported beer. Caterers may also offer some specialty drinks, such as piña coladas, margaritas, frozen daiquiris, martinis, or one that is created specifically for the event. Specialty and frozen drinks may be a challenge at an event, though, without the proper equipment or electrical hookups. Additionally, as blended drinks take longer to make, they can create longer lines at the bars and should be offered only if you are able to successfully execute during the event.

The top-of-the-line drink menu offers a wide selection of liquor brands, both imported and domestic. For instance, a guest who wants a gin and tonic does not have to settle for the one brand offered on the standard drink menu (the caterer's "well" or house brand). In other words, for at least some beverages, guests are offered two additional choices: call brands and premium brands, where they are able to specify the type of liquor as well as its brand name.

Some clients may want to specify each brand of alcoholic and nonalcoholic beverage offered during the beverage function. However, when shopping for beverage service, most clients will not want to select all brands, and most often opt for a level of liquors served. Usually some of them will choose only those few that absolutely must be offered in order to satisfy specific guests. Often clients will want to specify the exact varieties and brand names of wines served at catered meal functions, but not those liquors served during the pre-meal receptions.

Instead of specifying brands, most clients would rather concentrate on the price per drink, price per bottle, labor charges, specific needs (such as a particular style of cocktail service), or the price charged for each hour the bar is open.

This does not mean, though, that you should ignore the subject of well liquor versus call or premium liquor.

You will need to broach this subject with potential clients. One way to do this is to develop a drink menu that notes all brand names and the prices charged per drink. For instance, you might note that a well brand costs $6.00 + + per drink and that a call brand costs $7.00 + + per drink. A client may then mix and match well and call brands and create a unique drink menu.

Occasionally you will encounter clients or guests who have personal drink recipes they want your bartenders to prepare. For example, a guest may prefer a unique type of martini made in a special way.

There also may be times when a client will ask you to special-order a spirit, beer, or wine that you generally do not carry. While it is advisable to accommodate as many of these requests as possible, be sure to first check availability with your liquor distributor. In many areas, there are strict liquor laws restricting you to purchasing only from select vendors, so you cannot just go to the corner liquor store and pick up a bottle. In addition to ensuring availability, you will need to know if there is a minimum order quantity of the requested item. If there is, and it is not an item that you will likely sell to other events, you should advise the client and have him or her agree to purchase the minimum quantity of the product.

BEVERAGE CHARGES

Beverage functions sometimes include several different types of charges. The catering sales representative usually can offer a few alternatives to clients. However, before discussing pricing procedures with clients, it is important to determine if the beverage function will be offered as a cash bar, an open (or hosted) bar, a combination of cash bar and open bar, or a limited consumption bar.

Cash Bar

A cash bar is sometimes referred to as a no-host bar. To obtain drinks at a cash bar, guests pay for them personally. The guests may purchase drink tickets from a separate cashier and give them to the bartenders in exchange for drinks. Alternatively, the bartenders may take cash and prepare and serve drinks, thereby eliminating the cashier position. Consumption tax generally is included in the price of the drink and backed out by the caterer at the end of the event. Tips are up to each guest at the time of order.

Open Bar

An open bar is sometimes referred to as a host bar. Guests usually can drink as much as they want and what they want during the beverage function without having to pay. The client or a sponsor is paying for them. Consumption tax is generally not included in the price of each drink, but is added to the total bill, along with a gratuity or service charge. Tips can be a sticky subject with hosted bars. As the client is already paying a gratuity or service charge and does not want guests to feel obligated to leave a tip, most caterers do not allow tip jars on the bar for open bars. Some will allow a bartender to accept the tip discreetly, though, if the guest insists.

Combination Bar

A combination bar includes elements of the cash bar and the open bar. A typical combination bar arrangement involves the host paying for each guest's first two drinks, with the guests then paying for any subsequent ones. For instance, the host may purchase the first two drink tickets and issue them to each guest. After that, guests are on their own. If they want more drinks, they will need to purchase their own drink tickets.

Another variation of the combination bar is when the client hosts the bar for a specified period of time. For example, the bar may be hosted for the first hour during a reception and then convert to cash once the dinner begins.

The combination bar is the logical solution for the client who does not want to provide only a limited number of types and brands of liquor at an open bar, yet cannot afford to allow guests unlimited choices and consumption. The combination bar is also a good way to limit liability for the client and the facility by not providing unlimited consumption.

Limited Consumption Bar

A limited consumption bar is priced by the drink. The host establishes a dollar amount that he or she is prepared to spend. When the cash register/bar total reaches that amount, the bar is closed. The bar may reopen as a cash bar. This is only feasible on a per-drink basis when a cash register is used. The challenge with this combination is that the guest may be unaware of the limit. He or she may order one drink without paying and then later order a second and be caught off guard when the bartender asks for payment.

Types of Beverage Charges

The way in which liquor charges are set varies somewhat from food menu pricing procedures. Generally speaking, with food, the menu price offered to potential clients includes all relevant charges for food, labor, and direct and indirect operating expenses. With beverage, though, potential clients usually can pick and choose how they want to pay these relevant charges. They may pay one price for everything, or they may opt for an itemized list of charges and pay for each one separately.

The client sometimes can negotiate away some of these extra charges if a certain level of sales is attained, unless he or she requests something special not normally provided by the facility. For instance, some facilities will waive bartender charges if the beverage sales reach a predetermined dollar amount. However, with steadily increasing labor costs, this is less and less often the case. A client, though, may attempt to have the facility waive standard corkage fees on any beverages donated for the event or brought in by the client with the venue's permission.

For hard liquor, most establishments pour between 7/8 and 1¼ ounces per drink. It is recommended that, absent a computer bar system (usually only found at permanent bars), portion control measuring pourers, such as Posi-Pour, be used. This type of bottle measuring system ensures that bartenders do not free-pour and decrease the number of drinks per bottle. Some bartenders favor the measuring jigger, which is preferable to free pouring, but bartenders usually overpour while emptying the contents of the jigger into the glass.

1. *Charge per drink.* This is the typical pricing procedure used for cash bars. Normally the price charged per drink is high enough to cover all relevant expenses.

Individual drink prices usually are set to yield a standard beverage cost percentage set by the facility. For instance, mixed-drink prices usually are based on a beverage cost percentage ranging from approximately 12 to 18 percent; wines and beers usually are priced to yield a beverage cost percentage of approximately 25 percent. The menu prices will be lower only if a client pays separately for other relevant charges.

The price-per-drink method can also be used for open bars. Bartenders can keep track of all drinks prepared and served by ringing up each one on a pre-check machine. If a machine is not available, a starting and ending inventory of each bottle can be used to determine the usage. At the end of the beverage function, a total count will be computed and extended by multiplying the number of drinks consumed by the agreed-upon price per drink. Consumption taxes and gratuities are added, and the final accounting is presented to the client for payment.

Some clients may want the facility to charge a relatively low price per drink at cash bars in order to minimize the financial impact on guests. The caterer can suggest that to accommodate this, the client directly subsidize the drink prices by, for example, paying the facility $2.00 for each drink served.

An example of a by-the-drink menu follows:

Cordials, cognacs, international coffees, specialty drinks $8.00
Premium brands $7.00
Call brands or imported beers $6.00
Well brands $5.00
Wine by the glass or domestic beers $5.00
Bottled water, juices, or soft drinks $3.00

2. *Charge per bottle.* The charge-per-bottle pricing method is often used for hospitality suites or when poured-wine service is offered during a luncheon or dinner meal function.

A physical inventory of all alcoholic beverages is made at the beginning and end of the beverage function in order to determine usage. Many facilities will charge the client for each opened bottle even though all the alcoholic beverage is not used. In a hotel, the remaining liquor can be sent to the host's suite or remain in a hospitality suite. Alternatively, if a client has booked several catering events during a convention, the leftover opened liquor could be used at the next function. It is not a good idea to let clients take home the opened bottles, as this may be illegal in your area. Even if the facility has an off-sale liquor license, open containers usually are not allowed in automobiles.

If the client pays for each bottle instead of per drink, he or she may save money in the long run. For instance, if a liter of gin yields twenty-seven 1¼-ounce drinks at a price of $5.00 each, the expected revenue is $135.00 per liter plus plus. Generally, the per-bottle charge in this situation will be a little less. However, it cannot be significantly lower unless the client is willing to pay separately for other relevant charges.

Although the client is interested in saving money, it is easier for a caterer to sell $5.00 drinks than it is to sell a bottle for, say, $125. It may also be easier for the client to accept a $5.00 drink price; the bottle price in this example may cause sticker shock for most clients.

3. *Charge per person.* This pricing option usually is available to clients who want to offer open bars to their guests. Since the open bar reduces the facility's control over liquor consumption, the price per person usually is set fairly high to ensure profitability.

The amount charged per guest may also include a charge for food and beverage. The client's final billing usually is based on the type and amount of foods and alcoholic beverages desired and the amount of time the bar must remain open. For instance, if a client wants unlimited shrimp, expensive canapés, and quite a few premium brands, and wishes to have the bar remain open longer than normal, the catering executive will charge much more per person than if the client settles for standard offerings.

4. *Charge per hour.* This is similar to the charge-per-person pricing procedure. The major difference is that this pricing method may include a sliding scale of charges. For instance, for 150 guests, a client may have to pay $2,500.00 for the first hour of standard bar service and $2,000.00 for the second hour. Since most guest consumption usually takes place in the first hour, the caterer can offer a lower price for the second hour and still earn a fair profit. If you do offer this type of pricing, it is important to get an accurate count of the number of guests. Should the count go over the agreed number, the cost will increase.

To some extent, then, the charge-per-hour pricing strategy may have to be combined with the charge-per-person pricing strategy. For instance, you might charge $25.00 per person for the first hour, $20.00 per person for the second hour, and so forth. This combination strategy will usually satisfy those clients who prefer a fixed charge per hour. It also ensures the caterer will retain control over sales, expenses, and profits.

What is the best pricing procedure or combination of pricing procedures? The most profitable method of selling from the beverage function charges noted above will vary for the caterer based on each event. The caterer should take into account what clients are looking for, then determine which option is best suited for both parties. Whenever possible, he or she should focus on selling the combinations that will generate the most revenue.

As an example, consider the following:

- If the caterer charges $100.00 for a bottle of liquor that yields twenty-seven 1¼-ounce drinks, each drink costs the client $3.70 + +. If it is anticipated that guests will have two drinks each, for a one-hour reception of 1,000 people, the client purchasing by the bottle would pay approximately $7,400.00 ($3.70 × 2 × 1,000 = $7,400.00) + +.
- If the client purchases by the drink, at $5.00 per drink he or she would pay $10,000.00 ($5.00 × 2 × 1,000 = $10,000.00) + +.
- But if purchased at $12.50 + + per person (no food), the billing would be $12,500.00 ($12.50 × 1,000 = $12,500.00) + +.

In this example, the caterer makes more money selling per person, and the client saves money by ordering bottles. Note in the sample package plan on the next page, the charge is per person.

Package Plans

Most catering organizations offer a package plan. Following is a sample of how a package plan may read.

• PACKAGE PLANS •

Azalea Hotel Cocktail Reception Package Plan

The Azalea Hotel Cocktail Hour is a package designed to ease your budgeting plans for groups of 50 or more attendees. You will be provided a full-service cocktail reception with portable bars, experienced bartenders, and full setups.

Choose the package you prefer, and you will be billed per person, based on guaranteed attendance or actual attendance, whichever is higher.

The Azalea complete bar setup includes call or premium brand liquors, California wines, domestic beers, bottled water, and soft drinks. Bar service includes vermouth, mixers, juices, and garnishes.

Per-person charges:

Number of Hours	One	Two	Three
Premium Brands	$21	$25	$29
Call Brands	$18	$22	$26

Prices are subject to a 19 percent gratuity and 8 percent sales tax. A $100.00 fee per bartender will apply.

Labor Charges

Sometimes a caterer will waive labor charges. For instance, a very large party that generates considerable food and beverage (and, in the case of a hotel, sleeping room) revenues may receive complimentary bartenders and cocktail servers.

Labor charges may also be waived if the beverage function generates a specified amount of business, calculated by either dollar amount or number of drinks. For instance, the caterer may charge the client for three bartenders to staff a cash bar but note in the catering contract that half of the charge will be rebated if more than 300 drinks are consumed and all of the charge will be rebated if more than 500 drinks are consumed.

One bar and bartender for every 75 to 100 guests is standard for a hosted bar. Cash bars or bars that serve only beer and wine may adjust that ratio to one bar and bartender for every 100 to 150 guests. If all guests are arriving at once, or if the host doesn't want the guests standing in long lines, you can provide one bar and bartender for every 50 to 75 guests. Unless this is a very lucrative group, you would pass on these labor charges to the client. The catering executive must evaluate the overall event, though, including the length of the function, the demographics of the group, and so on, before agreeing to staffing the additional bartenders. While there is generally an initial rush at the beginning of an event or when guests arrive at one time, this typically levels off quickly and then the bartenders will not have enough to keep them busy. A suggested alternative would be to have the servers pass trays of beer, glasses of wine, bottled water, and so on as guests first enter. This adds a nice touch to the event and alleviates some of the pressure at the bars. If the food servers are going to be in the room anyway—say, for the dinner to follow—they can and should provide this service for the client. If, however, they are going to be dedicated cocktail servers for the entire evening, then there would be an additional charge.

1. *Charge for bartenders.* Usually clients must hire a minimum number of bartenders for a minimum number of hours. For example, a caterer may have a policy that all beverage functions must have at least one bartender working a four-hour shift.

2. *Charge for bar backs.* Generally speaking, there is no separate charge for bar backs. Their cost is normally included in the charge assessed for bartenders. For instance, if two bartenders are hired by a client, their cost will normally include the cost of one bar back needed to assist them in replenishing ice, stock, glasses, and so forth.

3. *Charge for cocktail servers.* Cocktail servers can cost almost as much as bartenders. For instance, if a client wants a few cocktail servers to pass trays of filled wine glasses, this little touch of luxury will add to the final bill.

Some clients view cocktail servers as an unnecessary cost. If a beverage function has two or three portable bars set up throughout the room, it may be more convenient to let guests give their orders directly to bartenders instead of to cocktail servers. In fact, the additional layer of service imposed by cocktail servers can slow service (unless a dedicated service bar is set up behind the scenes) as well as increase a client's costs.

There may be times, though, when it is best to schedule cocktail servers. For example, in an arena setting, a client, who does not have a private suite, may want to host beverages and food items for a group of guests attending a public event. If the client does not want guests to have to get up from their seats to go to a concession stand or dedicated bar, then cocktail servers can take orders at their seats and deliver the items directly to them. To accomplish this, a service bar needs to be set up for the exclusive use of the servers. There would be a labor charge for the cocktail servers, bartender, and possibly a food attendant if necessary. In some cases, because of the difficult nature of this position, the venue may assess an extra gratuity, over and above that added to consumed items, for the cocktail servers. Additionally, if you are offering food, there generally would be a minimum food purchase required to cover the associated costs of having these items available. This is an excellent upsell opportunity that should always be suggested when working with groups on a private event they are attending in the venue either before or after the main event.

4. *Charge for cashiers.* Some facilities will not allow clients to schedule cash bars unless they agree to employ at least one cashier. They do not let bartenders handle cash since the extra work of making change will slow down beverage production and service significantly. Bartenders handling cash also creates additional security problems. Separate cashiers are an excellent form of financial checks and balances and must be used if tight cost control is desired. Furthermore, money is dirty and can create a sanitation problem if bartenders handle money and beverages simultaneously.

5. *Charge for security*. It is unusual for a catered function to have extra security assigned to it. However, if a large beverage function has a cash bar arrangement or there are minors expected at the event, a client may feel more comfortable if the facility provides an extra margin of safety. Since in this situation the facility may be at risk, a client may expect the catering department to absorb the added security costs. However, since the typical facility employs an in-house, licensed security service to patrol the entire property, usually the client will need to pay for anything beyond this.

Some clients may be more than willing to pay a few extra dollars to hire additional security so that they have one less thing to worry about. The catering sales representative should broach this subject with clients because some of them may be unaware that they can employ additional plainclothes or uniformed security and thereby gain some additional peace of mind.

6. *Charge for corkage*. Some clients may want to bring in their own beverages and have them served at their functions, thinking they will save money by avoiding the higher prices charged by the facility. This is generally only allowed for a limited number of events, though, such as a charity fund-raising dinner where the product is donated, or if the actual winery or liquor company is holding the event. In other cases, though, clients are not concerned about cost but are motivated strictly by the desire to serve something special that only they are able to obtain.

Most facilities have policies prohibiting guests from bringing in their own food and beverage products. And some state and local government agencies, especially health districts, may not allow this type of thing. If there are no restrictions and the facility is willing to allow clients to use their own beverages, usually a corkage fee is charged.

The corkage fee charged is typically based on the facility's estimated labor cost needed to handle the products. For instance, you may need labor to receive a special delivery, store it, possibly refrigerate it, and deliver it to the portable bar. You also may need labor to set up a drink area, keep it clean, maintain clean glassware and sufficient ice, and so forth. The more expense involved, the higher the corkage fee must be.

Part of the corkage fee may represent a type of luxury or privilege tax assessed on clients. For instance, you may want to charge something for the privilege of bringing personal liquor into your licensed establishment to compensate for the profit you would have made selling your items.

Clients who want to bring in and serve their own beverage often will do so when serving wines. For instance, it is not unusual for a convention to have a few corporate sponsors, one of which might be a winery. Naturally the winery will want its wines served at one of the catered events. To keep the peace and accommodate a good client, the facility usually will make arrangements to honor this request.

A corkage fee is usually quoted on a per-bottle basis. For instance, you might charge $23.00 for each outside wine bottle brought in by the client and served by your staff; of this, $15.00 would go to the house and $8.00 to the waitstaff to offset the gratuity they would have made had the product been purchased from the facility.

A corkage fee might also be billed to the clients in the form of drink setup charges. For example, if a client brings in a very special, very old brandy that is unavailable locally, you may agree to handle it only if you can charge $2.00 per drink setup every time you use the liquor to make a finished drink.

TYPES OF BEVERAGE FUNCTIONS

As with meal functions, each type of beverage function presents unique challenges. In some cases, the number of challenges increases considerably if the beverage function must be arranged around a meal function. For instance, not only must a pre-dinner cocktail reception go off without a hitch, it also must set the stage for the dinner that follows. Any guest dissatisfaction erupting during the reception may carry over to the banquet service and cause additional unhappiness.

Cocktail Reception
The cocktail reception is one of the most common types of beverage functions. Those held during the workweek usually are scheduled during the early evening hours, just after the end of the normal business day. On weekends there is more flexibility, but as a general rule, cocktail receptions are usually scheduled after 5:00 PM.

Cocktail receptions oftentimes precede a dinner event. They usually are scheduled for only about forty-five minutes to one hour. And in almost all instances, at least a few foods are served along with the beverages.

Hospitality Suites

These functions are usually set up in a hotel suite that can accommodate the reception's production and service equipment, supplies, employees, and guests. These events generally have to be coordinated with the hotel manager and security, as high-level floors often have restricted access and require either an elevator key or security clearance to obtain entry.

In some cases, a hospitality suite is held in a public area, such as a small meeting room converted to a hospitality suite, or a restaurant banquet room. This may be less expensive for the client than reserving a hotel suite. In addition, it may be more convenient for guests. Other benefits include room for a band or disc jockey, room for a dance floor, and room for a buffet.

If a hospitality suite is held in a hotel suite, usually the hotel's room service department handles the event. Private hospitality suites are not usually serviced by the banquet staff. Generally speaking, catering is involved only when selling the event or when the hospitality suite is held in a public area.

The hotel suite on a sleeping room floor is generally set up like a home living room, with sofas, chairs, and coffee tables. These furnishings may become impediments to the flow of the event if it is overcrowded. However, these suites usually have great ambience, are comfortable, and often provide a great view.

Some hotels and restaurants have designated employees in the catering department whose primary function is to market hospitality suites to major conventions. In a hotel, the food and beverage service may be handled by the room service department, but the selling, planning, and coordinating activities in these hotels are usually the responsibility of the catering department.

Hospitality suites are an inextricable part of the convention business. Conventions have exhibitors, sponsors, and attendees who want to hold open houses. These affairs are primarily social events, but they also present opportunities for guests to network and discuss business.

Hospitality suites are normally open only in the evening, after the regular convention business day is over. Attendees who wish to expand their social horizons like to make the rounds of these hospitality suites in order to meet friends, acquaintances, and business associates, and to expand their network as far as possible.

Some hospitality suites are ongoing affairs. For instance, a convention sponsor may have an open house virtually around the clock. During the evening the open house serves alcoholic beverages, but during the rest of the day it resembles a refreshment break, with a continental breakfast in the morning and soft drinks and snacks in the afternoon. In this case, the sponsor is competing for attendees with other refreshment breaks and attractions located in the convention area.

Some hospitality suites offer a full bar; others are beer and wine only. Some offer a wide range of food; others provide only dry snacks.

If convention attendees have an open evening, you can promote more food. If they are coming directly from a dinner, you can suggest desserts, flavored coffees, and cappuccinos.

Many hospitality suites are not connected to meetings. A tourist destination city may wish to host a hospitality event for local travel agents to promote travel to their location. A corporation may wish to hold an event as a thank-you to its best clients.

A sensitive issue that tends to arise with hotel hospitality suites is the convention attendee who wants to offer an "underground" or surreptitious hospitality suite. It is not uncommon for attendees to go out to the local supermarket or liquor store and purchase wines, beers, spirits, mixers, paper and plastic supplies, and dry snacks. Not only does the hotel lose this revenue, but these clients and guests can increase nuisance noise for other hotel guests (since their room may not be in an area of the hotel suitable for larger gatherings) and increase the hotel's liability exposure.

Poured-Wine Service

This type of beverage service is part of a meal function. Many dinner events include one or more wines that are served by the food servers.

At more elaborate meals, cocktail servers, supervised by a sommelier, may be in charge of wine service. This is especially true if guests are offered a choice of wines. It is also more common when a rare or expensive wine is served with each course.

Caterers usually uncork most of the wine that is ordered for an event for ease and speed of service. Some cost-conscious clients will ask you to uncork wines as needed so unopened bottles can be returned to stock at no charge.

It is important to be familiar with your wine list. You should be prepared to offer wine recommendations that would complement your client's menu choices. When matching wine with food, the body and acidity of wine are as important as its flavors. A high-acid food, such as tomato sauce, would be best suited to a high-acid wine, such as Chianti.

White wines and blush wines are served chilled and best served with light dishes and delicately flavored foods. Red wines are served at room (cellar) temperature and are best served with medium to hearty foods.

One problem with serving well-known wines is that consumers know how much they pay at their local liquor store and don't understand the overhead and handling costs that a caterer must add, which of course makes the wine more expensive. One way around that is to stock a label that is sold wholesale only to hotels, clubs, venues, and restaurants. An example would be Whispering Peak's domestic wines.

According to *Food Arts*, generally wine should not exceed 20 percent of the total food and beverage billing for a typical catered affair. Many caterers use a standard formula for a seated affair, with about half a bottle per person. They add 10 percent to cover emergencies, then divide the number of bottles into the total wine budget to locate the appropriate price range.

The nature of the event should also be considered, including the average age of the guests (younger groups tend to drink more wine and beer, an older crowd more hard liquor), occupation, nationality, and other factors. Also consider the location. At an outdoor party more white wine will probably be used as a thirst quencher. Take into account season as well—more red wine is consumed in winter.

Occasionally you can offer a good client a special deal on wine if your pro-perty has received an exceptional price from the distributor or you have broken cases in your inventory. Broken cases (sometimes referred to as busted cases) are those where some of the bottles have been used, leaving less than a full case.

Pay attention to your glassware. Glass size affects consumption. Larger glasses tend to promote more consumption. Use the correct glass for the type of wine. Red-wine glasses are more bowl-shaped, whereas white-wine glasses are more cylindrical.

According to Korbel, when serving champagne, the best method of chilling is with ice. To achieve the best benefit from ice, fill the ice bucket or tub with equal parts of cold water and ice. Adding cold water allows for a more rapid exchange of heat out of the wine or champagne. Serving temperature can usually be achieved in twenty to thirty minutes, depending on the number of bottles, the size of the icing bin, and the amount of ice and water.

Chill only what you will need, as temperature fluctuations can lower the quality of the wine. Champagne and white wine bottles should not be left in the water indefinitely or the water will soak off the glue on the label.

When chilling large quantities of champagne for an outdoor party, you can use the cardboard case the product was shipped in. Simply remove the champagne and cardboard dividers, line the box with two plastic garbage bags, and place the wine back in the box with water and ice. Never allow champagne to get warm before chilling with ice. The sudden change in temperature may cause the champagne bottle to fracture, with explosive results.

Also, the champagne cork is treated with a lubricant that allows for easy extraction. Warm conditions, such as direct sunlight on the bottle neck, will cause the lubricant to soften to a degree that will permit the cork to fly out of the bottle when the muselet (wire hood) is removed. This is dangerous and could cause injury, so it is important to keep champagne buckets, tubs, and cases shaded while the bottles are chilling. Drape the bottles with linen cloths to reduce the exposure of the bottle neck to warmth and sunlight. The opposite effect occurs when bottles fall over in the iced water and become extremely cold. Now the cork lubricant hardens, making it very difficult to pull the cork. Never remove the wire hood prior to uncorking the bottle. You can pull away the lead foil in advance, but always leave the wire in place, as it is holding down the cork.

You could taste wine with your client as part of pre-event planning. Tasting wine, along with menu choices, can demonstrate how wine enhances the meal. If this is not feasible, at least include suggested wine pairings on your menu.

Special Events

Alcoholic beverages, especially wines, are oftentimes the stalwarts of special functions. For instance, many fund-raising events are centered around wine and cheese tastings, food and wine pairing dinners, and introductions of new wineries and new wine products.

Unique alcoholic beverage presentations are also used by convention clients to generate excitement and enthusiasm at one of their catered events. For example, you may encounter a client who wants to book a dinner at which Beaujolais Nouveau, the first of the season, is served. Or a client may request unique selections, such as martini bars, vodka imbedded in ice carvings, Bloody Mary breakfasts, or champagne parties. Mojitos have also gained popularity in recent years.

LIQUOR LAWS

Of all the products and services sold by caterers, none are subject to more governmental control and regulation than liquor sales and service. The facility must adhere to liquor laws enacted by the federal, state, and local governments. While there is some similarity in liquor laws throughout the nation, usually each state, and particularly each local municipality, has unique liquor codes. Catering salespeople must know and adhere to these rules.

Illegal Liquor Sales

No matter where the facility is located in the United States, there are at least four types of illegal liquor sales that must be avoided by a catering facility.

1. *Sales to minors.* In most parts of the United States, it is illegal to sell alcoholic beverages to anyone under twenty-one years of age. There are a few exceptions to this, though. For instance, in some states, it is legal to serve a minor if his or her parents are present, or if his or her majority-age spouse is present. Since it can be difficult to determine what the laws are in some states, it's probably better not to serve beverage alcohol to anyone under twenty-one years of age, no matter what state you are located in.

Usually the law allows you to refuse liquor service to anyone you suspect is underage. This is true even if someone shows you what appears to be an identification card that indicates legal drinking age.

Most parts of the country also prohibit minors from being inside a tavern or liquor store. The catering staff must ensure that minors are not allowed near the portable bar areas.

Admittedly it is very difficult to police guests' movements during a catered function. While public bars are ever vigilant, there is a tendency to relax normal crowd control procedures when serving a private party, especially if there is the feeling that clients will get upset if you adhere strictly to the letter of the law. However, the catering executive must not surrender to this temptation to relax standards. If you are caught serving minors, you can rest assured that the private-party defense will receive a cold reception from the legal authorities. Furthermore, the client will usually be one of the first to complain that you failed to exercise reasonable care. Caterers and facilities are increasingly vulnerable to lawsuits.

2. *Sales to intoxicated individuals.* It is illegal to serve alcohol to a person who is legally intoxicated. In fact, usually the law stipulates that you cannot serve alcohol to anyone who appears to be intoxicated.

In most states, a person is legally intoxicated if his or her blood alcohol concentration (BAC) is .08 percent. In some parts of the country a person is legally intoxicated if his or her BAC is .05 percent.

It is impossible for you to estimate accurately each guest's BAC. For instance, after consuming one drink, a young person may appear intoxicated, whereas an older guest who has considerable drinking experience may be legally intoxicated yet show no outward signs of intoxication.

The average person's liver needs about one hour to eliminate the alcohol in one drink. If he or she has more than one drink per hour, the BAC will increase quickly. For instance, if a person weighing 125 pounds consumes three average drinks (i.e., a drink that contains approximately ½ ounce of alcohol) in one hour, his or her BAC could be .08 percent or above. Unless this person reduces his or her liquor consumption significantly or refrains from drinking during the rest of the catered function, the liver will not have enough time to reduce the BAC to a legal level before the function ends.

Caterers use many strategies to prevent overconsumption. For instance, instead of dictating the number of drinks a guest can consume, you could offer mini-drinks or use low-alcohol liquors in all prepared drinks.

Another trend is for bars to offer frozen concoctions that have only a hint of alcohol. When the drink is frozen, the guest is less able to determine the amount of alcohol present. Furthermore, many guests seem to love these types of drinks. Unfortunately, they are much harder to prepare and serve, so you may have to charge more to cover the additional expense. They also take longer to drink, as the typical guest cannot take too much cold too fast. Consequently, since you serve fewer frozen drinks, you will need to charge more for each one in order to compensate for this revenue shortfall.

Some states and local municipalities allow the sale of low-alcohol products. For instance, instead of using an 86-proof bourbon, you might be able to purchase a 56-proof product in your area. Even though this product has less alcohol, it is a better choice than merely adding more mixer to the 86-proof product. Excess mixer tends to give the finished drink a washed-out character. The low-alcohol alternative tends to retain the characteristic flavor of the original beverage even though it contains less alcohol.

If there is any doubt about a person's BAC, you must cut off that person. When this is necessary, try to use peer pressure to your advantage. Attempt to check with the host of the function before taking action with an intoxicated guest. Ask another guest or the client to help you handle the situation. Be courteous to the guest and minimize the confrontation. Note that you cannot serve any more alcohol, but you can offer food or nonalcoholic beverage alternatives. Or you could see to it that the guest gets a safe ride home at that time. Retain a professional demeanor and do not prolong guest contact any longer than necessary.

Your company should have a policy on handling intoxicated guests. Some facilities participate in a designated-driver program, where at least one guest in a party consumes no alcohol so that he or she will be able to drive everyone home safely. You can offer free nonalcoholic drinks to encourage a guest to be the designated driver.

Unfortunately, this concept has backfired on some occasions. For instance, if you cut off a guest who is part of a designated-driver group, he or she may become quite agitated. After all, the guest may assume that the designated-driver program allows him or her to get completely sloshed. The fact that it is illegal to serve visibly intoxicated people may put you at odds with a customer who has arranged ahead of time for a safe ride.

You may encounter a similar problem with conventioneers who do not plan to leave the hotel after the catered function. Instead, they plan to go directly to their rooms and go straight to bed after a long night of partying. They feel that they should receive special consideration since they will not be driving that evening.

Our liquor laws are sometimes contradictory, as are some of the solutions that have been developed over the years to combat drunk driving. But that does not alter the fact that you cannot serve liquor to an intoxicated guest, even if that person is chained to a table and cannot drive. To do so puts your liquor license, not to mention your career, in jeopardy. In addition to being illegal, it is not good practice to continue serving intoxicated guests, as they may become sick or overly rowdy if they continue to consume alcohol.

3. *Hours of operation.* Most local municipalities restrict the hours during which liquor can be served in a commercial beverage establishment. For instance, many areas have blue laws, and so you may be unable to accommodate a client's request for a Sunday champagne brunch because no liquor can be served before noon on that day. Or a late evening event may have to stop liquor service at 2:00 AM. Some areas prohibit liquor sales while the polls are open on election day.

You will need to check the local codes to determine if these restrictions apply to private parties. If they do, you must ensure that you do not book alcoholic beverage functions during the prohibited hours.

4. *Liquor license.* To serve liquor, you must hold the appropriate liquor license. For instance, a full tavern license, or hard liquor license, is usually needed to serve spirits, wines, and beers for consumption on the premises. The typical on-premise catering facility usually holds this type of liquor license.

If the facility holds only a soft liquor license (a wine and beer license), it cannot serve distilled spirits. To say the least, this puts a large crimp in your ability to sell full-service catering functions. It is possible, though, that under these conditions clients may be able to bring in their own spirits, in which case you can earn your revenue by charging corkage fees or drink setup charges.

In some parts of the country, a hotel or conference center may be unable to serve liquor unless it holds a private club license. In this case, you cannot serve anyone who is not a member or a member's guest. Usually, though, you are able to grant memberships to any qualified clients and their guests. But since this adds to your administrative burden, you may need to charge a bit more for catered beverage events.

You may be in an area where the facility cannot purchase its own liquor. In this case, usually you must have a private club license or similar license in order to prepare and serve liquor brought in by the client. For instance, in some parts of the country, the guest must buy liquor at a state-operated liquor store, bring it to the facility, and give it to the bartender. The guest then pays a drink setup charge for each drink prepared and served. At the end of the function, the guest carries home any unopened leftover product.

It is important to note that a liquor license attaches to a specific location. An on-premise facility cannot produce an off-premise event in a park across town and assume its existing liquor license covers the event. You may need to obtain a temporary license for each event of this type.

Facilities with on-sale licenses cannot sell liquor to be taken off the premises and consumed. Some hotels have both on- and off-sale licenses, which is very expensive. You will usually see a bottle shop in the lobby at these establishments. Liquor stores have off-sale licenses, which means alcohol cannot be consumed on the premises.

Potential Liquor Code Violations

The catering executive must ensure that all local liquor laws are obeyed when booking and serving group functions. While the prohibited sales noted above are common throughout the United States, each local municipality usually has one or two unique regulations that place additional controls on the local liquor licensees. Those that usually affect caterers are:

1. *Food served with beverage.* In some parts of the country, the local alcohol beverage commission (ABC) may prohibit beverage functions that do not offer foods. In these areas, a person applying for a liquor license to sell and serve alcoholic beverages for on-premise consumption must show that he or she intends to serve foods as well.

Alcohol should never be consumed on an empty stomach. Without food to slow down the rate at which alcohol is absorbed into the bloodstream, guests run the risk of becoming intoxicated very quickly. If these guests leave the function and drive away in their cars, traffic accidents may occur. By requiring you to serve foods at all beverage functions, the local government authorities are giving society one more weapon to fight these tragic situations.

2. *Bring your own bottle.* Before allowing clients to bring in their own liquor, you need to check with the local ABC to see if the liquor code permits this. In some parts of the United States, you are not allowed to use liquor purchased from a retail liquor store in a bar operation that serves liquor by the drink for on-premise consumption. In this case, you must purchase all liquor from licensed liquor wholesale distributors or, in control states, from the authorized state liquor agency.

3. *Free liquor.* You may be prohibited from giving away any liquor during a catered function.

Similarly, you may be prohibited from offering sliding-scale pricing; you must sell the beverages for a fair market price. For instance, you may be unable to offer the first 250 drinks for $6.00 apiece and anything over that amount for $5.00 apiece.

Free liquor or reduced-price liquor tends to encourage overconsumption. By outlawing these types of pricing practices, the local ABC keeps a tight rein on the sale and purchase of alcoholic beverages.

4. *Self-service.* To control further overconsumption of alcohol, some local municipalities may prohibit guests from preparing their own drinks at group functions. If this restriction exists in your area, usually it does not infringe upon the hospitality suite host's ability to allow guests to mix their own beverages.

5. *Alcoholic content of liquor used.* There may be a regulation prohibiting the purchase and use of liquors that have an exceptionally high alcohol content. For instance, some parts of the country prohibit the use of any distilled spirit that exceeds 100 proof.

Some clients may be unaware of this type of restriction, so it is up to you to inform them. This is especially true for conventions that attract attendees from all over the country. Where this is true, you should let these clients know that some drinks, such as a traditional Zombie, cannot be prepared and served.

Similarly, if an out-of-town client wants to bring his or her personal liquor, and assuming the liquor code and your facility policy permits this, you must ensure that anything brought in does not violate alcohol-content restrictions.

6. *Amount of alcohol per drink.* Some local municipalities may restrict the amount of alcohol you can put into each drink. For instance, doubles, boilermakers, and pitchers of beer may be outlawed because they can spur overconsumption of alcohol. Likewise for drinks that contain more than one type of liquor. You may not be allowed to prepare and serve drinks such as the traditional Mudslide, Long Island Iced Tea, and Scorpion because they contain multiple liquors.

The major problem with a multiple-liquor drink is that one of them can have the same clinical effect on a person's central nervous system as three or four average drinks. Recall that the average person's liver can eliminate alcohol from the body only at the rate of about one average drink per hour. Also recall that the average drink, such as a typical highball, contains about ½ ounce of alcohol, but a traditional Mudslide contains approximately 1½ ounces of alcohol. If a guest consumes two Mudslides in one hour, his or her BAC may exceed .08 percent.

7. *Leftover liquor.* The local ABC may not permit clients or guests to take home any leftover liquor. If a client books a beverage function and agrees to pay for each bottle served as well as each bottle opened, you must let him or her know up front that no leftovers can leave the facility.

If you face this situation, you could charge clients the standard price for each full container consumed and a prorated amount for each partial container used. You should only consider offering this, though, if the bottles are in your control the entire time (that is, not left in a hospitality suite for guests to mix their own drinks). This probably will satisfy all clients, and work for the facility for all events except those who order something special that cannot be reused at one of the facility's other bars or other events.

Alcohol Awareness Training

Some local municipalities require anyone who sells, serves, distributes, or gives away alcoholic beverages to take an approved alcohol awareness training course before being allowed to work in a licensed establishment. These courses are similar in concept to the sanitation courses that some local health districts require all food handlers to take before they can work in a foodservice establishment.

The typical alcohol awareness training involves instruction in the following areas:

1. Dealing with minors
2. Telltale signs of intoxication
3. Dealing with intoxicated guests
4. Clinical effects of alcohol on the human body
5. Local liquor codes

Alcohol awareness training courses offered throughout the United States vary from about four to twenty hours of instruction. They usually follow the format initially established by the Techniques of Alcohol Management course or the ServSafe Alcohol program developed by the National Restaurant Association Educational Foundation.

Before hiring a permanent beverage staff member or putting anyone on the A-list or B-list, the catering executive must ensure that the job candidates have the appropriate training. Usually people receive a pocket card after taking the course that they can show to potential employers to prove they have been certified and the term has not expired. In some locations staff may be required to have the card with them every shift. In addition, most municipalities require certifications to be renewed periodically.

Third-Party Liability

If you serve an intoxicated guest (or a minor) and he or she goes out and hurts an innocent third party, the facility, server, and host may be liable for damages to the injured person.

Some states have passed dram shop laws that specify exactly your liability in these instances. Under dram shop legislation, if it is proved that you served a minor or legally intoxicated person who causes damage to a third party, you usually will be held at least partially responsible. For example, if a minor you served gets into a traffic accident and injures someone, the injured party can sue the driver, the server, the facility, and even the host. Chances are the minor does not have the same financial resources as the facility. Consequently, the facility stands to lose a great deal since it often has the "deep pockets" that a judge or jury can tap for huge financial awards.

In a state with dram shop laws, usually the facility cannot defend itself if it is proved that its employees served a minor or a legally intoxicated guest. You cannot, for example, tell the judge that the minor presented what looked like a legitimate ID card. Nor can you plead that the person appeared to be of legal age. Such defenses usually are not permitted where absolute liability has been legislated. As a result, if you serve a minor or legally intoxicated person who causes damage to an innocent third party, you can count on being held responsible, period.

It is important for clients to realize that some states have passed social-host laws. Social-host laws hold individuals liable for private functions hosted in their homes or at other locations. For instance, if a minor served at a private party held at a facility inflicted damage on an innocent third party, the function host and the facility would share responsibility for the accident.

Most states do not have dram shop or social-host laws. However, the facility, server, and client still could be held liable under common law. Under this system, an injured third party can sue you for damages, but it is up to him or her to prove you were negligent in serving the person who caused the accident. For instance, if you can prove that a minor whom you served falsified his or her age by showing what appeared to be a legitimate ID, chances are you would be absolved from liability, especially if you can also show that the minor appeared to be older than twenty-one. As long as you followed generally accepted beverage service principles and practices, usually you can mount an adequate defense. In a liquor liability situation, it is most likely that everyone involved in the incident, from top to bottom, will be sued, with all parties having to hire and pay lawyers to determine who is ultimately culpable.

In addition to the facility and the person causing the accident, hosts and servers can be named parties to a lawsuit under common law. Hosts with deep pockets can rest assured that one way or another they will be defendants.

It is imperative that clients realize the types of risks they incur when booking beverage functions. In some cases, they may need to be reminded of this if they expect you to cater a wild affair, such as a bachelor party. Entertainment options may be restricted if alcohol is served; for example, in Las Vegas, no female dancers are allowed to emerge from a cake if alcohol is served. A few minutes spent discussing legal and liability issues with clients should quickly dispel such requests.

SUMMARY

When planning beverage events, it is essential to understand the purpose of the function. There are several types of events where wine, beer, and spirits are typically served, including receptions and hospitality suites, and caterers have several options when charging clients for beverage functions. Whenever alcoholic beverages will be served, it is important to keep in mind all local liquor laws and liability issues.

KEY TERMS

Third-party liability	Spirits	Combination bar
Cash bar	Open bar	Limited consumption bar
Bar back	Corkage	Hospitality suite
Varietal wine	Dram shop laws	Alcohol awareness training

REVIEW QUESTIONS

1. What is an underground hospitality suite?
2. What is a neutral beverage?
3. What is the difference between a call brand and a well brand?
4. What is the difference between a cash bar and an open bar?
5. What is the difference between an open bar and a combination bar?
6. What is an advantage to the client of purchasing a limited consumption bar option instead of an open bar option?
7. When would a caterer require the client to pay a corkage charge?
8. What time of day are beverage functions usually scheduled?
9. What is another term for hard liquor?
10. What does the French word *terroir* refer to?
11. What is Posi-Pour used for?
12. What does BAC refer to?
13. What is one of the differences between a cocktail reception and a function held in a hospitality suite?
14. List two types of illegal liquor sales.
15. What is a dram-shop state?

Chapter 6

FUNCTION ROOM SELECTION

AND SETUP

The catering sales representative must select an appropriate function room or area to hold the event. Along with the client, he or she needs to consider several things when making this selection. The major factors influencing the selection process are a function room or area's appearance, location, utilities, and amount of floor space.

APPEARANCE

Oftentimes appearance is high on most clients' priority list. In fact, frequently a potential client is attracted to the facility primarily because of the ambience provided.

For instance, a function room in Caesars Palace in Las Vegas overlooks the Las Vegas Strip. At night, the view is phenomenal. Of course, many clients want to book this room regardless of any other advantages or disadvantages it offers.

Room dimension, ceiling height, number of columns, exits, entrances, restroom facilities, colors and types of floor and wall coverings, sound insulation, and lighting are also important, especially for those facilities whose function rooms do not enjoy breathtaking views.

The overall appearance of the room is very important. Consider the following characteristics of the room:

- Lighting
- Sound
- Colors
- Walls
- Temperature
- Smell
- Visibility
- Layout

Many clients will be turned off by a function room that is long and narrow with a "bowling alley" effect. This type of dimension precludes guest mingling, participation, and networking. It also harms service because many guests will tend to gravitate toward one end of the room; for instance, the bar at one end may be very busy, with the others having only a few guests. It is also difficult to place a speaker in a long, rectangular room, due to visibility. Although it is preferable for the speaker to be in the middle of the long wall, as opposed to either end of the room, guests on the far sides may find it difficult to see the person speaking. The use of audiovisual is also limited in a long, narrow room.

The typical ceiling height in hotel or convention center function rooms is approximately 11 feet. In many municipalities, the building code may require a higher ceiling. For instance, some building codes stipulate 14-foot ceilings in public areas, such as restaurants, theaters, and shops.

Columns are usually a negative in a function room. A few are acceptable, but too many will detract from the catered event unless the caterer can suggest a room setup that will minimize their negative effects. For instance, buffet tables can be arranged between decorated columns in a way that enhances the room's appearance. Or buffets can be wrapped around columns using hollowed-out circular tables. For a classroom- or theater-style setup, the seats can be arranged so that the columns are in the aisles.

Usually a function room has a sufficient number of entrances and exits because a local fire code requires them. Some clients who have speakers and audiovisual presentations or elaborate decor setups scheduled will want to know how easy or difficult it will be to transport their equipment in and out of the function room. Some rooms have outside entrances and loading docks.

Consider the room's location in the facility in relationship to the rest of the meeting rooms, restrooms, sleeping rooms, and other features.

The colors and types of floor and wall coverings are the first thing a client sees when viewing a function room. In addition to meeting building-code requirements, they should be free from stains and in good repair. They also should be in good taste and decorated with style.

As we noted in Chapter 3, guests tend to eat and drink more in brightly lit, colorfully decorated surroundings. Vibrant colors such as brilliant red, hot pink, and bright yellow stimulate the appetite. Dark tones dull the appetite. Examples of these colors are dark green, navy blue, gray, and black.

Some caterers consider how the clients are paying for receptions. If they are paying per person, it would benefit the facility to have the guests eat and drink less; hence locating them in a darker room would be a wiser choice. However, if clients are paying on a consumption basis, the facility's sales would benefit if the event is held in a brighter room.

Table placement at receptions also affects food consumption. An hors d'oeuvre table placed against a wall provides only 180-degree access to the food. A rectangular table in the center of the room, though, offers 360-degree access to the food and will result in greater food consumption. A round table in the center of the room gives an appearance of a lavish presentation, but since there is no way for a line to form to circle the table, guests have to work their way in and out at various points for each item they wish to eat, which may decrease food consumption.

If the function room directly abuts the kitchen, hallways, and service corridors, some action should be taken to prevent unwanted back-of-the-house noises from seeping into the function room. Employees moving about in these behind-the-scenes areas may occasionally cause distractions. For instance, some guests may be unable to hear a speaker if employees are overheard working, laughing, or talking. Employees should be trained to tread lightly in these areas in order to minimize noise pollution. Additionally, a podium or head table should not be located next to an entrance because the movement of those coming and going will disrupt the speaker.

A similar type of barrier installation will also be needed if you have to minimize the amount of ambient light seeping into a darkened room from around doors, draped windows, or production and service areas.

LOCATION

If the function room or area is a great distance from the kitchen, the menu planner may be limited to only those foods that hold up well.

The banquet staff also will need to use hot and cold transport equipment in order to preserve the foods' culinary quality en route. Without this equipment, food costs could increase because finished food items are more vulnerable to quality deterioration when they must be pre-plated and transported long distances. The extra effort also could increase labor costs.

UTILITIES

Meeting and convention clients are often concerned about the function room's utility capabilities. These clients tend to book functions that tax a function room's utilities. Usually the catering sales representative has schematic drawings of the room that illustrate them. These drawings should be included in any sales solicitation and on the facility's website.

The catering sales representative must be conversant with each function room's utilities. Clients will be concerned with:

1. Types of electricity available in-house
2. Types of electricity that can be brought in
3. Maximum amperage that can be used
4. Maximum lighting available
5. Number of separate lighting controls (for example, if a client will be using rear-screen projection, you will need to darken the area behind the screen while leaving the rest of the room light)

6. Heating, ventilation, and air-conditioning (HVAC) capacity
7. Closed-circuit TV, radio, and video system
8. Closed-circuit audiovisual (AV) system
9. Paging system
10. Number, types, and locations of:
    a. Electrical outlets
    b. Electrical floor, wall, and ceiling strips
    c. Phone jacks
    d. Dimmer switches
    e. Vents and ducts
    f. Built-in speakers
    g. Doors (open in or out, single or double)
11. If the function will be held in an exhibit hall, the client may also be concerned with the number, types, and locations of:
    a. Gas hookups
    b. Exhaust fans
    c. Drains
    d. Water connections
12. Wi-Fi, data ports for computers, Internet service providers, and other cutting-edge technology

SPACE REQUIREMENTS

The amount of floor space available is perhaps the function room's most critical feature. The caterer must assume responsibility for determining the amount of square footage needed. He or she cannot expect the client to make this calculation.

Room setup is often strictly regulated by the local fire marshal, and it is imperative that catering executives keep current on the applicable rules governing setups for their locations. Additionally, some locations require a diagram (drawn to scale) be submitted with a permit application for any room setup for larger groups. For example, in Las Vegas, if the event is expected to have 299 or more people, then a diagram must be submitted for fire marshal approval and a permit. As there is a fee for this, which is generally passed on to the client, you must advise them early in the planning stages not only of this fee but also that the fire marshal has final say on the room setup.

Several factors influence the amount of space needed. The most critical ones are:

1. *Number of guests.* The local fire code will dictate the maximum number of people who can legally occupy a function room. The number of guests allowed in any given room will vary based on the setup of the event. For example, a stand-up function, such as a cocktail reception, can accommodate more guests, whereas banquet or classroom setups will accommodate fewer people.

Generally speaking, for most meal and beverage functions, you would be unable to accommodate the maximum number of persons allowed by the local fire code. The room setups required for these types of events will usually reduce significantly the number of guests that can be handled efficiently and comfortably.

2. *Setup used.* You need to allocate about 10 square feet per guest if seating is at rectangular banquet tables. If round tables are used, you will need about 12½ square feet per guest (round tables are the easiest for the staff to service, and they maximize interaction among guests); whereas, you need about 20 square feet per guest for classroom seating. These estimates will suffice if you are using standard chairs whose seats measure 20 inches by 20 inches. You should adjust your estimates if you use smaller chairs (seats measuring 18 inches by 18 inches) or larger armchairs (which usually have a minimum width of 24 inches). Chair backs should be placed 2 to 3 feet apart. Adjustments may also need to be made based on the size and shape of the room. For example, smaller rooms have more dead space per person at the front, back, and sides.

3. *Aisle space.* Aisles are needed for server access and guest maneuverability. Aisles between tables and around food and beverage stations should be at least 48 inches wide.

When planning aisle space, remember to leave enough entry and exit room for guests. You must plan to allocate sufficient cross-aisle space (aisles through which guests funnel in and out of the function areas). A cross-aisle should be a minimum of 6 feet wide, and for larger events should be up to 10 feet wide.

Cross-aisle space is very important when setting large functions. For instance, for a function requiring 100 tables, you cannot set a square layout of 10 tables by 10 tables without allowing some additional space for guests to maneuver comfortably to the middle tables from the outside perimeter. As a general rule of thumb, if you need 100 tables, you should set up four blocks of 25 tables. Within the 25-table block, 48-inch aisle space is sufficient. However, there should be a 6-foot-wide cross-aisle surrounding each block of 25 tables. Tables should also be at least 48 inches from the wall, more if required by the local fire code.

4. *Dance floor space.* If the function includes dancing, you need about 3 square feet of dance floor per guest. If you use layout squares, most of these types of portable dance floors come in 3-by-3-foot (9 square feet) sections; plan on using one section for every three guests. A 24-by-24-foot dance floor covers approximately 600 square feet of floor space.

For very large functions, a second dance floor is convenient. Guests at the back of the room will not have to negotiate the long trail leading to the front where the single dance floor normally is located. On the other hand, this arrangement does divide the group into two subgroups. Two dance floors placed as diamonds with the points abutting keeps separate dance floors connected. Be sure the dance floor is safety-coated with an abrasive to improve traction. Also be certain that sections are flush against each other and there are no cracks in which a lady's high heel could get caught. All sides must be completed with trim pieces that slant and will not cause a guest to trip.

5. *Entertainment stage.* You should estimate about 10 square feet per band member. Drum sets usually require about 20 square feet. Large pianos, synthesizers, runways, and so forth need additional space. Disc jockeys may need less space to hold their equipment and music collection as much of it now is computerized and much smaller in size. You should check the entertainment contract, as it may set forth the floor space specifications.

Bands and other similar attractions are sometimes elevated on risers (also called platforms, daises, and staging). Risers come in many shapes and sizes.

Their purpose is to elevate speakers, other entertainers, or AV equipment so that a large audience can see what is taking place at one end of the function room.

Most risers are 4 by 8 feet or 6 by 8 feet folding risers that can be adjusted to several heights. While it may vary by manufacturer, low risers generally can be adjusted from 8 to 24 inches in height, and performance risers generally adjust from 3 to 6 feet high. Risers should be set up with steps with attached handrails and light strips. A lawsuit can occur if a guest falls from an improperly set stage.

6. *Other entertainment.* You may need to allocate additional floor space for strolling musicians and similar entertainment. Once again, you should check the entertainers' contracts for exact space requirements.

7. *Head table(s).* Head tables usually need about 25 to 100 percent more floor space than regular dining tables. Furthermore, if the tables will be placed up on risers, you must increase your space estimate accordingly to accommodate the riser area, the steps, and the need to spread the table-and-guest weight properly over the stage. For instance, if using typical riser sections measuring 4 by 8 feet, you would need to connect three pieces to have enough space to accommodate a dining table measuring 8 feet long by 3 feet wide. This allows for the 8-foot length of the table plus 2 feet on each side, the 3-foot width of the table, the chair, and space behind for a guest to safely get up without falling off the back of the riser.

A raised head table for twelve people plus a podium should be a minimum of 28 feet long. The rule of thumb is 2 feet per person, plus 2½ feet for the podium. For more comfortable seating, allow 2½ to 3 feet per person.

If you have head tables reserved for speakers, dignitaries, and other VIPs who will be addressing the guests after the meal, you may be asked to set up extra dining tables on the floor for these guests, near the head tables, so they can eat without feeling like they are on display. Some guests do not want to sit at an elevated table and eat. If there is enough space in the function room, they can eat at regular dining tables, and then move up to the head tables just before the program begins.

Setting up extra dining tables allows you to maximize the number of VIPs who can be accommodated at the head tables. For instance, if you have ten

VIPs and ten spouses, you can set up twenty place settings (covers) at regular dining tables. And if the client agrees, instead of setting up a head table for twenty, you can set one for only the ten VIPs. The spouses can remain at the dining tables after the meal.

8. *Line control.* A typical line control consists of posts (stanchions) and ropes set up to control guest traffic. You may want to use ropes and stanchions to control traffic around cashier and ticket-taker stations. If they are necessary, you will need to allocate more floor space to accommodate them.

9. *Reception needs.* If the function room is used to house a reception and a meal, you will need enough space to handle both phases of the catered event. In most cases, there is usually insufficient time to reset the reception area in order to accommodate meal guests. Furthermore, it is aesthetically unattractive to reset a room while guests are present.

To accommodate a reception adequately, you will need about 6 to 10 square feet of floor space per guest. With 6 square feet, guests will feel a bit tight; they also will have a bit less ease getting to the food and beverage stations. Consequently, they may eat and drink less. If a cost-conscious client is paying on a per-person basis, where guests can eat and drink as much as they want for one price, you might consider allocating only about 6 square feet per person to keep your food and beverage costs under control.

Adding a little extra space, so that there is 7½ square feet per person, creates what is considered to be a comfortably crowded arrangement. It is thought to be the ideal amount of floor space per guest for receptions and similar functions.

Ten square feet provides more than ample space for guests to mingle and easily access the food and beverage stations. It is an appropriate amount of floor space for a luxury-type reception. It is also an appropriate setup if the client is paying according to the amount of food and beverage consumed. You want guests to have enough room to eat and drink as much as they want so that your revenues are maximized.

10. *Buffet table.* All food stations need enough floor space for the tables and aisles. For instance, an 8-foot-long rectangular banquet table needs about 24 square feet for the table, and about 60 square feet for aisle space (if the table is against the wall); about 100 square feet for aisle space is needed if the table is accessible from all sides.

When determining the number of buffet tables needed, as well as the number of buffet lines required, you need to consider:

    a. Number of guests expected

    b. Length of dining time

    c. Amount of service equipment required

    d. Type of service equipment required

    e. Type of menu

    f. Style of service

    g. Amount of decor desired on the buffet line

    h. Amount of total floor space available in the function room

Generally speaking, you must allocate approximately 2 running feet of buffet table for each food container needed, plus an additional 2 feet for the plates. You should also allocate space on the buffet tables between and in front of food containers. Guests will need some "landing space" to set their drinks and other things they might be carrying while putting food on their plates. They also will need room on the table to set their plates temporarily while deciding what foods to take. Flatware should be placed at the end of the buffet (unless it is a station), so guests do not have to carry it the entire length of the buffet. Taking all the above into account, if you have to display three hot offerings, two cold offerings, and a condiment basket, you should set up a buffet table about 16 to 18 feet long. If you use two standard 8-foot rectangular banquet tables, you will need about 48 square feet of floor space for the buffet table and approximately 150 square feet of standard 3-foot aisle space surrounding the buffet table. The total allocation for this setup, then, is about 200 square feet.

    11. *Beverage station.* For self-service nonalcoholic beverage stations, the setups are similar to buffet table setups. For instance, a hot-beverage station will need about as much space as a buffet table laden with foods. Bars, though, will need more floor space because you need room to store backup stock, ice, and coolers to hold beer and some wines. You also need to allocate enough working space for bartenders and, if applicable, cocktail servers. Generally speaking, the smallest portable bar you can use measures approximately 6 feet by 7 feet, or about 42 square feet. However, when you take into account the aisle space and other space needed, you will need to allocate at least 150 square feet for the typical portable banquet bar setup.

If you are setting up portable bars for a large function, you may be able to reduce your space estimates if you can arrange to locate them in pairs. For instance, you may be able to locate two or four portable bars back-to-back in the middle of the function room so that the bars can share a common area where glassware, ice, wines, beers, and so forth are stored. This will eliminate duplicate storage areas, free up extra floor space, and increase guest access.

12. *Side stands and tray jacks.* Allow 3 square feet for each side stand or tray jack. The number of tray jacks needed will vary based on the number of guests. For plated service there are generally two tray jacks per team of servers. One is used to put down trays of plates, while the other is used to collect dirty plates. For receptions and buffets there is generally one tray jack per server, which is used to collect dirty plates, glasses, and utensils.

Tray jacks may also be used for guests to discard empty plates, glasses, soiled napkins, and waste. It can be located next to a bar or against a wall. When used in this manner, allow 4 square feet for each tray jack area. Widely scattered cocktail tables can also accommodate this need. You can reduce the amount of tray jacks needed and elevate the level of the event if attendants remove the discards quickly and often during the event.

13. *Action station.* Allocate a bit more floor space than for a buffet, so guests can gather and view the chefs' performance. Your floor space allocation also must be increased if the action station is elevated on a riser.

14. *Staging/storage area.* You may need to set up a temporary storage area in the function room. A band or disc jockey may need a place to store its shipping containers. A client may need space to store convention materials, party favors, and other similar items. You may need to allocate floor space to temporarily store lighting and sound equipment. Or you may need to set up a temporary service corridor at one end of the function room to store hot carts, cold carts, and gueridons. If you anticipate any of these needs, you must allocate sufficient space to accommodate them.

If you allocate floor space for a staging area, you should block it off with pipe and draping, or some other form of "camouflage," so that it does not interfere with the appearance and ambience of the catered event.

15. *Cashier.* Some functions, particularly beverage functions, may require floor space for one or more cashiers. For instance, the catered event might include a cash bar. If so, some facilities will require the client to use cashiers to sell drink tickets.

Generally speaking, you should allocate at least 25 to 30 square feet for one cashier station. If a security guard will be stationed at the cashier area, you will need additional floor space to accommodate this person.

16. *Display area.* Sometimes clients need space to set up their own cashier stations, registration or information tables, kiosks, booths, and so forth. For instance, a client may need a cashier station in order to sell meal tickets to guests who have not prepaid but who decide at the last minute to attend the event.

Selling individual event tickets is typical with association clients. Most associations give a set of event tickets (one ticket for each paid meal function) to each attendee who registers and pays in advance for the total conference. A few attendees, though, may decide to bring a spouse to a meal or register after the preregistration deadline passes to attend the conference. Or some may not want to attend every event; instead, they may show up for only one or two preferred events and pay only for these functions.

If guests need to use tickets to enter a function room, you will have to provide sufficient space for someone to collect the tickets. Usually the ticket taker has a spot reserved just inside or outside the front door. This space is sometimes the same space used to house the client's registration or information station. Guests, therefore, can check in and pay at one station. This is more convenient for guests. It also allows you to economize on your floor space requirements.

If you set up an area to handle all of the client's cashiering and check-in procedures, you must ensure there is sufficient floor space to accommodate one or more cashiers, desks, tables, chairs, backdrops, service corridors, telephones, waste receptacles, lockboxes (to hold the used tickets or receipts to prevent reuse), and so forth. Some clients may have lists of their display needs along with exact dimensions. If not, you should question them carefully about these requirements so that you do not have to rearrange the function room layouts at the last minute.

17. *Meeting activity during the meal.* A client may want to have a business meeting and the meal or reception in the same function room. For instance, an association chapter may want the function room divided into two sections: one section housing the reception, and the other housing an auditorium-style setup to accommodate the group's program.

The meeting activity can easily be accommodated if the function room is large enough to be divided appropriately. It cannot be accommodated as readily, though, if the meeting and the meal or reception must share the same space.

One way to handle smaller events where space must be shared is to use a different type of setup, such as conference room, U-shaped, or hollow square. For instance, with a U-shaped setup, guests can conduct their meeting and, when it is time to eat, roll-ins can be placed in the hollow section of the setup, or the back of the room, and foods arranged to allow self-service.

A conference room setup usually requires no more space than the typical meal function; however, the U-shaped or hollow square setups may need two to three times as much floor space. The U-shaped setup is the least efficient use of floor space, requiring about 42 square feet per person.

To calculate the proper meeting space for an auditorium-set general session, multiply the expected number of attendees by 12 square feet per person. For example, you would need 2,400 square feet for 200 attendees (200 × 12 = 2,400). For a classroom-style setup, plan for 19 square feet per person.

18. *Style of service.* This is important if you are planning to use French or Russian service, as these service styles require up to twice as much floor space than the others. Some buffets, especially those where beautiful displays and several tables are used, may also need extra space. For instance, if the function is very elaborate and you want to provide a luxury amount of space for all guests, you may want to increase the typical buffet floor space estimate by 50 to 100 percent.

19. *Audience separation.* If it is necessary to divide or separate the audience, you may need considerably more floor space. For instance, in locations that still allow smoking in public facilities, if you set up smoking and nonsmoking sections, you should set one or two extra tables in each section unless you know exactly how many smokers and nonsmokers to expect. In the worst-case scenario, you will have several half-used tables in each section.

20. *Accessible seating.* If you expect to have a physically handicapped guest, you will need to allocate additional floor space. A wheelchair-bound guest will need a bit more space at the dining table as well as a wider aisle in which to navigate.

21. *Props, decor, plants.* Some events use large props. In Atlanta, a prop of Tara is often used for *Gone with the Wind* parties; in San Antonio, a prop of the Alamo is often used. Even small props scattered around the room take up space that must be considered.

NONTRADITIONAL/CREATIVE FUNCTION SPACE

There may be times when it is necessary to use nontraditional space for catered events. This may occur when all of the other function space is booked or when your client is asking for a unique area to break up the routine of traditional meeting space.

The creative catering executive can increase sales by coming up with options in these instances. For example, a restaurant that is generally open only for dinner can be used for a convention luncheon. Events can also be held in showrooms, the parking lot, on top of the building, in the kitchen, and so on.

Before booking an event in a nontraditional space, though, you need to be sure that the space is conducive to the event, can be serviced properly, and meets all the necessary health and safety requirements to hold an event.

PLANNING THE FUNCTION ROOM SETUP

Function room setups must be established well in advance. Table locations, exhibits, displays, food and beverage station locations, table sizes, the head table, the seating mix (for example, number of rounds of 8, rounds of 10, and so forth), table spacing, table settings, and preferred decor usually are planned by the catering sales representative and the client. With the availability of graphic software, you are likely to encounter clients who bring in their own designs showing how they would like the room to be set up. However, some clients still do not want to be bothered with these details, do not have the software programs to lay out the setup, or they may be much more interested in focusing on the menu, price, and decor.

Using facility floor plans and other schematic drawings that show square footage, dimensions, doors, and other factors that may be important to the client, you can develop several visual plans using any one of the software programs readily available on the market.

You can also find room size calculators on various websites that will calculate the amount of space you will need. See, for example, http://www.hotelplanner.com/Common/Popups/SpaceCalculator.cfm.

If your facility can afford it, you should purchase customized computer software that will correlate the room's dimensions, location, doorways, service corridors, columns, protrusions, dead space, permanent service installations (such as a permanent stage, bar, or dance floor), and other limitations with the client's desires and draw several suggested layouts for consideration. (See Figure 6.1.)

For instance, the typical software program will draw a layout using industry standards as defaults (which can be changed) for such things as distances between rows of chairs or tables, aisle space needed, and the optimal angles that should be set to accommodate video presentations. Most of these software packages also will automatically generate standard seating styles. If you are unhappy with a computer-generated layout, you can alter the parameters and have the software draw another layout.

Before developing the final function room setup plan, it is important to estimate the amount of time needed to accomplish the client's layout and design objectives. When scheduling a function room setup, some of the critical factors are:

1. *Function room status.* Function rooms used as temporary storage or those being repaired or remodeled cannot be used. If a function room has an existing setup, additional time must be scheduled so that it can be torn down. Furthermore, it is important to know how the room will be used after the catered event ends. Similar functions should be scheduled in the same room. Breaking down one reception setup only to reset it in another function room is a waste of time, money, and effort. When schedules permit and group sizes are similar, a basic setup can be used several times.

2. *Timing of events.* If the function room will be empty several days before the catered event, its setup can be scheduled during slack periods. In this case you have more flexibility. Moreover, usually you can maximize labor productivity. On the other hand, if there is a meeting scheduled in a function room that ends at 5:00 PM and you need to turn over the room for a 7:00 reception, time

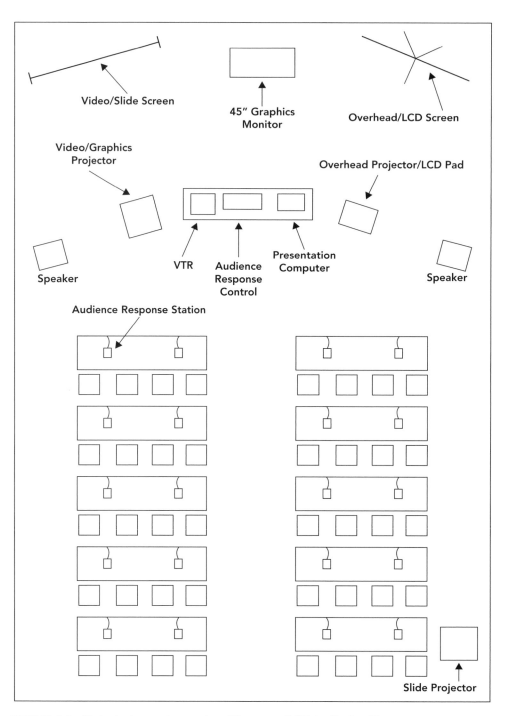

FIGURE 6.1 Today's electronic meeting. (Courtesy AVW Audiovisual.)

becomes your enemy. It may be necessary to advise the client(s) of the limited amount of time between events so that the early meeting does not run over and the reception client does not show up at 5:00 P.M. expecting a completely set room. This type of scheduling demand can increase your labor costs unless you plan very carefully.

Before breaking down a room, check to see what the next event in that room will require. You may be able to leave the setup in place, or at least leave the required chairs and tables in the room.

3. *Setup difficulty.* The amount of time needed to perform the final setup depends primarily on the type of setup required. For instance, a theater set requires less time than a classroom set, and a reception can be set up faster than a sit-down dinner.

4. *Function room layout and design.* Usually the catering manager or banquet manager is responsible for preparing the final function room layout and design for all catered events. In some cases, exact locations of food stations, bars, seating, decor, and other requirements must be communicated to the banquet setup team well in advance of the function dates. Standardized and frequently used setups, however, do not require complete instructions. Nor do they usually require a significant amount of advance notice. For instance, it is not necessary to draw a diagram of each standard classroom setup unless there is something unusual or distinct about a particular one.

Record special room setups and decorations by taking digital photos before the room is broken down. These photos provide a reference, so you will not have to rely on memory to re-create a theme or special setup. These photos are also handy to give or email to potential clients so they can see how the room would be set up for their event.

5. *Decor.* A theme party or similar function requires additional time to set up properly. Props, plants, flowers, lighting, and so forth must be delivered and located. The amount and type of decorations and whether they are stored in the facility or must be delivered and set up by outside contractors will determine when the function room can be set and how much of the function room can be set at one time. Larger props should be set first, furniture and equipment next, with smaller props then set around the furniture and equipment.

6. *Pre-movement.* Larger functions require additional planning primarily because it takes more time to transport the furniture and equipment. Pre-movement is necessary so that final room setups can proceed quickly. For instance, if a function requires 1,000 chairs, when the banquet setup staff have some extra time available, they should move the chairs as close to the function room as possible and store them temporarily. The final room setup can be handled quickly and efficiently if a good deal of furniture and equipment is pre-set this way.

Moving large quantities of furniture and equipment early allows time to handle any unforeseen delays that might occur. Forklift problems, employee sick calls, and equipment mishaps or miscounts can derail the final setup schedule. Time is precious when setting up a function room for a large event. Pre-setting furniture and equipment will increase productivity, eliminate the need to rush at the last minute, and decrease the chances of an accident occurring when moving items.

7. *Teardown.* When a function ends, the banquet setup staff must dismantle the furniture and equipment and return it to storage. Efficient scheduling can reduce labor requirements and increase productivity. For instance, if the next setup in the function room requires chairs, you should leave the required number in the room.

The cycle of delivering, setting up, and tearing down furniture and equipment is similar to a chess game, with all pieces subject to constant movement.

8. *Lighting and audiovisual.* Meetings and meal functions sometimes require extensive lighting and/or AV services. Function room setups that include these services usually require additional setup time, sometimes referred to as a "rehearsal set." While complete furniture and equipment setup is often not necessary for a rehearsal set, it can be essential if a band or keynote speaker wants to test the sound system with all furniture and equipment in place. Rehearsal sets increase significantly the time and effort needed to set up a function room properly.

Communication is critical for a rehearsal set. When will it take place and how long will it last? Will other setup work continue during the rehearsal set or must it be postponed until after the rehearsal ends? Unplanned rehearsals can seriously interrupt the overall setup schedule. Productivity is compromised if the setup crew must work in the dark or wait for access while a band is checking sound levels.

9. *Outside service contractors.* If clients are using outside service contractors, the banquet setup staff must ensure that their work dovetails nicely with the facility's standard operating procedures. For instance, if an outside service contractor is hired to handle all lighting installations and teardowns, the banquet setup team must coordinate closely with the contractor's crew to maximize productivity and eliminate unnecessary downtime.

Dining Room Layout

When you walk into the set banquet room, everything should be symmetrical. Round tables should be evenly spaced so that the eye can view attractive, neat rows. All of the table legs should face the same direction, and the points of square tablecloths should form V-shapes over the table legs. When the banquet room is completely set, the client should be able to look down a row of tables and see a consistent line of V-shapes surrounding each table leg.

The tables used should be the standard ones that measure 30 inches from the floor. Some clients may specifically ask for rectangular dining tables because they want picnic-style seating, or a mix of round, rectangular, triangular, and oval tables for variety and interest. Generally, though, rounds are the most popular style of dining tables, except where U-shaped, hollow square, or conference room setups are required. For instance, a small luncheon with a guest speaker can be more readily accommodated with the U-shaped arrangement. The riser, podium, and supporting props can be set up at the top of the U before the meal is served. The speaker can begin right after dessert, and guests will not have to change seat locations.

The typical tables used in catering are:

1. *5-foot (60-inch) round.* Typically called a round of 8, or 8-top. It is usually used to seat 6 to 10 guests.

2. *6-foot (72-inch) round.* Typically called a round of 10, or 10-top. It is usually used to seat 8 to 12 guests.

3. *5½-foot (66-inch) round.* A more recent compromise table size, it is designed to take the place of the 60- and 72-inch rounds. It can seat 8 to 10 guests. If it uses this table, the facility may be able to minimize the different types of tables it carries in stock.

4. *6-foot banquet.* A rectangular table, measuring 30 inches wide by 6 feet long. Can seat up to 8 guests.

5. *8-foot banquet.* A rectangular table. It measures 30 inches wide by 8 feet long and can seat up to 10 guests.

6. *Classroom or schoolroom table.* Similar to the 6- and 8-foot banquets. It can be 18 or 24 inches wide and 6 or 8 feet long. Used mainly for business meetings where classroom presentations are made. Seating is usually on one side only. Can also be used as one-half of a buffet table or for registration and display tables where space is limited.

7. *Serpentine table.* An S-shaped table typically used with rounds or 6- and 8-foot banquet tables to add curves to a buffet line.

8. *Half-moon table.* A half-round table. It is typically used to add another dimension to a buffet line. It can also be used by itself to hold, for example, a few dry snacks at a beverage function.

9. *Crescent-shaped table.* The typical size used is one-fourth of a hollowed-out round table, though you can purchase one that is one-fifth of a hollowed-out round table. They are used with 6- and 8-foot banquet tables to add curves to a buffet line. They also can be used to create a hollowed-out circle, where foods can be displayed on the tables and some sort of attraction (such as a floor-mounted fountain) can be displayed in the center.

10. *Cocktail table.* A small round table, usually available in 18-, 24-, 30-, and 36-inch diameters. You can use 30-inch heights for sit-down service, shorter tables for displays, or taller (bar height) ones, sometimes referred to as highboys, for stand-up.

11. *Oval table.* A table of varying proportions, used primarily as a dining table. The typical one used for catering measures 54 by 78 inches. It can be used to increase room capacity; for instance, you can fit ten ovals in place of eight rounds. The oval table also allows a more elegant seating arrangement, in that a host can sit at its head. But oval tables do present some drawbacks. For instance, they are more difficult to drape with linen, and their shape makes it more difficult for servers to work around them efficiently. Guests seated on the narrow ends may feel cramped and crowded. And if a few foods are pre-set in the middle of the table, some guests may be unable to reach them easily.

When taking round banquet tables from storage, never roll more than two at a time. When opening and setting them up, be sure that the legs are locked properly. This will prevent accidents that can occur if the tables are not set up and adequately secured. If locking bolts are exposed incorrectly, a guest could scratch his or her legs.

You also must ensure that the table legs lock properly when tearing down the tables and putting them away. And if the tables are stored on a dolly, they must be secured correctly to prevent accidents and damage.

The seat height of the chairs used should measure 17 inches from the floor. The most common seat cushion dimension is 20 inches by 20 inches. The typical banquet stacking chair meets these specifications. Folding chairs usually do not; they are usually lower (15 inches high) and less comfortable. Folding chairs should only be used for outside events or for emergency backup. Ensure that all chairs are sturdy, safe, clean, and in good condition.

The placement of chairs and tables in a room can significantly affect the outcome of a function. Unsuitable arrangement or cramped seating can spoil an event. Consider the objective of the function. Is there a speaker? Is interaction desired or are the attendees expected to just listen? Can everyone see the speaker? Can everyone see the audiovisual presentation?

Ultimately, the seating arrangement used will depend on the purpose of the catered event. For instance, the purpose of the function also will indicate if a head table is appropriate. With a head table, it is important to specify if it is to be on a riser because, just like a dining table, the riser must be set up and dressed appropriately. The appropriate riser height also must be determined.

Before the banquet setup crew is finished, they must be certain that all ancillary tables, chairs, and equipment are set up, such as podiums, AV equipment, cashier stations, registration and information tables, kiosks, booths, and display attractions.

Bar Layout

Bar setups are easier to plan than food events. Unlike food, alcoholic beverage service tends to be very standardized. Also, you do not normally set up portable bars with the wide array of equipment needed to prepare and serve a complete line of specialty drinks. Simple mixed drinks, wines, and beers are more commonly served; unique specialty drinks are not commonly available.

Bar setups are also easier to plan because the facility may have permanent, self-contained banquet-bar installations in some function rooms or banquet areas. These bars need only a bartender or two, some inventory, and clean glassware and they are ready to go.

A bar also does not pose the same quality control problems as food does. The product is very standardized. It is a manufactured item, with standardized packaging, quality, and servable yields. And, except for beer and some wines, the inventory has a virtually unlimited shelf life.

Ideal locations vary depending on the size of the room, the location of the doors, and the placement of the food and the dance floor. Avoid placing bars too near the entrance, which may create a bottleneck at the door, or grouping bars too closely to food stations, which could cause crowd buildup. In a large room, open the bars further from the entrance first in order to encourage guests to move into the room.

Even in function rooms that use portable bars, the facility often has designated locations for them that are always used. These locations provide the appropriate utilities, space, and accessibility. When planning beverage service, therefore, the catering sales representative and client need only work around this preallocated space. In effect, you are working with semi-permanent bars that tend to be almost as convenient as permanent ones.

If portable bars are used, and if you need to allocate space for them, the planning is a bit more challenging. You will need to ensure that they are set up to:

1. *Serve all function needs*. For instance, if there is a reception with dinner following, the bars may have to accommodate both events. This implies that there must be enough room to allow guests to approach the bars during the reception, and also sufficient service bar area to accommodate cocktail servers who may need to handle poured-wine or table cocktail service.

2. *Provide sufficient working space*. Normally you will need at least one bartender and one bar back per bar. If you are catering an upscale function and are using a sommelier, you should allocate some working space so that he or she can handle wine service correctly. Depending on the type of function, you may also need cocktail servers.

3. *Provide sufficient storage space.* A busy bar will need a back area in which to store additional inventory. Portable refrigerators, portable ice carts, glassware, and paper supplies should also be available so that service does not lag.

4. *Enhance cost control procedures.* There must be enough working space to eliminate bottlenecks, which can lead to overpouring and spillage. With cash bars, if there are no cashiers scheduled, the facility may bring in cash registers for the bartenders to use to ring up sales and hold cash receipts. If drink tickets are sold by a separate cashier, the bar will need a lockbox to store used drink tickets. Furthermore, sufficient standardized portion control devices, such as Posi-Pour color-coded pour spouts and standardized glassware, should be used.

5. *Prevent access by minors.* A permanent or semi-permanent bar installation usually is positioned to avoid this problem. Portable bars may not be so closely watched. However, local liquor codes usually demand that you provide some type of separation to prevent underage drinking.

6. *Allow adequate space for other items.* Required cocktail tables and chairs, tray jacks, cashiers, and ticket takers, will need an appropriate amount of space.

7. *Accommodate special customer requests.* For example, a client may want you to provide a separate draft beer station, wine-tasting station, and spirits and mixed-drinks station. In this case, you will need to plan your setup very carefully in order to prevent overcrowding.

8. *Allow for a proper accounting of all drinks served.* If the bar service is set up to charge the client for each drink consumed by his or her guests, you will need to allocate space for pre-check cash register machines to record the number of drinks served.

9. *Enhance security.* Liquor theft is all too common in our industry; tight security will minimize this problem. It is best to transport all liquor stock in a portable, locked cage. You also will want to leave the cage near the portable bar so that if the area must be unattended, the liquor stock can be secured. You can have the portable bar and locked cage set up well before the catered event is scheduled to begin; when the bartenders and bar backs come on duty, they can unload the liquor cage and set up the bar.

Coffee Stations and Refreshment Breaks

Coffee may be the simplest and most profitable service you provide. There are more compulsive coffee drinkers in the United States than there are compulsive liquor drinkers, and they need coffee throughout the day. Coffee drinkers are generally impatient and want their coffee right away, especially in the morning. The setup must be simple to understand. You must make access easy. Traffic must flow smoothly with no backtracking.

Attendees can draw 5 gallons of coffee from a single urn in fifteen minutes. You can anticipate fifteen 8-ounce cups of coffee per gallon.

It takes twice as long to add cream and sugar as it does to pour coffee, so cream and sugar should never be placed directly in front of the coffee urns. By placing these items away from the urns, the line will move much faster. For larger events, you may want to set up a separate condiment station to ensure constant access to the coffee urns.

If you are providing food as well as drinks, it should also be placed away from the coffee urns, or on a separate table.

From left to right, items should be placed in this order to facilitate the traffic flow:

- Cups
- Regular coffee
- Decaffeinated coffee
- Hot water for tea
- Tea bags, sugar, sweetener, cream, lemon slices
- Spoons
- Food

Buffet Layout

Buffets allow guests to choose their favorite menu items. Guests also have some personal control over the portion sizes. And chefs can use their creative talents to decorate the foods and buffet tables.

Buffets are generally faster and more efficient than table service, assuming that there are enough buffet lines to accommodate the guests quickly and efficiently. Potential disadvantages of buffets, though, include the possibility that some guests will finish eating while others are still waiting in line and the fact that buffets take more space to accommodate than a plated meal.

There are times when buffets are the only feasible option for an event. For example, at an outdoor tailgate event, where guests are coming and going over the course of several hours, a buffet is the only form of food service that makes sense. Buffets usually provide an acceptable level of customer service for all but the most formal events.

When laying out the buffet stations, you should try not to put salads, entrees, and desserts on the same table. This will slow down service, as the guests will attempt to take everything at once. Most guests cannot carry two plates, but this does not stop them from trying. The inevitable result: spillage and other food-wasting accidents.

You should avoid setting up the buffet tables near doors or other entryways, where they can cause traffic jams. If the buffet line will be longer than 16 feet, it should be two tables wide (i.e., about 4 to 6 feet wide). A long, narrow line is unattractive. A wider line allows you to spread out the foods, create a more aesthetically pleasing arrangement, and enhance the setup with decorations and food displays. If you must use long, narrow lines, you should use a combination of straight tables and curved ones to eliminate the "skinny" look.

If the buffet line will include an action station, you will need to allocate enough space to accommodate the in-process inventory of food, preparation and service equipment, the chef, and guests who will want to congregate and watch the chef create the finished items.

If the action station will be put toward the center of the function room instead of up against a wall, you will need more floor space. An action station in the round usually is set up with several inside tables and outside tables to allow for maximum chef maneuverability and exposure and guest accessibility.

The number of action stations needed depends on the amount of time needed to prepare and serve the foods, as well as the estimated number of customers who will want them in lieu of the other foods displayed on the buffet line. At the very least, you should expect that half of the guests will want something from an action station.

Some buffets incorporate a bit of cafeteria service. If so, there must be enough room allocated so that food servers and chefs can maneuver adequately.

For any group over 50 people, you should use double-sided buffet tables whenever possible. They can save as much as 20 percent of your available floor space, and guests will be able to go through much quicker. At times, a double-sided buffet may mean only that guests can go on either side of the table, but all utilize the same serving vessel. For larger groups, though, the double-sided buffet means there is a duplicate setup on both sides of the table. When service slows near the end of the meal, you can close one side of the line and consolidate all foods on the open side.

Whenever possible, beverages, such as wine, hot coffee and tea, and soft drinks, should be served at the table. This provides a bit of personalized table service that guests appreciate. It also makes the overall service much quicker and more efficient. Experience shows that guests take a long time at beverage stations and that bottlenecks are inevitable. If beverages are not to be served at the tables, place them on a separate table.

If possible, you should use small containers of food on the buffet line. Try to use containers that hold no more than 25 to 30 servings. They will be more attractive than large, elaborately garnished containers. Keep in mind that only the first few guests through the line will see the beautifully garnished large presentations before they are disturbed. Though small containers will need frequent replacement, experience shows that guests will take smaller portions from smaller containers and larger servings from bigger containers. The result: you save more on food cost than you spend for any extra labor. Furthermore, smaller containers usually mean fresher, more attractive presentations.

Most meal buffets are usually set with one line for every 100 guests. (One line is one side of a buffet table; if you are using two sides, that is considered two lines.) The maximum number you can serve efficiently with one line is 120 guests. Generally speaking, you should have one line for every 100 guests, but you should have two lines if the number of guests ranges from 120 to 200.

For some luncheons with limited time, it might be a good idea to set one line for every 50 guests, which means you can feed the entire group in about fifteen minutes. The first guest will take about five minutes to go through the line. After that, there will be about four guests passing through the line every minute.

If hors d'oeuvres are served buffet-style during a beverage function, industry experts recommend setting one table for every 50 guests. Using fewer larger tables tends to interfere with bar traffic.

If you set one buffet table for every 50 guests, you may need more labor to prepare multiple containers and replenish food supplies. You will have more product distribution problems unless you set up enough service corridors to handle replenishment. And you may have more leftovers with several small buffet tables unless you consolidate some tables toward the end of the event.

For breakfast functions, you may be able to get by with one buffet line for more than 100 guests. Unlike luncheon guests, breakfast guests tend to arrive a few at a time. For instance, many convention attendees will drift in throughout the meal. Even though the typical breakfast buffet will have a guest rush during the last fifteen minutes of the meal period, usually enough guests will have already been served to prevent any service glitches.

Display tables, unless decorative and attractive enough on their own, need to be draped to the ground with linen or skirted. Skirting is draped along the side of the table. It is connected on the table's edges and allowed to fall to just above the floor.

Skirting is usually attached with clips. Plastic clips with Velcro on one side have made installation and removal easy, as they attach to Velcro on the inside of the skirt. Clips come in two sizes, standard and angled. Standard is made to fit a ¾-inch-thick tabletop, and angled is used for ½-inch-thick tabletops.

Table skirting is usually 29 inches in length to accommodate the standard 30-inch table height. Riser skirting is used to dress risers and is available in lengths ranging from 6 inches to 36 inches. Longer skirting is available for portable bars or tall cocktail tables. If the standard lengths do not meet your needs, you may want to use pipe and draping or other fabric to dress anything taller.

For some skirting, you will need to use a skirting liner. For instance, if you plan to use sheer or lace skirting, you will need to line it so that the uncovered areas do not show through.

Traditionally, all buffet tables, display tables, and risers were skirted. Some dining and meeting tables may also be skirted. For instance, a head table usually is skirted on three sides. The skirting provides a vanity shield as well as an attractive presentation.

When calculating the amount of skirting needed, you must be very careful to compute the correct total. If, for example, you need enough skirting to fully cover an 8-foot banquet table, you will need about 22 running feet (i.e., two 8-foot sides and two approximately 3-foot sides equals about 22 running feet). If the table is against a wall or you intend to leave a portion of the table without skirting (for example, at a registration table, where people will need to sit and be able to push the chair in), then you will need about 16 running feet of skirting.

In lieu of skirts, caterers can use table drapes. Table drapes are a combination of a tablecloth and skirting that rests just above the ground. It is a one-piece item that slips over the table and has a fitted look. Radial tablecloths that cover a banquet table are now commonly available as well. The radial cloth drapes over a table and falls to just above the ground, but is a less fitted look, similar to that of a round tablecloth that falls to just above the ground on a round table.

The trend lately, though, is to use tables that are more like furniture, or decorative in some way so that skirting is not needed. Many different options are now used to create buffet tables. Examples of these include using tables and bookshelves that look just like the furniture in someone's home or in an upscale hotel lobby, or using tables made out of plexiglass or stainless steel.

Tablescapes: The Tabletop

The top of the table is the "stage." Once guests are seated they will spend the rest of the meal function looking at the table. The table presentation sets expectations for the meal and should reflect the theme. All dining tables and buffet tables must be dressed and outfitted appropriately. The type of meal function, menu, and style of service will influence the quality and type of table decor used.

Tables should be padded whenever possible, so that table noises are minimized. The typical dining table and buffet table at high end or formal events often have padded underliners placed underneath the tablecloths. This pad can be permanent—you can buy a roll of padding, cut pieces to fit each table, and staple them to the tabletops. Or the pad can be temporary and placed on the table prior to adding the tablecloth. You can purchase tables that are pre-padded. Generally, though, these tables are much more expensive than unpadded ones.

Almost all tables require linen. Buffet tables and display tables, unless decorative on their own, will need tablecloths. And dining tables will need tablecloths and napkins. You will also need linen for most of your beverage stations. For instance, the alcoholic and nonalcoholic beverage stations will likely need tablecloths, coasters, and napkins (though normally you will use disposable paper coasters and cocktail napkins for the stations).

Linen adds warmth and color. In the public's eye, cleanliness is its most important attribute. Crisp, clean, stain-free linens helps create a favorable impression. The colors of the linen should not clash with the carpet or wall treatments.

Previously most linens used were made from polyester (the easiest to clean), cotton, or a poly-cotton blend. However, recently there has been an abundance of new fabrics introduced to the special-events market. Everything from silks and velvets to hemp, denim, and organza is now readily available from standard and specialty rental companies.

White is the most traditional color used for linen. Other light colors, such as ivory, are used when white does not provide the background desired. Darker colors can be used when a stark contrast is desired or for all-day functions (such as permanent refreshment centers) where the linen, which will get soiled during the day, cannot be changed easily. And darker colors (often green, burgundy, or brown) are used for schoolroom tables so that convention attendees can take notes without battling the glare that white linen gives off.

Sometimes you may want to use two or more colors to dress a table. This can be an excellent upsell opportunity, as caterers generally carry only a few neutral linen colors. An almost endless color palette is available through most local rental companies. For instance, a beautiful shade of eggplant may be appropriate for a buffet table overlay (a contrasting cloth laid on top of the base cloth), while a white tablecloth with a gold overlay may be just right for a table used to display door prizes. Black tablecloths with brightly colored napkins (such as fuchsia, gold, or white) can provide a contrasting visual effect.

Special linens can be rented in a variety of materials and patterns. A beautiful tablecloth and complimentary napkin help set the stage for a memorable event. Pintucked cloths, exquisite designs, or festive patterns and fun plaids can help set the mood of a catered event. White lace overlays, sheer organzas, or l'amour satin are appropriate for a wedding.

Chair covers can be a great addition to the event. They help to transform the look and feel of a room and can camouflage chairs that may not go with the theme or color palette selected. Chair covers may be formfitting or loose and finished with a tie, band, bow, or other decorative touch.

When ordering linen or requisitioning it from a linen room, you will need to specify the exact measurements needed. For example, if you use round tables, for most functions the tablecloth should be approximately 30–48 inches wider than the table diameter so that about 15–24 inches of cloth will drape over the sides. If the tabletop diameter is 60 inches, you would use a 90-inch round cloth. A 72-inch-diameter table should be fitted with a 120-inch round cloth. The more formal the meal or occasion, the longer the drop generally is.

For some formal dinners, if floor-length tablecloths are desired, allow 29 inches on each side, so for a 72-inch round table, you would order a 130-inch round tablecloth. When using floor-length tablecloths, be sure that the setup crew does not push the chairs in so far that the cloth is not hanging straight down to the floor.

When placing the tablecloths on the tables, you should keep the hemmed sides down and the creases up. If the tablecloths were pressed incorrectly and the creases and hemmed sides both face in the same direction, you should keep the hemmed sides down even though the creases may not be attractive. In this case, you must select the lesser of two evils. If this does occur, it is best to use a steamer on-site to release some of the crease whenever possible.

The napkin fold and placement of the napkin on the table can add interest. The napkin can be placed in the center of the cover, set to the left of the forks, or decoratively folded and placed in stemmed glassware. An interesting twist would be to have each napkin a different color or with a different fold. The layout must be symmetrical and pleasing to the eye.

Caterers usually consider more than just color for the napkin fold. The type of fold is determined by the formality of the event, the amount of time available for setup, the type of fabric used for the napkin, and the location of the napkin on the table. A flat fold would be preferable if a standing menu or a name card is used. Flat folds are usually a better choice for outdoor events, which could be windy.

The napkins used must be laundered and handled correctly so that they have enough strength to hold whatever fold you want to use. For instance, you can use the more common napkin folds, such as the pyramid, goblet fan, or Lady Windermere's fan, or you can use something more adventurous and unusual, such as the rosebud, bishop's mitre, or candle fold. A website with napkin-folding instructions is www.napkinfoldingguide.com; for additional folds, type "napkin folds" into Google or another search engine.

A nice touch is to have the servers unfold the napkins for the guests and lay them across the lap just after they are seated, and to refold the napkin if a guest leaves the table during the event. If a group is having several banquets, use a different fold for each meal.

If you are using a casual buffet-style service, you may opt to provide the napkins at the end of the buffet line. For speed and efficiency at casual events, you could roll the flatware inside the napkins.

Your dining tables will also need plates, cups, saucers, flatware, water goblets, wine glasses, roll baskets, condiment containers, wine coolers, carafes, show plates, and other appropriate items, which must be pre-set on the dining tables in a symmetrical pattern. As with napkins, though, if you are using a buffet-style service, you could let the guests help themselves to some tableware on the buffet line.

There are many other types of tableware needed that usually are not pre-set on the dining tables. You may need teapots, pitchers, mugs, serving platters, serving bowls, ramekins, and specialty utensils.

Glassware includes stemware, tumblers, goblets, parfaits, decanters, pony glasses, snifters, pilsners, bottles, punch bowls, and cake plates. Food service facilities usually purchase glassware that has been produced with a heat-treatment and rapid-cooling process that ensures durability and long-term attractiveness.

Each place setting is referred to as a cover. The cover should never be empty (what is called a "naked cover"). A show plate, folded napkin, menu, or pre-set first course should be placed between the flatware.

The standard cover includes a plate set in the center with flatware placed on either side. Forks are placed to the left of the cover, knives and spoons to the right. Some dessert and coffee flatware may be placed above the center plate.

Flatware is placed in the order in which it will be used by the guest, from the outside in. The soup spoon would be on the outside and far right, as soup is usually an early course. The knife would be closest to the center plate, with the blade edge facing the rim of the plate. The smaller salad fork would be set to the left of the dinner fork on the left side of the plate.

Dessert pieces set above the plate would have the bowl of the spoon facing the guest's left, and the tines of the fork facing the guest's right.

The exact place setting depends primarily on the menu and style of service selected by the client. Many catering executives have sample covers set out on credenzas in their offices so clients can view them. Clients can also redesign the sample place settings in order to develop something unique.

Coffee cups should not be pre-set at a formal dinner. They should be placed on the table after dinner, or poured and served on trays by the servers when coffee service begins.

When selecting decorative items or serving containers, you must be careful to use only those intended to hold foods. For instance, an imported serving bowl could contain lead in its glaze. Care must be taken to ensure that these types of containers are used only to hold or display nonfood items.

Some dining tables may need nameplates or personalized menu cards. If you are setting a head table, you must see to it that the head table guests are seated correctly. For the head table at a formal event, the first guest of honor should be seated to the right of the host, with the second guest of honor seated on the left. If a third guest of honor is present, he or she should be seated to the right of the first guest of honor. If there are other dignitaries, they should be balanced back and forth according to rank or prominence.

For the head table at a wedding, the bride and groom should be seated at the center, with the bride sitting on the groom's left. On the bride's left will be the best man, followed by a bridesmaid, groomsman, bridesmaid, groomsman, and so forth. On the groom's right will be the maid of honor, followed by a groomsman, bridesmaid, groomsman, bridesmaid, and so forth. There should be enough room allocated at the head table to accommodate the entire wedding party, but if this is impossible, you should seat the most important members at the head table, with the others seated at the dining tables closest to the head table. Many bridal couples are electing to do varied arrangements at the head table. These include having all the bridesmaids to the left of the bride and all the groomsmen to the right of the groom, or selecting instead a "sweetheart" table that is set just for the bridal couple while the remainder of the bridal party is seated at the guest dining tables.

Your table setting is not complete without some sort of additional decoration. Most catered events, especially dinners, have centerpieces on the dining tables. They also have similar attractions on the buffet tables. Interesting centerpieces can be made from fresh flowers, baskets of bread or fruit, or various types of food. Centerpieces can be highlighted with small spotlights (pin spots) from the ceiling.

According to decorator John Daly, floral arrangements are a manifestation of beauty that can add a unique dimension to an event, filling the eye with beauty. The bases of any arrangement are style, shape, size, color, texture, scent, and location.

Before setting the tables, the banquet manager must specify the exact setup needed for regular dining tables, head tables, beverage stations, and buffet tables. It is a good idea to diagram in advance the required setup so that the setup crew do not have to scurry around at the last minute for directions. If special center-pieces must be placed on the head table, the setup crew must know about this before they go to work.

A client may request a smoking section, assuming the law allows the caterer to set one up in the facility. If a smoking section is allowed, the banquet setup crew will need to set out ashtrays on the tables in the smoking section and "Thank You for Not Smoking" signs on those tables in the nonsmoking section. If these signs are not on tables, guests may think someone merely forgot to put out ashtrays; they may just go ahead and light up without thinking about it.

Sometimes the caterer may have to set up tables for a function to exceed the number of guaranteed guests. Usually these tables do not have a complete tablescape and should have a reserved sign on them so they are not used unless needed. This procedure is referred to as an overset or set-over-guarantee. It represents the number of covers set up in the dining room that surpass the guarantee. The caterer will do this because if unexpected guests arrive at the last minute, it will be easier to accommodate them without disturbing everyone.

Dining room layout, bar layout, buffet layout, required table settings, and other pertinent information will be listed on the banquet event order (BEO). Some BEOs also include a room diagram. Working with the specifications outlined in the BEO, the banquet captain usually sets a captain's table—a sample cover—as a guide for the servers to follow when setting the dining tables. While the typical BEO details very specifically the dining room, bar, and buffet layouts, it does not always include an exact description of the required table settings. If the client wants menus, brochures, and handouts placed at each cover, this information must be noted on the BEO. Every detail, no matter how small, is important to the client. You cannot afford to let any get lost in the shuffle.

Wall and Ceiling Treatments

Many events require wall or ceiling treatments. Walls can be draped, floor to ceiling. Ceilings can be given a tent look or simply hung with swags or baffles that are transformed by lighting.

Make sure to find out about any fire regulations and insurance considerations before hanging anything from the ceiling or draping fabric. Never hang anything off a fire sprinkler.

Tables and chairs should not be set up in the room until the ceiling treatment is finished. In some cases, chandeliers must be removed to accommodate production lighting.

Lectern or Podium?

There is some confusion over the terms *lectern* and *podium*. Some people say a lectern goes on a table, while a podium goes on the floor. Others say a podium is a base, like a riser, and that you stand on it. The most widely accepted use in the industry now is *podium*, and so this should never be used as a term for something that you stand on. If your facility carries both, you will need to discuss with the client, and specify to staff, whether a tabletop (half) podium or a standing (full-length) podium is needed. Podium placement can vary based on the event. Most often it is placed in the front of the room in the most visible area. When combined with a head table, it is commonly in the center, whether it is on top of the table or on the riser with a head table on each side.

Flag Placement

The American flag should always be placed to stage right in the United States (the host country always has its flag to stage right). Stage right is determined by the right side of the speaker as he or she is facing the audience. So stage right would be to the left as the audience views it.

If a state flag is used, it would go stage left, with the podium in between. If the organization or association has its own flag, it would go far stage left, on the left side of the state flag.

When international flags are displayed in the United States, the American flag would go to far stage right.

Restroom Facilities

If the location has permanent restroom facilities, be sure they are unlocked, clean, and well lit. It is a good idea to offer upscale bathroom amenities for certain groups, possibly for an additional charge. For example, adding mouthwash, hairspray, cloth hand towels, and a fresh floral arrangement is a very nice touch.

If your outdoor location is not equipped with restroom facilities, arrange for one portable toilet for every 100 guests. Deluxe portable sanitation facilities are available in mobile trailers and provide regular commodes, sinks, and lighting, rather than the portable single-stall potties seen on construction sites. Hand-washing stations, whether inside the potties or separate, must also be provided and are regulated by the local health department in many areas. Hand sanitizer dispensers should also be provided. Be sure there are adequate directional signs indicating the location of all restrooms.

Room Temperature

Attendees often complain about the temperature in the room during a function. Most newer facilities today have energy management systems that turn the air conditioner on automatically to pre-cool the meeting room about an hour before the banquet or meeting.

Many facilities set the thermostat at 72°F unless the planner requests a different temperature. Some planners have been known to request a 69°F temperature. The important thing is to know the group. If there are to be 90 percent men, keep the room cooler, as men tend to wear more clothing than women. If it is an evening function and the women are wearing cocktail dresses, you may need to go as high as 74°F.

Tents

Functions are often held in tents, which are usually rented. Many sporting events, such as golf tournaments or football games, will have a variety of corporate tents set up to host their best clients. These would be off-premise events unless the facility holding the event has an on-premise catering department, such as at a golf course, stadium, or arena.

Some facilities short of function space may opt to increase saleable space with a tent. Or a resort with a golf course, beachfront property, or other scenic amenity may wish to hold events on the property, but away from the main building.

If a tent is infeasible, you might want to expand your saleable area with awnings. An awning is a roof-like structural overhang that is attached to a permanent building in case of rain or for shade.

At one time, all tents were made of canvas, which is cotton treated with mineral oil to make it waterproof. However, canvas has fallen out of favor because it is highly flammable. There are a number of other tenting materials now available.

Tents must be anchored, usually with stakes, water barrels, or sandbags. There are mechanical stake drivers and stake pullers, which makes the job of erecting and removing the tent considerably easier than in years past. If you are installing or allowing a tent to be installed on your property, it is important to ensure that the holes are filled after the tent is removed. This is particularly true if the area used is a parking lot, as it can create a trip hazard if the holes are left unfilled. If the tent is being installed onto a surface that you do not wish to have damaged by holes, then be sure to advise the tent company that the tent must be secured by either sandbags or water barrels. There is generally an additional cost for the water barrels, due to the labor involved in filling the barrels and transporting them, so when ordering a tent you will need to be sure of all costs so you can correctly bill the client.

A clear span tent has a structure that allows it to function without internal poles for support. This is preferable to having to work around poles. Some tents are modular, in that several standardized sections function together as one system.

Many tents now have clear vinyl roofs, windows, and doors, to let the light in and eliminate the claustrophobic feeling. It would not be advisable to use vinyl tents in very cold climates, because when the temperature falls below 0°F they often crack.

Tents now come with a number of optional accessories, including:
- Flooring or carpet
- Dance floors
- Heaters, air conditioners, fans
- Power generators
- Lighting, including specialty chandeliers
- Hinged doors

When erecting tents, make sure the ground is level. If the ground is not level and it rains, the inside of the tented area could get water runoff and become quite muddy. It may be necessary on some surfaces to first put down a subflooring to have a more stable ground for guests to walk on inside the tent.

Portable air conditioning or heaters are optional. When placing tents with clear vinyl on one side, be careful not to position the clear side toward the west if the party will be taking place during sunset hours.

Tents can be used solely for protecting the food area, or may contain an entire party. It is common for one or more sides to be open to allow free movement and air flow in and out.

"Tent seating" refers to the number of people who can be accommodated under a tent. Following is the information needed to determine the size of tent you need:

A 20-by-20-foot tent will hold:

- 50 people for a reception
- 30 people for a buffet with seating
- 30 people for a served dinner

A 20-by-30-foot tent will hold:

- 75 people for a reception
- 30 people for a buffet with seating
- 40 people for a served dinner

A 30-by-30-foot tent will hold:

- 110 people for a reception
- 50 people for a buffet with seating
- 60 people for a served dinner

A 40-by-40-foot tent will hold:

- 200 people for a reception
- 100 people for a buffet with seating
- 110 people for a served dinner

CLEANING AND MAINTAINING THE FUNCTION ROOM

Dirty windows, walls, or floors can reduce a function room's quality level and cause guest dissatisfaction. Guests notice poor maintenance such as burned-out lightbulbs in chandeliers or stains on walls.

Function rooms must be vacuumed before each function setup (when the room is empty), with one final sweep or vacuum just before the catered event is scheduled to begin. Post-function cleaning is equally vital. Trash and leftover materials must be discarded promptly.

Some rooms have a door leading onto a loading dock or outside area through which dirt can be tracked into the room area. Trucks, forklifts, and carts that enter the function room will hasten carpet deterioration and generate a considerable amount of working dirt. Covering the floor near the loading entrance with old carpets and plastic sheeting can be an effective dirt catcher. Pre-cleaning ramps and loading docks can also reduce the amount of dirt tracked into the room.

Restroom, trash can, and public area cleanliness requires constant care during peak periods and must be scheduled to ensure an attractive atmosphere.

Torn wallpaper, ripped carpet, and broken equipment must be replaced or repaired quickly so that the function rooms remain presentable and safe. Quick room turnarounds and constant movement of heavy furniture and equipment will cause damage to doors, floors, ceilings, and walls. These details must be monitored consistently.

Frequent inspection and repair can reduce wear and tear on the facilities as well as create a favorable guest environment conducive to memorable, exciting catered events.

It is a good idea to remove the meeting space from service during slow periods to have it deep-cleaned and repaired as necessary. Try for quarterly, or at least twice a year.

EMPLOYEE UNIFORMS

A good deal of a catered function's visual impact can be attributed to the type and style of employee uniforms and costumes used. The typical client does not think about this unless he or she requests a specific theme, in which case special uniforms and costumes will be needed to carry out the theme.

Often a facility uses a standard server uniform for breakfast and luncheon meal functions, with a slightly different, more formal server uniform used for evening affairs. The evening uniform may include a vest with a tuxedo, or a black or red bow tie, to provide for some variation. It is a good idea to mix up uniforms when possible for multiple-day events.

Bartenders, cocktail servers, bar backs, and buspersons also wear a standard outfit. These standard uniforms are designed to suit most food and beverage functions adequately.

If the client is a bit more adventurous and has a bit more money to spend, the catering sales representative may wish to broach the subject of alternative employee attire if he or she thinks it would add significantly to the function's success. For instance, you could suggest renting unique garments specifically for the meal function. This little extra touch can be just the thing to make a good event a great event. As noted in Chapter 3, service personnel in costumes are referred to as "moving decor."

COMMUNICATION WITH FUNCTION ROOM STAFF

Facilities with several function rooms in various locations require coordination and control of banquet staff. It is difficult to monitor employees who are constantly on the move. Managers must select an appropriate method to supervise and communicate quickly with all employees.

One basic, low-cost method of control is the callback method. In this situation, an employee must contact a supervisor when his or her assigned task is completed. The supervisor will know how much time it normally takes to complete the task and can therefore anticipate a pattern of calls from his or her employees. As calls come in, new tasks are assigned on a priority basis. Furthermore, if a last-minute request is received, the supervisor will be able to assign it to the first employee who calls in.

A common method of communication control involves push-to-talk (PTT) devices, whether via radio or cell phone. Push-to-talk devices are generally given to key staff on each shift so they have constant communication with supervisors. With PTT, supervisors can also monitor the conversation between employees and keep up-to-date on the movement of furniture, equipment, and labor. For instance, if a request is broadcast to one employee to locate some equipment, another employee monitoring the broadcast can break in with some pertinent information.

PTT can also be issued to a client, but this should be done only if a separate channel is available. It is not advisable to have the client on the same channel with all the staff, as airtime may be cluttered and the client will be able to hear all the details the staff is discussing.

In addition to PTT, lead employees and supervisors can be assigned cell phones and thereby become privately accessible to each other and to clients.

Many cell phones today are less expensive, smaller, and easier to handle than their predecessors. Some larger groups choose to rent them from one source so they can connect with hotel staff at no charge for minutes or expense to their personal cell phones. Last-minute changes can be communicated immediately. Clients are very impressed when their requirements change and employees respond to them instantaneously.

EQUIPMENT INVENTORY

The catering facility uses a considerable amount of specialized furniture and equipment to set up the function room and serve the catered event. The director of catering should ensure that complete, up-to-date lists of these items are kept by banquet setup staff and other relevant employees so that the catering staff knows what is available and what will need to be obtained from a rental company. These inventory lists, which are often kept in a software program, should note all chairs, tables, easels, tripods, stanchions, dance floor, AV equipment, gueridons, rechauds, china, glass, flatware, linen, skirting, serving utensils, side stands, trays, bus carts, hot carts, cold carts, permanent centerpieces and other decor, portable bars, and other furniture items kept in-house.

Equipment lists should be updated monthly. A complete physical inventory should be taken at the end of each quarter so that damaged items can be repaired and missing ones replaced quickly. If there is a good deal of catering business, there might be an above-average loss due to damage or theft. If so, a physical inventory should be taken more frequently.

SUMMARY

This chapter focuses on choosing and setting up an appropriate function room to hold the event. Factors to consider include the appearance of the room (including colors, views, and so on), the location within the facility, and proximity to restrooms. Also important are the types of utilities needed, including electricity, phone, and Wi-Fi, and amount of floor space necessary to accommodate tables, chairs, dance floors, bars, buffets, decor, and any other equipment.

KEY TERMS

Podium	Serpentine table	Half-moon table
Ambient light	Cross-aisle	Ropes and stanchions
Tray jack	Staging area	Pre-movement
Tablescape	Clear span tent	Captain's table
Linens	Skirting	Function room layouts

REVIEW QUESTIONS

1. What considerations should be made when using a room with columns?
2. How does table placement at receptions affect food consumption?
3. What is the ideal amount of floor space to allocate per guest at a reception?
4. How many square feet of dance floor should you allocate per guest?
5. Where should the American flag be placed when in the United States?
6. Why should you avoid holding an event in a function room that is long and narrow?
7. What type of color stimulates the appetite?
8. What type of color dulls the appetite?
9. If you are planning a cocktail reception with food, why should you avoid placing a round table of food in the middle of the function room?
10. If round dining tables are used for a sit-down meal function, how much space should be allocated for each attendee?
11. If rectangular banquet tables are used for a sit-down meal function, how much space should be allocated for each attendee?
12. Assume you have a group of 100 attendees for an awards banquet (with dancing) on the convention's final evening. Approximately how much dance floor space should you have?

13. Approximately how much more space is needed for a head table than for a regular dining table?

14. Assume you are planning to use two standard 8-foot rectangular banquet tables for a buffet. Approximately how much total floor space should you allocate for the complete buffet setup?

15. Approximately how much floor space is needed to accommodate the typical portable banquet bar setup?

16. Approximately how much space per attendee does a classroom-style setup require?

17. What are serpentine tables typically used for?

18. How many attendees can be seated at a 72-inch (6-foot) round dining table?

19. Why is it easier to plan bar events than food events?

20. At a coffee station, why is it a bad idea to place cream and sugar on the same table as the coffee urns?

21. What is a captain's table?

22. What is an overset?

23. Assume that you are scheduling a reception for 50 attendees that will be held in a tent. What size tent should you rent to accommodate this group?

Chapter 7

PRODUCTION AND SERVICE

PLANNING

Production and service planning must be correlated with client needs to ensure smooth-running functions, satisfied guests, and fair profits. All factors must be evaluated so that the appropriate plans can be developed and implemented. Coordination is vital. Attention to detail is critical. And every detail is significant. You cannot take anything for granted.

PRODUCTION PLANNING

A production plan lists the types and amounts of finished foods and beverages needed, when they must be ready, and when they should be produced. The chef and banquet manager must have copies of the banquet event orders (BEOs) in advance of the event so that they can incorporate them into the daily production and work schedules.

Quantity of Foods Needed

The chef needs to requisition foods from the property's storeroom (or order them from a distributor if the chef is responsible for purchasing). If the kitchen staff needs something unusual that the catering operation does not normally carry , he or she will need to prepare a purchase requisition a few days (or possibly up to two weeks, depending on the item) before the meal function and give it to the purchasing department. The purchasing agent will then have enough time to shop around for the product and get the best possible value.

The amount of food that must be requisitioned and produced depends primarily on these factors:

1. Number of guests expected
2. Style of service
3. Expected edible yields

You should plan to prepare enough foods to handle the guaranteed guest count, plus a set percentage above that amount. Generally speaking, you should plan for 5 percent more than the guarantee; if the guarantee exceeds 1,000 guests, you should plan for 3 percent more.

If the guests are having a sit-down, pre-plated meal, it is less difficult to compute the food requisition amounts because you can control the portion sizes. For instance, if the main course is roast bottom round of beef, the serving size is 6 cooked ounces, and the expected edible yield percentage for the raw roast beef is 75 percent, you will need to requisition approximately 53 pounds of raw beef for a party of 100 guests. Fifty-three pounds will serve 105 guests, 100 plus an extra 5 guests. The calculations are:

1. Divide serving size by edible yield percentage. This will tell you how much raw product you need per serving.

$$6 \text{ ounces} \div .75 = 8 \text{ ounces}$$

2. Divide 16 ounces by the amount of raw product needed per serving. This will tell you the number of edible servings you can get from one pound of raw roast beef.

$$16 \text{ ounces} \div 8 \text{ ounces} = 2 \text{ servings}$$

3. Divide the number of guests by the number of edible servings per raw pound. This will give you the amount of raw roast beef you must requisition.

$$105 \text{ servings} \div 2 = 52.2 \text{ (53 rounded) raw pounds}$$

If you plan to use reception or buffet service for a meal function, it is more difficult to determine the amount of foods to requisition and produce. There are some rules of thumb that can help you make a reasonable estimate. For instance, in a reception where foods are displayed on buffet tables, guests will generally consume approximately seven hors d'oeuvres during the first hour of a reception, and less during the succeeding time.

Guests will typically consume less if the event emphasizes socializing, which tends to keep them away from the food trays.

Another rule of thumb suggests that blue-collar people will eat and drink more than white-collar and pink-collar employees. And if you crowd people into a room, they tend to eat and drink less than if they have more space to roam around. A crowded room makes it more difficult for guests to revisit the buffet tables.

Recall that the way in which you display your foods on a buffet table will encourage or discourage overconsumption. For instance, putting the less expensive items up front, placing the more expensive items further back, and having chefs portion and serve some of the entrees can give you an extra margin of control.

In some cases, you may not be too concerned if you overproduce foods for a buffet. For instance, if you can get the client to agree to eat the same types of menu items that are used in your other food outlets or if you can use the foods for another event on the same day, overproduction may not be a problem because you can reallocate any remaining food that has not been put out. If the menu items cannot be reallocated, either you must have a sharp pencil when making your estimates or you will need to increase your competitive bid price for the catered meal function to take into account the additional food costs. This is even more stressful if your facility has a policy that absolutely forbids running out of any food. Unfortunately, it is very difficult to make an accurate determination of the amount of food to requisition and produce when you are dealing with self-service buffets and receptions unless you sell foods by the piece and clients agree to purchase a set amount. For that matter, even per-person pricing can be based on a specific amount and types of food items offered.

For some menu items, you may always have to prepare more portions than you want to. For instance, with the roast beef example above, it is unlikely that you can purchase exactly 53 raw pounds. Unprocessed and minimally processed foods like raw roast beef, fresh whole salmon, or raw turkeys, do not come in sizes that meet your exact needs. When you buy these types of products, you usually need to purchase what is called the "catch weight." Catch weight is an approximate size. To ensure that you obtain 53 pounds of raw bottom rounds, you may have to purchase three or four bottom rounds that together weigh at least 53 raw pounds or more. Or if the food distributor sells this item in case lots, you may need to buy a case that contains 60 raw pounds. The concept of catch weight is similar to going to the supermarket meat counter and rifling through the prepackaged meats looking for one that has the weight best suited for your needs at home that night. Under these circumstances, you can view this as being a built-in hedge against running out of product (or a built-in waste factor, depending on how you feel about this purchasing limitation).

If there are no restrictions placed on the self-service function, you cannot compute reasonably accurate estimates unless there is a great deal of relevant historical data upon which to base them. But even if you do take a lot of time to estimate your needs, you have limited control over the serving sizes. As a result, you must always add a margin of safety to avoid running out of food.

Quantity of Alcoholic Beverages Needed

It is much easier to determine the quantity of alcoholic beverages you will need than it is to forecast your food requirements. Unlike food, beverages are standardized, manufactured products. By and large, you do not have to worry about spoilage and variations in quality and yield. Furthermore, as long as your liquor storeroom is well stocked, you should never run out of product. You cannot quickly prepare and serve an extra roast beef dinner if you are out of cooked roast beef, but as long as there are alcoholic beverages in-house, you can make drinks.

Usually the banquet and reception bars are set up with a par stock (i.e., the maximum amount of inventory you want to have on-hand) of beverages, ice, glassware, garnishes, and other necessary supplies about a half-hour to an hour before the catered event is scheduled to begin.

The normal par stock used is influenced by the:

1. Number of guests expected
2. The caterer's experience with similar events
3. Amount of storage space available at the bar

Generally, you should expect liquor consumption to average at least 2 drinks per guest during a one-hour reception, particularly if the event attracts a mixed-company crowd. Average consumption tends to drop at very large receptions and usually increases at men-only events. However, if you schedule enough help and stock enough inventory to handle 2½ drinks per hour, you should be able to accommodate any type of beverage function adequately.

If the beverage function's drink menu varies significantly from the type you normally serve, bartenders will need to change the types and amounts of alcoholic beverages usually stocked at the portable bars. For instance, if a drink menu will offer only red and white wine, gin, bourbon, vodka, scotch, and an assortment of soft drinks, the bartender will need to adjust the typical opening par stock requisitioned from the liquor storeroom.

Usually you do not need to worry about stocking an exact amount of beverage at the banquet or reception bars because you can always depend on the bar back to replenish the supply quickly. You should make an effort to forecast your needs as accurately as possible, though, because this will help ensure a smooth-running event. In addition, if some items need to be iced down, it behooves you to make sure that you have plenty of ice available; you cannot take a room-temperature item and chill it quickly unless you have the specialized equipment needed to do this.

In most instances, it makes no difference if you overstock a banquet or reception bar because the merchandise can be used at other bars in your property. However, if you need to purchase specific products for the function that will not be used in other bars, you will need to compute as accurately as possible the amount you should order.

For example, a meal function might require a unique dinner wine that must be special-ordered. If the expected guest count is 100, you will need to order enough wine to handle 105 people.

Usually you will estimate 2½ servings of wine per guest for the typical dinner banquet. In this example, you will need to order enough wine to serve 263 glasses (105 × 2.5). Since the standard wine glass holds a 5-ounce portion (approximately 148 ml), you will need to special-order fifty-two 750-ml bottles of wine. The calculations are:

1. Divide the amount of liquor per 750-ml bottle by the serving size. This will tell you how many potential drinks you can obtain per container.

$$750 \text{ ml} \div 148 \text{ ml} = 5.07 \text{ potential drinks per bottle}$$

2. Divide the number of servings needed by the number of potential drinks per container. This will tell you how many containers you will need to special order.

$$263 \text{ servings} \div 5.07 = 51.87 \text{ (rounded to 52) 750-ml bottles needed}$$

If you take into account overpouring, waste, and the fact that usually you cannot get every last drop out of a bottle, you will need to increase the size of your special order. For instance, if you assume that you will lose 1 ounce (approximately 30 ml) per 750-ml bottle, your order will be about fifty-five bottles. The calculations are:

$$(750 - 30) \text{ ml} \div 148 \text{ ml} = 4.86 \text{ potential drinks per bottle}$$
$$263 \text{ servings} \div 4.86 = 54.11 \text{ (rounded to 55) 750-ml bottles}$$

Some liquor distributors may not allow you to place a special order in anything less than case lots. In our example, then, you may need to special-order sixty 750-ml bottles (five cases, twelve bottles per case) because the liquor distributor may not want to break a case for you. When special-ordering product, generally you would have the client commit to the full amount ordered unless you are certain you can sell any remaining product to another event.

As you could lose profit if you are unable to sell any remaining product to another event, it is important to price the special-order item at a level that will not compromise your beverage pour cost.

Unopened leftovers could find their way into complimentary fruit baskets for favorite clients who generate a good deal of business for you. Or if the catered event is held in a hotel or country club, opened and unopened wine could be sent to the client's hospitality suite or used for another function the client is planning. For instance, if the client has booked three meal functions, perhaps the leftover wine can be used for the next event.

The liquor distributor may be willing to exchange unopened leftovers for something you normally use. While the typical supplier may not want to take back one or two bottles, he or she is usually willing to take back unopened cases in trade. If the client agrees, you could charge the client by the case, order an extra case or two, keep the few leftover loose bottles, and return the unopened cases to the liquor distributor for credit.

Finally, you could charge the client by the bottle or by the case and let him or her take home any leftover wine. Before you do this, though, check the local liquor code to see if it is legal. For instance, your property may need to hold a package-goods liquor license before you can let the client take home unopened liquor. And opened stock may have to be served solely for consumption on the premises.

To avoid the problem of leftovers, you could special-order, say, four cases of wine (forty-eight 750-ml bottles), serve all of this wine first, and when it runs out, back it up with another wine from your standard wine list. However, make sure that you advise the client before doing this.

Quality of Foods Needed

The quality of foods used is dictated by product specifications and by standardized recipes prepared by management. For instance, a catering operation that is part of a chain organization typically will have a vice president of purchasing and a vice president of food and beverage operations on the corporate level, who usually have the final responsibility for making these quality determinations.

Before you requisition foods, you must examine the standardized recipes very carefully so that you know exactly what you need. For example, if the corporate recipe calls for Kraft cheese, you must requisition this brand name. You cannot requisition another brand of cheese because the recipe is specifically geared for Kraft. Since other brands are not quite comparable, the finished product will not be the same if you substitute another brand.

Likewise with other product identification factors. You must requisition the correct product quality, size, color, package size, degree of preservation, type of processing, and so forth, if you expect to maintain quality control. Actual quality that differs from the expected quality, no matter how slightly, is unacceptable.

In addition to quality control, product specifications and standardized recipes help ensure cost control. When you cost out your standardized recipes, you will use purchase prices based on the types of ingredients noted in them. If you use a substitute and do not account for any difference in cost, your final accounting will show an actual food cost that is more or less than what you budgeted. If the actual cost exceeds the budgeted standard cost, the operation will suffer a loss. If the actual is less than the standard, clients may be cheated because they will have received foods that were inconsistent with the menu prices quoted.

Quality of Alcoholic Beverages Needed

As with food, the quality of alcoholic beverages served will depend on the product specifications and standardized recipes used to prepare finished drinks. Unlike food, though, there usually is one more thing to consider: the client's desires to have certain brands of liquor served at the catered event.

Some clients will not specify brand names. Since well brands usually cost less than call brands, some clients will be satisfied with them. Consumer preferences, though, indicate that while people are drinking less, they are drinking higher-quality products. Premium brands are in vogue, and more clients today are asking the caterer to provide a choice of high-quality wines, spirits, and beers.

Brand names are the primary selection factor used when developing alcoholic beverage product specifications, standardized recipes, drink menus, and stock requisitions. However, when requisitioning these items from the liquor storeroom, there are a few additional factors that must be noted.

For instance, you will need to note the container sizes for each product needed. Generally speaking, for spirits, you will use 750 ml or 1 liter bottles if you free-pour the drinks, and 1.5 liter or 1.75 liter bottles if you use an electronic dispensing unit to prepare drinks.

When requisitioning beers, more than likely you will want 12-ounce bottles or cans. If you have a portable draft-beer dispensing unit, you would requisition the appropriate keg size that fits it.

Wines come in various container sizes. Generally this flexibility allows the client more cost-saving opportunities. For instance, you can purchase wines in 750 ml and 1.5 liter bottles. Less expensive products, such as well wines, can be purchased in larger bottles and in bag-in-the-box containers (a large plastic bag of wine inside a cardboard box that is designed to be used as a self-dispensing package).

As with food, your drink product specifications and standardized recipes help ensure cost and quality control. Without these guidelines, it will be very difficult to forecast accurately the beverage costs. In this case, price quotations offered to potential clients may not be as competitive as they should be.

Food Pre-Preparation

Food pre-preparation activities generally are performed a day or more before the meal function. They include all the food production steps that can be performed ahead of time that will not compromise the quality of finished menu items. For instance, if the menu calls for vegetables and dip, a pantry person can prepare these items the day before and refrigerate them. Or if the menu calls for an egg action station, a cook can pre-prep the egg mixes, dice the vegetables, and lay out the bacon on sheet pans the night before.

Generally speaking, the larger the function, the more pre-prep that must be done in advance. For instance, a banquet of 5,000 prime rib dinners may require you to start pre-plating the meals several hours in advance and put them in a holding cabinet (hot box). The best cook-and-hold equipment will maintain the product's temperature and culinary quality for several hours.

Some caterers have adopted the sous-vide form of pre-preparation. This involves the production of finished or semi-finished menu items about a week or more before they are needed. After they are produced, the foods are then vacuum-packed and stored in the refrigerator until needed. Commercially prepared sous-vide products are also available.

Sous-vide production has expanded the number and type of menu items that can be pre-prepared. For instance, if you have a party next week and grilled salmon will be on the menu, today you can sear, season, and vacuum-package the filets, then cook them in their plastic pouches. When done, the individually packaged salmon portions must be cooled rapidly and stored in the refrigerator. A few minutes before service, you reheat and plate them.

Sous vide offers several culinary advantages. For instance, with normal cooking procedures, you would be unable to serve grilled salmon to a large group of people while simultaneously maintaining quality control.

Unfortunately, sous-vide procedures can contribute to food-borne illness if they are not monitored closely. Sanitation is extremely important when food is vacuum-packaged. If harmful bacteria are left in the package, some guests consuming the food may become ill.

The catering executive should try to include as many pre-prep items as possible. This makes it much easier to plan food production. It gives you more control over the labor work schedules. You can utilize production labor more efficiently. And it ensures that the correct amount of foods will be available when it is time to prepare the finished products.

Bar Pre-Preparation

Bar pre-prep is much easier than food pre-prep. Generally, it includes stocking the portable bars with all non-perishables whenever it is convenient to do so. Then, just prior to service, you pre-prep your garnishes, requisition the items needed, load the ice bins, and ice down water bottles, soft drinks, wine bottles, and bottles or cans of beer.

If the banquet bars are permanent or semi-permanent fixtures and can be secured, bar backs and/or bartenders can restock them after a catered event according to the specifications noted on the banquet event order for the next function. For instance, when a party is over, the manager can take an ending inventory and determine the liquor usage for that function. The bar back or bartender can then replenish the bar with non-perishables so that the bar production workers the next day need only spend a few minutes pre-prepping the perishables.

Food Preparation

Food preparation activities are performed just prior to the point of service. For example, your preparation schedule for hot foods should dovetail with your guest service schedule. You would not want to produce these products too far in advance, or else they will lose culinary quality. Nor would you want to produce them to customer order, (except at action stations), as this will slow down service.

A good food production schedule combines the pre-prep and prep activities. For instance, if you have a baked chicken item on the menu, you can do some pre-prep work the night before, such as washing the products, seasoning them, and laying them out on sheet pans. About an hour or so before service, you will prep them, putting them in the oven to cook.

Finish Cooking

Finish cooking involves cooking to guest order. For instance, the chef usually does not prep steaks in advance; he or she must wait for the guest to order.

Finish cooking is the most difficult part of the food production plan. It is also the most labor-intensive. You need to schedule a lot of worker hours. And the worker hours must be provided by highly skilled food handlers who can work under the demanding conditions that accompany most finish-cooking activities.

For instance, a chef working at an egg action station must be quick, efficient, and accurate. He or she normally will be producing two or three guest orders at a time and will need to remember them as well as those that are coming in from other guests waiting in line.

Bar Preparation

In most instances, bar prep is synonymous with bar service—that is, the same person who prepares the drink also serves it and, if applicable, collects cash or a drink ticket.

In those instances where cocktail servers use a service bar to obtain drinks for their guests, the prep and service activities are separated; the bartender preps drinks only when the servers order them. For cost control purposes, usually a server must give a drink ticket or cash to the bartender before a drink can be prepared, unless the entire bar is hosted.

Food Workstation Setup

Action stations, serving lines, and buffet tables must be set up prior to service. In some catering operations the kitchen staff has this responsibility, while other properties split the work between the kitchen and service staffs. For instance, cooks may be responsible for setting up the serving lines in the kitchen or in the service corridor and setting up the action stations, while the kitchen and banquet setup crews together set up the buffet tables. Generally speaking, the kitchen handles the foods and the service staff handles the table setups.

Replenishing the Food Workstations

The kitchen normally is responsible for replenishing the food supplies on buffet tables, action stations, and serving lines. Usually a food runner is employed to handle this task. In some cases, though, the service staff might take on this duty. For instance, the kitchen crew may be responsible for stocking backup foods in hot boxes and delivering them to a service corridor. A food server can then be assigned to replenish depleted food stations with foods taken from these hot boxes.

Employees assigned this responsibility typically must do more than merely refill serving containers. They must be able to anticipate customer needs, combine half-empty pans and make the combination appear as attractive as any other container, and react to the chef's last-minute instructions. It is important to note that combining food trays or pans on any buffet should be done in the back of the house, not in the room while guests are present as this type of work can be unsightly, messy, noisy, and slow down the line. They also may need to pitch in and help keep buffet tables clear of soiled tableware and trash.

Replenishing the Bars

Bar backs are responsible for replenishing liquor, ice, garnishes, glassware, and direct operating supplies, such as coasters, stir sticks, and cocktail napkins. Most bartenders will also jump in and help restock merchandise in an emergency, such as when the bar back is helping out at another beverage function that is shorthanded.

Cocktail servers may also help out in a pinch. For instance, if there are one or two special drink requests that cannot be prepared by the bartender because he or she does not have the stock available, a cocktail server may go to another bar to fill them. Or during a particularly busy period a cocktail server may jump behind the bar temporarily and help the bartender get caught up.

Number of Food Production People Needed

While the banquet service staff concentrates solely on the scheduled meal function to which it is assigned, the typical food handler likely juggles many tasks. For example, food handlers may be responsible for food production for multiple events. Catering in a hotel or club may be part of the central kitchen's duties, with food handlers also responsible for other restaurants.

It is therefore a bit more difficult to determine exactly how much food production labor is needed for a particular meal function. On one hand, the cooks on duty in a restaurant outlet may be able to handle the entire catered event along with their other responsibilities. At the other end of the spectrum is the catered function that requires a completely separate kitchen crew. For some meal functions you may not have any additional variable labor costs, whereas for others the food production payroll will be a significant portion of total expenses.

In general, the number of food production work hours needed for a catered event will depend on several factors:

1. *Number of guests.*
2. *Amount of time scheduled for the catered event.*
3. *Applicable union and company personnel policies.*
4. *Type of service style used.* For instance, action stations require more production labor, whereas the typical buffet that offers only standardized menu items will need less.
5. *Amount of convenience foods used.* Processed foods are less expensive to prep and serve. You need fewer labor hours to reconstitute them. You also avoid expensive labor expertise because the products require less skill to handle. However, their purchase prices usually are very high because of the built-in labor, transportation, packaging, and energy costs that the manufacturer must

recapture. You may not use processed foods often, though, if they are not of high enough quality to maintain your standards. Also, many consumers have become less willing to accept processed foods that contain chemical preservatives, trans fats, or high-fructose corn syrup.

6. *Amount of scratch production.* This is the opposite of convenience foods usage. The closer a food ingredient is to its natural state, the lower its purchase price will be. A significant amount of scratch production results in a low food cost. However, you will end up with a higher labor cost since you take on all of the pre-prep and prep burdens. If the local labor market is tight, the resulting labor cost incurred may be prohibitive.

7. *Amount of finish cooking needed.* Too much finish cooking wreaks havoc with a food production labor budget. If the client wants a great deal of this, chances are he or she must be willing to pay a handsome labor surcharge.

8. *Type of menu items offered.* Some products take more time to pre-prep and prep. For instance, it takes more time to produce meat loaf than roast beef, vegetable soup than onion soup, and galantine of capon than roast duckling.

9. *Number of last-minute requests.* Flexibility is one of the hallmarks of a successful catering operation. You must be flexible enough to accommodate some unscheduled requests. For instance, you should be ready to produce one or two vegetarian meals on a moment's notice. Ideally clients will inform you well in advance about special needs; however, chances are there will always be at least one guest requesting an off-menu item at the last minute.

10. *Number of special diets.* It can take almost as long to produce two or three meals for special diets as it does to take care of fifty standard guest meals. If you know about these needs in advance you can be ready for them. Furthermore, once you start producing a different menu item for each guest, you immediately lose the labor and food cost advantages that catering enjoys over regular restaurant food production and service.

11. *Accuracy of mealtime estimates.* It is not unusual for a meal function to start late and end late. This, unfortunately, may result in overtime pay for some production staff. It also can necessitate overtime pay for other employees, such as servers, housekeeping, and security, because their work schedules may be thrown off.

When catered functions run behind schedule, you must expect to incur a higher labor cost. It is also likely that the foods may have lost a good deal of their culinary quality. Unfortunately, when these things happen, the caterer's costs increase and the quality of the entire event decreases. These things will happen once in a while. That is why it is very important to diplomatically remind clients that the property needs to stay on schedule as much as possible.

In most operations it is the chef's responsibility to prepare staffing charts to help determine the number of food production work hours needed, how many people to call in to work the function, and how these people should be scheduled. (In some very small organizations, catering managers handle these responsibilities.) These charts usually relate the number of work hours needed to the number of expected guests. For instance, if you expect 100 guests, you go down the column headed by 100 and in each cell there will be a number of suggested work hours needed for each job classification.

Assume you are allowed 16 food production hours for 100 guests. If the meal function will last four hours, you can divide the 16 work hours into four 4-hour shifts and bring in four people. You also can schedule one 8-hour person and two 4-hour employees, or any other acceptable combination.

Distributing work hours over a work schedule also depends on how many food production people you want on board before, during, and after the meal function. Usually you will need to stagger the work schedule in such a way that most of your production work hours are used when the lion's share of the production must be completed, with the remaining hours left to cover the start-up and teardown periods.

Staffing charts work well in service planning because once you know the timing of the function, the menu, the number of guests, and the style of service needed, you can usually lock in a standardized work schedule.

Kitchen staffing charts must be continually revised unless your catering business settles into some sort of predictable pattern. The chef will usually keep a close eye on the staffing chart and change it as needed. He or she also will be forever looking for that elusive pattern, which can make it much easier to forecast food production payroll expenses and develop accurate food production work schedules.

Number of Bar Backs and Bartenders Needed

The number of bar backs needed for a catered function will depend primarily on these factors:

1. Number of bars scheduled
2. Capacity of each bar to hold in-process inventories
3. Distance between the bars and the kitchen and storerooms
4. Degree of ease or difficulty associated with retrieving backup stock
5. Number of guests
6. Hours of operation
7. Variety of liquor stock, glassware, garnishes, and direct operating supplies needed at the bars
8. Applicable union and company personnel policies

Unless the catered event is very small, you will need at least one bar back. The typical banquet bar, especially the portable one, does not have a lot of storage capacity and usually will need periodic replenishment.

The number of bartenders needed for a catered event will depend primarily on these factors:

1. Number of bars scheduled
2. Whether the bar is cash or hosted
3. Types of drinks that must be prepared
4. Number of drinks that must be prepared
5. Number of guests
6. Hours of operation
7. Amount of bar-back work that must be performed
8. Applicable union and company personnel policies

You will need at least one bartender for each bar location. For large beverage functions, you usually would schedule two bartenders for each bar plus any wine service personnel needed for the meal.

The standard in the industry is one bartender for every 100 guests for a hosted bar. For cash bars, where guests tend to consume less, that is sometimes adjusted to one bartender for every 125–150 guests. Some meeting and event planners will request a ratio of one bartender for every 75 guests. The catering executive must evaluate the overall event before committing to this request. The 1-to-75 ratio may be necessary if you expect all guests to arrive at the same time. If you do not have enough bartenders when a crowd hits the door, some guests may have to wait longer than your standard to get a drink.

If you have more than 1,000 guests, the ratio of one bartender to each 100 guests is appropriate. With a large crowd, guests cannot move around as much. And with ten bartenders, the preparation and service tends to be quicker and more efficient because the bartenders can help each other and keep the lines moving.

The timing of a beverage function can also influence the number of bartenders needed. For instance, if 200 people are leaving a business meeting and going directly to a cocktail reception, you may want to set a ratio of one bartender for each 50–75 guests so that they will be served quickly. If there is a break period between the end of the business meeting and the beginning of the cocktail reception, so guests can take the time to go home or to their hotel rooms to freshen up, they will not arrive all at once. As they will usually come in a few at a time, you could use fewer bartenders to handle this group.

To alleviate pressure on the bartenders, you could schedule a few servers to pass glasses of champagne, wine, bottled water, and other beverages. This also adds an extra touch of elegance to the event.

A food server, busperson, captain, or other member of the catering and kitchen staffs could be used to help out the bartenders and bar backs. For instance, it might be more economical to schedule one 6-hour busperson to handle busing and bar back duties than to schedule one 4-hour bar back and one 4-hour busperson.

If you decide to mix and match job classifications and adopt these types of creative scheduling techniques, you will need to check the union joint bargaining agreement, if applicable, and the company's personnel policies and procedures manual to see if they are permissible. Furthermore, you must ensure that the relevant staff members have received the proper type and amount of cross-training needed.

Number of Cashiers Needed

If a cashier is required to sell drink tickets, you will need at least one on duty. Normally you will need only one cashier if the catered function is small or if it is a leisurely event where guests are not pressed for time. Larger functions, as well as those where speed is essential, require more cashiers. Under these conditions, generally you will have to schedule one cashier for every two bartenders.

If you are using cashiers, you may want to schedule a plainclothes security guard to supervise and protect the cash-handling operations. A plainclothes guard sometimes is preferable to a uniformed guard because some guests may become a bit anxious if they see uniformed security.

If you have a security guard scheduled to supervise the beverage function, and if the group being serviced is not too large, he or she could also oversee the cash-handling operations. With a large group of guests, though, you should consider scheduling at least one security guard to supervise liquor preparation and service and one to oversee the cash-handling procedures.

Number of Ticket Takers Needed

If guests must use tickets to enter a function room, or if they need to use them to get into a meal or beverage function, you may or may not have to schedule a ticket taker to collect them. In most cases, clients will handle this chore personally; however, on some occasions you will be asked to provide this service.

You should avoid coming between the client and his or her guests in what sometimes could be a confrontational occurrence. You do not want to be put in a position where you must impose client sanctions on guests. Furthermore, some guests may not appreciate the caterer assuming this control position.

Drink tickets and other similar tickets (such as entree tickets used by guests at buffet functions) do not usually cause confrontational problems. Consequently, if guests are required to use them, there generally is no need to schedule separate ticket takers. In these cases, bartenders and servers can collect them.

Number of Banquet Setup Crew Members Needed

The number of people needed to set up, tear down, and clean a function room will depend primarily on these factors:

1. Amount of lead time available
2. Size of the catered event
3. Size of the room or other location
4. Whether the room or other location is on your property or off-site
5. Amount of time available between functions (for example, how much time you have to tear down and clean up after a breakfast function and set up for an afternoon reception)
6. Amount of setup (for instance, if you are catering off-site, the client may handle part of the setup, or if you are catering a meal function at a local hall rented by the client, part of the rental fee may include room setup)
7. Applicable union and company personnel policies

If you have a lot of time available or if the function planned is for 50 guests or less, usually you can get by with only one crew member. For larger functions, or if time is precious, usually no fewer than two people must be scheduled. Two or more crew members may also be needed if some tasks require the strength and agility of at least two people to accomplish. For example, setting up risers, rolling out and setting up a portable dance floor, or hanging signage or decorations often requires two people working in tandem.

Usually a caterer wants function rooms set up as soon as possible. All nonperishable items should be set out in advance so that staff members can concentrate on the last-minute details and not have to worry about doing things during prime times (times when guest service is a priority) that could have been done quite comfortably during slack times (times when guests are not being served).

SERVICE PLANNING

Unlike production planning, service planning is a much easier task. Once you know the timing of the function, the menu, the number of guests, and the style of service, you usually can forecast an accurate estimate of the number of service work hours needed, the number and types of servers required, and the most efficient work schedule that should be followed.

Types of Servers Needed

Depending on the type of catered event, the banquet manager will need to schedule one or more of the following types of service personnel:

1. Captain
2. Food server
3. Bartender
4. Cocktail server
5. Sommelier
6. Food runner
7. Busperson

Service Duties

Service personnel are responsible for a wide array of duties. Unlike production staff members, servers are often called upon to jump in at a moment's notice and handle unscheduled requests and/or activities. For instance, while the typical client would not consider asking the chef to change the menu at the last minute, he or she may not be shy about asking the captain to set up an extra dining table, slow down service because the speaker is running a bit late, or push two tables together so that a larger group can create its own party atmosphere.

Service personnel must be very flexible. All of them should be trained to perform the following functions:

1. Napkin folds
2. Table settings
3. Placing table pads and tablecloths
4. Pre-setting foods on dining tables
5. Greeting and seating guests
6. Taking food and beverage orders from guests (if guests have a choice of entrees and beverages)
7. Serving food and beverages

8. Submitting guests' food and beverage orders to chefs and bartenders (if guests have a choice of entrees and beverages)

9. Opening wine bottles

10. Pouring wine

11. Hot beverage service

12. Cold beverage service

13. Crumbing tables

14. Busing tables

15. Carrying loaded cocktail, oval, and crescent-shaped trays

16. Stacking trays

17. Emptying trays

18. Tableside preparation

19. Using different service styles

20. Handling last-minute requests for food, beverage, and service

21. Handling complaints

22. Directing guests to other locations in the property or general area

23. Handling disruptions

24. Dealing with intoxicated guests

25. Refusing liquor service to minors

26. Requisitioning tableware and linens

Service Ratios

Service ratios—the number of service personnel needed to handle a given number of guests—are usually established by management. These ratios are the heart of the service staffing guide.

The number of service personnel needed depends on many factors. The primary ones are:

1. *Number of guests.*

2. *Length of the catered function.*

3. *Style of service used.*

4. *Menu, especially its length and complexity.*

5. *Timing of the event.* For instance, you may need fewer servers if there will be a considerable amount of time between courses because of speakers, dancing,

or stage shows. Similarly, if the group needs to be fed very quickly, you will need more service personnel (though, since you will not need them very long, you might be able to handle the catered event adequately without exceeding your labor budget).

6. *Room setup.* Are the layout and design conducive to quick, efficient service, or are bottlenecks expected?

7. *Location of function room.* How much distance is there between the kitchen and the function room? Is there enough aisle space? Is the service corridor large enough? Are there enough service elevators?

8. *The probability that overtime must be scheduled.* For instance, experience may suggest that a particular type of catered event or a particular type of group will tend to run late. This could result in overtime pay for a few service personnel. However, if you can anticipate this problem, you should be able to schedule enough employees to handle the event properly without resorting to overtime.

9. *Number of guests at the head table.* These guests require much more service attention than do the others.

10. *Number and type of extraordinary requests.* For instance, a client may want extra labor to seat guests after they go through a buffet line. Some guests may request extra condiments, which will add to the service workload. And some clients, at the last minute, may want the room rearranged somewhat; usually the service personnel have to handle this type of last-minute request because the setup crew may be unavailable on short notice.

11. *Applicable union and company personnel policies.* Unionized caterers must schedule at least the minimum number of service personnel called for in the union contract. Nonunion properties whose competitors are unionized may also follow these standard ratios.

Experience shows that the minimum number of servers as well as the minimum number of each service job classification that must be scheduled according to union regulations usually are insufficient to provide the level of service required by most catered events. You generally will need more servers if, for example, you need to serve a large luncheon very quickly, or if you must provide French service for a dinner function.

The union's collective bargaining agreement typically provides enough servers to accommodate only small and easy-to-handle groups. These service minimums, though, at least give you something to work with when forecasting the number of servers needed.

Many caterers develop strict service ratios and do not vary from them even though a particular situation may call for it. For instance, some properties will budget one server for every 32 guests regardless of the style of service, the type of menu, or whether the servers are responsible for wine service.

If you adhere strictly to this 1-to-32 ratio, you may risk customer dissatisfaction. Some catered events can be handled adequately under this formula. However, most full-service meals will need more help or else they cannot be serviced efficiently.

Irrespective of the quality of a catered function's food and beverage, room setup, and overall ambience, poor service reduces significantly the guests' appreciation and enjoyment of the event. Customer surveys consistently show that patrons rank the quality of service very high on their list of desired catering attributes. They usually place it no lower than second on their lists, ranking it just slightly behind the quality of the food and beverage.

Poor service will overshadow any other favorable aspect of the event. Guests will never be pleased if the service is lacking. They will usually remember a bad experience much longer than a good one. The catering executive who tries to shave service costs to the bone will undoubtedly make a lot of clients and guests unhappy. He or she will also jeopardize repeat patronage.

If you are on a very tight labor budget, at times you will be between a rock and a hard place. You will be asked to maintain the budget, yet provide a level of service that will satisfy guests and encourage clients to return. You cannot risk coming in over budget. If the catered event's projected revenue will not cover the extra labor costs, the least you should do is ask the client to alter his or her menu or service requirements, or agree to pay a modest labor surcharge so that you can schedule adequate staff.

Experience shows that the number of service personnel needed can vary from a low of about one staff member for every 8 guests at a high-end plated dinner to a high of approximately one staff member for every 75 guests for a casual reception.

Industry experts suggest that the minimum service ratio for conventional sit-down meal functions with plated (American) service with some foods pre-set is one server for every 20 guests. If you are using rounds of 10, you should schedule one server for every two dining tables. If you are using rounds of 8, two servers should be scheduled to handle five dining tables.

The minimum busperson ratio for this sit-down meal is one busperson for every three servers. If you are using rounds of 10, you should schedule one busperson for every six dining tables. If you are using rounds of 8, one busperson should be scheduled for every eight dining tables.

Some caterers will schedule one busperson for every two servers. This is usually done for functions that include several VIPs or where extraordinary service is requested by the client. Generally speaking, though, you can make do with one busperson for every three servers because servers normally are expected to perform some busperson work during the catered event.

If the conventional sit-down meal function includes Russian, French, or poured-wine service, you normally will need one server for every 16 guests. You should schedule one server for every two rounds of 8, or two servers for every three rounds of 10. One busperson for every six rounds of 10, or every eight rounds of 8, will usually suffice.

If the meal function includes Russian or French service along with poured-wine service, generally you will need at least one server for each dining table and one busperson for every three dining tables. This ratio is appropriate whether you are using rounds of 8 or rounds of 10.

If the meal function is served buffet-style, usually servers and buspeople can handle significantly more guests. For instance, the minimum service ratio of one server for each 20 guests and one busperson for every three servers could very easily be increased to one server for every 40 guests and one busperson for every four servers.

In some cases you may want to maintain the ratio of one server for each 20 guests for a buffet-style meal function. For instance, if the kitchen schedules a small crew, or if it has to handle several parties, it may be unable to refresh the buffet tables and help serve guests. You could use the balance of your waitstaff to focus on these tasks.

If the buffet requires considerable replenishment during the meal, you may need to schedule servers to handle the food-running chores. In this situation, normally one food runner (or other service employee) is needed for every 100 to 125 guests. You will need more runners if they are expected to accommodate several buffet stations spread throughout the function room. Conversely, if there are only a few buffet stations or a limited menu, other food servers could share the workload, and you should be able to schedule fewer runners. Moreover, if the chef schedules food runners, scheduling servers will be a bit easier.

Head tables usually receive the best service. If the catered function has head tables, you should plan to schedule at least one server for each head table. If a head table includes more than eight guests, you should assign two servers to accommodate them.

Ideally, the head table would have its own busperson. If you cannot afford this or do not need a separate busperson, you should assign the head table and one or two other nearby dining tables to one busperson. If possible, you should not have head-table servers handling both the serving and busing chores. They should devote their efforts to guest service.

If you need to staff a reception, you must schedule enough servers to supervise the food stations. Generally speaking, you should have one server responsible for every three food stations. If the stations are spread throughout the function room and there is considerable distance between each one, you will need more servers.

The servers responsible for overseeing the food stations can also perform some busing duties. For instance, they can help replenish the tableware, bus the area, and remove waste. Depending on the size and complexity of the reception, you may be able to get by with few or no buspeople.

You will need more servers if you intend to pass food trays butler-style during a reception. For a small catered event, one or two servers would suffice. As the function size increases, you normally need to schedule one server to handle one-fourth of the function room, one-eighth of the function room, and so forth. Generally speaking, you should plan to schedule at least two servers for every 75 guests. To reduce the amount of food consumption, servers can be sent out in waves at timed intervals. Servers should be assigned to specific sections of the room to ensure that all guests have access to the food.

You also will need more buspeople if you have servers pass trays during the reception. The servers usually will be unable to pitch in and help with the busing duties because they will be too busy with guests. You should expect to schedule at least one busperson for every three to four servers.

Even if there is no food served during a reception, you still should schedule at least one or two buspeople to pick up discarded glasses, napkins, and other trash. Perhaps a busperson or two could be brought in earlier than the others to cover the reception's busing needs; then after the reception, they can help out during the meal function's rush period.

If you are using beverage servers during a reception to pass trays of pre-made drinks, you will need at least one beverage server for every two to three food servers. Usually you need considerably fewer beverage servers than food servers in this situation because guests tend to approach the food servers more frequently than they do the cocktail servers. For instance, a guest might take a glass of wine from a tray and nurse it throughout the reception, whereas he or she will usually take more than one piece of food.

Very few catered events use cocktail servers to take guest drink orders, return to a service bar to fill them, and then go back on the floor to serve them. This type of service is infeasible for large group functions. Generally it is done only for small functions, especially those that cater to VIPs. The type of service most often used for standard catered events requires the guests to approach the portable bars, get their drinks, disappear into the crowd, and return when they want more drinks.

If you do use cocktail service to take guest orders, though, your labor costs will increase significantly. In this situation, at best a server can usually make only three or four passes per hour through his or her assigned floor area. During each pass, he or she will usually be able to carry, at the most, only twelve to sixteen drinks. In the best-case scenario, then, you would need one cocktail server to handle forty-eight to sixty-four drinks per hour. Furthermore, since this type of service is less efficient and requires more coordination and effort, you will need more bartenders to handle the workload. Many receptions last only about one hour. Some will last up to two hours. If it is a one-hour period, you normally expect each guest to consume at least two drinks. For a two-hour period, you expect each guest to consume at least three drinks. If you have a one-hour cocktail reception for 100 people and the client wants cocktail servers to take drink orders from guests, you will need about two bartenders and four or five cocktail servers to handle the drink orders efficiently. If you have a two-hour reception, though, guests will not drink so quickly, and some of them will leave before the reception ends; consequently, you may be able to get by with fewer bartenders and cocktail servers. Unfortunately, in this instance most guests will do the bulk of their drinking during the first hour, so you may be unable to reduce your service requirements significantly.

When clients are faced with the exorbitant labor cost associated with having cocktail servers take guest orders, they generally decide against it. But even if a client is willing to pay the extra labor charges, you still might want to discourage such a labor-intensive style of service because there are too many opportunities for the catered event to bog down. For instance, at a pre-dinner reception, if guests need to wait too long for their drinks, the reception, and ultimately the dinner, will probably run much longer than scheduled.

On the other hand, sometimes slower cocktail service can be a cost savings for a client. If there is a host bar at a cocktail reception, for example, guests may be tempted to overindulge, whereas if they give their orders to a server, their consumption will probably be much less.

Regardless of the style of service or type of event, you usually will need to schedule at least one floor supervisor. This supervisor could be a banquet captain or a lead server.

Generally speaking, you should plan to schedule at least one banquet captain for each catered event. For very large meal functions, you should plan to schedule one banquet captain for every block of 250 guests (i.e., for every block of 25 rounds of 10). Alternatively, you could schedule one banquet captain for every ten to twelve servers.

The banquet captain for a small catered event can supervise both the meal service and the reception service. For example, if there are only 100 guests, one floor supervisor is sufficient to handle both segments.

If you need to schedule more than one banquet captain, you should assign one assistant banquet manager to coordinate their duties. For instance, if you have a meal function for 1,000 guests, typically you would assign one assistant banquet manager and four banquet captains to supervise service. If there is a pre-meal reception, the assistant banquet manager should supervise both the meal service and the reception.

You should not try to serve a function without a sufficient number of floor supervisors. These men and women play an extremely important role in coordinating service and seeing to it that all guests are served efficiently. As one example, with a sit-down meal function it is important to have all the guests served a course at approximately the same time. This will not happen by itself. It is a difficult feat to achieve, and it is almost impossible to accomplish without adequate supervision and coordination.

Work Scheduling

The banquet manager usually sets aside enough time one day each week to prepare the service work schedules for the following week. Each week he or she must prepare a fixed work schedule and a variable work schedule.

The fixed schedule represents the minimum number of people and number of work hours needed to keep the catering operation open and active, regardless of the volume of business expected. For instance, if there is at least one catered function each day, you will need a handful of permanent full-time or part-time people scheduled to provide the level of service expected by guests.

If you do a great deal of catering business, these permanent employees can be scheduled solely for catered functions. If the catering business varies, with several peaks and valleys, you can still have permanent staff members assigned to catering, though you might have to share them with another department. For instance, in a country club, you might have a full-time employee assigned to catering, with the understanding that if catering business is slow, he or she will work in the main dining room also.

The more fixed employees you have, the easier it is to prepare your weekly work schedules. It is also more conducive to employee satisfaction. Permanent employees usually have steady, predictable work schedules. They will appreciate the ability to plan their personal lives more accurately.

Variable labor is incremental labor. It will fluctuate with the volume of catering business. The caterer usually must schedule a large number of variable employees each week. Unlike the typical restaurant operator, the variable work schedule will usually need to be prepared each week. Catering business can be predictable for some companies, but the uniqueness of each catered function forces you to contact A-list and B-list employees every week in order to prepare a proper work schedule.

The work schedules will be based primarily on these variables:

1. Types of functions booked that week
2. Expected lengths of each function
3. Number of guests anticipated
4. Styles of service required
5. Allowable labor costs
6. Employee availability
7. Degree of guest satisfaction required (that is, how much pampering you have to provide)

Typically you would use this information, applicable union regulations, and the staffing guidelines set forth in the staffing charts to prepare the appropriate work schedules.

When preparing work schedules, you will need to allocate a sufficient number of work hours to cover the pre-opening and teardown periods. You should stagger your servers so that some arrive and leave earlier than others. You should aim to have the maximum number of workers available when the catered functions are in high gear and fewer scheduled at function beginnings and endings.

Scheduling the appropriate number of work hours while simultaneously adhering to your labor budget may be hard to accomplish in some situations. For instance, if you are working in a union property, the union contract may require you to guarantee each employee you call in a minimum four-hour work schedule that day. If you need a few people one day to cover three-hour shifts, you are free to schedule them for three hours apiece. However, you must pay them for four hours.

It was noted earlier in this chapter that the minimum number of servers required by the typical collective bargaining agreement usually does not cause problems for you because this minimum normally is insufficient to handle most types of catered events. However, the minimum number of guaranteed work hours can cause problems if you have several bookings that lend themselves to scheduling several service personnel for less than the minimum.

Even a nonunion property may have a policy of paying a minimum number of work hours, so as to compete with unionized operations for workers. To say the least, this will make it more difficult to economically schedule some catered functions.

Timing of Service

The client and the catering sales representative normally discuss the timing of the service and these desires are relayed to the service staff. The banquet manager must take these desires and develop a plan that will provide maximum efficiency with minimum bottlenecks.

Service will make or break a catered function. If half the guests are waiting for their entrees while the other half are eating dessert, there is a problem. Also, if the guests at the head table, which usually receives the best service, are finished before other guests, they will have to wait for the others to finish or will have to begin the program while some guests are still being served or are still eating.

Timing problems can be minimized or avoided by scheduling extra servers. However, the cost may be prohibitive.

An inexpensive way to minimize timing problems is to pre-set as much food and beverage on the dining tables as the client and menu will allow. This is especially important if the client is in a hurry. For instance, if the group has only one hour for lunch, many food items, such as appetizers or salads, rolls, butter, condiments, and desserts, can be pre-set on the dining tables.

Some caterers can offer luncheons that are entirely pre-set. For instance, salad and/or sandwich luncheons can be pre-set in such a way that guests can sit down and eat quickly. Servers would need to handle only cold beverage refills, coffee service, and special requests.

To ensure proper timing as well as smooth service, the banquet captain will normally call the roll of all service personnel about two hours before the catered function is scheduled to begin. All employees are called by name to confirm attendance. Work stations are assigned. Servers are informed of the menus, any special diets, special service requests, and so forth. Also during the roll call, the captain will describe all menu items so that guest inquiries can be answered without the need for servers to run back to the kitchen and check with the chef. Providing servers with a printed copy of the menu will make answering guest questions easier.

For most receptions, normally there is a scheduled starting and ending time. Usually only a few guests will arrive at the very beginning of the event. By the time the reception is half over, all guests will usually be present. Toward the end of the reception, you should begin to see guests leaving a few at a time.

Some receptions will have all guests there when they open. For instance, a cocktail reception that begins immediately after a convention group's last business meeting of the day usually will have maximum attendance when the doors open.

About fifteen minutes before you want the meal service to start, you should begin calling guests. You can start the music, dim the lights in the pre-function area, ring chimes, or make announcements to signal guests that it is time to enter the dining room. Servers should be standing ready at their stations when guests walk into the room, not against the wall talking with each other.

For most conventional sit-down meal functions, the salad course will usually take about twenty to thirty minutes, and the entree about thirty to fifty minutes, from serving to removing of plates. Dessert can usually be handled in approximately twenty to thirty minutes. Normally the entire banquet service will be about one and a quarter hours for the typical luncheon and two hours for the typical dinner event.

More elaborate meal functions may take a bit more time to serve. While the added diversions can enhance the dining experience, long meal functions tend to make guests a little anxious. Even if you are using elaborate service styles or other similar attractions, guests will begin to think something is wrong with the catering operation if the meal lasts much longer than two hours. In addition, recall that some potential guests will be very reluctant to attend the catered event if they suspect it will run on too long.

Teardown Procedures

As the function winds down, servers can begin performing a bit of teardown work. For instance, prior to serving dessert, they can crumb tables and remove nonessentials such as salt and pepper shakers and extra flatware. While the guests are enjoying their dessert, the servers can begin to refill the condiment containers in the back of the house and put them away.

As guests begin to trickle out, servers can see to it that all utensils and tableware are cleaned and returned properly. They can inventory all service equipment. And they can see to it that any necessary paperwork, such as drink and meal ticket accounting, is completed correctly.

Soon after all guests have left, all dining and buffet tables must be stripped. Soiled linens must be collected for cleaning and leftover clean linens must be returned to storage. Unless the tables must be set up for the next function, they will need to be broken down and put away by the banquet setup crew.

In properties such as hotels, the housekeeping or convention service staff members will need to come in and clean the floors, walls, hallways, mirrors, windows, and fixtures. In some properties, servers may help; for instance, at the end of the function, a server may run a vacuum cleaner over the heavy-traffic areas.

While housekeeping or convention service may be handling the cleaning chores, a server or two might be able to help set up for the next scheduled function. For instance, if you are tearing down after a luncheon and there is a dinner scheduled later, the banquet setup crew might want to get a head start by simultaneously tearing down and resetting the room. The crew would most likely appreciate any help service personnel can contribute. The kitchen staff may also need to reallocate a few leftover foods. Sometimes these foods can be used for the next catered function, by a property's restaurant outlets, or for employee dining.

If the leftover foods have lost some of their culinary quality, they should not be served again. For instance, foods that have been on a buffet table for an hour or more may be perfectly edible, but have deteriorated to the point where their appearance, taste, and texture are below your quality standards and should not be offered to other guests.

CATERING SAFETY AND SANITATION

Food and beverage production and service must be carried out in a safe and wholesome manner. Anyone handling foods and beverages must be trained to practice safety and sanitation procedures to ensure that employees and guests do not fall victims to accidents or food-borne illnesses.

All commercial foodservice operations must adhere to the sanitation standards set forth by their local health districts. These agencies periodically inspect food and beverage production and service personnel, equipment, and facilities to ensure that they comply with local rules and regulations.

Catering executives should consider following the sanitation guidelines developed by the National Restaurant Association Educational Foundation when training employees. In fact, any employee who completes successfully the Foundation's ServSafe sanitation course will earn a certification that is viewed favorably by all local health districts. If an employee successfully completes an advanced course, he or she will earn the Hazard Analysis and Critical Control Points (HACCP) certification.

Production and service equipment and facilities must meet pertinent standards of safety and sanitation. For instance, in most cities and counties in the United States, all food-contact equipment must display the familiar blue seal of the National Sanitation Foundation (NSF) International. Equipment that does not carry this seal usually cannot be used in commercial food and beverage operations.

Underwriters Laboratories (UL) and the American Gas Association (AGA) inspect and certify equipment compliance with generally accepted safety standards. For instance, a gas oven displaying the AGA seal is safe to use in commercial production. All commercial construction must meet building code guidelines. Most local building codes usually require all equipment and permanent installations to meet or exceed safety standards promulgated by these types of independent inspectors.

The safe and sanitary food and beverage operation also meets standards set by other local government agencies. For instance, the fire marshal will inspect periodically for fire hazards, such as blocked exits, overcrowding, and discharged fire extinguisher systems.

The Department of Labor is another agency concerned with safety matters. For example, if you hire a few teenagers to work as buspeople or food runners, they will not be able to perform all types of work. Usually people under eighteen years of age cannot operate machinery such as slicers, food processors, and dough-cutting machines. They also typically cannot fill, refill, or light fuel containers, such as Sterno pots.

The state workers' compensation agency is responsible for providing insurance to employers to cover employees against job-related injuries. And the Occupational Safety and Health Administration (OSHA) enforces federal regulations detailing required health and safety requirements for businesses. Caterers can call upon these agencies to help them develop effective employee safety training guidelines. Furthermore, the agencies can visit your property, point out areas of concern, and note what you can do to eliminate these hazards.

There are several safety and sanitation problems that must be controlled by the catering executive. Experience shows that the major ones are:

1. *Tableside and action station cooking.* Exhibition cooking poses many risks, even if it is performed by trained professional chefs who have a great deal of experience with this type of work.

Some parts of the country may prohibit exhibition cooking. You should check the local fire code to see if it is allowed in your area. If it is allowed, check further to see if there are any restrictions.

Action station cooking does not seem to be nearly as dangerous as tableside cooking, because usually there is sufficient aisle space set up to minimize the threat of accidents at the action station. Tableside cooking, especially the type involving flaming dishes, poses the most serious risk, and many companies have policies prohibiting this practice.

Rarely does tableside cooking result in a major fire. The accident would have to be very serious for any fire to overwhelm the modern property's sprinkler system. However, guest injury is another matter. Flaming dishes are an attractive addition to the catered event, providing an exciting and entertaining change of pace, and clients and guests are always pleased with these types of presentations. Unfortunately, the curious guest who gets a little too close to the action is liable to inhale hazardous gas or come into contact with a spark or flame.

Usually whenever you flame a dish, an extra server is stationed nearby to observe the spectacle and react to any emergency. This minimizes the fire hazard. However, you may not be able to control gases because usually you cannot see them leaking until some harm occurs.

You must be very careful when using Sterno, butane, propane, or other types of cooking fuels. Propane is especially troublesome and risky. When using propane, it does not matter how much training the chef has had. A leaking tank is not obvious. Furthermore, lighting the burners can provide some anxious moments if too much gas is allowed to enter the burners before you light them. It is recommended that propane be used only outdoors. It is so combustible that, depending upon temperature, humidity, and the amount of air space between the tanks and the grills, there is as much as a 60 percent chance that the equipment will malfunction and cause a serious accident.

Most tableside cooking units use butane as fuel. It is much safer than propane. It also is preferable to Sterno because you can control the temperature and size of the flame much better with butane than you can with Sterno. Another option is to eliminate the fuel by using induction cooking equipment; this is a safer procedure because there is no lighted gas burner or noxious odors.

Tableside cooking should be limited to a single sauté or wok station that is no closer to guests than the diameter of a 60-inch round dining table. The work area must be well ventilated. You should not allow exhibition cooking in a low-ceilinged room or in a room that does not have proper ventilation.

If a client prefers the excitement and attraction of tableside cooking, you can indulge this request safely by providing a flaming display on an elevated riser situated away from the dining areas on one side of the function room. The display can be used to prepare a handful of portions, with the bulk of production performed in the kitchen.

Another compromise is to have a flaming parade around the perimeter of the function room with the lights dimmed. For instance, food servers can carry a few flaming baked Alaska desserts or a few flaming kabobs from the kitchen to a dining room service area. Once there, servers can douse the flames, plate up the foods, and serve a few guests. After the flaming display, the remaining production and pre-plating can be done in the kitchen.

2. *Burns*. Even if you do not provide tableside cooking, guests are still subject to accidental burns. For instance, if you have unprotected candle flames on each dining table, napkins can be set afire if the candles tip over. Or guests may accidentally burn themselves or their clothing if they reach over the flame without realizing how hot it is. If you want to put candles on each table, you should use votive-type, flameless candles, containers or chimneys, which can prevent accidental burns or fires. In many areas the local fire marshal has banned the use of open flames. When they are allowed, there may be restrictions on their use. For example, they may need to be enclosed in a non-combustible container that is at least 2 inches taller than the height of the flame. Be sure to check your local fire codes before using open flames for a catered event.

Buffet service also presents several potential hazards that can cause burns. For instance, hot chafing dishes can be very dangerous to the unsuspecting guest. Handles and utensils can get very hot. And the steam created by the typical chafing dish may build up and escape suddenly, seriously burning someone standing nearby.

If Sterno or a similar gel fuel is used to keep the contents of chafing dishes hot, the fuel can "flame out"—that is, if the lid on the Sterno container is left open too wide, you may suddenly have a flame surrounding the bottom of the pan and possibly even enveloping the whole chafing dish.

If you use Sterno, do not allow anyone to refuel the little pots while they are in use. Sometimes you cannot see the slight flame emitted by the fuel. If you try to refuel while the pot is still burning, you may burn yourself very badly. In fact, many years ago, a young chef in a Las Vegas hotel lost his life when his chef's jacket caught fire while he was trying to refuel Sterno pots on the buffet table.

Hot carts positioned throughout the function room pose another burn hazard. Portable steam tables can be a problem as well. Similarly, hot-beverage setups may be dangerous. To prevent these types of accidental burns, you must see to it that any exposed hot surface is clearly marked. For safety purposes, most manufacturers will place warning signs that identify potentially hot surfaces at the factory when the equipment is being manufactured; your municipality may require this type of marking before the equipment can be used in local commercial foodservice operations.

3. *Falls.* Guests are always subject to falls. Most of them are unfamiliar with the function room. Some of them are not careful when roaming around the room, thereby bumping into other guests and servers. And many of them may not immediately recognize electrical or sound drop cords laced throughout the area.

To minimize the possibility of guests falling, you should never allow any loose item to be placed on the floor. For instance, if a drop cord must be used, it should be secured and marked conspicuously.

Similarly, if there is a slope in the floor, it should be marked clearly. Furthermore, all tables, carts, tray stands, and other equipment must be placed in the correct locations and secured properly.

4. *Broken glass.* Broken and chipped tableware is another hazard that seems to be more prevalent in catered events than in regular restaurant service. The time pressures associated with most catered functions increase the risk that guests will inadvertently find damaged items.

Usually chipped plates can be found and removed from service before they end up in front of guests. However, the same cannot always be said about broken glassware. Indeed, the possibility of guests finding a piece of broken glass is always present whenever employees are rushing to serve a group of people.

Hurried bartenders, buspeople, and other employees who clear buffet and guest tables may also increase the number of broken glasses and thus the possibility of a guest getting a piece of glass in his or her food or beverage.

Buspeople should be taught to dump ice out of glasses before placing them in bus trays. The ice overloads the trays. It also causes glasses to slip around and bang into each other. Either way, the potential for chipped and broken glassware increases, along with the increased possibility that glass chips will get into the food and beverage supply.

Likewise, glasses should not be stacked in bus trays. Flatware should never be put into glasses. And plates should not be mixed with glasses. All of these actions increase the possibility of broken glass getting into a guest's drink or meal.

Ice or cold water should never be put into hot glasses. The glasses may crack and split. This would not be troublesome if the glass broke completely before it was served to a guest. There is a serious problem, though, if the glass merely sprouts a hairline crack; when the guest sees this, he or she will be leery of all other food and beverage offerings. Worse yet, if a guest actually drinks from this glass, he or she might receive a cut lip.

Glasses should never be used to dip ice out of an ice bin. If the glass breaks, you will need to empty the bin and clean it thoroughly. You should use plastic scoops to dip ice and put it into glasses; metal scoops should not be used because they can chip the glasses. The last thing you want is a guest receiving a piece of glass in his or her drink.

5. *Food-borne illness.* One of the caterer's worst nightmares is to cause an outbreak of food-borne illness. Imagine the agony and negative public relations you would suffer if guests became ill after consuming contaminated food at one of your events.

Food-borne illness can be traced to many sources. Products may be contaminated when purchased. They may become contaminated during production and service. Or they can become contaminated if stored under improper conditions.

Improper storage for an excessive period of time generally is the biggest problem faced by the typical catering operation. The time/temperature dilemma rears its head whenever potentially hazardous foods must be held for long periods of time on a buffet table.

Potentially hazardous foods must be stored at 40°F or below or at 140°F or above. The 40°F-to-140°F range is the danger zone. If potentially hazardous foods must go through the danger zone (such as when they are cooked), they must spend as little time there as possible because at these temperatures harmful bacteria will thrive.

Foods on a buffet table are especially vulnerable to the time/temperature problem. For instance, if you offer a lasagna entree, a chafing dish may be unable to maintain the temperature required. If a guest or employee contaminates this cooked food and the food is not served for a while, harmful bacteria can multiply and eventually someone may become ill.

If you are serving potentially hazardous cold foods on a buffet table, they must be kept at or below 40°F. For instance, a cold potato salad made with protein-rich ingredients should never be allowed to sit out unrefrigerated for more than a few minutes. It should be displayed on a cold table.

To prevent these time/temperature problems, you must ensure that the service equipment can hold foods at the proper temperatures and see to it that foods are not kept on the buffet table any longer than necessary and certainly no longer than the time allowed under local health codes.

You could also minimize these types of problems if you are willing to forgo the use of some of the more troublesome foods. For instance, if eggs are to be used in a menu item that will not be cooked, such as hollandaise sauce, you could use pasteurized refrigerated or frozen eggs instead of fresh shell eggs. You also could refuse to serve items with raw eggs (such as Caesar salad), items with raw meat (such as steak tartare), or raw seafood.

SUMMARY

Essential elements of production planning include determining the quality and amount of food and beverage needed and scheduling and service timing. Service and service standards are an integral part of any catered function, and safety and sanitation standards are critical to avoid guest illness or accidents.

KEY TERMS

Par stock	Sous vide	Finish cooking
Action stations	Scratch production	Staffing charts
Service ratios	Collective bargaining agreement	Teardown
HACCP	UL	AGA
OSHA	Prime time	Slack time
Production plan	Service plan	A-list
B-list		

REVIEW QUESTIONS

1. Is it easier to determine the amount of food or the amount of beverage needed for an event? Why?
2. What usually occurs when catered functions run behind schedule?
3. What is the industry standard ratio of bartenders to number of guests for a catering function?
4. What are the primary factors that determine the number of service personnel needed?
5. How can timing problems be minimized?
6. Where should propane be used?
7. Given the following data, calculate approx. how many raw pounds of salmon you need to purchase (or requisition from the storeroom) to serve 100 guests:
   Serving size: 6 ounces, cooked
   Edible yield % of raw salmon: 80%
8. Given the following data, calculate approx. how many 750-ml (25.4 ounces) bottles you need to purchase (or requisition from the storeroom) to serve 100 guests:
   Expected no. of drinks per guest: 2.5
   Serving size: 5 ounces
9. What is the primary selection factor buyers use when developing liquor product specifications?
10. Describe the sous-vide food production process.
11. What is the difference between food preparation and finish cooking?
12. When is it appropriate to schedule one food server for every 20 guests for a meal function?
13. Many receptions last only about _____ hour (s).
14. For very large meal functions, the caterer should schedule one captain for every block of _____ guests.
15. What is another term for incremental labor?

Chapter 8

INTERMEDIARIES AND SUPPLIERS

Some catered events require much more than food and beverage service. In addition to food and drink, some clients will need staging, unique decor, photography, entertainment, audiovisual, and/or lighting services. Some will require specialized dining table and buffet table presentations. And others may need something else unique to ensure that guests come away from the functions with many happy memories.

Clients who are planning several meal and beverage functions within a short time span, such as meeting and convention clients, also may ask for something more than food and beverage service, if only to relieve the monotony. They may also want something unusual to recharge guests' batteries so that they have an extra storehouse of energy to draw on when tackling the remaining business sessions.

Unique attractions are also used by clients to highlight celebratory catered events. Awards dinners, weddings, new product introductions, and the like are made more exclusive and memorable if clients provide a medley of food, beverage, and other services specifically designed to maximize their impact on guests.

Caterers can sometimes be in a conflicted position when dealing with clients who want other services. After all, if clients spend a lot of money for these things, how much will they have left over for food and beverage? You certainly do not want to speak ill of clients' ideas, but it is your responsibility to point out that they should strike a proper balance between decor and food and beverage. In the long run, we know that guests are most impressed with the quality and value of food and beverage received, and that other services cannot overcome mediocre products. You need to be cautious, though, when discussing these points; at no time should you attempt to feather your nest at the expense of the client's needs and desires.

The catering executive must be prepared to entertain a variety of special requests for other event services. Usually only the small, refueling type of catered meal functions are built solely around food and beverage service.

Most events require some sort of additional service. It can range from the mundane (such as the need for a DVD player, TV monitor, LCD projector, or screen) to the spectacular (such as the client who requests a skydiving stunt).

The caterer will need to coordinate many special requests. He or she will need to help plan, organize, and implement an assortment of unusual and unique requirements. He or she may also need to advise clients of the most effective and economical combination of special services needed to ensure success. Like a bandleader, the caterer must see to it that all food, beverage, and special services are playing from the same "sheet music."

PROVIDING OTHER CLIENT SERVICES

Caterers specialize in providing food and beverage service. While some are capable of providing additional services, others prefer to leave these to outside experts.

A caterer cannot be all things to all people. He or she realistically must draw the line somewhere. Cost and space considerations render it virtually impossible to store all of the specialties that clients might potentially need.

When dealing with services other than food and beverage, usually the caterer is faced with five options: (1) provide as many of them as possible; (2) steer the client to outside service contractors; (3) expect clients to find their own outside service contractors; (4) authorize concessions, that is, provide in-house space for outside service contractors to set up shop; or (5) use some combination of these four possibilities.

Facility-Provided Services

A facility usually will provide its own special services only if it is economically feasible to do so or if there are no other outside alternatives that can be trusted to do the work correctly and efficiently.

Some properties have their own in-house destination management departments. That way the caterer doesn't have the added responsibility of dealing with things that may be beyond their experience, yet the facility still retains 100 percent of the business and guest satisfaction. This arrangement provides one-stop shopping for the client.

Some special services can be very profitable, particularly if they are not labor-intensive. For instance, providing a few pieces of audiovisual equipment and one technician to a group usually does not involve a lot of variable costs. Consequently, its contribution margin can add considerably to overall profits.

Providing a full range of AV services, on the other hand, can be an expensive undertaking. AV technology changes so rapidly that it is difficult to keep pace. A complete in-house AV system is a major investment, but one that is required in conference centers, exhibition halls, and resorts located in rural areas where outside service contractors are not readily available.

Many other special services are similarly capital-intensive. For instance, most lighting equipment is very expensive. In addition, some equipment tends to become obsolete very quickly, thereby requiring you to replace it periodically with even more expensive items. It is cost-prohibitive to let such equipment sit idle. Unless the facility uses it often, you may not earn an adequate return on your investment.

In some instances, a facility may be happy to break even with such services as lighting and sound if it means that clients will spend freely on food and beverage services. The facility also needs to take into account what its competitors offer. In some markets, standard lighting and sound are included with most facilities, and being unable to provide these could cost your company business. In these cases, it may be good business to offer the client a loss leader if it helps secure other, profitable business for the facility.

Outside Service Contractors

Clients occasionally will require other services the facility is unable to provide. If outside service contractors must be used, the facility may have an approved supplier list for the client's convenience. If not, it is up to the client to secure the necessary services and coordinate them with the catering executive. Some facilities will take on the role of working with the outside contractors on behalf of the client. This may make it easier for both the client and the facility. The client deals only with the facility representative, not multiple outside companies. If the charges are added to the overall event bill, then the client has to pay only one entity, not multiple vendors. For the facility, it can be easier too, as the catering executive can ensure that all elements will coordinate, that the vendors are reliable, and that the facility can have control over delivery, installation, and other aspects of combining these services. When working with outside vendors, typically the facility is given a discount off the retail price. This percentage is retained by the facility (the retail price is charged to the client) as compensation for its work and coordination.

The most common types of other service contractors used by clients are:

1. Decorator, service contractor
2. Designer, event planner
3. Audiovisual
4. Photographer, videographer
5. Transportation
6. Specialized security
7. Computer equipment, printing
8. Host/hostess
9. Talent bookers, entertainment or production companies

10. Florist
11. Specialized food (e.g., subcontracting a sushi bar from a local Japanese restaurant)
12. Furniture, equipment
13. Exhibit equipment (e.g., pipe and drape, pop-up booths)
14. Wireless Internet access
15. Ice company

Some caterers have a list of approved outside service contractors that they recommend to potential clients whenever special services are needed. These contractors usually are the ones the facility feels are capable of doing the job properly. As mentioned previously, these outside companies offer a discount to the caterer that is an added source of revenue to the facility while being no more expensive to the client. Before adding a contractor to the approved list, he or she normally must have adequate references and proof of adequate insurance. The director of catering must review the list regularly to ensure the companies are maintaining the level of service, product, and pricing expected. A caterer does not want to risk recommending someone whose ineptness will cause the client and his or her guests dissatisfaction and ruin the chances of repeat patronage.

Service contractors range from full-service to single-service. Full-service general service contractors, such as the Freeman Companies or GES Exposition Services, rent pipe and drape, dance floors, risers, temporary carpeting, furniture, audiovisual equipment, exhibits, and a variety of other items. Single-service contractors include florists, photographers, limousine companies, and so on.

Some caterers may not want to recommend outside service contractors because it represents a possible conflict of interest. They fear someone may accuse them of taking kickbacks (i.e., illegal gifts given by the contractor to caterers if they agree to help defraud their clients). They also run the risk of clients complaining they were steered to inadequate, costly outsiders whose incompetence should have been well known to the catering executives. As most clients will ask you for a recommendation (particularly if they are from out of town), it is critical that you be selective about whom you recommend and that you do not make a recommendation unless you are confident about the vendor's services and standards.

Sometimes a client may want to use an outside service contractor that the caterer would like to avoid. Generally, though, you must be willing and able to work with any outside service contractor selected by clients.

Many potential clients, especially large conventions that hold events throughout the country, have long-term contracts with several outside service providers. This is an effective and cost-saving procedure for them, since a service contractor will normally offer clients a generous volume discount if they purchase a large amount of services. The caterer will need to work with these outside companies if it wants to book the catering business.

If you book a very large catered function, subcontracting may be the logical way to handle the event. For instance, if a caterer has to feed 50,000 people at a large convention, different parts of the meal could be subcontracted to other caterers. In some cases, especially with subcontracted food or beverage, the caterer will add a profit markup of between 20 and 125 percent to the subcontractor's charge, depending on the item.

In-House Concessionaires

Large hotels, convention centers, and conference centers that do not want to provide their own special services, yet do not want to inconvenience potential clients, may grant a few outside service contractors concession status. These contractors will automatically receive a client's business unless he or she wants to make arrangements with another service contractor and receives permission from the facility to do so. The facility usually allocates the concessionaire some storage space within the property so that necessary equipment and materials can be kept on-site. The concessionaire will also need a bit of space to house employee work areas. Usually the concessionaire has its own backup warehouse facilities off-site. By granting it on-site space, though, you can ensure that clients will be serviced quickly and efficiently. Furthermore, emergencies or last-minute requests can be handled immediately when employees, product, or equipment is available at a moment's notice.

Facilities usually charge a commission to in-house vendors. It is important to understand that these costs must be passed on to the end user, and with high commissions, your mutual clients may end up paying $75.00 to $100.00 or more for a simple screen.

Some facilities impose a surcharge on outside vendors for the right to work in the venue. This is done to discourage the client from using a different vendor. Instead, the client must use the in-house vendor. This ensures that the caterer will not lose its commission.

Some properties state in sales contracts that convention groups must use in-house AV for breakout sessions, but can use their own equipment or the services of an outside vendor for general sessions, or vice versa. If a group brings in its own projector, for example, the hotel may charge an accommodation or support fee. The principle is that when you go to a nice restaurant, you wouldn't bring in your own steak to have them cook it. That would take away the property's opportunity to conduct business. This fee also covers the facility's costs, such as electrical usage, that would be covered with the rental of the item from the facility.

Combination of In-House and Outside Services

Occasionally the facility may provide some services itself while the client is expected to secure others. For instance, if a convention needs specialized sound and lighting services, you may be able to provide microphones and speakers, but the client may have to use an outside service contractor to provide the necessary lighting.

Usually a facility can provide a handful of the most commonly needed client services. For instance, it is the rare property that cannot provide the basic audio-visual equipment, such as screens, microphones, speakers, LCD projectors, TV monitors, and DVD players. If the property is new or has undergone recent renovations, it might have several of these items built in. If nothing else, it can rent a few of these items and relieve the client of this chore.

Occasionally a facility may want to offer a few complimentary client services in order to secure a large catering contract. For example, if a client needs a microphone for the luncheon speaker, a facility may provide it free of charge.

This type of service is relatively inexpensive to provide because you can often tap into a house sound system (for example, a public address system) very easily. The client will appreciate the additional consideration and remember it when it is time to plan the next catered function.

GUIDELINES FOR SELECTING SOME OUTSIDE SERVICES

Some clients may need to engage some specialized outside service contractors on their own, or they prefer to do so even though the caterer is willing to do it for them. Usually caterers have compiled approved vendor lists, mostly through personal experience. The vendors on this list—florists, balloon artists, photographers, music, rental agencies, and the like—usually are the ones most often hired by the typical client. These outside service contractors know the property and do not need a lot of handholding. This efficiency makes life much easier for the caterer. It also can be a solid source of additional revenue, in that commissions and surcharges, as modest as they may be, add up quickly.

Guidelines for using vendors may vary regionally; however, certain rules of thumb may apply. For instance, after price, product, service, and reliability comparisons, select one or two primary suppliers for each service when possible. For example, call the same florist for all of your floral orders.

There can be benefits to establishing a list of preferred vendors. Developing a working relationship may result in better service and greater in-house discounts. For example, using the same booking agency for all entertainment may result in a free band for the employee holiday party.

Agree up front and in writing what discount the vendor will provide (though the agreement should not in any way imply that you will do business with only that vendor). Discounts normally range from 10 to 20 percent. The guest is charged the published price, so you aren't adding to the cost, and an amount equivalent to the discount comes directly to the facility. For example, a vendor normally charges $450.00 for a wedding cake. You can charge a client that same price, but with a 10 percent discount from the vendor, however, you will pay just $405.00. The $45.00 difference goes straight to the bottom line.

This is a source of income that is often overlooked but requires little time and effort. Following are guidelines to help you select and work effectively with vendors.

Florists

Contact a reliable vendor and show him or her your meeting and event space so that floral arrangements can be balanced with the colors in these areas. Ask the florist to provide photographs of several arrangements in different styles and price ranges. Provide clients with photographs of centerpieces and arrangements that are in line with what they are looking for. As flowers are a seasonal item, it may be difficult to list a firm price with the photographs, and it is always best to reconfirm current pricing with the florist before quoting it to the client. Many business clients are happy to give you a budget for the florals and let you work with the florist to design the best possible arrangement within that cost.

Bakeries

If your facility does not have its own bakery, establish a working relationship with a good bakery in your area that can provide the facility with a wide assortment of breads, decorated cakes, and standard and unique pastries. Collect a list of available styles and flavors of birthday, wedding, and other special-occasion cakes, and use that information along with photographs and a price list as sales aids.

For specialty items, particularly wedding cakes, you may need to work with the bakery to provide sample cake, filling, and frosting selections to the bridal couple to try before they make their selections.

Rental Agencies

Many caterers do not wish to own and store equipment that is not used often. Nor are they able to own if they do not have sufficient financial resources or space. In many cases it is too expensive and inconvenient to own. Generally, when specialized equipment is required, it is more economical to rent it, as off-premise caterers usually do. The cost, of course, is either passed on to the client through separate, itemized billing or included in the per-person charge.

Caterers typically will rent the following types of equipment:
- Portable cooking equipment for off-site events, including refrigerated storage and generators
- Transportation
- Tables and chairs
- Tableware (flatware, china, etc.)
- Service utensils (chafing dishes, ladles, etc.)
- Linens and chair covers (often clients want colors, patterns, or items the facility does not own)
- Centerpieces (if the client doesn't have their own)
- Lighting
- Tents

Create and maintain a list of rental agencies in your area, with phone numbers and other pertinent information, so that you can respond readily to special requests. The client may need all kinds of equipment and extras, from silver punch bowls to tuxedos or specialty linens.

Printer

A printer can provide everything from invitations to banquet menus, place cards, or signs. The best printers to use are the ones who have quick turnaround times and specialized, sophisticated, cutting-edge equipment. It also helps if they are located very close to your facility, can accept projects via email, and are able to deliver finished items.

Photographs

Professional photographers are in demand for many types of functions, from weddings to awards banquets. When comparing prices, be aware that some photographers charge separately for time, a disc of photos, and printed pictures.

AUDIOVISUAL

Audiovisual services are probably the most common type of additional services needed by catering clients. You must be able to counsel your clients regarding the best options for them to use. You should be able to help them match their particular needs with the most effective and efficient AV systems.

The main purpose of AV is to communicate. Presentations are made to sell, train, inform, and entertain. The most effective and memorable presentations use AV to "show and tell." Without AV, presentations are apt to lack the punch and power needed to make a lasting impression on guests.

Typical AV Equipment Needed

The most common pieces of AV equipment used are:

1. *Microphone.* Can be a table, podium, floor, handheld, or lavalier (lapel) type. Most microphones are available either with or without a cord. While cordless models are more expensive, they allow greater freedom and flexibility for the speaker and can also be passed around the audience for questions.

Using more than one microphone in a room usually requires a mixer. Standard mixers have four channels, handling four microphones. A sound technician should be hired when large or multiple mixers are used.

2. *Screens.* There are two basic types of projection screens: front-screen projection and rear-screen projection. With front-screen systems, the projector is placed in front of the screen and can be seen by the audience. Rear-screen systems have the projector behind the screen, where it is not visible to the audience. They also require additional room for setup, as these generally require a 20-foot or more throw distance (the distance from projector to screen).

When comparing the two, the advantages to rear-screen projection are that there is no interference with the projection beam, there is no tripping over cords or other equipment, and the lights do not need to be dimmed, allowing the audience to take notes. The disadvantages are the additional space needed for the throw distance and that the area behind the screen must be dark. Function room size, function room layout, and audience size are all important factors in determining the correct screen size.

3. *Projection/video equipment.* Most clients have their presentation on a laptop and will need a hookup for their computer. Others may need the total computer/ projection package. Overhead projectors, carousel slide projectors, and VCRs are all but obsolete; DVDs are more common. PowerPoint is the presentation medium most clients prefer.

Selecting an AV Service Contractor

When a client needs to use an outside AV service, you may be asked to recommend one. You should have one or two reliable companies on your list of approved suppliers.

Before adding a firm to your approved supplier list, you must be sure it is able to adequately handle clients' needs.

1. Assess the reputation of the AV professionals. Ask for references. Call the references and ask:

    a. How capable technically and professionally were the AV representatives?

    b. Did the firm have all necessary equipment? Was it up-to-date and in good working order?

    c. How responsive was the firm to last-minute requests?

    d. Was the final bill equal to the original competitive bid?

2. Check the AV service contractor's certifications. Look for a contractor with communication technology specialists certified by the International Communications Industries Association. An AV firm with these specialists on staff is committed to continuing education within this highly technical and ever-changing industry.

3. Check the proximity of the AV firm to the facility.

4. Determine the availability of deliveries and installations after normal business hours.

5. Inquire about the number of field representatives.

6. Find out how many delivery vehicles the contractor has.

7. Check the availability of field representatives and drivers. Do they all carry cellular phones so that they can be contacted quickly?

8. Get a list of rental charges for equipment. Ensure that you learn the total charge for delivery, setup, and post-production.

9. Find out if there is a charge for backup or emergency equipment.

10. Determine if deposits are required.

11. Get information on the contractor's refund policies. For instance, if an equipment order is canceled at the last minute, will some of the deposit be returned? Inquire also about the procedures used to reconcile disputed charges.

12. Determine how much setup time is needed.

13. Find out how much rehearsal time is required.

14. Ask if staging areas are required.

15. See if client assistance is provided. Many clients will need help planning their AV needs. The approved AV service contractor must be able to provide sufficient input and assistance in developing these plans.

16. Get information on labor charges. This can be the biggest part of a client's AV budget. However, armed with the correct information about the catered event, the AV firm will be able to develop a detailed labor schedule that complies with union contracts (if applicable) and gives the client a realistic expectation of actual labor costs.

Unfortunately, actual labor charges tend to exceed the budgeted ones because the client and the AV service contractor cannot anticipate everything about the scheduled function. For instance, there may be a problem getting into the facility to set up sound equipment because another catered function is running late. Events that run longer than scheduled, tight turnarounds, last-minute on-site changes, and incomplete agendas are the most common reasons for labor cost variances.

These cost variances may increase if union labor must be scheduled. Many facilities and AV companies have contractual agreements requiring union labor for AV services. With complex, elaborate setups, more than one union may be involved. Since most labor contracts include hourly minimums, meal penalties, overtime rates, and show calls, the actual labor charge can be significantly greater than the budgeted one.

17. Assess the firm's ability to coordinate with other service contractors. For instance, if a separate lighting service contractor is required, the firms will need to work together smoothly to avoid glitches that can add to final costs and cause guest dissatisfaction.

Accommodating a Client's AV Needs

If a client is using AV services, the catered function must be held in a room where sound is transmitted effectively. The walls should have absorbent panels and be at least 1 inch thick. If air walls (moving partitions) are used, they should be 2 to 4 inches thick, with seals and gaskets that are intact and tightly secured to prevent sound leaks.

Wool or other thick pile rugs are excellent floor coverings. These will absorb unwanted sounds, such as those created by footsteps and moving equipment.

The function room's ceiling should not be too high or else sound can reverberate. If the local building codes require very high ceilings, you will need to have some sort of acoustical material installed to reduce this effect or, if the client and room setup allows, position the speakers appropriately so that this problem is minimized. Usually if there is any potential for sound reverberation, you can quickly overcome it by temporarily installing fabrics, tiles, baffles, or other acoustical material.

If a client is using an outside AV service contractor, be certain that the firm is apprised of the facility's logistics. For instance, the firm must be aware of accessibility, freight elevators, height and width of the doorways, and so forth in order to plan and implement the project correctly. The firm should also be informed of other events in the facility that could interfere with installation and teardown procedures.

Finally, make certain the client realizes that all outside services will be billed at the actual cost, which may or may not be the same as the original competitive bids submitted.

ENTERTAINMENT

Many catered events include some type of entertainment. The offerings run the gamut from the common to the spectacular. At one end of the spectrum might be the strolling violinist, while at the opposite end are internationally famous singers headlining major show productions.

Music is one of the most common types of entertainment the caterer will encounter. Consequently, you should include bands, disc jockeys, and other musical entertainment as part of your catering packages. Know which rooms accommodate a dance floor or stage. Know where the electrical outlets are located and the power capacity of the facility. Be aware of union regulations for musicians in your area.

As with any outside service contractor, the facility should have at least one or two entertainment companies on their approved supplier list for potential clients to use. This would be relatively easy for those facilities that offer entertainment in their restaurant and bar outlets or have a corporate entertainment director.

If a client requires entertainment, though, usually the responsibility for booking, scheduling, and coordinating falls on the client's shoulders. The caterer's major involvement in the entertainment decision is to take it into account when planning the catered event. For instance, if a dance band is scheduled, everything from banquet setup to work scheduling will be influenced. Considering the major impact that entertainment will have, the catering executive cannot work effectively unless he or she is privy to this information.

The caterer must also know if there are any additional services that will have to be provided. The entertainment contract will indicate what they are and who is responsible for securing them. Require the client to show you the entertainment contract prior to signing it. There may be conditions that you cannot meet or that will require you to add extra charges.

Generally speaking, the key variables the caterer must consider are:

1. *Lighting requirements.* Will the entertainment provide its own? Will there be a separate outside lighting service contractor? Will the facility's permanent system suffice?

2. *Number of dressing rooms and production offices needed.* Also note where they must be located and specifics of what must be included. For example, some entertainers require that there be a minimum of one full-sized sofa, two oversized club chairs, a cocktail table, two end tables, and a full-length mirror in the room. If you do not have this in the dressing room, you will need to rent the items and pass the expense on to the client.

3. *Sound systems and back line.* Many entertainers have their own sound systems, back line (equipment such as instruments, etc.), and technicians. Your responsibility is to provide sufficient space and electrical power. Policy may require you to charge the client for this extra space and electrical power.

4. *Rehearsal time and facilities needed.* If you need to hold the function room space for a day or two before the event so that rehearsals can be held, you will probably need to charge the client extra for this accommodation, as you will be unable to book the space for another event.

5. *Setup time.* In lieu of rehearsal time, or in addition to it, you may need to hold a function room for an extra day or two so that the entertainment production can be set up properly.

6. *Security.* Some entertainers have their own security guards. Others may depend on the facility for all security or for additional security to supplement their own.

7. *Staging requirements.* In addition to setting up a stage and runway, you must know if you need to dovetail with the lighting and AV service contractors.

8. *Dance floor.* You also want to know if one or more dance floors are needed.

9. *Buffer area.* This is the space between the entertainers and the audience. Some big-name acts want quite a distance between them and their fans, primarily for security purposes.

10. *Liability.* A glance at the contract will tell you if there is any potential liability concern. For instance, some magicians employ unusual and potentially dangerous props that could expose the facility to a lawsuit if guests are injured. You also need to know if the facility will be responsible for the entertainer's personal property. If so, you must control the handling of these items.

11. *Complimentary food, beverage, and sleeping rooms.* Depending on the entertainers and their requirements, you may want to offer entertainers the hospitality of the house as a goodwill gesture. Generally though, the client is responsible for paying their tabs.

12. *Operational logistics.* Some entertainers have demands that may impact the facility. For instance, a singer may require a larger dressing room with a shower and specific furniture. Or an entertainer may request special foods and beverages. Ask to see the entertainment contract "rider" that outlines special requirements to ensure you are able and willing to fulfill those requests.

LIGHTING

Lighting is most commonly used to provide safety and security. It is primarily used to illuminate public and work areas properly so that they meet local building code requirements as well as create a relaxed atmosphere.

Lighting, though, can be much more than this. Lighting is a great opportunity to upsell. Pin spots on centerpieces, uplights around the rooms with complimentary gel colors, and lighting for bars and buffets really enhance the look of the room.

Lighting can be used to overcome a plain, pedestrian environment; highlight people, products, and specific function room decors; illuminate speakers and entertainers; focus attention on a particular spot; create a more exciting and dramatic dance floor; frame an area; follow awardees from their seats to the stage; and provide other decorative touches.

Lighting can also be used to tell a story. For instance, you can project company logos, pictures of award recipients, names of VIPs, and so forth on a wall so that guests can see them when they enter the facility.

Depending on the client's needs, he or she can use the facility's permanent lighting system or employ a qualified lighting service contractor. The typical facility does not own specialized lighting equipment that can be used to create light shows or any other type of unusual production. Normally it can provide a few spotlights and other similar equipment. However, it is not set up to accommodate unusual requests, for which an outside service contractor will be required. In some cases, sufficient electrical power, space, overhead beams, and so forth are included in the original building design in anticipation of these needs.

Conference centers, arenas, resorts, and hotels in rural areas may have sufficient lighting equipment and resources to handle most special requests. These properties may feel obliged to provide such services because clients expect this type of convenience, and when the facility is located in an out-of-the-way area, there may not be nearby service contractors.

INTERMEDIARIES

At times the caterer will not work directly with a client. Instead, he or she will be dealing with a third-party intermediary hired by the client to arrange a catered function. Examples of some major companies are Maritz, Carlson, and Helms Briscoe. Wedding receptions and some high-end social events often have a third-party planner to assist with all aspects of the event.

Clients such as corporations or associations often outsource all or parts of an event to intermediaries. For instance, if there will be several meal and beverage functions, two or more facilities involved, and many outside service contractors, a potential client may feel more comfortable employing a seasoned professional experienced in producing these types of detailed affairs.

Intermediaries are often used for civic and political fund-raising events where it is necessary to solicit financial support and to sell tickets. For instance, fund-raising fashion shows, theme parties, charity auctions, and art shows are typically planned and implemented by professional intermediaries.

The catering executive typically has mixed feelings about intermediaries. Their professionalism may be welcome, depending on the event and the person planning it. They generally know what they are doing. Unlike some clients, they do not need to be educated about every little detail. Furthermore, the client is paying for their work.

On the other hand, intermediaries generally are more astute shoppers than typical catering clients. They tend to drive harder bargains. They sometimes want more control over events than the typical catering executive is willing to surrender. And there may be some uneasy moments if, in addition to getting a fee from the client, an intermediary solicits a commission from the facility for including the property in the event. As some properties will not pay this type of commission, a client may not be exposed to all potential facilities capable of handling his or her needs.

Given the growing number of wedding and other event planners (some seasoned and some not), the caterer may encounter inexperienced planners who take more of the caterer's time to work with. Planners may suggest ideas that the caterer knows will not work well in his or her facility. The caterer will need to find a balance between working with the planner and ensuring the best possible outcome for the client.

Independent Meeting Planners

Professional meeting planners, sometimes referred to as "contract planners" or "multi-management companies," are probably the most common type of intermediary used by clients. A client can hire them to plan and implement the entire function. Or they can be used to perform specific services, such as site selection, negotiations, or registration of convention attendees.

Independent meeting planners specialize in producing convention programs, business meetings, training programs, and similar events. They are capable of coordinating all necessary business functions, meal functions, beverage functions, and outside service contractors. They usually meet the needs of small and medium-sized companies that require professional assistance yet do not have the resources to hire full-time in-house planners. Most government clients also engage these types of intermediaries.

Special-Events Planners

These intermediaries are sometimes engaged by corporations to plan and implement company parties and other similar affairs. They usually have a select clientele list that are served on a periodic, predictable basis. For instance, a special-events producer may plan a particular company's annual picnic every year. Clients tend to prefer this type of long-term arrangement because it ensures continuity and variety.

Professional sports teams typically use special-events planners to coordinate after-game parties, halftime events, parades, and so forth.

Major events such as the Olympics, corporate centennial celebrations, high-profile openings, presidential inaugurations, and so forth usually use several planners. For instance, the Coca-Cola Company's 100th birthday celebration in Atlanta required the services of several special-events specialists, with each one responsible for one specific part of the celebration.

If several special-events planners are used, one of them may be responsible for overseeing and coordinating everyone's efforts. He or she may also need to develop a master plan for the overall event and decide how each planner will be used.

Independent Party Planners

These intermediaries are similar to special-events planners. The primary difference is that independent party planners tend to work more often with non-corporate clients. For instance, a small group of people wishing to organize a 20th high school reunion will tend to use this type of intermediary to help publicize, plan, and implement the function.

High school reunions are the most common type of reunion function. However, other reunions, such as college, family, military, company alumni, and so forth, are quickly becoming commonplace as clients realize how easy it is to accomplish what was once thought to be an impossible task.

Independent party planners usually take over all aspects of the function: booking the site, handling mailings, booking entertainment, preparing a memory book, and so forth. Many of them also "lend" clients the deposits required by caterers, thereby allowing volunteer clients to avoid paying out of pocket for up-front expenses; the client can wait until the guests pay before having to pay the planner.

Many independent party planners are brokers who subcontract most or all portions of the function. For instance, if a group wants to hold a prom function, it may contact this type of intermediary, who will then select the caterer, help plan the menu, hire a decorator, and engage the appropriate entertainment.

Travel Agency

The travel agent's typical responsibilities are to sell individual or package tours, rental cars, sleeping rooms, and transportation tickets. Some of them, though, have expanded their role to include meeting-planning services. For instance, if a client uses a travel agent to secure airline and sleeping room reservations, it is a small leap to use the agent to book a meeting room and catered luncheon for the client who wants to deal with only one person for all services. With the increase of travel purchases over the Internet, travel agents are looking to generate other sources of revenue. However, some caterers are not comfortable working with travel agents, who expect commissions on all bookings, including catered events.

Travel agents are usually uncomfortable with guarantees. They are used to "breakage," the cushion of money tour operators make when they include in a package the cost of something that winds up not being used. For example, if a tour group is given coupons for a breakfast buffet and half of them decide to sleep in instead of eating, they do not turn these coupons in to the facility.

The facility, then, does not have the coupon to submit to the tour operator for payment. Since the cost of the buffet was factored into the cost of the package, the tour operator gets to keep that money. Contrast that with having to give a caterer a guarantee and having to pay for the guaranteed number, whether the people show up or not.

Combined Travel Agency and Independent Meeting Planner

Travel agencies and independent meeting planners are specialized intermediaries that sometimes merge. The travel agency has the transportation expertise, and the planner has convention and meeting-management abilities. Together they make a formidable option for clients. In fact, in many instances, this combination gives even the smallest client a one-stop shopping opportunity.

Destination Management Company

A destination management company (DMC) is a liaison between out-of-town clients and services that the host property does not offer. DMCs range from those that provide very specialized services to full-service firms capable of handling all logistics. For instance, some DMCs provide only ground transportation (such as buses, limos, and vans), while others can handle personally or can subcontract everything a client needs. Full-service firms can book entertainment, plan theme parties, coordinate tours and spouse programs, and handle off-site events (including catering) at museums and other local attractions.

Full-service firms can also provide personnel. For instance, exhibitors may want to hire local models to work exhibit booths. Trained registration personnel can also be hired. "Moving decor," such as costumed models, caricature artists, and celebrity look-alikes, can be used to help carry out an event's theme. Generally speaking, it is much cheaper for out-of-town corporate and association clients to hire people locally than to pay transportation and per-diem maintenance for company employees.

Destination management companies are oftentimes used to secure props for theme parties. For instance, a DMC can see to it that a 1960s party has a vintage Mustang or Corvette display. Appropriate balloon art and pyrotechnics displays can also be coordinated by this intermediary.

Many out-of-town clients are willing to pay a local destination management company to provide guidance in an unfamiliar area. It is very difficult for a client to judge the quality of services available if he or she has never visited the area. This intermediary can relieve the client of this burden. Furthermore, it can handle negotiations and oversee every detail, thereby ensuring a successful event.

Clients whose events are held in a different area every year prefer working with destination management companies. These intermediaries have made it easy for clients to indulge this preference by locating themselves in major convention cities. In fact, some national firms, such as USA Hosts, have local offices in several major convention cities that provide large corporate clients with one-stop service as well as favorable quantity discount prices for this service.

Of course, there are independent DMCs that work only one part of the country. Because of their specialized approach, clients may find them to be the best option. The Association for Destination Management Executives can be visited at www.adme.org

Convention and Visitors Bureau

The local convention and visitors bureau (CVB) is an attractive option for the out-of-town client who wants to book an event in a local area but is unfamiliar with it. The CVB can provide useful information about the area, such as attractions, transportation, hotels, and amount of available exhibit hall space, that a client can use to evaluate the location's suitability for an event.

The CVB can be an extremely valuable one-stop-shopping source for clients. For instance, if a client wants to plan a convention, he or she can send the CVB a request for proposal (RFP)—a list of requirements for meeting and sleeping accommodations, meal and beverage services, and any other required services. The CVB will distribute the leads to local hotels and outside service contractors, thereby relieving the client of the tedious task of shopping around. Many CVBs now accept RFPs online.

The CVB's most tangible benefit for clients is the time saved. In addition to providing suitable alternative selections for clients, it can provide considerable logistical support at the local level.

Since the typical CVB is usually funded by local member hotel properties and a variety of taxes, a client can usually use its services inexpensively or free of charge. The CVB can also offer promotional material at no expense to clients. For instance, oftentimes clients can get free name-tag holders, brochure shells, small mementos, registration personnel, and similar support. Most bureaus will use their advertising budgets to absorb these types of costs.

Ground Transportation

Some ground transportation firms specialize in providing limousine service for clients. They can pick up and drop off guests as well as be on call for personal needs during weddings, conventions, meetings, and so forth. Shuttle or motor coach service often is needed by the large convention clients because it is more efficient and, in most cases, a lower-cost alternative to using taxicabs.

A few ground transportation companies specialize primarily in entertainment. For instance, some trips, such as charter boat rides and trail rides, are planned strictly for their entertainment value.

Some ground transportation firms specialize in transporting a client's personal property. A local transport operator may pick up air-freighted or rail-freighted convention materials, such as equipment and product samples, and deliver them to the exposition hall. The same firm can also retrieve leftover material and return it to the airport or railway yard after the event.

Generally speaking, the large convention or meeting client will spend more time lining up motor coach transportation than any other type of ground transportation. The caterer is oftentimes asked to take on this burden, especially if the clients are from out of town and are unfamiliar with the area. There are several things to keep in mind before selecting this type of service contractor:

- Motor coaches usually are booked per coach on a four-to-five-hour minimum rate.
- Motor coaches can be booked on a daily rate if you need them all day. A daily rate is usually less expensive than booking them for only a few hours.
- Motor coaches charge from the time they arrive at the pickup site to the time they drop off passengers; however, some calculate their time

from garage to garage. In this case, the meter is running from the time the coach leaves the company's site until it returns to the company's site. Most companies do not charge garage to garage, but if it is a busy time, a regional coach company may not have the inventory; in that case, it would subcontract the job to a coach company that is outside the city. When this happens, the client usually would be charged garage to garage.

- Driver tips and gas may or may not be included in the charges; you will need to check.
- Ask whether staff will be on-site to load luggage, coordinate the transfers, and communicate with dispatch. If so, what are the charges for staffing? How many staff are needed? Typically, the staff are paid on a four-hour minimum; the cost also includes a positioning fee (parking or cab fees, etc., for the staff person).
- Find out if there will be signage on the coaches.
- Determine if staff will have communications with all other staff, dispatch, and drivers.
- Establish where the motor coaches will stage, (the location they will wait before guests board), and how long before the event they will stage.

Caterers can spare themselves some headaches by contracting with a DMC or ground company to handle some or all of these logistics. They know the good companies and will steer them in the right direction. However, caterers who subcontract these tasks will earn less profit.

Remember, the coach company is in the business of keeping its wheels on the road. Not all coach companies provide an on-site supervisor or staff; they may devote all of their human resources to driving, not to support services. Sometimes drivers are on break or can't be found when the group is ready to reboard after completing a visit on a scheduled tour, and sometimes a bus breaks down and there is no backup to rescue the group.

If, for example, a client needs to transport a group from the hotel to an off-premise site for dinner, you can't assume the driver is going to show up, clean, in uniform, with directions in hand, and know exactly where he or she is going. You don't want to stay up at night printing maps from the Internet, spend time explaining directions, or send drivers on a practice run prior to the event. Again, a DMC or ground company can be subcontracted to handle these kinds of challenges. A DMC or ground company will have extra maps, will make sure the driver understands instructions, and so on.

Government Agencies

You may need to work closely with government agencies when planning a special event. For example, you may need to inform the fire department if you are putting on a pyrotechnics display. You will also need to make sure that the pyrotechnic company producing the display acquires the appropriate liability insurance, typically a minimum of $2 million.

The fire department may also need to oversee and inspect any portable tent and canopy structures and electrical power setups to ensure they are installed and grounded properly and safe for use in a public area. In some jurisdictions, a fire marshal must approve banquet room and exhibit setups to ensure that guests will be able to evacuate safely in the event of a fire.

The local health district needs to approve kitchen facilities, temporary tents, cooking lines, serving lines, and so forth to be sure you are not violating health guidelines.

You may need special parking permits for buses, parade permits, or a temporary off-site liquor license.

If a client has a public official, such as a mayor or governor, speaking at a meeting, you may be dealing with bodyguards or, in the case of the president of the United States, the Secret Service.

COOPERATING WITH OTHER FACILITIES

Some catered events are so large that two or more caterers must cooperate in servicing them. Attendees are often shuttled back and forth. If you are involved in this sort of cooperative venture, someone will need to coordinate and direct it. The client will usually handle a great deal of the organization needed, but the individual caterers must go beyond this. Without communication, guests may not receive enough menu variety.

SUMMARY

In the course of planning an event, it will often be necessary for the caterer to work with outside suppliers. Examples include rental companies, audiovisual companies, entertainment and lighting services, ground transportation, and government agencies. In all cases, the caterer will need to evaluate the supplier's services and work directly with them to meet the client's expectations. Occasionally caterers may also need to work together cooperatively with other catering facilities to plan and execute a major event.

KEY TERMS

Client services

Outside service contractor

In-house concessionaires

Rental procedures

Selecting rental companies

Lighting

Independent meeting planner

Independent party planner

Destination management
    company (DMC)

Ground transportation

Cooperating with other facilities

AV equipment

Kickbacks

Accommodation or support fee

Selecting outside contractors

Entertainment

Intermediaries

Special-events planner

Travel agency

Convention and Visitors
    Bureau (CVB)

Government agencies

REVIEW QUESTIONS

1. How might a caterer be in a conflicted position when clients want recommendations and advice on whom to hire for services the caterer does not provide?

2. Name one type of caterer that is most likely to personally provide clients a complete in-house audiovisual system instead of requiring clients to purchase it from an outside supplier.

3. List some of the most common types of outside suppliers used by clients.

4. What is an in-house concessionaire?

5. Describe how caterers usually select a florist to recommend to clients.

6. Describe some of the factors caterers should consider when evaluating an outside audiovisual service they are thinking about using for an upcoming event.

7. Assume a meeting planner is planning to book a big-name musical act for the gala party on the last night of the convention. List some of the key variables the caterer and meeting planner should consider when arranging for this type of entertainment.

8. What is lighting most commonly used for?

9. Usually motor coach companies charge from the time they arrive at the pickup site. However, at times they may charge from garage to garage. Which procedure is more expensive to purchase? Also, list an example of when a motor coach company is most likely to charge from garage to garage, even though ordinarily it would charge from the time it arrives at the pickup site.

10. What is a positioning fee?

11. What does DMC stand for? List some services a DMC provides.

12. Cite an example of when a client and the caterer may need to work closely with a government agency when planning a special event.

Chapter 9

STAFFING

One cannot overestimate the importance of staffing in the service industry. The catering department's reputation rests on its ability to prepare and serve a consistent quality of food and beverage. Without the proper amount and type of personnel, a caterer cannot hope to develop or maintain a sterling reputation.

What motivates a client to book business with a particular caterer? What is the difference between one caterer and another? Certainly each caterer lays claim to some sort of unique benefit that it alone can provide to clients. However, if you scratch the surface of any caterer's reputation, chances are you will find that its perceived level of service is one of its most important features.

One of the best things that can happen to you is for clients to say yes, they did spend a great deal, but they got their money's worth. In other words, they received value for their dollars.

Conversely, one of the worst things that can occur is for clients to perceive that they did not get a good value. No matter how low the price is, if a client does not perceive value, it is too high.

Staffing is critical. It is an organization's lifeblood. Experience shows that customer satisfaction and repeat patronage are influenced primarily by food and beverage quality, service, sanitation, and cleanliness. An inadequate, undermanned, undertrained staff is incompatible with the successful catering operation.

Finding the proper balance between staffing enough labor to successfully execute an event and overstaffing that costs the company profit can be very tricky. To ensure that your labor dollars are used effectively, it is imperative to hire the best employees.

EMPLOYEE RECRUITMENT

Even if you are in a large departmentalized company, you should not rely solely on the facility's human resources department to secure adequate staffing. You cannot merely pick up the phone and call the employment manager whenever you have a job opening. Rather, it is very important to adopt a proactive stance in order to satisfy your staffing needs.

Staffing is an ongoing activity primarily because the typical catering department's staffing requirements fluctuate widely. This is especially true for the group of employees who work part-time or very unpredictable schedules.

There is a critical core of permanent, fixed-cost, full-time and part-time managerial and hourly staff members. Many of these people are career-oriented or otherwise satisfied with their current positions. Consequently, they are apt to remain with you. This does not mean, though, that this core will never change. As with anything else, it is subject to change at a moment's notice. For instance, a permanent part-time head bartender may suddenly leave you to take a full-time bartending job elsewhere.

The majority of your staff consists of variable-cost employees who often tend to work for more than one caterer. While many of them prefer part-time status, some of them are looking for full-time employment. If they secure something permanent, they may leave you on short notice.

Variable-cost employees may be busy when you need them. For instance, some of them may be working their regular jobs and cannot break away to help you, while others may be working for another caterer that day.

Maintaining an adequate number of qualified employees is no easy task. No one likes to encounter severe employee turnover. However, the fluctuating demands for staff members in the catering industry have resulted in a certain amount of structural (i.e., unavoidable) turnover that you must deal with daily.

The caterer must be willing to constantly cultivate potential employees. This is especially important for your hourly staff. Your A-, B-, and C-lists can never be too long. You do not want to get to the end of them and find that you still do not have enough staff for their upcoming catering events.

You also need to cultivate and develop your fixed-cost employees. Since the typical way of doing this is to promote people from the variable-cost employee group, it is even more important to spend as much time as possible recruiting entry-level employees.

Job Specification

For management positions, a job candidate must have technical work experience along with the requisite human skills. For many hourly positions, you also prefer job candidates with a reasonable amount of catering work experience. However, conceivably you could hire people for many positions who have minimal or no work experience in our industry if they possess other qualities you are looking for.

If a person has the willingness to do the work and possesses customer contact skills and a positive attitude toward the catering industry, he or she can be trained to perform capably. For instance, with patience and understanding, you can turn energetic people into excellent food and cocktail servers.

The lack of technical skills, though, can place an additional burden on you and the rest of your staff because of the extra training that must be done. Generally speaking, managers in the foodservice industry are accustomed to hiring and training neophytes. In fact, many of them prefer to do this because they do not have to retrain new hires and break old habits. They feel that it may be much easier to start with a blank slate.

It is one thing to hire someone without catering work experience, but quite another to hire a person who has no work experience in customer-contact positions. There generally is no way to predict how someone will react when put into a high-pressure situation where guests are blowing off steam. Experience shows that the various personality tests available do not adequately predict a newcomer's initial reactions.

Likewise, if you contemplate hiring someone who has never worked a paid job outside the home, you encounter all the problems associated with hiring someone with no catering work experience plus those that crop up whenever someone is introduced to the realities of the workplace. Not only must you teach novices how to perform their jobs, you also must teach them the protocols of working for a living.

When recruiting job candidates, you must see to it that they possess the appropriate credentials. For instance, some positions may need to be staffed solely with union members. A few jobs may require college degrees or similar training. Clerical staff should be knowledgeable about basic computer software, email, catering software, record keeping, and related tasks. Other positions may require people who have current alcohol server awareness training certificates. And some employees may need current health cards issued by the local health district.

Minimum age is another job specification for job candidates who prepare, sell, or serve alcoholic beverages. In most parts of the United States, these people must be at least twenty-one years old. As a general rule, facilities will hire minors for kitchen pre-prep, food runner, and other similar jobs. However, the catering department usually will not hire minors for front of house positions because it is almost impossible to keep them away from alcoholic beverage service.

Job Description

It is imperative to maintain up-to-date, current job descriptions so that job candidates know exactly what to expect if they come to work for you. You do not want to be put into the position of relating inaccurate information. This will cause unnecessary grief, job dissatisfaction, and avoidable employee turnover.

Job descriptions should paint accurate pictures of all job duties that must be performed. Experience shows that oftentimes job candidates misinterpret job parameters because the job descriptions are too vague. The recruiter may compound this problem further by failing to address the specific job needs during the interview process.

It is thought that misinterpretation of what a job requires is one of the key variables responsible for excessive employee turnover. Generally speaking, if you can keep an hourly person for thirty days and a management person for one year, chances are that he or she is satisfied with the job and the company and is likely to remain for a while. If you paint a realistic picture up-front and then see to it that reality does not vary significantly from this description, your employee turnover will probably be much lower than the industry average.

Labor Pool

The catering executive should work closely with the human resources department or hiring manager to develop an adequate labor pool. He or she should inform them of potentially fruitful areas to seek job candidates so that their efforts are not wasted. For instance, if you feel that the local college will generate adequate job candidates, you should encourage the human resources department to recruit on campus.

A catering organization also should not be afraid to adopt a proactive stance. It should have a long-term staffing plan that notes expected terminations and resignations along with anticipated total staffing needs. It should take the lead whenever possible and seek out job candidates and send them to human resources for interviewing and possible hiring.

The following labor pool sources can yield capable job candidates:

1. *Promote from within.* Employees like promotion-from-within policies since this gives them an opportunity to move up in the company. Experience shows that career ladders attract potential employees who otherwise would not perceive your facility as a good place to work.

2. *Job referral.* Current catering employees may have friends or relatives who might wish to apply for job openings. This could be a win-win situation, in that the current employee may receive some type of bonus while the catering organization gets another good employee who knows what to expect. Unfortunately, some conflict-of-interest and nepotism problems could arise. Because of these problems, some caterers severely restrict this hiring practice.

3. *Use employees from other departments/areas.* A part-time employee in another department may be a good addition to your A-list or B-list. This can be another win-win situation, assuming it does not violate corporate policy. You must be careful when doing this, though, because some jealousy and hard feelings can develop. For instance, it could be rather ticklish if a part-time kitchen employee finds the catering service area more inviting and requests a transfer.

Using other department employees also could cause overtime problems. For instance, if in one week an employee works five full days in the kitchen and one full day as a food server, he or she would have to be given overtime pay for the sixth day. Federal regulations mandate that an employee must be compensated at one and one-half times his or her regular rate of pay for all hours worked in excess of forty per week. Furthermore, in some states an employee may be entitled to overtime pay for all hours worked in excess of eight per day (if the normal workweek is five days, eight hours per day) or ten per day (if the normal workweek is four days, ten hours per day).

4. *Union hiring hall.* A unionized facility may need to use the union hiring hall for permanent and temporary hires if the jobs are unionized. In some cases, the union may sponsor internships and apprenticeships that can provide you with a steady, albeit ever-changing, supply of young, enthusiastic workers.

5. *Culinary schools.* This is a good source of permanent, full-time employees. It also represents a good pool of part-time workers who need to earn work experience hours to complete their degree requirements. As an aside, the instructors may be interested in working part-time. Or they may be willing to work for you during their summer vacations.

6. *Colleges and universities.* You should concentrate your recruiting efforts on the many universities and two-year colleges offering hospitality management training. You may be able to attract graduates for full-time positions. And since most college programs require students to earn a minimum number of work hours in the hospitality field, you should try to set up a system whereby your part-time staff is continually replenished with students.

Many other college majors might be willing to work part-time. Our industry is flexible enough to work around most school schedules. Students are usually favorably disposed to part-time catering work because of its ability to match almost anyone's personal schedules. You should call schools' placement offices and ask them to post job openings on their job bulletin boards. If your local college has a hospitality program, contact that department directly. Many colleges maintain listservs (through Yahoo Groups or Google Groups) to send job information directly to students who subscribe via email.

7. *Homemakers.* These are one of the best sources for A-, B-, or C-list people. Experience shows, though, that you will need to be extra flexible with them because they will not work if your needs conflict with their family responsibilities.

8. *Seniors.* Many retired people want to keep active in the work world. They are becoming more and more of a fixture in many part-time labor pools. Several types of foodservice operations are anxious to hire them on a part-time basis. They usually bring a favorable combination of work experience, enthusiasm, patience, personality, availability, and dedication that makes them extremely valuable employees.

9. *Private industry councils.* Many businesspeople support institutes and other similar organizations that can be good sources of full-time and part-time labor. These groups are very active in sponsoring employment job fairs, apprenticeship programs, and job training opportunities that can dovetail very nicely with your employment efforts.

10. *Employment agencies.* Public and private employment agencies may yield full-time job candidates. Public agencies operated by state employment departments can be good sources of hourly workers. They may be preferable to private employment agencies because they do not charge fees for their services. Usually because of the fees involved, employers tend to use outside private headhunters only when it is necessary to hire middle and top management personnel.

11. *Government job-training agencies.* There may be one or more local government agencies sponsoring job-training programs on their own or with the cooperation of the federal government. For instance, state departments of labor or OSHA offices may sponsor rehabilitative training programs for injured employees who cannot go back to their old jobs. You could be part of these training efforts by providing jobs for the trainees. In some cases, your cooperation can result in payroll savings, since some programs grant tax credits and/or pay part or all of the wages during the training periods. Moreover, a successful trainee could end up taking a full-time, permanent position with your property.

12. *Day labor operations.* These organizations are similar to public and private employment agencies. The major difference is that they usually "lease" people to you on a daily basis. For instance, if you need a few extra hands to set up an outdoor tent, a call to a local agency could yield the exact number of workers required. You get only the amount of help needed, and it is more convenient to pay one price for it rather than putting everyone through the normal, expensive hiring procedure.

Day labor operations may hire street people. This tends to turn off the typical employer. However, experience shows that if you use these organizations properly and assign workers only those jobs they are capable of doing, you can obtain favorable results.

13. *Other caterers.* While it is not neighborly to steal employees from your competitors, you should not let this stop you from spreading the word about job opportunities at your company. Furthermore, since all caterers use part-time people, there is ample opportunity to offer someone one or two workdays at your property while allowing him or her to keep the other job.

Usually some of your employees are working for several caterers anyway. For example, a few of them may be on the B-list of every major property in town. You might as well take the initiative and maximize the potential of this labor source by using good taste in publicizing your job opportunities.

14. *Outside staffing agencies.* Some locales have agencies that specialize in providing part-time, temporary employees to the hospitality industry.

15. *Professional associations.* This is one of the most prolific sources of sales and management personnel. Many hospitality managers belong to one or more professional associations. For instance, many catering professionals belong to the National Association of Catering Executives (NACE, www.nace.net) and/or the International Caterers Association (www.internationalcaterers.org).

One of the benefits association members enjoy is being kept apprised of current career opportunities available in their field of expertise and interest. You should use these built-in grapevines to advertise current job vacancies.

16. *Social media.* Many savvy caterers are looking to Twitter, Facebook, LinkedIn, and other forms of social media to spread the word of job opportunities.

Job Application

The job application is the most common method used to screen potential employees. Usually applications are filled out in the human resources department by walk-ins, that is, people who respond to classified ads or who merely stop by to see if you need help. Many hotels and other types of catering operations have an online application process.

The job application can be an excellent prescreening device. The employment manager can use it to weed out unqualified job candidates who do not possess the requisite experience, education, and other pertinent background characteristics.

If you find someone to fill a job position, you would still need him or her to complete a job application and go through the rest of the job-processing procedure.

Job Interview

If a walk-in candidate seeks a job and the job application reveals some promising information, usually the person is given a prescreening interview. Typically the prescreening interview involves a discussion of things such as: When can the person report for work? What is the depth of his or her work experience? Will the person feel comfortable working under your property's particular rules and regulations?

A prescreening interview is also an excellent opportunity to determine if a job candidate is likely to succeed at your facility. Some facilities use a prescreening process to determine if a job candidate has the proper attitudes, skills, and work habits needed to perform effectively.

If a job candidate passes the prescreening interview, the interviewer should take the time to check references before moving him or her along in the job-processing procedure. Telephone calls should be made to verify information indicated on the job application and during the prescreening job interview.

A facility may also include some testing procedures. For instance, your facility may have a policy of giving all job applicants a tray test to see if they can successfully balance a tray full of plates or glasses, or an integrity test, drug test, physical exam, and so forth, before they can qualify for the next step in the employment process.

If the reference check yields favorable information, the job candidate usually is then formally interviewed by you or someone on your staff. In some cases he or she may be interviewed by you and other management personnel. This is especially true if the person is applying for a sales or management position.

After this interview, it is usually up to you to determine if the facility should offer the position to the job applicant. Many facilities require a pre-employment drug test. If the person passes that, and you determine you want to hire the person, you or human resources will then extend the job offer formally, complete the employment process, and schedule the new hire's first workday.

ORIENTATION

In a large facility, the human resources department is responsible for orienting all new hires. This procedure normally takes the better part of one workday. Smaller facilities should also complete some or all of the following steps.

Orientation usually involves providing new hires with information that is not directly related to the various job tasks a person is expected to perform, such as health benefits, location of the employee dining room, or introducing management staff.

For instance, new hires are usually:

1. Introduced to the company's philosophy
2. Fitted for uniforms
3. Given an employee handbook and explanation of the information it contains
4. Welcomed by the general manager and other key personnel
5. Given an overview of property security procedures, company history, career opportunities, and so forth
6. Given a property tour
7. Assigned locker room space, a parking place, a name tag, and so forth
8. Introduced to supervisors and coworkers

TRAINING

Usually the human resources and catering managers share the training efforts. For instance, human resources may provide general training in life safety, customer courtesy, complaint handling, telephone procedures, drug and alcohol awareness, and so forth, with catering taking responsibility for initial and ongoing specific job-related training.

The Food and Beverage Committee of the Hospitality Sales and Marketing Association International developed training guidelines that can be used to familiarize a catering department's new hire with all pertinent operating and non-operating activities. While these guidelines were developed for management positions in hotels, depending on the facility and the position, any new hire should be familiarized with some of the following areas:

1. *Catering sales manual.* All catering sales representatives should be familiar with your catering policies and procedures. New entry-level salespeople who are unfamiliar with the general sales systems used in catering should pay particular attention to the following:
   a. Catering files and filing procedures
   b. Tracing procedures
   c. Solicitation procedures
   d. Catering sales analysis
   e. Booking procedures
   f. Procedures used to prepare banquet event orders, pre-function sheets, and convention resumes
   g. Dates and space reservation procedures
   h. Confirmation procedures
   i. Cancellation procedures
   j. Specific job responsibilities
   k. Sales techniques
   l. Credit procedures
   m. Guarantee procedures
2. *Food and beverage department.* If relevant, the new hire should be exposed to some or all of the following food and beverage operating procedures:

   a. Food and beverage controller's office
- **i.** General catering food and beverage cost requirements
- **ii.** Exposure to catering food and beverage cost calculations
- **iii.** General food and beverage accounting procedures
- **iv.** Food controls
- **v.** Beverage controls
- **vi.** Guarantee and attendance calculations
- **vii.** Variance analysis
- **viii.** Profit-and-loss statement analysis
- **ix.** Computing total banquet costs
- **x.** Percentage analysis
- **xi.** Payroll cost analysis
- **xii.** Profit ratios

   b. Kitchen
- **i.** Executive chef's responsibilities
- **ii.** Banquet chef's responsibilities
- **iii.** Catering menus
- **iv.** Banquet change orders
- **v.** Staffing
- **vi.** Stock requisitions
- **vii.** Food pre-prep
- **viii.** Food prep
- **ix.** Banquet dish-up
- **x.** Evaluating potential menu items
- **xi.** Month-end inventories
- **xii.** Portion control

   c. Steward
- **i.** Payroll forecasts
- **ii.** Review of banquet menus
- **iii.** Staffing
- **iv.** Stock requisitions
- **v.** Equipment preparation
- **vi.** Equipment inspection

       vii. Equipment storage

     viii. Coordination with kitchen and service

       ix. Salvage procedures

        x. Sanitation procedures

       xi. Refrigeration

      xii. Equipment par stocks

     xiii. Equipment inventories

      xiv. Supplies storage

      xv. Equipment and supplies purchasing

d. Banquet manager

        i. General service procedures

       ii. Coordination with kitchen and steward

      iii. General supervisory procedures

      iv. Banquet rooms

       v. Function room setups

      vi. Pre-meal service meetings

      vii. Seating charts

     viii. Function room maintenance

       ix. Menu meetings

        x. Pre-convention meetings

      xi. Coordination of tableware and napery

      xii. Payroll forecasts

     xiii. Rehab meeting (forecasted repair and maintenance needs)

      xiv. Work scheduling

      xv. Housekeeping worksheets

     xvi. Styles of service

e. Beverage

        i. Catering menus

       ii. Coordination with steward and banquet manager

      iii. Stock requisitions

      iv. Change orders

       v. Guarantees

      vi. Sales and cost data

        vii. Pre-function meetings—roll call and briefing

      viii. Stocking bars

        ix. Bar teardown

         x. Beginning and ending bar inventories

        xi. Cash reconciliation

      xii. Drink ticket reconciliation

     xiii. Month-end inventories

     xiv. Work scheduling

  f. Room service

       i. Hospitality suites

      ii. Liquor control

     iii. Room service checks

     iv. Coordination with room setup

      v. Amenity service packages available

  g. Food and beverage manager

       i. Daily revenue and payroll report

      ii. Filing system

     iii. Restaurant outlets

     iv. Bar outlets

      v. Forecasting

     vi. Payroll analysis

    vii. Menu analysis

   viii. Coordination with the district or regional director of food and beverage (if applicable)

     ix. Coordination with the corporate vice president of food and beverage (if applicable)

3. Purchasing

  a. Product availability

  b. Seasonal variations

  c. Special items not commonly used

  d. Banquet menu reviews

  e. Banquet order sheets

  f. Order sizes

    g. Ordering procedures

    h. Purchase price trends

    i. Plant visits

4. Convention service

    a. Review of function-room setup checklists

    b. Banquet room assignments

    c. Event room capabilities and limitations

    d. Hospitality suites

    e. Clearing space for catering functions

    f. Pre-convention meetings

5. Tour and travel

    a. Travel agents

    b. Tour wholesalers

    c. General sales procedures

    d. Meal coupons

    e. Other coupons

    f. Product and service prices

6. Front office

    a. Reservations

    b. Front-desk procedures and software

        i. Check-in

        ii. Checkout

        iii. Baggage handling

    c. Coordination with sales department

    d. Room and suite tours (if applicable)

    e. Bell desk

    f. Concierge

7. Credit/accounting

    a. Credit procedures

    b. Deposit requirements

    c. Collections

        i. Procedures

        ii. Problems

      iii. Outside collection agencies

      iv. Types of accounts

8. Human resources

  a. General personnel procedures

  b. Coordination with other departments

  c. Compensation packages

9. Engineering

  a. Sound

  b. Lighting

  c. Utilities available in function rooms

  d. Charges for utilities, labor, and equipment

10. Public relations and advertising

  a. Food and beverage promotions

  b. Newspaper clippings and online articles

  c. Outside calls

  d. Attend functions at other catering operations

  e. Contact individuals responsible for buying catered functions

  f. Familiarization with competing catering organization's offerings

11. Safety

  a. Recognizing safety hazards

  b. Slippery floor procedures

  c. Customer safety

  d. Proper utilities hookups

  e. Setting up crosswalk areas

  f. Fire codes

  g. Health codes

  h. Evacuation routes

12. Laundry and valet

  a. Linen controls

  b. Stock requisitions

  c. Soiled linen storing procedures

  d. Usage charges

  e. Uniforms and costumes

The department head should use these suggested training guidelines to develop an appropriate training program for each new hire. The new hire's progress should then be monitored, with the department head submitting a training report to the director of catering at the conclusion of the training period.

The training report should be reviewed with the trainee before preparing the final draft. For instance, each time an entry is made in the report, the trainer and trainee should confer for a few moments to discuss the entry and determine if any changes need to be made in the program. This is also a good time to discuss the trainee's progress and clear up any questions or concerns.

For some new hires, it would be useful to have them prepare a personal report at the end of their training period. For instance, if you are training a new catering sales manager, you may want to ask him or her to submit a written report detailing what was learned after visiting and working in all other departments. This report can give you a valuable insight into the trainee's communications skills. It can reveal if additional training is needed. And it can also tell you if future training programs need to be modified.

COMPENSATION

The typical compensation package includes a combination of some of the following: salaries, wages, gratuities, commissions, bonuses, tips, required employee benefits, and discretionary employee benefits. In large facilities, compensation packages are developed and coordinated by the human resources department. You should know specifically the types and amounts of compensation allowed for each job classification so that potential job candidates will not be misled when you are cultivating them.

Management personnel normally receive predetermined salaries unrelated to the amount of time worked. Some managers, though, may receive performance bonuses or commissions. For instance, a catering sales manager may receive a modest fixed salary plus a percentage of either all business booked or all gratuities collected. Non-management positions are usually compensated on an hourly basis. Some of them may also receive a predetermined split of the gratuities collected for each catered event. If a client leaves a tip, the hourly employees typically will share it as well.

Required employee benefits are usually referred to as payroll taxes. They include primarily the employer's contribution to the federal government's social security, Medicare, and unemployment tax programs. Some states also require employers to contribute to their unemployment tax programs and the state-operated workers' compensation programs.

As a general rule, the minimum cost of required employee benefits is equal to about 15 to 18 percent of your total payroll expense. For instance, if you pay a server $10.00 per hour, the employer's out-of-pocket expense for this employee is about $11.50 to $11.80 per hour after factoring in these payroll taxes.

In some parts of the country, the total payroll tax expense is much higher because for most employees, the tax percentages will be applied to the payroll expense plus the amount of gratuities and declared tips they earn. For instance, if a $10.00-per-hour server averages an additional $5.00 per hour in gratuity and tip income, the hourly payroll tax expense for this employee will be about $2.25 to $2.70 (15 to 18 percent of $15.00). The hourly out-of-pocket expense for this employee, then, is about $12.25 to $12.70.

Typical discretionary benefits are health, dental, vision, and life insurance offered to employees at a reduced rate. Some companies also provide stock-option plans, profit-sharing plans, 401(k) plans, free or reduced-cost meals, matching contributions to selected charities, paid vacation days, paid sick days, reduced-cost vacations, insurance coverage for dependents, formal training, career opportunities (such as promotion from within), reimbursement of educational expenses, flexible work scheduling, uniform allowances, and reduced-cost meals, beverages, and sleeping rooms at other company-owned or -operated properties.

Generally speaking, only full-time employees qualify for the full range of discretionary benefits. Some facilities may offer a limited number of discretionary benefits to part-time employees who work at least twenty hours per week. Employees working nineteen hours or less per week usually do not qualify for discretionary benefits.

Some facilities, especially unionized properties, have generous overtime pay policies that exceed those mandated by federal and state labor regulations. They may also have very generous holiday pay policies. For instance, union or company policy may require you to pay double time instead of time and a half for all overtime worked, straight time for all state and federal holidays not worked, and double time for all state and federal holidays worked.

SUMMARY

The importance of staffing cannot be underestimated. The reputation of the facility depends on the quality of service provided by the staff. When recruiting job candidates, you must seek those who have skills and knowledge of the job, but who also have a good attitude. Caterers use a significant number of variable (on-call) employees, in addition to the fixed (steady) employees.

KEY TERMS

Job specification	Job description
Labor pool	Orientation
Overtime	Variable-cost employees
Discretionary employee benefits	Required employee benefits
Training	Job interview
Job application	Employee recruitment

REVIEW QUESTIONS

1. What is a job description?
2. What is a job specification?
3. What types of things motivate a client to book business with a particular caterer?
4. What is typically included in an employee's compensation package?
5. What does structural labor turnover refer to?

6. What is the difference between A-list and B-list employees?
7. What is an advantage of hiring senior citizens to work part time?
8. What services does a day-labor operation provide?
9. What is the difference between employee orientation and employee training?
10. What is another term for required employee benefits?

Chapter 10

FINANCIAL CONTROLS AND REPORTS

Control procedures must be used to ensure that actual performance is in line with the planned performance. The control cycle begins when a potential client considers booking business with your company and it does not end until the catered event is completed to everyone's satisfaction.

Before a control system can be implemented, you must set standards of performance. For instance, if you book a beverage function and you expect each bottle of liquor to yield approximately fifteen drinks, the actual number of drinks served per container must be consistent with this standard. If your bartenders pour more or less than fifteen drinks per container, you may have a control problem. If they pour too many drinks per container, the customers are probably receiving a reduced portion size. If they pour too few drinks per container, there is excessive waste or customers are receiving excessive portion sizes.

It is management's duty to set the required standards and policies by which all catered events will be run. All operational procedures—booking the business, purchasing, receiving, storing, issuing, producing, serving, function room selection and setup, final bill tabulation, and bill collection—must be standardized. If all employees follow the standard operating procedures, chances are you will reach your cost control and quality control goals with minimal difficulty.

One of management's primary responsibilities is to see to it that actual results are in line with the standards. To do this, management must develop data-gathering and data-analysis procedures that can be used to compute actual results and compare them to the standards. If there are variances between the standards and the actual results, management must move to identify and solve the underlying problems. Experience shows that this correction phase of control is the most difficult one because it is not always easy to diagnose what went wrong. If you cannot get at the root of the problem, it is impossible to solve it.

For example, if your bartenders are consistently pouring more drinks per bottle than you expect, there are many potential causes for this variance. Unintentionally underpouring each drink is the most logical cause, though mechanical problems with the liquor-dispensing machinery, inadequate record keeping, and failure to account properly for those guests who ask for short pours are also possible reasons.

Another difficult aspect of the control process is the potential for overcontrolling everything. You must be careful to not cost-control yourself out of business. You cannot spend a dollar to control a dime. There comes a point where some controls are not cost-effective. For instance, computerized automatic liquor-dispensing units will increase your ability to control drink service. Unfortunately, these systems are expensive and your investment may not be recovered in a reasonable period of time.

Overcontrol can also put a manager in the position of concentrating solely on inanimate objects and ignoring clients and guests. You cannot dwell so much on cost-related matters that you begin to lose sight of the customer. You must satisfy your clients and guests. However, if you are spending too much time gathering, processing, and analyzing data, you may be neglecting them.

It is very difficult to strike just the right balance between effective control and customer service. Experience shows that if you take good care of the guest, your expenses and profits will fall into line. But if you concentrate solely on every penny, eventually you will not have to worry about control because you will have no business left to control.

Michael Hurst, past president of the National Restaurant Association, summed it up best when he remarked that you could achieve maximum control by closing your business; this is the only way to avoid control problems. If you want to stay in business and build it into a profitable enterprise, he suggested, manage from the front door, not the back door. Taking care of the clients and guests and providing consistent value is the best recipe for success in the food and beverage industry. After all, clients don't select the caterer who has the best accounting and record-keeping systems.

The purpose of this chapter is to discuss the generally accepted control procedures used in the on-premise catering industry. By adopting them, the director of catering takes a giant step toward minimizing variances and maximizing client and guest satisfaction.

BANQUET EVENT ORDER

The banquet event order (BEO), sometimes referred to as the function sheet or just the event order, is the basis of the property's internal communication system. It also forms the agreement between the company and the client about all specific aspects of the event. Some larger properties also utilize a meeting event order, which is similar to a BEO except that it is used for an event without food or beverages. Smaller properties generally use one form regardless of whether there is food and beverage service or meeting only. These forms are the basic building block upon which the catering department's accounting and record-keeping systems are constructed.

A BEO is prepared for each meeting, meal and beverage function, or other event, and sent to the client for approval and signature. Copies are then sent to the departments or employees that will be directly or indirectly involved with the events.

Usually all departments receive a copy of each BEO a week or more before the catered function is held. This ensures that all department heads have enough time to schedule and complete their necessary activities that support the events.

BEOs are usually numbered sequentially for easy reference. If your software program does not automatically do so, it is important to manually assign an identifying number to each BEO. This way, department heads, or the catering executive and the client, can ensure they are discussing the same event to review any specifics or questions easily and quickly. For instance, if banquet setup is unclear about a particular event's requirements, it can call the catering office for additional information regarding BEO #175. This is certainly easier and more accurate than using clients' names or other forms of identification, particularly for clients that have multiple events.

The typical BEO contains the following information:

1. BEO number
2. Function day and date
3. Type of function
4. Client name with signature line
5. Client address
6. Client contact person, or person in charge
7. Person who booked the event and authorized signature(s)
8. Name of function room
9. Beginning time of function
10. Expected ending time of function
11. Number of guests expected (guarantee)
12. Number of guests to prepare for (caterers typically prepare a percentage over the guarantee to cover those who just show up)
13. Food and beverage menus
14. Style of service
15. Function room setup
16. Special instructions (audio-visual equipment, centerpieces, parking details, miscellaneous labor charges, linens, table sets, bar arrangements, props, entertainment, electrical or engineering needs, unique underliners, VIPs, other special amenities)
17. Prices charged
18. Billing instructions, with master billing account number if applicable
19. Reference to other BEOs or other relevant records

20. Date BEO was completed
21. Signature of person preparing (or approving) the BEO

PRE-FUNCTION SHEET

Some catering companies want to advise all employees well in advance of future catering activity. For instance, management may want everyone to have a good idea of the amount and types of catering business booked for the next month. This can be done by preparing a monthly pre-function sheet that briefly notes the types of events and number of guests expected the following month.

The pre-function sheet serves many purposes. Its major advantage is that it allows each department head to pre-plan his or her staffing needs for the long term. Other advantages are that the kitchen and purchasing departments can use this information to plan tentative ordering, pre-preparation, and preparation schedules; the storeroom can plan its inventory management procedures more effectively; convention service and the steward departments will have plenty of time to secure additional furniture, equipment, and tableware if needed; and housekeeping can plan its heavy cleaning routines much more easily if it knows what to expect.

CHANGE ORDER

Usually clients have opportunities to make alterations in their booked functions. For instance, they may be able to make changes to the menu one week before the event is scheduled, adjust the time of service three days before, and decide to add extra bars twenty-four hours in advance.

At times several changes must be made at the last minute. For example, if a function that initially expects 400 guests suddenly expands to 600 guests, the property may need to move the buffet line into the pre-function space in order to accommodate additional seating.

Sometimes a change may be suggested by the caterer. For instance, if there is a challenge getting a particular wine, the catering sales representative will discuss with the client alternative options that can be served for the same price.

These types of alterations must be communicated to all employees involved with the catered event. The most efficient way to do this is to prepare an addendum to the original BEO.

The BEO addendum is usually referred to as a banquet change order, banquet change log, or banquet change sheet. It contains the original BEO's identification number as well as other pertinent identifying factors, and it notes very specifically the changes that must be made. The caterer must specify clearly what must be eliminated, added, or changed in regard to the scheduled catered event.

Some software programs will prompt you to do a change order each time a BEO is revised. With these systems, you may hold all changes and then print and distribute them once per day. This can prevent support departments from being inundated with numerous change orders at various times throughout each day.

Some caterers use a paper color-coded system to ensure that changes are recorded accurately. For instance, they may use a color-coded system: white for the original BEO, canary for revised BEOs, and pink for change logs. In this case, if a change must be communicated, all relevant departments will receive them on canary or pink paper, update their original BEOs, and retain only one copy. A similar system that is computerized can further reduce the paper flow.

RESUME

A resume is a detailed summary of all relevant aspects of a convention or meeting. Included is information on the group itself and the purpose of the convention or meeting. It may or may not contain all of the BEOs for an event. If the program is large, often an outline is created of the meeting space needed along with room setup type, rather than including each individual BEO.

Generally speaking, the resume includes:

1. Function days and dates
2. Types of functions
3. Client name
4. Client contact information (address, email address, and cell phone number)
5. Client contact person, or person in charge

6. Person who booked the events along with authorized signature(s)

7. VIPs

8. Overview of all meeting space used, including:

   a. Beginning and expected ending times of functions

   b. Function room names

   c. Function room setup

   d. Number of attendees

9. Room rental charges

10. Original sleeping room block

11. Actual pickup of sleeping rooms

12. Amenities

13. Transportation

14. Special instructions

15. Security arrangements

16. In-room dining

17. Bell desk room drops and deliveries

18. Business center equipment and services needed

19. Housekeeping notes

20. Front desk notes

21. Group arrival and departure information

22. Estimated charges and deposits folio

23. Master billing account number

24. Billing instructions

25. Reference to other relevant records

26. Date convention resume was completed

27. Names of sales manager, convention services manager, and catering manager

28. Signature of person preparing (or approving) the resume

29. List of departments receiving a copy of the resume

For sample resumes, please see the Event Specifications Guide on the Convention Industry Council's website, www.conventionindustry.org. Choose Apex, and select "Accepted Practices," then click on event specification guides.

CATERING CONTRACT

Caterers typically require clients to sign formal catering contracts before the events are scheduled to take place. This is especially true when dealing with large functions.

Sometimes a property will forgo the use of formal contracts and instead rely on signed BEOs or signed letters of agreement. These documents may be every bit as legally enforceable as formal contracts. Usually, though, they do not include the typical boilerplate language (the standardized legalese) found in most formal contracts. Signing an agreement is much less threatening to most people than signing a contract.

You should never book and confirm a catered event without a signed agreement. Usually an unwritten contract cannot be legally enforced in a court of law unless you are dealing with an agreement worth $500 or less. But even with small parties, it is good business practice to detail in writing both your and the client's responsibilities and obligations.

If you have standardized contract forms, you can give a copy to a potential client to read and study before progressing any further. This gives the client enough time to examine the terms and conditions and to ask questions if anything is unclear.

Many properties develop standardized contracts that contain a considerable amount of boilerplate with enough blank space available to write in specific details as needed. For typical functions, the standard contract will usually suffice. But if there is anything unusual that must be addressed, the caterer's legal counsel or other representative must add it.

If a convention client requires uncommon services, the facility's and client's legal representatives may work together to negotiate a mutually agreeable arrangement. This can then be added to the standard boilerplate contract, or it can be written as a stand-alone contract.

Some catering departments do not have to get involved with contract preparations. For instance, if you are part of a hotel sales department, the director of sales may handle all contract negotiations for groups that require sleeping rooms as well. He or she may take care of adding clauses, explaining policies, detailing the property's responsibilities and obligations, and so forth. Only occasionally would you need to participate in these developments. However, catering managers at these properties will likely need to do contracts for groups that hold events at your facility with no sleeping rooms attached.

The basic catering contract usually includes the following details:

1. Contract date
2. Function days and dates
3. Function times
4. Appropriate client and facility signatures
5. Function rooms tentatively assigned, with room rentals if applicable
6. Function room setups
7. Overset policy
8. Outside food and beverage restrictions
9. Display limitations
10. Licenses and permits required
11. Substitution procedures
12. Insurance requirements
13. Cancellation policies
14. Other client services as appropriate, such as:
    a. Audiovisual options
    b. Sleeping rooms and rates
    c. Transportation guidelines
    d. Security requirements
15. Food and beverage minimums (and/or head count guarantees per function)
16. Estimated cost summary
    a. Food and beverage charges
    b. Consumption taxes
    c. Gratuities and service charges
    d. Labor charges
    e. Room setup charges
    f. Deposits
    g. Other charges

17. Amounts and due dates of deposits
18. Billing procedures and collection procedures
19. Procedures that must be used if changes are necessary
20. All catering policies (see Chapter 1)
21. Client's responsibilities and obligations
22. Other standard contract language, such as:
    a. Person signing contract represents he or she has full authority to legally bind the client
    b. Contract to be binding upon the parties, as well as their heirs, administrators, executors, successors, and assigns
    c. Client has read the contract and completely understands its contents
    d. Client stipulates he or she is not signing the contract under duress

CREDIT MANAGEMENT

Usually very few clients are eligible for or are extended credit. As a general rule, clients are expected to pay the full estimated total in advance.

Probably the major reason caterers are reluctant to advance credit is the fact that the services provided are completely consumed. You can repossess a car or other tangible asset if a customer reneges, but this option does not exist when selling catering services.

Most hotels and conference centers offering catering services operate their own credit department for corporate or association groups. Since many of these functions exceed several thousand dollars, bank or travel-and-entertainment credit cards may have insufficient credit lines to be used to pay for them. The typical hotel will usually take a credit card payment only for small to midsized functions. For example, if you are serving a business luncheon for 25 guests in a private dining room, you may be willing to treat this event as if it were a normal restaurant transaction.

If a client is eligible for credit, the venue's credit manager will evaluate the client's credit rating and, if credit is approved, set up a master account number. He or she will then detail the property's deposit requirements and billing procedures.

Deposit

All but a very few select clients are expected to put up a deposit of 25 to 50 percent of the estimated final bill, depending on the size of the catered function, to hold the date and space. The remaining balance is then due two weeks prior to the event.

When taking a deposit, the credit manager or catering executive will issue a receipt to the client, and the deposit will be recorded in the client's file.

Forms of Payment

Personal or company checks are generally accepted as long as there is a minimum of fourteen working days prior to the event. This allows enough time for the check to clear.

Other acceptable forms of payment are cash, cashier's check, wire transfer, or credit card.

Many caterers allow clients to use their personal or company credit cards to pay for catering services. This procedure virtually eliminates credit risk. It also makes the caterer's job a lot easier since the credit card company handles all the credit verification chores and billing procedures. Unfortunately, when a client uses a credit card, caterers must pay a fee, called a merchant fee or discount rate, to the credit card company. The fee is usually a percentage of the amount of money charged. Depending on the type of card used, you can pay as much as 5 to 6 percent of the charge. Some caterers will pass on this merchant fee to the client while others absorb this as a cost of doing business.

Settlement

Stadiums, arenas, and other facilities that sell tickets to an event promoted by a client may handle payment via settlement. Settlement is the process of taking all revenue collected by the venue in the form of ticket sales and subtracting all event expenses, such as catering, rent, production, staffing, and so on. Any remaining balance is given to the promoter as profit. Generally no deposit is required for these types of events. However, if ticket sales are not going as well as expected, the venue may require the promoter to put up a deposit prior to the event to ensure that all minimum building expenses are met.

Billing Procedures

When dealing with clients eligible for credit, the credit manager will bill them according to the terms and conditions noted in the catering contract. The final accountings will be prepared immediately after the catered events. Some clients will be billed for the total amount due, while others will be given a credit period during which they are required to follow a specific payment schedule.

In a few cases, credit-worthy clients will not have to pay immediately after the event. Usually the facility will set up a billing cycle that is mutually agreeable to both parties. Moreover, tradition and competition sometimes enter the picture, whereby specific credit periods are granted to certain clients as a matter of standard operating procedure. For instance, some corporate clients are accustomed to billing cycles ranging between seven and sixty days for all their purchases. Government clients are also accustomed to these billing cycles. You may need to offer these credit terms in order to be competitive with other caterers soliciting such clients.

Most caterers, though, and particularly small organizations that have difficulty extending credit for events they have already paid expenses on, require full prepayment prior to the event. Typically a client will have to spend at least a certain amount to apply for a direct bill (invoicing procedure where a client is sent a bill after the event and has a specified period of time to remit payment), and this amount needs to be agreed to a specified number of days prior to the event.

Collection Procedures

If a client fails to make a scheduled payment, the credit manager usually sets into motion pre-planned collection procedures.

If a client is late, normally the credit manager will call the client immediately and discuss the problem and possible solutions. If this effort fails to produce results, sterner measures are instituted. For instance, a registered letter may be sent, or the bill may be faxed or emailed. These procedures take away the opportunity for the client to say that the bill was lost in the mail.

If all these efforts yield nothing, then the manager may turn the problem over to its corporate credit department. This office usually has more sophisticated collection procedures. It also will take the drastic step of turning over the account to an independent bill collection agency if necessary.

Other Credit-Related Issues

The catering executive or credit department may need to be involved with other credit-related issues. The credit manager, either alone or in conjunction with the catering executive, could be faced with the following:

1. Tax-exempt clients must demonstrate this status by providing their tax-exempt number and any other related documentation.

2. If clients are promised complimentary products or services, the final billings must be adjusted accordingly.

3. Some caterers pay referral fees or other types of commissions. If so, the credit manager may need to provide data necessary to compute them correctly.

4. A property may want to offer clients discounts if they pay their bills in cash or before the due dates. If so, the final billing will need to be adjusted; alternatively, a cash rebate may be mailed to clients.

5. If a client cancels the catered event, the credit manager or catering executive will need to determine if he or she will forfeit the entire deposit or if part of it can be refunded. In some cases, particularly when clients cancel at the last minute, perhaps the deposit is insufficient consideration. If so, the appropriate charges will need to be computed and collection procedures will need to commence.

6. Some clients may have refunds due. For instance, you may want a client to put up a refundable deposit for audiovisual equipment. When the equipment is returned on time and in an acceptable condition, the deposit will be credited to the final billing, or a separate refund check may be issued.

Another form of refund is buying back drink tickets from guests who did not use all of them. Usually a caterer will not buy back those that were purchased by the client and given to the guests. However, if a guest purchases extra drink tickets and does not use them all, the caterer may have a policy of repurchasing them.

7. Returns and allowances may need to be factored into the final billing. For example, if you had to make a last-minute menu substitute that is less expensive than the original selection, you may need to adjust the final billing. Conversely, if the chef had to use a more expensive substitute, the manager may not wish to pursue the matter because it is not the client's fault that the original item could not be procured. However, the client and catering executive may meet in advance of the event and perhaps agree to split the difference if such circumstances arise. If so, this may need to be taken into account when processing the final billing.

FOOD AND BEVERAGE COST CONTROL

Effective product cost control is based on standardized operating procedures. To ensure consistent, predictable business results, top management must establish budgetary standards, quality standards, labor standards, layout and design standards—the list is endless.

If there is one major, overriding problem afflicting many businesses in the food and beverage industry, it is the lack of standards. This is understandable due to the fact that they are difficult to establish, implement, monitor, and revise. The poorly trained manager only has so much time. When rushed, he or she may neglect company standards and permit unacceptable practices.

Even establishments that have complete sets of standards can fall prey to the inability or unwillingness of managers to apply them consistently. The best control procedures are worthless if they are not used correctly.

Management must develop and implement a consistent cycle of control. Moreover, it must monitor the control system continually so that needed changes can be made quickly and efficiently.

The food and beverage operation's cycle of control begins with the purchasing function. It continues through receiving, storing, issuing, production, and service. Checks and balances are inserted throughout the cycle in order to pinpoint responsibility and reveal any problems.

The main purpose of product cost control, or any other expense control, is to ensure that actual costs parallel standard (budgeted) costs. Unlike the typical restaurant business, catering is in a better position to minimize variances between standard and actual costs. After all, you know what to expect and when to expect it. Consequently, it is easier to forecast your needs and prepare for them accordingly.

Experience shows, though, that catering's advantage over the typical restaurant operation is not as large as it may initially appear. For instance, even though you know what to expect, guests are notorious for arriving late, leaving late, and requesting special attention at the last minute.

As a general rule, the potential to minimize variances between actual and standard costs is a bit easier for the typical catering organization. But while this may be true, the system is not error-free. It can be as close as possible to being error-free, though, if you pay close attention to every major operating activity.

Purchasing

The food and beverage cycle of control begins in the purchasing agent's office. This person is responsible for selecting and procuring the needed products for the most economical prices. Values obtained by the purchasing agent establish initially the ultimate costs of doing business.

Probably the most critical cost control tool used by the purchasing agent is the product specification. Food and beverage costs, as well as the quality of finished menu items, cannot be predicted accurately unless you are using standardized, consistent product specifications. You must use the same ingredients time after time or else the finished products' costs and culinary qualities will vary unpredictably.

Another major cost control technique is to identify appropriate suppliers who can handle your needs adequately, and include them on an approved supplier list. When ordering, only these approved suppliers should be used. Exceptions must be authorized by top management.

The purchasing agent also contributes to cost and quality control by preparing and entering the optimal order sizes for each ingredient purchased. If you order too little, you risk running out of an item, which can result in unhappy guests. If you order too much, you risk spoilage and excessive inventory carrying charges.

Catering lends itself nicely to computing optimal order sizes because, unlike typical restaurant service, most catered events are very predictable. If, for instance, you expect 100 dinner guests and you normally prepare for 105, you then order enough merchandise to prepare and serve 105 meals. In most cases, you do not have to anticipate customer demands because you know about them well in advance. Furthermore, if the ingredients used for catered events are also used in other outlets in your property or for other events, you can even order a little additional safety stock and not worry about it going bad in storage.

Receiving

Unlike the typical restaurant operation, hotels and other large catering companies usually do a very good job receiving their shipments. They usually assign at least one full-time receiving agent to ensure that deliveries are consistent with purchase orders and the product specifications.

Many caterers follow the invoice receiving technique. This system requires the receiving agent to:

1. Compare the delivery slip (invoice) to the purchase order. You must be certain that the shipment is the correct one and that it contains all the items originally ordered.

2. Compare the products delivered with the invoice and the purchase order. All three must match.

3. Inspect the quality of each item. The shipment must meet the product specifications. If not, it should not be accepted unless a supervisor authorizes receipt.

4. Inspect the quantity of each item. Weights, volume, counts, and so forth must be accurate.

5. Arrange for credit from the supplier, if applicable. If there is any problem with product quality or quantity, the receiving agent must get a credit slip from the driver. If the driver is an independent trucker, you will need to send a request-for-credit memorandum to the supplier's credit department. Before the bill is paid, any and all credits must be properly accounted for.

6. Sign the invoice, retain a copy for payment, and arrange to store the shipment.

Storage and Issuing

The major purpose of storage is to protect the merchandise from theft and spoilage. Theft is minimized by keeping everything under lock and key, restricting access to the storeroom facilities, and using a standardized issuing system whereby anyone wanting merchandise from the storeroom must complete and sign an authorized stock requisition and take responsibility for the products.

Spoilage is minimized by maintaining appropriate sanitation standards and rotating the stock correctly. Products must also be stored in the appropriate temperature, humidity, and ventilation environment.

Canned goods and other dry storage groceries should be stored at about 70°F (50°F is ideal), with approximately 50 percent relative humidity.

Frozen foods should be stored at 0°F or less. Refrigerated meats, seafood, and poultry should be stored at the coldest temperature possible without freezing, dairy products at about 34 to 38°F, and produce at about 36 to 40°F. Each of these product categories requires approximately 85 percent relative humidity. Ideally, you will have at least three separate walk-in refrigerators so that the recommended temperature and humidity can be maintained.

Products in the typical food service operation's storage facilities normally do not spoil to the point where they are inedible. Usually they lose just enough culinary quality to render them unfit for service. For instance, flaccid lettuce could be eaten without risking food-borne illness; however, you cannot expect customers to pay for it. The challenge of maintaining culinary quality is a little more daunting in the food and beverage industry than it is, say, in a home kitchen.

Production

Pre-prep and prep procedures offer several opportunities for cost overruns. To combat this tendency, the catering executive should work with the chef and food and beverage director to develop adequate production controls. The major production controls that should be emphasized are:

1. *Always use standardized recipes.* Standardized recipes are just as important as product specifications. It is useless to purchase the same quality of merchandise every time if you do not use consistent pre-prep and prep procedures.

2. *Develop a standardized production plan.* The timing of pre-prep and prep activities is another crucial factor impacting product costs. This is particularly true for foods, since if you produce foods too far in advance, chances are you will have a lot of finished items that are past their peak of culinary quality and cannot be served.

Since you have a good idea of how much to produce and when the finished items will be served, you normally can develop a very accurate production plan. It is this knowledge that gives you a cost control advantage over the typical restaurant operation; predictability minimizes cost variances.

3. *Supervise portioning procedures.* Experience shows that we tend to over-portion foods. Guests who help themselves tend to take more than they can eat. And employees have the tendency to put a little more on the guest's plate, especially if the guest is witnessing the dish-up process.

It is also true that we have a tendency to create excess waste during the production process. This is especially the case if we are rushed. Since you usually have sufficient lead time and know what to expect, chances are correct production planning can virtually eliminate this problem.

Many foodservice experts believe that if you use standardized product specifications and recipes, make a conscious effort to reduce avoidable waste, and maintain portion control, the odds are excellent that your actual costs will be in line with your standard costs. Minimizing or eliminating cost variances should be one of the food production manager's major goals.

Service

Usually if you have enough servers, you will not encounter any significant service problems that could cause cost and quality variances. However, good service does not just happen. Someone must supervise and monitor the service function to ensure cost and quality standards are met and all guests are satisfied.

The most critical aspects of service control are:

1. *Plating should be done as close as possible to service time.* Culinary quality suffers if finished items have to sit any longer than necessary. Products past their peak of quality cannot be served; usually they end up in the garbage, with your product costs increasing and profit percentages decreasing accordingly. Service costs may also increase if you need to plate and serve quite a bit of food to replace products that cannot be served.

2. *An expediter should be used to coordinate production and service.* This person usually sees to it that servers' needs are communicated properly to production people and that guest orders are delivered from the kitchen and served to the guests in a timely manner. Usually a supervisor or manager fills this critical role as part of his or her overall responsibilities.

3. *A food checker should be used to inspect the quality of finished menu items.* He or she should also be responsible for ensuring that only the correct portion sizes of meals and beverages are served. Also, as meals are carried from the kitchen to the banquet room, the food checker will keep a running tally of them and compare the total served to the expected number of guests noted on the banquet event order. As with the expediter position, this role may be filled by a supervisor or manager.

In some cases the expediter could also perform the food checker's duties. For small catered events, he or she could keep the tally as well as maintain coordination between production and service.

Food and Beverage Cost Control Record-Keeping System

Your cost control efforts are incomplete if you do not have some way of gathering and analyzing cost data.

You will need an effective data-gathering and analysis procedure for at least two reasons: one, you must have some way of calculating standard and actual product usage, and two, these data might be needed to calculate a client's final billing.

If you are primarily interested in calculating standard and actual costs, you should use the standard-cost record-keeping system.

The standard-cost system is a rather long, arduous procedure that is not usually performed in the typical foodservice operation unless it is fully computerized. It is usually too difficult and time-consuming to operate this system by hand.

The system requires you to calculate the standard cost for each menu item. You must pre-cost each menu item—that is, you must determine the exact standard cost for each one. This requires you to cost out each recipe and calculate the expected (or potential) product cost per serving.

Once you have the potential product cost for each serving, you need to multiply it by the number of servings used. This gives you the total standard cost.

To compute the total actual cost, you must take a physical inventory of all foods and beverages left at the end of the catered function and cost it out. This ending inventory is then inserted into the following formula in order to compute the total actual cost:

> Beginning inventory (the previous ending inventory)
> + Issues from the storeroom
> + Direct purchases (i.e., deliveries that bypass the storeroom and go directly to production)
> − Ending inventory
> _____
> = Total actual cost

The total standard cost is compared to the total actual cost. If there is a significant variance, you need to go back through the cycle of control and see if you can spot the problems. That is to say, you must examine your purchasing, receiving, storing, issuing, pre-prep, prep, and service procedures to see what needs to be corrected. You then make the necessary corrections so that future catered events do not suffer the same fate.

Experience shows that if there is a significant cost variance, the problem is typically due to one of five reasons:

1. *There may be errors in the record-keeping system.* This is oftentimes the primary reason. It is always best to check this first, for just as a nonworking piece of equipment can easily be caused by failure to plug it in, small arithmetic errors can cause huge variances.

2. *Check your purchasing and receiving procedures.* Sometimes the products ordered are not consistent with the specifications; for instance, you may be ordering a more expensive product without realizing it. Or you may be receiving an incorrect product, one that either costs too much or does not work properly in your recipes.

3. *Review your standard recipe costs.* Sometimes these data are out-of-date and cannot give you an accurate analysis.

4. *Be alert to overproduction and overportioning.* If the first three reasons are not the problem, you can usually expect that excessive leftovers or portion sizes are the culprits.

5. *Someone may be stealing.*

Some foodservice managers will cost out recipes only once in a while, while others will cost out each event. When submitting a competitive bid to a client, the catering executive should always calculate current recipe costs. Likewise, you may need the current standard costs if you book an event that will be priced according to the amount of food and beverage consumed.

Another way of gathering and analyzing cost-related data is to use the product analysis record-keeping system. This system (sometimes referred to as the critical item inventory system) concentrates on food and beverage usage, not on their costs.

This system is not as accurate as the standard cost system, but it is much easier to use. However, while it exchanges a bit of accuracy for time saving, the information it yields is sufficient to control product costs. Experience shows that it is the most common type of product cost record-keeping system used in the foodservice industry.

In a nutshell, this system involves a comparison of banquet room counts to production counts. For instance, if the kitchen plates up 125 steak dinners, the banquet records should reveal that 125 guests were served. The kitchen usage should compare favorably with head counts, plate counts, meal tickets, entree tickets, or any other service records used. Any variance must be investigated and the underlying problems corrected.

The products counted are usually only the critical (expensive) items. For example, if you book a party for 100 T-bone steak dinners (and plan to prepare 5 percent more than over the guarantee just to be on the safe side), you tend to concentrate your food cost control efforts solely on the meat. You should take the time to compare kitchen counts with banquet room counts. In addition, you should match these data with the stock requisition records and check for consistency. If everything works out right, there will be 105 T-bone steaks noted on the stock requisition and/or direct purchase invoice, 105 prepared, and 105 served or otherwise accounted for.

Some foodservice experts are critical of this system primarily because you neglect other product costs. However, the product costs you neglect are not nearly as high as the ones you monitor. As a result, while not infallible, the system does provide a reasonable measure of product cost control. Furthermore, this system provides enough information to calculate the final billings of those catered functions that are priced according to the amount of guest consumption.

Foodservice experts also may criticize this system because if you rely on it exclusively, you will ignore raw product purchase prices and edible portion costs. If this happens, you may not have sufficient data upon which to base menu prices. You also do not know if your month-end actual cost calculations reflect reality because you have no standard cost with which to compare it.

It would appear that the product-analysis system will be with us for some time since the standard-cost system cannot effectively be used unless the food and beverage operation is fully computerized or a large central accounting staff is maintained. The cost of an integrated property computer system is expensive and may not be cost effective for the typical food and beverage operation. However, without a sophisticated, expensive computer system that links all operating activities performed by the property, it is difficult and time-consuming to maintain accurate, current recipe costs.

A form of product analysis that is used exclusively for beverages is sometimes referred to as the ounce system of control. Under this procedure, the manager establishes a standard number of drinks that should be poured from each container, and the actual number of drinks served should be consistent with the standard.

For instance, if you use 1 liter containers of vodka and the average drink size is 1½ ounces, the potential number of drinks per bottle is 22.5 (33.8 ounces ÷ 1.5 ounces = 22.5 drinks). At the end of the beverage function, if you note that 2.7 bottles of vodka were used, the sales records for vodka should reflect approximately 60 drinks served (2.7 bottles × 22.5 drinks = 60.75 drinks). In this example, after taking an ending inventory and calculating the expected number of drinks served, you should have approximately 60 drink tickets, or the cash equivalent, for the vodka.

At the end of the beverage function, the manager will calculate the usage of each brand of liquor and determine the total number of potential drinks served. This total serves as your basis of comparison, the standard to which is compared the actual number of drink tickets/cash collected.

Generally speaking, you expect the actual number of drinks served to be a bit less than the standard. For instance, if the bartenders do not use a liquor-dispensing machine and have to free-pour, chances are there will be some overpouring. Furthermore, with free pouring, you cannot get all the liquor out of the bottle; some of it will remain in the bottle since you usually do not have time to wait for every last bit to drip out.

Faced with this situation, you may need to adjust your standards. For instance, you may plan to lose, say, ½ ounce of liquor per container and revise your standards downward. For instance, in the vodka example noted above, you might expect 22 drinks per container instead of 22.5.

For complete control, when selling beverage tickets by a cashier, you will need to relay the beverage usage data to the head cashier so that he or she can audit the performance of the cashier assigned to the beverage function. The basic comparison here is between the number of drink tickets sold, the number collected by bartenders, and the amount of cash collected. The cash collected and the number of drink tickets sold should match exactly. However, you expect the number of drink tickets collected to be a little smaller than the number sold and the cash collected because a few guests may not use all the drink tickets purchased.

If the bartenders collect cash from guests, you might want to use the standard sales record-keeping system for beverage functions. This system (sometimes referred to as the potential sales system) is very similar to the ounce system, in that it concentrates on usage and not on product costs. The major difference is that it allows you to control cash as well as product usage.

To use this system, you need to calculate a bottle value for each container of liquor stocked in inventory. The bottle value represents the amount of sales revenue a container of liquor should generate. For instance, if the 1½ ounce serving of vodka noted in the example above sells for $5.75 per drink, the bottle value of a liter of vodka is approximately $129.38 (33.8 ounces ÷ 1.5 ounces = 22.5 drinks; 22.5 drinks × $5.75 = $129.38). If you note at the end of the function that 1.7 liters of vodka were used, the cash collected should be approximately $219.95 (1.7 bottles × $129.38 = $219.95).

At the end of every beverage function, you must calculate usage rates for each brand of liquor. Each brand's usage rate must then be converted to its standard sales revenue. After calculating each brand's standard sales revenue, a grand total of standard sales revenue must be determined. This grand total serves as your overall standard sales figure, which is then compared to actual sales revenue (the total cash collected). The comparison should show very little variance.

A variation of the standard sales record-keeping system is to keep track of disposable glassware usage. For instance, if you use 9-ounce plastic cups for mixed drinks that are sold for $5.00 apiece, and there are 100 cups missing at the end of the event, the cash collected should equal $500, and the beverage inventory should be consistent with the preparation and service of 100 mixed drinks.

Controlling Product Costs for Buffets, Receptions, and Open Bars

If guests are able to serve themselves or can order drinks without using drink tickets or other forms of documentation, your cost control procedures need to be adjusted to take into account average usage figures. Since you do not control portions or guest usage rates, your purchasing, production, and service strategies must be based on historical averages. This requires you to analyze previous catered events periodically in order to keep up-to-date on average customer usage in your property.

Another key area that will need revision is the record-keeping system used. If you use the product analysis system, you must be sure to use relevant averages or else you will have no control over the critical items. For instance, if you are serving veal cutlets on an all-you-can-eat buffet line for 100 guests, and in the past you note that each guest takes, on average, 1½ servings, at the end of the event the kitchen and banquet room counts should balance at around 150 servings.

Unfortunately, when working with averages, there is a greater opportunity for inventory shrinkage (loss of product). For instance, in the veal cutlet example, you have no way of knowing if five of the 150 servings were pilfered by employees unless you use additional subtle cost control procedures designed specifically to thwart this activity. This is particularly troublesome if the client's final billing is based on guest consumption.

Unfortunately in our industry, there are many opportunities for undetected pilferage if you must work with average cost data. Mystery shoppers, extra supervision in the function room and kitchen, web-cams, and similar techniques usually must be deployed to minimize them.

Product Cost Reduction Techniques

While cost reduction technically is not the same as cost control, many people see no difference between them. The typical food and beverage operation spends about one-third of its sales revenue on product costs. Any little decrease, therefore, will have a major favorable impact on net profits.

Some of the more common product cost reduction techniques used in the foodservice industry are:

1. *Seek long-term competitive bids from suppliers.* This allows you to maximize your purchasing power. Suppliers may be willing to offer price concessions if they can count on your business.

2. *Qualify for purchase-price discounts.* For instance, many suppliers will grant quantity discounts if you purchase a huge amount of one type of item. Before agreeing to a very large purchase, though, make sure that you will be able to use the item in a reasonable amount of time and have enough storage space and cash or trade credit available to handle it.

If you submit large purchase orders, you may qualify for a volume discount. This type of discount is offered if you purchase a large dollar amount of several types of items.

Some suppliers offer promotional discounts, whereby they may reduce the purchase price if you agree to promote their products in your operation. For instance, if you allow them to put table-rent advertisements on your dining room tables, you might receive a 1 or 2 percent price reduction.

Cash discounts may also be lucrative alternatives. These are granted by some suppliers if you pay your bill before the due date. Purchasing agents will routinely ask suppliers if they offer any type of discount for prompt payment.

3. *Other purchasing opportunities.* Suppliers occasionally offer other cost-reduction opportunities the caterer may find attractive. For instance, you may be willing to take advantage of:

a. *New products.* These usually carry some sort of temporary introductory price that is much lower than normal. You could stock up on some of these things and use them to accommodate a few catering functions. For instance, a new pre-prepared chicken hors d'oeuvre may come on the market. You may be able to get two free cases for every one you purchase at the regular price. If you have the storage room and the money, you could stock up on this product and offer it as a low-cost alternative to some of your clients who are on tight budgets.

b. *Discontinuation sales.* Similar to the new product introductory prices, these money-saving items can increase your net profits or allow you to be more competitive when soliciting cost-conscious clients.

c. *Consider trading for products instead of paying cash.* Many businesses have trade-out arrangements with certain suppliers. For instance, instead of paying cash for your canned groceries, you might find a supplier who is willing to accept payment in kind. While trading is not commonly done for food commodities (it is more common with services, such as outdoor advertising), it is worth pursuing because bartering can save a good deal of money. It is cheaper to pay a $100 invoice with $100 worth of menu items because your out-of-pocket costs are much less than $100. And if you allow these trade credits to be used only during your slow periods, there will be no extra pressure on your production and service staffs.

4. *Use more raw food ingredients.* These are much cheaper than pre-prepared convenience items. Unfortunately, you will usually spend more for labor and energy since you will need to do most, if not all, of the pre-prep and prep work. Generally, though, except for the restaurant operation, the typical on-premise caterer has sufficient production space and labor on hand to make raw-ingredient use an economical option.

LABOR COST CONTROL

Foodservice experts agree that there are usually two main lines of defense against labor cost variances: maximize sales revenue and use effective work scheduling techniques.

As with most cost control problems, your troubles seem to vanish whenever you have a great deal of business. For example, an extra server's salary doesn't seem important when you are busy every day. It is usually so small in comparison to the heavy volume of business that it probably would not show up in a cost analysis. Excessive sales revenue cures many ills.

The manager's second line of defense against labor cost variances is the work schedule. Your work scheduling skills will have a major impact on your ability to minimize variances between standard and actual labor costs.

The work schedule represents the standard labor cost. It is based on the property's staffing guide. And the staffing guide is based primarily on the number of guests expected. As the guest count increases, the number of work hours and staff members needed also increases.

Unfortunately, the relationship between number of guests and number of work hours and staff members needed is not easily predictable. For instance, there is no neat formula that tells you how many work hours you need for each guest, nor is there a calculus that reveals the additional number of work hours that should be scheduled if five more guests show up. Furthermore, you cannot always predict if you need more staff members to handle a few more guests; for example, if one server can usually handle 14 guests, he or she may be able to handle 16 with no additional trouble.

The optimal labor cost is a very elusive figure in the foodservice business. Unlike food and beverage costs, labor costs are not completely variable. They have been tagged with several descriptions, such as semi-variable costs, semi-fixed costs, and step-wise variable costs. The fact remains, though, that if you plot labor costs against sales revenue on a graph, you will not get a straight line.

Factors Affecting Labor Cost

The optimal labor cost is a bit unpredictable because there are so many factors affecting it. While some factors are controllable, many of them are not.

And the degree of control that can be exercised can vary considerably among catering operations. Indeed, if you manage a particular property and have mastered its labor cost control vagaries, you may find that a transfer to another property will cause you to regress temporarily to the bottom of the learning curve in that some things you did at the old property cannot be effectively used at the new one.

The key factors that affect the amount and cost of labor needed are:

1. Menu
2. Style of service
3. Guest count
4. Guest arrival patterns
5. Facility layout and design
6. Type of equipment
7. Employee tenure
8. Employee turnover
9. Local labor market conditions
10. Hours of operation
11. Union regulations
12. Federal and state labor department regulations
    a. Minimum wage
    b. Tip credit
    c. Meal credit
    d. Child labor restrictions
    e. Overtime pay
13. Amount of payroll taxes
    a. Social security
    b. Medicare
    c. Unemployment insurance
    d. Workers' compensation insurance
14. Amount of other discretionary employee benefits (e.g., health insurance, holiday pay)

Labor Cost Control Record-Keeping System

As with any type of cost control record-keeping system, the primary objectives are to compute standard and actual costs, compare them, and evaluate and correct any unacceptable variances.

The standard labor cost is computed by costing out the work schedule and tacking on the cost of payroll taxes and other employee benefits. If you are lucky, a healthy part of the work schedule will be fixed. But if the bulk of your work schedule is variable, you might have to calculate standard costs daily.

The caterer must expect the typical work schedule to lean heavily in the direction of variable-cost employees since many catered functions booked in your property may need completely different crews. Furthermore, if the client is paying separately for labor, you will need to cost out the entire work schedule.

You cannot avoid calculating standard labor costs. Competitive bids rely on accurate cost estimates. Since labor is a considerable chunk of the total cost needed to prepare for and serve a catered event, chances are the catering sales representatives will continually need current labor cost estimates.

Actual labor costs are computed by costing out the time records and adding the appropriate amount of payroll taxes and discretionary employee benefits. Some time records are fixed; for example, the salaries of assistants, supervisors, and managers may not vary. However, variable-cost employees normally use a time clock or sign a time sheet.

The fixed and variable work hours are converted to a total actual labor cost. This actual is then compared to the standard. As always, if there is a significant variance, the problems must be uncovered and corrective action taken.

If there is a significant variance, chances are you can trim your labor force a bit without compromising guest service. But usually you cannot eliminate smaller variances unless you increase your sales revenue. This is why upselling is so critical. The added revenue allows you greater flexibility, which in turn enhances service and pleases clients and guests. Long after the catered events are over, clients will be talking about the food, beverage, and service they received. Rarely will they even remember the price paid.

Labor Cost Reduction Techniques

The typical food and beverage operation spends at the very least approximately 30 percent of each sales revenue dollar for payroll, with another 5 percent or more going for employee benefits. In some cases, payroll, employee benefits, and payroll-related administrative costs can exceed 40 percent of a foodservice operation's sales revenue. As a result, no labor cost control procedure is considered complete unless it includes one or more cost reduction techniques.

Some labor cost reduction techniques used in the hospitality industry are:

1. *Employee leasing.* Instead of hiring employees, you lease the entire staff from a company that specializes in this. These companies oftentimes provide other related services, such as payroll processing for your entire staff. In some cases this can save money because the company consolidates and handles all the human resources administrative details, thereby relieving the caterer of this costly burden. The company also can consolidate several small employers' employee benefits needs, qualify for large-employer discounts, and pass on some of the savings to its clients. According to the employee-leasing industry, clients typically save between 2 and 4 percent of their current labor costs by using employee leasing.

2. *Hiring "rehab" employees.* In some instances, if you agree to participate in rehabilitative efforts by hiring physically or mentally challenged individuals, allowing the local department of labor to place trainees in your property, or hiring individuals in certain targeted social or income groups, you may receive a monetary reward. For instance, the department of labor may pay part of a trainee's wages for a few weeks. Or you might qualify for an income tax credit if you hire a person in a targeted group.

3. *Use independent contractors in lieu of employees.* For some tasks, you may be able to employ independent contractors instead of hiring employees to do the work. For instance, instead of hiring coat check or valet parking attendants, you might want to hire an independent service. This can be more convenient in the long run since you do not have to maintain extensive personnel files, process payroll checks, and handle other relevant administrative details. You merely send a check once a month to the service and use the time saved to pursue other, more profitable activities.

4. *Use part-time employees in lieu of full-time employees.* Usually part-time employees working nineteen hours or less per week do not receive discretionary employee benefits, such as health insurance. They also grant you a great deal of flexibility. The down side, though, is that you need to have more people on the payroll, which can increase significantly your uniform, employee meal, management time, and other personnel-related costs.

5. *Use more pre-prepared convenience foods.* When using convenience foods, you do not need as many employees, nor do you need very many highly skilled (hence costly) employees. The drawback, though, is increased food costs and potentially substandard products.

Purchase prices are much higher for convenience products because they include not just the cost of food but also the cost of the labor and energy needed to produce them. Generally, though, frozen food items can be used to maximize the productivity of current production labor, as it allows food handlers to increase significantly the numbers of guests that can be served during the day.

6. *Institute more self-service options.* This reduces payroll at the expense of food and beverage costs. The hope is that the extra foods and beverages guests will take when left on their own will not wipe out entirely the labor cost savings. Unfortunately, when guests help themselves, they take more time to go through the lines, the event will tend to drag on, and some guests may be displeased with the slow pace.

7. *Eliminate overtime pay.* Labor laws as well as union regulations require you to give employees overtime pay under certain circumstances. (See Chapter 9 for a discussion of overtime pay.)

At times you may fall victim to this problem because some catered events are bound to run over schedule and you will need to keep some people on board to take care of the stragglers. If these overruns are common, you would be much better off scheduling one or two people to come in later during the event. They can stick around and take care of closing down. And instead of being stuck paying overtime, you would be able to pay the more economical straight-time wage.

Another way to prevent overtime premium pay is to advise clients in advance that if the events run over, they will be responsible for paying the additional labor charges.

Alternatively, you could schedule a supervisor or manager to handle any last-minute extended events. Usually management employees do not have to be compensated at overtime rates. They normally receive straight salaries that do not vary with the amount of hours worked.

8. *Reduce costly employee turnover.* Proper employee selection, orientation, and training should help reduce employee turnover and the subsequent costs of hiring replacement personnel.

9. *Institute a profit-sharing plan.* This and similar employee motivation techniques can reduce employee turnover as well as increase employee productivity. Over the long haul, the extra pay and benefits given to long-term employees usually pale in comparison to the increased sales revenue and profits generated by experienced staff members.

10. *Use labor-saving equipment.* Under some circumstances, you may be able to reduce your labor costs by investing in labor-saving devices. For instance, a computerized automatic bar may increase worker productivity enough for you to reduce the number of bartenders needed. It can also enhance your quality control efforts.

The expensive investments that usually must be made in this type of equipment, though, may not be recovered easily. Chances are you will not see enough of a labor cost reduction to justify any major investments. However, if an investment can pay for itself in about three years or less, generally it is considered a good choice.

Be careful, though, when estimating the cost savings that supposedly accompany labor-saving equipment. Our industry has been unable to take full advantage of many labor-saving technological advances since, after all, we are in the personal service business. It can be easy to overestimate cost savings, particularly if we rely on enthusiastic equipment salespeople for these estimates.

CONTROL OF OTHER EXPENSES

Usually the catering executive concentrates on controlling product and labor costs primarily because they represent a very large chunk of the sales revenue dollar. This "prime cost" (product cost plus labor cost) is about 55 to 60 percent of the typical foodservice operation's sales revenue. Consequently, it is understandable that a manager's cost control efforts will be aimed in this direction.

But there are a handful of other controllable expenses that deserve some of your attention. Generally speaking, these are: direct operating expenses (such as linen, tableware, soaps, chemicals, and paper products), utilities, repairs and maintenance, and administrative and general expenses (such as telephone, postage, and office supplies).

The key to controlling these expenses is to be on the lookout for waste, pilferage, and incorrect equipment use.

Waste is a typical problem when using paper products, production equipment, soaps, chemicals, and other similar items. For instance, it is not uncommon for employees to use too much chemical in the rinse water, be overly generous with the use of paper napkins and doilies, turn on the oven long before it is needed, and neglect to sort soiled linen correctly. While individual actions do not necessarily cause significant decreases in net profit, they will add up quickly if you do not monitor them.

Office supplies and telephone use are subject to employee pilferage as well as to waste. Personal use of the company's email server and Internet connection can also eat into profits. Subtle controls, such as taking inventories of office supplies and restricting long-distance telephone use, should be applied in order to minimize these problems.

Employees must be trained adequately in equipment use before allowing them to operate it. If they do not know how to use equipment correctly, they may injure themselves and the equipment. In addition to increased workers' compensation costs, experience shows that incorrect equipment use is the major cause of exorbitant repairs and maintenance expenses. Moreover, incorrect equipment use will drastically reduce the equipment's useful life. One of the paradoxes of the food and beverage business is that we would never allow someone to drive a car without a driver's license, yet we may be willing to let someone operate a $50,000 dish machine without proper training.

COMPUTERIZED CONTROL PROCEDURES

The caterer can gain many benefits by computerizing its operations and information systems. However, since computerization can be an expensive undertaking, to justify its investment, a computer system must offer substantial benefits to the property and to its guests, such as:

1. Improved guest service
2. Streamlined handling of paperwork and data
3. Improved control over day-to-day operations
4. Timely, accurate report generation
5. Reduced cost of paper supplies
6. Increased sales revenue
7. Increased employee productivity
8. Reduction of clerical staff
9. Job enrichment, due to the reduction of repetitive tasks
10. Ability to keep current sales and expense data on file

Selecting a Computer System

You should take your time and consider carefully all available options before making a computer-investment decision. Some catering executives suggest that you let the following rules guide your decision:

1. Never be the first user of a computer system. The first user usually is placed in a high-risk position.

2. Avoid purchasing or leasing a computer system from a firm that has many large clients, unless you are one of them. The largest users will receive priority service from the computer firm.

3. Before buying a system, always observe someone else using a similar system at a similar property. Interview the users and seek their opinions.

4. Decide specifically what you want the system to do for you. This tells you the type of software you will need to purchase or rent.

5. Once the software is selected, look for the appropriate hardware. Be certain that the hardware is compatible with other computer systems used at your property. If possible, never select hardware that requires you to take data from one machine, reformat it, and enter it into another machine. Data reentry

significantly reduces the benefits of computerization and increases the potential for error.

6. Select an adequate computer service firm. The firm should provide sufficient training and technical backup. The company should have a help hotline. Furthermore, the firm must be able to adapt the standard software to coincide with your property's overall system.

A good backup service is important even if the caterer has computer people on staff. Many on-site computer people are front-office- or back-office-oriented and may find food and beverage perplexing.

Computer Uses

Software available to the food and beverage industry can be purchased to perform the following tasks:

1. Desktop publishing for menus, brochures, and other promotional materials
2. Sales analysis
3. Bookings analysis
4. Cancellation report
5. Group booking log
6. Daily tracer list printout of current and previous clients
7. Sales call report
8. Group profile sheet
9. Banquet event order
10. Function resume
11. Lost-business report
12. Pre-function sheet
13. Catering contract
14. Daily event schedule
15. Forecast
16. Daily function room schedule
17. Work schedule
18. Room layout
19. Space management

20. Link to outside suppliers and service contractors
21. Payroll processing
22. Recipe costing
23. Menu pricing
24. Inventory management
25. Recipe nutrition analysis
26. Invoice control
27. Product cost analysis
28. Labor cost analysis
29. Equipment scheduling
30. Word processing
31. Time clock
32. Production schedule
33. Break-even analysis
34. Menu planning
35. Tip reporting
36. Tip allocation
37. Server analysis
38. Stock requisition
39. Department-by-department comparison
40. Open guest check report
41. Cashier analysis
42. Communication with other departments
43. Link with corporate headquarters
44. Banquet checks/billing
45. Inventory reorder
46. Yield management
47. E-commerce opportunities

Function Book

The function book, or diary, is critical for the smooth running of the facility's operations. Previously paper books of various size and complexity were used to suit the needs of every type of catering operation. The traditional paper function book has been nearly phased out in all but the smallest of venues, in favor of a computerized version available on many software programs. Moving to a computerized function book has allowed caterers to become more organized, streamline processes, and improve the efficiency of the organization.

Regardless of the system you use for a function book, the same basic principles apply:

- Only designated personnel should be allowed to make entries and changes.
- Tentative bookings should be indicated as such.
- The function book must be readily accessible so that available dates and space can be determined.
- A phone should be in close proximity so availability can be checked immediately.

When a potential client inquires, the first order of business is to see what space is available on the date and time requested.

Prospective entries are inquiries. Tentative entries actually hold space for a certain period of time and indicate that a proposal or contract has been sent. Definite entries occur when the signed contract is returned and the deposit arrives. All entries should be initialed or otherwise coded. In computer software, generally the letters T (tentative) or D (definite) are used, or color coding entries is used.

Catering Software Options

There are many different software programs currently available on the market. The cost of the program, ongoing support costs, and included features vary widely. Each catering organization will need to evaluate the available options and determine which one is best for it.

Some of the more commonly used programs include:

Delphi by Newmarket

Caterease

Caterware

Total Party Planner

POST-EVENT EVALUATION

As one of the final control steps, it is important to review each event in terms of profitability, challenges, and desirability of rebooking. A sample post-convention report form is available in the Appendix (see page 462).

For larger groups, it may be advisable to hold a post-conference (post-con) meeting with the event planner. This gives clients an opportunity to discuss what they think went well and what could have been done better, while it is still fresh in their minds. It is important that clients feel free to discuss their thoughts openly, and therefore the post-con is best facilitated by someone other than the catering executive who handled the overall event.

SUMMARY

Control procedures are vital for the financial health of the facility. This starts with setting standards and policies for service and production. The BEO communicates the parameters of each function to all stakeholders. Contracts are essential to the process, which includes granting credit and cost control (controlling the cost of both labor and food).

KEY TERMS

Banquet event order	Pre-function sheet	Change order
Resume	Expediter	Food checker
Catering contract	Credit management	Cost control
Computer software options		

REVIEW QUESTIONS

1. What is a BEO/Banquet Event Order?
2. Who is responsible for selecting and procuring the needed products?
3. What is the role of the expediter?

4. List 5 things that can cause a significant cost variance.

5. Before a control system can be implemented, you must set _____ .

6. When does the food and beverage cycle of control begin?

7. What is a disadvantage of overcontrolling?

8. What is the main purpose of the pre-function sheet?

9. What is a change order?

10. What information does the resume typically include?

11. A contract in excess of _____ dollars must be in writing or else it cannot be legally enforced in a court of law.

12. Usually a client is expected to put up a deposit of _____ to _____ percent of the final bill.

13. What is probably the most critical cost control tool used by the purchasing agent?

14. What is the purpose of having an approved supplier list?

15. What is the role of the food checker?

Chapter 11

WORKING WITH OTHER DEPARTMENTS

The catering department does not operate in a vacuum. While it often is the only department visible to the client, it depends on many other departments for its success.

The catering department cannot perform all the tasks involved in putting on an event. It must have the cooperation of other employees. One could think of the catering department as the orchestra leader. It assembles the players, develops the music, and supervises the performance. A successful catering event, like a pleasing musical performance, comes about when all the people involved play their roles well.

The purpose of this chapter is to note the other departments that contribute to the catering department's success and to discuss the major relationships that exist between them and the catering staff.

KITCHEN

It is extremely important to have a good working relationship with the chef and his or her staff. These food experts are perhaps the most important players in the catering orchestra. At times they will be your salvation.

The chef must know as soon as possible the menu, the number of guests, the timing, and all other relevant aspects of booked functions. He or she must ensure that the proper amount and type of foods are ordered, production is scheduled properly, and an adequate and appropriate workforce is retained for each event.

The chef also must be privy to any and all budgetary constraints. He or she is the last word in costing the menu. If, for example, the catering sales representative is preparing a competitive bid for a corporate meeting planner, the chef's food cost estimates must be obtained.

The chef can work with you in combating budgetary constraints, planning heart-healthy meals, outlining theme parties, and developing other customer-pleasing suggestions. He or she usually knows what will be in season, menu trends, typical customer likes and dislikes, cost trends, quality trends, and product availability. Chefs usually love the opportunity to contribute. Many of them enjoy being creative when given the opportunity.

In most properties, the catering staff participates with the chef in developing standardized catering menus. Usually the food and beverage director and purchasing agent are also part of the menu-planning team. The menus prepared by this group become one of the major tools in the catering executive's sales kit.

It is essential to check with the chef before committing to any off-the-menu selections. Many clients want something special and spurn the standardized menus. While you may want to accommodate them, you cannot do so without checking with the executive chef or the sous chef in charge of banquet functions.

Some off-the-menu selections may not be feasible because they cannot be prepared in bulk. For instance, it is likely futile to ask the chef to prepare individual chocolate soufflés for 1,000 guests, club sandwiches for 750, or Maine lobsters for a group of 500. These food items usually are impossible to produce correctly for large groups.

Some menu items also may be impossible to produce and serve because the facility does not own the necessary equipment. For instance, is there enough broiler and oven space to prepare 2,000 New York steak dinners? Are there enough slow-cook ovens to cook and hold prime rib for 1,500 guests? Can the kitchen prepare and hold 1,000 chef's salads with the available refrigeration space?

A menu item may not be feasible because the property does not have the appropriate labor to do the work. There may not be a sufficient supply of labor or there may be a lack of the labor skills needed to prepare a specific menu item. For instance, is there enough skilled labor to produce an ice carving, a five-tiered wedding cake, or fancy carved vegetable garnishes?

According to John Steinmetz, to get along well with the chef, you should adhere to the following rules:

1. Always consult with the chef before promising a special menu or any changes to a standardized menu.

2. Ensure that the chef receives the menus well in advance of the events. You should notify the chef at least ten days in advance.

3. Ensure that the chef receives timely updates of guarantee changes, special needs, and other major alterations. Do not wait until the last minute.

4. Do not spring any surprises on the chef.

5. Do not make it difficult or impossible for the chef to achieve his or her budgeted food, labor, and other operating costs.

BEVERAGE

Large hotels, clubs, conference centers, stadiums, and arenas employ a beverage manager who reports to the food and beverage director. His or her job description is similar to the chef's in that they both administer departments that produce finished menu products and serve them to guests.

The beverage manager usually oversees the facility's main bars, service bars, special-events bars (banquet bars), room service beverage deliveries, hospitality suite bars, and individual-access bars (locked bar cabinets located in sleeping rooms).

Catering typically works with the beverage manager when developing beverage functions, planning beverage menus, and evaluating product and service options.

The beverage manager may also help catering managers schedule the appropriate number of bartenders, bar backs, cocktail servers, and bussers.

PURCHASING

Most large facilities employ a full-time purchasing agent. His or her primary responsibilities are to prepare product specifications for all foods, beverages, and supplies, select appropriate suppliers, maintain adequate inventories, obtain the best possible purchase values, and ensure that product quality meets the property's standards.

The purchasing agent normally works very closely with the kitchen and beverage departments. He or she needs to be made aware of all catering events booked in order to purchase the necessary stock.

On a day-to-day basis, the purchasing agent orders sufficient merchandise to satisfy the property's normal business needs. Catering, though, may be additional business and must be handled accordingly. For instance, if there is a party scheduled for which you will need 2,500 chicken breasts, the purchasing agent must order enough to satisfy all other event and other food outlets' needs as well as the additional 2,500 needed for the party.

Standard catering menu items are usually readily available from local purveyors. In fact, a menu item may be standardized primarily because it is easy to obtain. If a catering sales representative is negotiating for off-the-menu item selections, though, the purchasing agent should be consulted to see if the products are available, what they cost, and how long it will take to deliver them to the facility.

If the catering executive is considering a menu revision, he or she will also need to check with the purchasing agent to see if the planned changes are feasible. Cost and availability trends must be evaluated very carefully in order to avoid menu planning mistakes.

RECEIVING AND STOREROOM

All but the smallest caterers have a central warehouse storeroom (sometimes referred to as the commissary) where all food, beverage, and supplies are kept under lock and key. Only authorized people are allowed to enter the storage areas or obtain products from the storeroom manager.

Storeroom personnel work closely with the receiving department. In some operations, both functions are housed in one department. Receiving agents check in deliveries and storeroom clerks help them move shipments from the receiving dock to the warehouse. The merchandise remains in the storeroom areas until department heads requisition them.

In order to obtain these products, a department head must fill out a stock requisition and hand it to a storeroom clerk. These requisitions establish the fact that the department head is now responsible for these items.

Once the requisition is processed, the department head can pick up the products or, alternatively, have them delivered by a storeroom attendant.

Production and service departments that are handling the booked event requisition most of the products needed to service a catered event. For instance, the kitchen will requisition food and the beverage department will requisition beverage. The catering staff, though, also will need to requisition some things, such as paper products, decorations, and office supplies.

HOUSEKEEPING AND CUSTODIAL

A hotel or conference center housekeeping department's primary responsibilities are to clean sleeping rooms, function rooms, and all public areas. It also works with maintenance to ensure that the property is kept in good repair. Many restaurants, clubs, stadiums, and arenas have custodial departments that are similarly responsible for cleaning event space and all public areas as well as routine maintenance.

In some properties, housekeeping is responsible for selecting replacement carpeting, upholstery, and fabrics. If you are involved with these decisions, be sure to avoid light colors and materials that do not have a pattern. Stains and spills show up quickly on light-colored materials and are quite obvious on unpatterned carpets. Incidentally, repeating patterns on carpeting are excellent guides for setting out tables and chairs symmetrically.

The housekeeping department in some organizations is the source of table linen, employee uniforms and costumes, laundry, and dry cleaning. Other catering organizations have a separate linen room that is under the supervision of the banquet setup staff. Regardless of which department is responsible, the catering staff must see to it that the linen room manager has sufficient lead time to ensure that all necessary supplies are available.

In some properties, housekeeping or custodial is responsible for pre-cleaning function rooms and other public areas as outlined in the catering department's instructions or in the convention services department's directives. It also may be involved with cleaning up after functions are completed. These personnel must be informed of special functions well in advance so that the necessary work can be scheduled and carried out properly. If housekeeping or custodial is not responsible for these tasks, then they generally fall under the direction of the banquet manager and are handled by the convention setup staff or by porters. This is particularly true for very large hotels that specialize in the convention business, or non-hotel organizations that do not have a separate cleaning and maintenance department.

Function rooms must be cleaned in plenty of time to avoid any embarrassing situations. For example, you do not want last-minute vacuuming to mar an otherwise successful event.

Function rooms need to be torn down and cleaned immediately after guests depart. If you wait too long to do this, stains have time to set in upholstery or carpets, and vermin will be attracted to the debris. Immediately after an event or meeting, the catering or convention setup staff strip the tables, and housekeeping staff, convention setup staff, or porters should come in and clean the walls, carpets, and furniture. Any items needing repair should be reported to the maintenance department.

Pre-function spaces require continuous attention. These are areas adjacent to function rooms that may be used to house registration tables, display booths, and so forth. Guests will assemble here throughout the day, especially just before it is time to enter the function rooms for events. While in these areas, they might leave soiled plates, cups, newspapers, and so forth lying about, and these should be removed as quickly and unobtrusively as possible. Routine dusting, polishing, trash removal, and vacuuming should be done when guests are not around.

Public restrooms especially are in need of constant attention. Many people abhor a dirty restroom and are quick to lose respect for the facility and management if one is encountered.

At the very minimum, restrooms must be cleaned thoroughly twice a day. They must be checked constantly for quick cleanups and restocking of tissue, seat covers, towels, and toiletries. Attendants also need to check periodically for equipment failure and must report any problems to the maintenance department.

A few properties sometimes use an outside contract cleaning service to handle certain housekeeping tasks. For instance, if you do not have the proper equipment or employee talent, you may not want to try cleaning large quantities of linen, large chandeliers, outside windows, or copper facades.

BANQUET AND CONVENTION SETUP AND SERVICE

Some hotels, conference centers, stadiums, and arenas have both a banquet manager who is in charge of banquet service and a banquet setup manager who sees that the room is set up. Banquet servers report to the banquet manager, and housemen report to the banquet setup manager.

The banquet setup division is responsible primarily for setting up function rooms, tearing them down, and putting away the furniture and equipment.

Banquet setup works hand-in-glove with banquet service. The banquet service division is responsible primarily for providing meal service. It may also be responsible for providing beverage service.

In lieu of a banquet service department, banquet setup and service activities may be performed by the catering staff, or by the catering staff in cooperation with other departments. For instance, catering may share this work with the kitchen and housekeeping staffs.

Smaller operations tend not to have separate banquet service departments. Their small size usually requires them to allocate the necessary duties to other departments.

Banquet service activities can be housed in various departments and can have many names. Banquet setup, banquet service, convention porters, and housemen are just a few of the titles used to describe these important activities.

Banquet setup is the backbone of the catering and convention departments. Function room setup and teardown, room maintenance and cleaning, transporting furniture and equipment throughout the function room areas, and related duties must be performed quickly and efficiently. All catered functions depend on the swift completion of these critical activities.

The major activity of banquet housemen is function room setup. This involves many aspects, the most critical of which is the need for all furniture and equipment to be in place by a certain time. Foremost in function room setup is receiving the proper information from the catering or convention manager. He or she must have a good working knowledge of the type, amount, and capabilities of the furniture, equipment, staff, and facilities so that clients can be advised correctly when they are planning their events.

Function room setup begins with information obtained from the client. This information must be complete and conform to the property's physical constraints. Table sizes, exhibit booths, registration needs, and so forth require physical setups. Someone has to obtain the proper furniture and equipment, transport it to the correct location, and install it properly. Before this can be done, banquet setup employees must know and understand the client's needs.

There are usually three types of banquet setup employees. The first is the regular or full-time employee. This employee is scheduled for a full workweek or is the first person called when a function room must be set up.

The second type of employee is the steady extra. This person is on call but is considered a permanent employee. Although this type of employee does not receive full employee benefits, he or she usually receives prorated benefits based on the number of hours worked. The primary advantages steady extra employees provide to the employer are that you can use them only when they are needed, but when they are called to work, they are as productive as full-time employees because they are familiar with the job, property, furniture, and equipment.

The third type of employee is the one-time recruit hired on a temporary basis to help set up an unusually large function or to assist regular employees temporarily overburdened with large or back-to-back catered functions that require quick turnarounds. This type of employee usually receives limited training and is not around long enough to become familiar with your property. Consequently, these employees are used primarily to move furniture and equipment and perform other manual labor.

Convention setup requires an adequate storage facility to house all necessary furniture and equipment. Storage of these items, though, involves more than just the housing of tables, chairs, portable dance floors, risers, meeting equipment, and convention materials when not in use. The storage area must be large enough as well as convenient to the function rooms in order to facilitate the constant movement of furniture and equipment in and out of the function rooms. Unfortunately, adequate storage in the convention setup department is sometimes overlooked when hotels, conference centers, clubs, and arenas are designed and constructed. This can cause continual problems and frustration.

A proper storage area allows you to store all furniture and equipment as well as transport equipment needed to move these items. For instance, you need enough room to store table and chair carts, which are used to transport several tables and chairs at one time, thereby allowing quick and efficient movement to and from function rooms.

The storage area should be large enough to house and organize an inventory of spare parts. For instance, if a houseman loses a piece of portable dance floor trim and cannot find another one in storage, you increase the risk of someone tripping on an improperly installed dance floor. If you lose one section of a portable dance floor, it decreases the size of the floor and increases the risk of guest dissatisfaction. Adequate storage space and proper storage procedures can prevent problems associated with misplaced, lost, or stolen pieces.

The storage area also must allow you to store furniture and equipment as close as possible to the function rooms. For instance, a portable dance floor should be stored near the function rooms because it is too heavy to transport easily.

Dance floor movement is a major concern. Heavy-duty carts are typically used to transport the 3-by-3-foot squares of wood and metal. Each full cart can weigh over 500 pounds, and improper movement and handling can damage walls and doors as well as injure employees. The probability of damage increases if this heavy load must be transported a great distance.

If applicable, the storage area must be able to accommodate meeting equipment such as whiteboards, blackboards, easels, podiums, water pitchers, glasses, pads, and pencils. It also may need to house audiovisual, computer, and lighting equipment. In some properties, some or all of this equipment is stored in other departments. Convenience, though, quickly overrides departmental lines, and convention setup typically finds it necessary to store many items that were originally intended to be stored elsewhere.

Some clients send convention materials, such as registration packets, machinery, and sample products, to the property via independent carrier services. These materials are extremely important to clients and their attendees. A lost or misplaced package can be devastating to a meeting planner.

All delivered convention materials must be signed in, counted, and inspected for damage at the point of transfer from the independent freight company. Properties assume a liability in the form of a bailment when they take possession of items they do not own, so it behooves them to ensure that all shipments meet client standards.

Generally speaking, a property's receiving and storeroom departments do not want to store convention materials. The primary reason is that their facilities are not designed to hold the varying types and amounts of materials that arrive for different groups. Client storage also has several potential liabilities, such as having unauthorized people in the back of the house, increased labor costs for the handling of the items, and placing the responsibility for safekeeping on the property.

A secure and central location is usually provided in a banquet room the group has on hold or in small closets attached to a registration desk. Convention setup is responsible for the safe delivery of these materials to the appropriate person at the right time and in the right place. Additionally, the client (or client representative) must sign for the delivery so that the property is relieved of any responsibility for materials that are subsequently lost. Although receiving convention materials may be the responsibility of other departments (particularly dedicated business centers in larger hotels and convention centers), convention setup accepts responsibility when taking the goods out of the warehouse.

It is important to maintain clear records of all client shipments. Clients must ensure that their instructions are communicated to the property. This is very important because receiving clerks usually are not allowed to accept a client's shipment unless they know in advance when it will be delivered and what inspection procedures they must follow. If clerks refuse to accept shipments, they can create tremendous difficulties for unsuspecting clients.

A clear audit trail must exist in order to track any client materials delivered to the property. The property that denies receiving a client's shipment loses that client's respect when the independent carrier service can show a copy of the packing slip signed by an employee who received the shipment. Liability exposure increases if the convention materials are misplaced internally and this causes the client embarrassment or monetary losses. You risk losing future business if potential clients suspect your property will mishandle their convention materials.

Housemen or convention porters must sign for convention materials when they obtain them from the receiving department or storeroom. The materials must then be taken directly to the appropriate function room areas.

When the function is completed, convention services usually is involved with shipping unused convention materials back to the client's home or place of business. When shipping materials, you must be apprised of the client's shipping and payment instructions. Nothing can be shipped without this information.

Usually the property will comply with the client's shipping and payment instructions, with the exception of cash-on-delivery (COD) shipments. Most properties do not want to ship anything COD. If the addressee for any reason refuses a COD shipment, it will be returned to you and you will be billed by the independent carrier for the shipping costs. It may then be very difficult or even impossible to get reimbursed by the client. As an alternative, you could ship the items for the client and bill the fees with the other event expenses if the client has either a credit card on file or approved billing set up in advance.

Banquet setup and banquet service are two of the most visible activities in that the results of almost all their work are witnessed firsthand by the clients and their guests. These departments are responsible for the staffing, service, and successful completion of each catered event. They are usually second only to the kitchen and beverage departments in terms of their influence on client and guest satisfaction.

FACILITIES

The facilities department is in charge of all property maintenance and repairs. Its employees perform routine maintenance, such as calibrating oven thermostats, oiling motors, and changing filters. They also are responsible for repairs, such as fixing broken water pipes, changing burned-out lightbulbs, and reconditioning worn equipment.

If the catering department has a repair need, normally it must fill out a repair requisition and send it to the maintenance department supervisor. The supervisor then prioritizes these requisitions and prepares work orders for maintenance employees. The employees work their way through the prioritized stack of work orders. If you are under a time constraint and need work done quickly, you will need to note on your requisition that the matter is urgent. This will move you up on the priority list, but top management may have a policy of charging a department's budget a little extra for express service, since it usually will disrupt the normal work schedule and could require some employees to work overtime.

ENGINEERING

The engineer generally is responsible for all major property systems, such as heating, ventilation, and air-conditioning (HVAC), refrigeration, electrical, plumbing, and sewer. He or she also supervises the property's energy management systems. Furthermore, the engineering department usually works hand-in-glove with facilities to ensure complete, coordinated control of the physical plant; in some organizations engineering and facilities are combined in one department.

If dictated by property arrangements, the catering staff must see to it that the engineer is contacted whenever a booked function requires sound system or computer hookups. While the AV department normally handles the delivery and setup of this equipment, the engineering staff typically is responsible for hooking them up and unhooking them. Alternatively, the AV department will handle all AV setups, including power installation.

The engineering department will need to know each function's energy requirements so that it can accommodate them. For instance, if a banquet needs several buffet stations, it may be necessary to install several electrical drop cords when the room is being set up by the banquet setup crew. In addition, if there are any unique lighting needs, the engineer must see to it that the appropriate power is available and that the systems are set up and torn down properly.

Engineering also must be aware of each function's beginning and ending times, as well as the expected number of guests, so that the proper amount of heating or cooling can be directed to the meeting and banquet rooms. Most function rooms are usually not heated or cooled during times when they are not in use. The engineer must have advance notice when they will be used because it takes anywhere from about twenty minutes to one hour to adjust a room's temperature.

When determining room temperature needs, the engineer will take into account the size of the room, number of attendees, time of day, solar load (heat that the building absorbs from the sun), type of HVAC system, ceiling height, heat given off by appliances, amount of insulation, outside weather conditions, amount of body heat given off by employees and guests, and type of function. For instance, a large room requires more heating or cooling. And a large group of people will quickly raise the temperature of a room.

PROPERTY MANAGER

The property manager is responsible for all outside areas. Normally he or she supervises landscaping, snow removal, pool and spa maintenance, and parking lot and sidewalk maintenance.

In some large facilities, there may be a separate property management department working independently and reporting directly to the general manager. In others, and in smaller properties, property management functions may be housed in the engineering or facilities departments.

In some small facilities, an independent service contractor may handle part or all of the outside groundskeeping. For instance, facilities may handle the pool maintenance and cleaning chores, while an independent gardener may stop by once or twice a week to take care of landscaping needs.

At times a catering sales representative will book a function to be held on the grounds. In particular, weddings are often held outside, including the ceremony, reception, dinner, and entertainment. To service these events properly, the catering staff will need to coordinate its efforts with the grounds crew to ensure that any needed tents are erected, sprinkler systems shut off, parking lots roped off, portable heaters installed, portable lights erected, and so forth.

STEWARD

The typical hotel, conference center, or club employs an executive steward whose major responsibilities include supervising kitchen sanitation and the china, glass, and silver stockroom. He or she provides one of the key links connecting the kitchen and other food and beverage production areas to guest service.

The catering staff must work with the executive steward to ensure that sufficient employees are scheduled to clean the dirty dishes, pots, pans, silverware, and utensils generated by catered events. Adequate work hours must be scheduled to perform the necessary kitchen, bar, and pantry cleanup after the functions end. If specialized china, glass, or silver is needed, the catering staff usually must requisition it from the executive steward.

Some properties employ kitchen stewards. Their responsibilities are similar to those of the executive stewards, except they also have food purchasing duties. Normally the smaller properties use kitchen stewards to oversee the kitchen sanitation crew, handle the chef's and bar manager's food and beverage purchases, check in shipments, and monitor all storeroom facilities. Being relatively small, these properties do not have separate purchasing agents, receiving supervisors, and storeroom supervisors. In this case, it may be easier to coordinate your efforts with only one person instead of several.

PRINT SHOP

Many large operations have a central copying center to handle their most common printing needs and a contract with an outside printer to handle jobs that cannot be done in-house. For instance, the central copying center may have the desktop publishing capabilities to print standardized menus, but its equipment may be insufficient to produce glossy four-color convention programs.

A few large operations do all of their printing in-house. This allows them to maximize quality control as well as keep an eye on expenses and profits. It also gives them maximum flexibility since they do not need to accept an outside printer's scheduling requirements. Furthermore, an on-site print shop might be the most economical option.

The catering department will use a lot of printed materials. Many catered functions call for printed programs, menus, name badges, place cards, and signage. While clients can opt to select their own printers, the convenience of an on-site print shop is a much appreciated benefit.

When the catering staff has a printing need, it usually must fill out a work requisition form and give it to the print shop or central copying center manager. He or she then prioritizes the work and assigns it to the appropriate employees, or if necessary subcontracts the order to an outside printer.

ROOM SERVICE

A hotel or conference center room service department usually handles all guest room food and beverage service. It is responsible for delivering food and beverage menu items and retrieving leftovers, soiled tableware and linen, tables, and equipment.

Generally speaking, catering does not get involved with guest room functions. However, occasionally the catering staff may need to coordinate with the room service crew to handle hospitality suites or small, intimate meal and beverage functions held in a guest suite. For instance, a major corporate convention may have several VIPs who require extensive room service. It may host several hospitality suites during the cocktail hours. Or it may decide to hold a board of directors luncheon in the president's suite instead of in a function room.

HUMAN RESOURCES

The human resources department's primary responsibility is recruiting, developing, and maintaining an effective employee staff. It is also responsible for administering many personnel-related matters. For instance, it must process all relevant government paperwork, handle grievances, work with union representatives, and manage employee compensation packages.

The director of catering will work with human resources whenever there are job openings in the catering department. The human resources department in a large property has an employment manager whose main activities include helping department supervisors develop job specifications and job descriptions; the employment manager also develops and implements recruiting programs, job application procedures, interviewing procedures, and methods used to process new hires.

When the catering department needs a new employee, the director of catering may need to fill out a job opening form listing the job classification, work hours, skills required, and other pertinent job information.

For entry-level, non-management catering jobs, the employment manager conducts prescreening interviews of job applicants, develops a list of one or more qualified job candidates, and sends it to the catering department. The catering manager then makes the final hiring decision, usually after personally interviewing qualified applicants.

For supervisory and management catering positions, oftentimes the director of catering finds a qualified candidate and sends him or her to the human resources department for processing. For instance, a catering executive may find an appropriate supervisory candidate through his or her membership in the National Association of Catering Executives (NACE). In fact, this professional organization publishes employment openings in the job bank section of its website (www.nace.net).

The director of catering also may uncover viable managerial job candidates through his or her memberships in other professional organizations and other contacts in the foodservice and food supply industries. For example, a few telephone calls to respected food suppliers in your local area can quickly reveal qualified people who are looking to make a career move.

Occasionally the catering executive may find a potential job candidate to fill an hourly position. If a current staff member recommends a friend to fill a job opening, the catering executive would send this person to the human resources department so that all necessary processing can be performed. As a general rule, though, hourly job candidates are generated by the human resources department.

Once a person is hired, he or she is processed by the employment manager. Generally speaking, this process involves an employee orientation, uniform fitting (if applicable), ID preparation, and assignment of a payroll authorization number, parking place, and employee locker.

The employment process may be shortened a bit for part-time catering employees. For instance, employees on the A-list and B-list may be scheduled temporarily at the discretion of the catering director. However, the employment manager must process them initially before they can be placed on these lists.

The employment manager may also provide a bit of training to new employees. Usually, though, the large human resources department employs a director of training who shoulders this responsibility. The director of training often will provide some basic training as part of the orientation process. Most frequently, though, job-related training is an effort shared by the training director and catering director.

The director of catering will be involved with human resources whenever employee problems arise. Usually large human resources departments have an employee relations manager to handle these types of situations. However, if there is a problem with a catering employee's paycheck, for example, the catering director must be part of the solution. This is also true if there is an employee benefits dispute, disciplinary problem, union contract dispute, or employee grievance.

CONTROLLER

The controller is responsible for securing all company assets. He or she normally supervises all cost control activities, payroll processing, accounts payable, accounts receivable, data processing, night audit, and cashiering.

The catering department's major relationships with the controller involve report preparation, cashiering, and accounts receivable.

All departments prepare reports. Generally speaking, many of them are coordinated and printed by the controller's office. For instance, budgets, profit-and-loss statements, and activity reports are usually prepared in final format by the controller's management information system (MIS) data-processing center based upon information provided by the departments.

Many catered events have cash bars. The controller's office may assign cashiers to sell drink tickets to the guests, if this is not handled by the beverage manager. At the end of the function, the cash collection will be compared to the ticket count and the pre- and post-event beverage inventories. If everything goes according to plan, these three totals will be consistent with each other.

With open bars and some meal functions, drink and meal tickets may be purchased in advance by the client and distributed to the guests. The controller's office will ensure that used tickets are consistent with the amount of food and beverages consumed.

Credit checks and granting credit generally are done under the jurisdiction of the controller. If a client has requested credit and is denied, the catering sales representative contacts the client and tries to resolve the problem. If this is not possible, the client will need to prepay all estimated expenses unless the credit manager is willing to change his or her mind and make other arrangements.

As noted earlier, most caterers are not in the habit of granting clients favorable credit terms. For instance, political functions and social events such as weddings are seldom granted the luxury of post-event billing.

The controller's office also generally prepares final billings and sends invoice statements to the clients. It handles collections and processes payments. If there are any problems, such as invoice disputes, late payments, or bounced checks, the catering department may need to help the credit manager resolve them.

SECURITY

This is often the property's least visible department, but by far not the least important. You know it is doing an effective job when guests do not recognize its presence.

Catered events present unique security challenges. Large groups may need someone to control foot traffic. Some groups may have considerable personal property that must be protected. Certain functions may include VIPs who require additional attention. Groups may attract disruptive protesters. And some events have the seeds of potential disruption; for instance, proms and fraternity parties must have security guards to prevent underage drinking and rowdy behavior.

The catering department must keep the security department apprised of all special functions because there may be some potential security problems that the department head can spot that would go unrecognized by the catering sales representative and client. If so, the chief of security would have an opportunity to resolve them beforehand.

Usually the chief of security receives copies of all group resumes and large-event BEOs in advance. This allows him or her to schedule the appropriate amount and type of security. It also gives the security chief sufficient lead time to process special needs, such as hiring temporary security guards, renting special equipment, and setting up perimeter barriers.

SALES

In most hotels and conference and convention centers, the sales director is responsible for selling, advertising, promotion, public relations, marketing research, and other relevant marketing efforts. Usually the sales department handles all local business on its own, but if the property is part of a chain organization, it is backed up by a corporate sales and marketing staff that solicits and coordinates regional and national business.

Recall that in some properties, the catering department is part of the sales staff. In this situation, catering sales and service employees report to the sales director, while kitchen and bar staffs report to a banquet manager employed by the food and beverage director. In this type of organizational structure, a convention services staff housed in the sales department may provide some or all catering services.

Catering must work hand-in-glove with the sales staff. At times their efforts might overlap. For example, a convention sales representative may be trying to sell sleeping rooms, function space, and meal functions to a meeting planner, while at the same time the meeting planner may be working with a catering sales representative to schedule a trial event, such as a small luncheon or reception. To say the least, a great deal of coordination and cooperation must exist in order to avoid any duplication of efforts and to ensure that the more profitable business is booked first, thereby maximizing function room space utilization and sales revenue.

FRONT OFFICE

The front office is considered to be the heart of hotels and conference centers. It is the hub of activity. It is usually the second contact (reservations being the first) individual guests make with the property. And it tends to be the place that influences customers' first and most lasting impressions of the property.

The front office normally includes the reservations, PBX phone system, registration, cashier, and guest services sections.

The catering department will need to work closely with reservations whenever conventions are booked. Reservations will keep a running tally of sleeping rooms blocked and sleeping rooms booked. The catering staff will use this information to forecast attendance at the various catering events scheduled by convention clients.

The PBX department is the property's communications hub. Catering will cross paths with this front office section whenever telephone calls are routed to its department, messages are taken and delivered, or clients request specialized communications service.

A catered event may require extraordinary communications service or equipment. If so, PBX may be part of the team handling these needs. For a large convention that requires several phones in the reception areas, PBX may deliver and retrieve them, engineering may hook them up and tear them down, and PBX may provide an operator or two to monitor incoming and outgoing calls.

The registration desk is the source of sleeping room occupancy statistics. If, for example, a large convention is checking into the property, the catering director will want to be kept up-to-date on the number of registrants so that accurate guest count estimates can be computed for each catered event. Catering will also need to know if the number of sleeping rooms booked meet the required number clients must achieve to receive discounts, such as free use of a function room or upgraded reception service. If the number is less than it should be, usually a contract clause referred to as "attrition" kicks in. Attrition refers to how much of these benefits clients have to give back because they did not meet their obligations.

The front desk cashier handles guest checkout. Normally this involves guests paying sleeping room, room service, gift shop, restaurant, lounge, and other incidental charges. At times, though, the costs of catered events may be part of a departing guest's final accounting. If so, the catering staff must ensure that accurate data are made available to the front desk clerks and cashiers so that guest folios can be posted correctly and the proper accounting prepared in the time frame required.

Guest services include the bell desk, valet parking attendants, door attendants, concierge, and property hosts.

Bell desk employees are trained to promote the property's amenities, especially the restaurant and lounge outlets. They also can put in a good word for the catering staff. At times, bell desk personnel may be involved more directly with catered functions. For instance, some of them may serve as ushers, tour leaders, or airport shuttle drivers for convention attendees.

Many properties provide valet parking services. Usually these services are under the direction of a parking supervisor or garage manager. The typical guest usually must pay for reserved parking lot space and valet parking services. An extra daily charge normally is added to the guest's folio since the standard sleeping room rate does not include this amenity. If a guest is part of a catered event, he or she may not have to pay separately for parking; it might be part of the total package price quoted by the catering sales representative for the entire function. Parking charges might be waived by the catering sales representative if the event booked generates considerable other income for the property, or to be competitive with other catering organizations. If parking charges are typically very high, you may not be allowed to waive them; however, usually you can discount them for large groups.

If the parking facility is operated by an outside parking concession, usually the parking charges cannot be waived. In some cases, though, the concession agreement may grant the property some discount privileges that can be passed on to certain catering clients and their guests. Absent such an agreement, either the client or the catering department must pay the concessionaire.

The concierge is an important part of the guest services team. This person specializes in providing information to guests about on-property activities and amenities and off-property attractions, such as where the best shopping, restaurants, and tourist attractions are located. Some catering clients and their guests undoubtedly will be influenced by this person's advice.

A number of properties employ property hosts to service their high-spending clients. For instance, in Las Vegas, most properties employ casino hosts to cultivate high rollers.

To some extent, catering sales and service representatives are similar to property hosts in that they try to cultivate long-term relationships with profitable clients. A catering client or group may be so pleased with a particular catering executive that the group is liable to stick with this person even if he or she moves to a competing property.

AUDIOVISUAL

Some large hotels and arenas and almost all convention and conference centers, have AV departments that are responsible for maintaining an inventory of AV equipment. In-house AV departments are also commonly found in large rural resorts that do a considerable amount of convention business.

The AV department may own the equipment or rent it from an outside service as needed to accommodate an event. It may also be involved with delivering the equipment to function rooms and retrieving it when guests are finished. And it may be responsible for providing AV technicians.

Many properties do not want to operate an AV department. The equipment inventory is very expensive. Repairs and maintenance are quite costly. And the equipment can quickly become obsolete and need to be replaced well before its useful life expires.

While properties are reluctant to operate their own AV departments, they do want to make this convenience available to the guest. This is absolutely necessary if you want to offer clients one-stop shopping.

One way to provide in-house AV services economically is to grant an outside AV company an exclusive concession inside the property. Ideally, the concessionaire will have adequate in-house storage space so that services can be provided quickly and efficiently.

Catering clients may opt to use their own outside AV services. For instance, a major convention client may have a long-term contract with a large national firm that provides a wide array of meetings and conventions services. In this case, a client will save money because of the quantity discounts available with national contracts. An added benefit is that over time, the national firm will learn and understand the group's unique needs and preferences and tailor its services accordingly.

Experience shows that most catering clients will not use off-premise AV companies unless the property's AV equipment is priced exorbitantly. They prefer the convenience of an on-site department. For instance, when the department is located at the property, a client can see the equipment beforehand, backup equipment can be retrieved quickly, and qualified technicians are on-site and can respond immediately if problems arise.

Catering must see to it that the AV manager is kept apprised of all client AV needs. The equipment, its delivery and pickup, and any necessary technicians must be scheduled well in advance. Sometimes the property is so busy that the AV manager must use and reuse a particular piece of equipment several times during the day, for several functions. On high-volume periods, close communication is necessary in order to pull off these scheduling miracles.

RECREATION

Many properties offer several types of guest recreation activities. Properties frequently have swimming pools, health clubs, and spas. Some have additional recreation amenities such as golfing, tennis, beaches, trail riding, and boating.

Salespeople tend to use the property's recreation offerings as a loss leader when trying to influence a meeting planner's property selection decision. For instance, a meeting planner could be offered free use of the spa for all convention attendees. If this complimentary amenity is used to secure a booking, it is imperative that the spa manager knows about it well in advance so that he or she can be ready to serve the extra guests properly.

Providing complimentary recreation amenities sounds like it might be an expensive giveaway, but in reality it costs the property very little. For example, many attendees will not use the spa facilities; however, they will be favorably impressed with the perceived value offered. Also, the property does not incur an out-of-pocket cost by promising clients preferred tee times or tennis court times. The only time this type of loss leader has a significant impact on the bottom line is when a guest recreation activity (such as golfing) is provided by an outside source. In this case, the outside contractor typically will expect a minimum payment regardless of the number of guests taking advantage of the amenity.

ENTERTAINMENT

A few properties employ entertainment directors. These executives are responsible for dealing with agents, booking entertainment acts, and interfacing with entertainment licensing authorities. For instance, the American Society of Composers, Authors, and Publishers (ASCAP) and Broadcast Music Incorporated (BMI) collect fees from businesses that provide musical entertainment to their guests for profit-making purposes.

If a catered event requires some sort of entertainment, the entertainment director may be involved with the decision. If clients book their own entertainment, the entertainment director may still be involved, perhaps providing a list of available acts to them, helping them contact a speakers bureau, or helping to schedule the events.

The entertainment director must always be made aware of catering activity in the property because this could influence his or her selection of acts. For instance, if a western-wear association convention is booked, the entertainment director may want to arrange to have a country-and-western act performing in the lounge.

BUSINESS SERVICES

Business services are clerical, secretarial, and Internet services provided by the facility to its guests. Properties that accommodate business travelers and meetings and conventions business typically make them available to all guests for an additional charge.

Many catered events require some business services. For instance, a convention may need copying and typing services. It may need someone to take minutes, collate reports, or handle incoming and outgoing messages. Some clients might need photographs or video coordinated for a presentation. And some may need a "computer doctor" to help them prepare or revise a PowerPoint presentation.

As with guest recreation activities, a few properties may provide a modest amount of complimentary business services to clients who book a large volume of catering business.

The business services manager must know as soon as possible the types and amounts of business services clients will need. This is very important because most employees working in this department are on-call, temporary employees who usually have full-time jobs elsewhere. They will need advance notice so that they can adjust their schedules accordingly.

SUMMARY

This chapter focuses on all of the other departments and personnel that interface with the catering department. It is imperative to have a good working relationship with these other departments, because the catering department does not work in isolation. Catering depends on all of the other departments to help produce the event successfully. The kitchen must prepare the food, the purchasing department must purchase the food, the housekeeping or custodial department must clean the facility, and so on.

KEY TERMS

Receiving	Requisition	Pre-function space
Houseman	Steward	ASCAP
BMI	Banquet setup	Banquet service
Guest services	Employment manager	Employee-relations manager

REVIEW QUESTIONS

1. Why is it essential to consult with the chef before committing to off-the-menu selections?
2. What is the role of the beverage manager?
3. What is the role of the controller?
4. Which department is considered to be the heart of the hotel?
5. In order to obtain products from the property's warehouse, a department head must fill out a _____ .
6. What hotel department is responsible for cleaning function rooms and other public areas?

7. What does pre-function space refer to?
8. What is the difference between the banquet-setup and the banquet-service divisions?
9. What is the banquet-service division's main activity?
10. List the three types of banquet-setup employees.
11. List an example of convention materials clients might ship to the caterer's property.
12. What is the role of the engineer?
13. What is the role of the steward?
14. What is the role of the employment manager?
15. Which department is often the property's least visible one?

Glossary

Action station

Similar to an attended buffet, except food is freshly prepared as guests wait and watch. Sometimes referred to as a performance station, live action station, or exhibition cooking.

Affiliate booking

Business that piggybacks on existing convention business. Another term for "in conjunction with" (ICW).

Afterglow

Relaxing time just after dinner but before dessert. Guests are asked to get up and move about a bit before tackling the sweets. To encourage this, afterglow food and beverage stations are placed throughout the function room or in a separate function room.

Air wall

Portable floor-to-ceiling divider used to partition a large function room into smaller rooms.

A-list personnel

These are steady extras, not full-time employees. They are the first ones called by the manager when help is needed.

Ambient light

Unavoidable light seeping into a darkened room from around doors, draped windows, or production and service areas.

American service

The most common type of table service in the United States. Food is plated in the kitchen, then served to individual guests at the table. Also referred to as plated service.

Amuse-bouche

A single bite-sized hors d'oeuvre. Generally it is served free of charge, typically for upscale events, is meant to tempt the taste buds, and offers a glimpse into the chef's style of cooking.

Assistant banquet manager

Reports to banquet manager; supervises table settings and decor placement. There may be two (or more) assistants: for example, there may be one for the day shift and one for the swing shift.

Assistant catering director

Services accounts; helps with marketing.

Attendant

Refreshes meeting rooms (does spot cleaning and waste removal during break periods and replenishes supplies such as notepads, pencils, and water); responds to requests for service by the client or a member of his or her staff. For some functions, there may also be restroom attendants or coat check attendants.

Attended buffet

Attendees are served by chefs or attendants; they do not have to help themselves. Much more elegant than the standard buffet.

Attrition

Contract clause that refers to how much the client will have to pay, or how many complimentary items (comps) received that he or she will have to give back, to the caterer if a guarantee is not met.

AV

Acronym for *audiovisual*.

Auditorium setup

Chairs are arranged in rows facing a head table. If the chairs are facing a stage and there are no tables used, it is usually referred to as a theater setup.

Bank maze

Consists of posts (stanchions) and ropes set up to control guest traffic.

Banquet change order

Form used to communicate alterations to booked functions that occur close to the date of the event. Sometimes referred to as a banquet change log or banquet change sheet.

Banquet Event Order (BEO)

A written documentation of all aspects of an individual event, as agreed to by both the client and caterer. Includes not only client contact information but also relevant details of the event including location, times, number of guests, menu, set up, service and special arrangements. Also forms the basis of the caterer's internal communication system between departments. Sometimes referred to as the function sheet.

Banquet French service

Platters of food are assembled in the kitchen. Servers take the platters to the tables and serve from the left, placing the food on a guest's plate using two large silver forks or one fork and one spoon.

Banquet manager

Implements the director of catering's instructions; oversees room captains; supervises all functions in progress; staffs and schedules servers and bartenders; coordinates all support departments. He or she is the operations director, as opposed to a catering executive, who handles primarily the selling and planning chores, or the banquet captain, who manages the floor during food and beverage functions.

Banquet service division

Responsible primarily for providing meal service. May also be responsible for providing beverage service.

Banquet setup division

Responsible primarily for setting up function rooms, tearing them down, and putting away the furniture and equipment.

Banquet setup manager

Supervises the banquet setup crew (housemen); orders tables, chairs, and other room equipment from storage; supervises teardown of events.

Banquet table, 6-foot

A rectangular table, measuring 30 inches wide by 6 feet long.

Banquet table, 8-foot

A rectangular table measuring 30 inches wide by 8 feet long.

Bar back

Provides backup and assistance to bartenders; his or her primary responsibilities are to stock initially and replenish the bars with beverages, ice, glassware, and other supplies and to empty waste receptacles.

Bartender

Concentrates on alcoholic beverage production and service. He or she may hand off finished drinks to other servers or may serve them personally.

Base plate

Large empty plate set in the center of each place setting and used as a base for several courses. Usually removed before serving the entree course. Also commonly referred to as charger.

B-list personnel

Part-time labor used to fill in the gaps when there are not enough A-list personnel available.

Block

The number of sleeping rooms reserved for a large group.

Blue collar

Consumer market consisting of persons whose jobs involve manual labor.

Book

To reserve a piece of business; to sell a catered event.

Boxed

Draped with a tablecloth that is folded, creased at the corners, and pinned.

Box lunch

Light lunch in a box packed to take out.

Breakage

The difference in revenue between meals and beverages sold and meals and beverages actually consumed. Revenue from breakage is almost entirely profit.

Breakout session

A session during which smaller groups, divided off from a large group meeting, discuss specific details or have presentations on topics relevant to the general, large-group meeting.

Buffet service

Food is attractively arranged on tables. Guests serve themselves and then take their full plates to a table to sit and eat. Beverages are usually served at the tables.

Busperson (buser)

Provides backup to servers; the primary responsibilities are to clear tables, restock side stands, empty waste receptacles, and serve ice water, rolls, butter, and condiments.

Butlered service

At receptions, butlered service refers to having hors d'oeuvres and/or beverages passed on trays, where the guests help themselves. At dinner, butlered is an upscale type of service, with food often passed on silver trays. Attendees use serving utensils to serve themselves at the table from a platter presented by the server.

By the bottle

Beverages served and charged for by the full bottle or container. Usually all bottles that have been opened must be paid for by clients.

By the drink

Beverages served and charged for by the number of drinks prepared and served.

By the piece

Food served and charged for by the piece. A billing procedure often used for a reception.

Cafeteria service

Similar to buffet service, except guests do not serve themselves; they are served by counter attendants and usually use trays to carry their selections.

Call brand

Refers to a particular spirit that customers order by brand name. *See also* Well brand; Premium brand.

Canopy

Portable cover used for outdoor events. Does not have sidewalls and is generally used to provide shade for food and beverage stations and/or guest seating.

Captain

In charge of service at meal functions; typically oversees all activity in the function room, or a portion of it, during a meal; supervises servers.

Captain's table

A sample table. It is a guide for the servers to follow when setting the dining tables.

Cart French service

See French service—cart style.

Carver

In-room attendant who carves and serves meats, poultry, or seafood during a reception or buffet service.

Cash bar

Attendees buy their own drinks, at times purchasing tickets from a cashier to exchange with a bartender for a drink. Sometimes referred to as a no-host bar.

Cashier

Collects cash at cash bars; sells drink tickets; may also sell meal, event, or concession tickets.

Cater out

Term used when an on-premise caterer does off-premise catering.

Caterer

Person or company providing food, beverages, equipment, and other services. May be on-premise or off-premise.

Catering manager

Maintains client contacts; services accounts.

Catering sales manager (CSM)

Oversees sales efforts; in some properties administers the sales office. Often used interchangeably with "catering manager."

Catering sales representative

Involved only in selling; handles outside and/or inside sales. In some smaller facilities, this position, the catering manager, and the catering sales manager are one and the same. In such cases, the rule seems to be "If you book it, you work it."

Centerpiece

Decorations or flowers placed in the center of a banquet, conference, or buffet table.

Charger

A large plate, usually used as a platter. Also used as a term for base plate.

Chef's choice

Selection of food items (such as types of vegetables) determined by the chef to accompany an entree.

City-wide

Generally refers to a corporate or association event that is too large to fit all guests at one property and so uses multiple hotels or event spaces throughout a city.

Classroom-style setup

Rows of tables with chairs where all attendees face the front of the meeting room. Each attendee has a space for placing books, laptops, and other materials. Also referred to as a schoolroom setup.

Clerical person

Handles routine correspondence; types contracts and banquet event orders; handles and routes messages; distributes documents to relevant catering staff members and other departments involved with the event.

C-list personnel

Labor used infrequently to fill in the gaps when there are not enough A- or B-list personnel available. Generally this group of employees are only scheduled for very large events or when a property has a large number of events. Most of these employees work at one or more other jobs.

Cocktail reception

Common type of beverage function. Often precedes a dinner function, in which case it usually is scheduled for forty-five minutes to an hour. In almost every instance, at least a few foods are served.

Cocktail table

A small round table, usually available in 18-, 24-, 30-, and 36-inch diameters. Generally available in two heights, low for seating or tall for standing.

Combination bar

A blend of the cash bar and the open bar. For instance, the client can host the first hour, after which the bar reverts to a cash bar.

Combination buffet

Inexpensive items, such as salads, are presented buffet-style, where guests help themselves. Expensive items, such as meats, are served by an attendant.

Concession

The privilege of maintaining a subsidiary business within a facility. Alternatively, a location where items are available for guests to purchase on their own. For example, during a trade show or large convention, a property may set up a concession stand when the host or organizer of the event is not hosting food or beverages.

Conference room setup

Rectangular or oval tables are set up with chairs placed around all sides. Also referred to as a boardroom setup.

Congestion pricing method

The price is based on demand. High demand results in a high price. Low demand results in a low price.

Continental breakfast

Light morning meal usually consisting of rolls, pastries, butter, jam or marmalade, chilled juices, and hot beverages.

Contract

Voluntary and legal agreement, by competent parties, to do or not do something. In almost every case, it must be a written agreement in order to be legally enforceable.

Contribution margin (CM)

The difference between sales revenue and variable costs. It is the amount of money left over that is used to cover all fixed costs plus profit.

Contribution margin (CM) method

Pricing procedure. The per-person price is equal to the average fixed expenses plus the average cost of food, beverage, and other variable costs, plus the profit markup.

Controller

Person responsible for securing all company assets. He or she normally supervises all cost control activities, payroll processing, accounts payable, accounts receivable, data processing, night audit, and cashiering. Also referred to as a comptroller.

Convention

Traditional annual meeting. Attendees come together for meetings, general sessions, and so forth, to further a common purpose.

Convention resume

A summary of all pertinent aspects for a convention or meeting; includes such things as sleeping room use, function use, room setup instructions, and VIPs. Sometimes referred to as a resume.

Convention services

Department that handles banquet setup and banquet service.

Convention services manager

Also called a conference services manager. Handles room setup in hotels, conference centers, and convention centers; sometimes handles catering for meetings and conventions.

Convention services setup division

Another term for banquet setup division.

Corkage

Charge placed on beverages (often wines) purchased elsewhere by the client, or donated on behalf of the event, and brought into a catered event or a restaurant. It represents compensation to the food and beverage operation for opening and serving the items and for loss of revenue, as well as gratuity for staff who serve the items.

Cover

Term used to describe a place setting on a dining table. Alternatively, refers to one customer or one meal.

Covers

Actual number of meals served at a catered meal function or in a foodservice facility.

CPRN

Acronym for "catering per room night." Refers to the minimum amount of food and beverage clients must purchase for each night they stay at a hotel. *See also* Minimum purchase.

Cross-aisle space

Aisle used for guests to collect and funnel in and out of the function areas. A cross-aisle should be at least 6 feet wide.

Cutoff date

Time when clients must release tentatively reserved function room space or commit to its purchase.

Dais

Another term for head table.

Damask

Woven silk or linen fabric used for tablecloths and napkins.

Dead space

Area(s) in a function room where sound is absent or unintelligible.

Deep market

Market segment that involves especially fancy, upscale functions. Price takes a backseat to quality and service.

Demographics

Population statistics. Examples are average age, gender, ethnic background, and socioeconomic level.

Deposit

Money or other asset used to ensure that future products or services will be provided. Alternatively, money or other asset used to ensure that the total amount of the final billing will be paid. Alternatively, money or other asset that can be retained by the injured party if a contract is not satisfied.

Destination management company (DMC)

Company that possesses extensive knowledge of the local area and is able to help clients design and implement events, activities, and tours. A great resource for meeting planners who are unfamiliar with the area.

Dinner

Evening meal for a group.

Direct bill

Invoicing procedure where a client is sent a bill after the event and has a specified period of time to remit payment.

Director of catering (DOC)

Assigns and oversees all functions; oversees all marketing efforts; interacts with clients and catering managers; coordinates with sales staff; creates menus in cooperation with the chef, beverage manager, and/or food and beverage director.

Double cloth

Another term for an overlay.

Drapery (valance)

Decoratively arranged tablecloths, fabric, or skirting on the front of head tables and around reception and buffet tables.

Dual entree

Serving two entrees, such as surf and turf. Usually the entrees are smaller portions than if they were served alone.

Dualing menus

Another term for dual entree.

Energy break

Refreshment break at which nutritious foods and beverages are served. May also include stretching or other forms of exercise.

English service

Also called family-style service. Attendees are seated, and large serving platters and bowls of food are placed on the dining table by the servers. Guests pass the food around the table.

Engineer

Provides necessary utility services, such as setting up electrical panels for major exhibits; hangs banners and other signage; prepares special platforms and displays; sets up exhibits; maintains the catering department's furniture, fixtures, and equipment (FFE). May also handle audio visual and lighting installation, teardown, and service.

Entree

In the United States, refers to the meal's main course. In Europe, the term refers to the appetizer.

Epergne

A container used as part of a centerpiece on a dining table. It has a slender center portion that does not obstruct the view across the table.

Family-style service

Another term for English service.

FFE

Acronym for "furniture, fixtures, and equipment."

Finish cooking

Preparing menu items to order.

Floor-length linen

Covers tables across the top and down to the floor.

Foams

Flavored toppings and garnishes. They are prepared in such a way that they can be sprayed onto a food or beverage from an aerosol container. They resemble whipped cream toppings purchased in aerosol containers. As with many foods, chefs can purchase them already made or make them in-house.

Food handler

There are various types, and their titles vary. A person handling food for a banquet or other similar event may be referred to as a cook, line cook, assistant chef, sous chef, banquet cook, cold food chef, or food steward. He or she prepares finished food products noted on the banquet event order and is responsible for having them ready according to schedule.

Food runner

Person assigned to supervise and replenish some or all of the food stations during a catered event.

Free pour

Liquors poured by hand without using shot glasses or other measuring devices.

French service—banquet style

Platters of food are composed in the kitchen. Each food item is then served from the guest's left by the server from platters. Any course can be "Frenched" by having the dressing put on the salad or having sauce added to an entree or dessert after it has been placed in front of the guest.

French service—cart style

This pattern of service involves the use of serving pieces (usually silver), heating and garnishing of food tableside by a captain, and serving of food on a heated plate, which is then placed before the guest by a server. Plated entrees are usually served from the right, bread and butter and salad from the left, and beverages from the right. All are removed from the right.

Front office

The heart of hotels and conference centers. It normally includes the reservations, PBX phone systems, registration, cashier, and guest services sections.

Function

A catered meal or beverage event.

Function sheet

Another term for banquet event order.

Full-service contractor

Outside supplier capable of providing several services to the client. Some contractors are capable of providing a one-stop shopping option.

Ganging menus

Occurs when two or more groups in a catering facility have the same menu on the same day. It can result in cost savings since food production can be more efficient. The caterer may also qualify for supplier discounts when purchasing a larger amount of food. These savings may then be passed on to clients.

Gel

A heat-resistant, colored transparent material placed in front of a light lens to bathe an area in a particular color.

Gratuity

Mandatory charge added by the caterer that typically is used to compensate the service staff. The typical gratuity for catered food and beverage events is about 18 to 22 percent of the food and beverage bill, depending on the type of property, location, service level, etc. Gratuities may be split between servers and other catering personnel. For instance, in Las Vegas, servers typically receive 86 percent of total gratuities while the remainder goes to the sales and operations management staff.

Green Book

Among other things, this publication explains how service is to be conducted for U.S. presidential protocol. It is not available for purchase since it contains information on presidential security.

Green event

An event that is planned and carried out utilizing only eco-friendly (biodegradable, compostable, or otherwise environmentally responsible) items and practices.

Guarantee

The minimum number of servings to be paid for by a client, even if some are not consumed. A caterer usually requires this type of guarantee to be solidified at least 72 hours in advance. Alternately, the amount of catering or noncatering business a client is expected to purchase (such as a specific number of sleeping rooms or minimum number of meals) in order to receive complimentary items (comps) from the caterer (such as free rental for a function room or upgraded meals at no extra cost).

Gueridon

A tableside cart with wheels.

Half-moon table

Half of a round table, or two quarter-round tables attached to make a half-circle. Also referred to as a half-round.

Hand service

There is one server for every two guests. Servers wear white gloves. Foods are pre-plated. Each server carries two covered plates from the kitchen and stands behind the two guests assigned to him or her. At a signal from the room captain, all servings are set in front of all attendees at the same time, and the plate covers removed.

Head count

Actual number of people attending a catered function.

Head table

Table used to seat VIPs, wedding parties, speakers, and other dignitaries; it is often elevated.

Hollow square setup

Tables are arranged to create a square pattern. Used for meetings where all attendees need to face each other and interact in discussions. Uses a large amount of space and generally is not conducive to large groups.

Hospitality suite

A place for attendees to gather outside of the meeting venues. It is normally open after dinner and typically begins after 10:00 PM. Occasionally it may open earlier in the day. Typically a variety of food and beverage is served.

Host bar

Another term for open bar.

Hosted bar

Another term for open bar.

House brand

When referring to spirit, it is another term for well brand. Alternatively, a product the restaurant serves when a guest orders something that is identified by a generic name, such as salad dressing, bread basket, or sweet rolls.

House wine

Wine recommended by the catering sales representative to clients who are on a tight budget. It is the caterer's well brand.

Houseman

Person who performs convention service activities. Physically sets up and tears down rooms with risers, hardware, tables, chairs, and other necessary equipment. Sometimes referred to as a porter or convention porter.

HVAC

Acronym for "heating, ventilation, and air-conditioning."

Incentive event

Celebratory event intended to showcase people who meet or exceed sales or production goals.

Incentive travel

A reward given by companies to employees who meet or exceed sales or production goals.

Inclusive price

Price that includes all food and beverage charges, applicable taxes, and gratuities. Sometimes referred to as an out-the-door price.

In conjunction with (ICW)

Affiliate events, or business that piggybacks on existing convention business. For example, an exhibitor may host a hospitality suite. The business exists solely because the main convention is being held. This type of business may make a group more valuable to the caterer.

Indemnification

Form of insurance. It is an agreement to hold harmless a party to a contract against any claims, losses, and damages, except those due solely to negligence or willful misconduct.

In-house service

Service provided directly and entirely by the facility in which an event is held.

Inventory shrinkage

The loss of products between point of manufacture or purchase from supplier and the point of sale. It relates to the difference in the amount of profit a retailer, such as a caterer, can obtain. Sometimes referred to as shrink.

Jigger spout

Adapter on a liquor bottle, used to pour a premeasured amount of liquor.

Job description

List of duties that make up a particular job position. May also include additional information, such as the job position's supervisor.

Job specification

List of qualities (such as type and amount of work experience and formal education) a job applicant must have in order to be considered for a particular job.

Jockey box

Portable unit that contains all the equipment necessary for cooling and dispensing keg beer. Ice water needs to be added to ensure temperature control. Typically used at outdoor special events and parties where electricity is not available. Sometimes referred to as a cold plate box or coil box.

Keg

Container holding bulk quantities of beer, wine, soft drinks, or soft drink syrups.

Kickback

An illegal gift given by a vendor or sales rep. to someone if he or she will agree to help defraud the catering operation. Alternatively, an illegal gift given by an outside service contractor to the caterer if he or she agrees to help defraud a client.

Labor cost

Includes the payroll cost plus the required employee benefits and discretionary employee benefits.

Landing space

The area where attendees can discard empty plates, glasses, soiled napkins, and waste. It can be a tray on a folding tray jack located next to a bar or against a wall. Alternatively, the area on a buffet table where attendees can place a drink or plate while deciding what foods to take.

Lectern

The preferred term for podium. A stand that rests on the floor or on a table. Speakers use them to hold their notes. The speaker usually stands behind the lectern, or slightly off to the side. Table lecterns are not floor height.

Leko light

Used for a long throw distance; creates a narrow beam of light. The design allows the use of shutters that can shape the beam of light.

Letter of agreement

Document used in lieu of a formal contract. It lists services, foods, beverages, prices, and so forth. It becomes binding when signed by the facility and the client.

Level pricing method

Pricing procedure. The caterer sets varying prices for similar functions and services. For instance, he or she may offer an economy-priced chicken dish, a high-end chicken dish, and other price points in between. In this example, clients can comparison-shop for different chicken dishes.

Light tree

Contains a base with two pipes forming a T. Lights hang off the crossbar.

Limited consumption bar

The client establishes a maximum dollar amount that he or she is prepared to spend. When serving drinks, the bartender rings up the price of each one, and when the maximum is reached, the bar may shut down. Typically, though, the bar stays open but reverts to a cash bar.

Linen

Tablecloths, napkins, and other table coverings.

Liqueur cart

Rolling cart that contains a selection of cordials and other types of after-dinner drinks.

Loss leader pricing method

Pricing procedure. The price covers at least the variable costs plus a little bit of profit; the caterer does not make the normal profit but neither does he or she have any out-of-pocket expense.

Maître d'hôtel

Floor manager in charge of all service personnel and oversight of all service aspects during meal and beverage functions. Sometimes referred to as a banquet captain.

Manpower agency

Firm specializing in providing day-labor workers.

Market segment

Group of potential customers who caterers focus on in order to attract their business. Major market segments include: business, association and SMERF, (social, military, educational, religious and fraternal). Some caterers focus instead on geographic location of where the client originates. Within all types of markets there are three financial levels; low (shallow), mid, and high (deep).

Meeting planner

Person who develops, executes, and coordinates every detail of a meeting, convention, conference, trade show, exhibition, or other similar function or event.

Merchant fee

Fee caterers pay for accepting credit card payments instead of cash or check. The fee is usually a percentage of the amount charged by the client.

Midlevel market

Market segment consisting primarily of association and business clients.

Minimum purchase

Smallest revenue amount required, or smallest number of covers or beverages that a caterer will agree to serve at a catered event. A surcharge may be added to a client's bill if the minimum is not reached.

Molecular gastronomy

The use of scientific practices and principles in cooking and food preparation.

Multiplier method

Pricing procedure. A variation of the contribution margin (CM) method of pricing. An item's price is calculated by multiplying the variable cost associated with the item by a factor that typically varies from about 3 to more than 7.

Napkin fold

A decorative way of folding a napkin.

Off-premise caterer

Most or all production is performed at a location that differs from the location used to service the event.

On-consumption pricing

The caterer charges clients only for the amount of product a group consumes.

On-premise caterer

Provides production and service in the same location.

Open bar

Guests do not pay for their drinks. The client or a sponsor takes care of paying for everything. Sometimes referred to as a host bar or hosted bar.

Open-space setup

Seating for meal functions is not assigned. Also, different types of seating arrangements may be offered. For instance, guests may be able to select sofa seating, stand-up tables, high-top tables, banquettes, and so on in addition to traditional seating at dining tables.

Oval table

A table of various proportions, used primarily as a dining table. The typical one used for catering measures 54 by 78 inches.

Overlay

Use of two tablecloths on a banquet table for decorative purposes. Usually two different colors are used, and the top cloth is smaller than the bottom one, allowing both to be seen.

Overset

Refers to the caterer's willingness to prepare a certain number of meals over the guaranteed number and to set aside some additional tables that are at least partially pre-set so that they can be pressed into service quickly, if needed. The purpose of an overset is to accommodate unexpected attendees who show up. If used, the typical overset is about 3 to 5 percent above the guaranteed number of meals. Also referred to as a set-over-guarantee.

PA system

A facility's in-house public address system.

PAR light

Used for short-throw distances; creates a wide beam of light. Can produce an intense oval pool of light.

Par stock

The maximum amount of a product you want to have on-hand. When reordering the product you want to buy (or requisition) just enough to bring you up to par.

Party planner

Works with clients to design and implement private parties.

Payroll cost

Includes the cost of wages and salaries.

PBX

Stands for "public branch exchange"; a type of phone system. The property's communications hub.

Per diem

Per day; also refers to a limited amount of money that an attendee or government employee is allowed to spend per day on food and other expenses.

Per person

A method of pricing food and/or beverages according to the number of guests expected to attend a catered event.

Pink collar

Consumer market consisting of people working in relatively safe, clean environments in traditionally female jobs. These jobs typically require less professional training than white-collar jobs.

Pipe and drape

Lightweight tubing and drapery used to separate exhibit booths, staging areas, or similar locations.

Place setting

Another term for cover.

Plated buffet

A selection of pre-plated foods is set on a buffet table for guests to choose from.

Plated service

Attendees are seated and served food that has been pre-portioned and plated in the kitchen. Also referred to as American service.

Plus plus

Addition of gratuities and taxes to the standard prices charged for food and beverages. Designated on a catering contract and BEO by the notation "+ +."

Podium

Another term for floor lecterns.

Poured-wine service

If part of a meal function, the wines may be opened and served at the dining tables. At more elaborate meals, cocktail servers or food servers may be supervised by a sommelier. If part of a reception, usually bartenders will pour wine, and in some cases servers will serve poured wine butlered style.

Pre-convention, (pre-con), meeting

Another term for pre-event meeting.

Pre-event meeting

Meeting between client and caterer to review the upcoming function and make last-minute adjustments.

Pre-function meeting

Another term for pre-event meeting.

Pre-function space

Area adjacent to a function room that may be used to house registration tables, display booths, and so forth. Alternatively, area adjacent to a function room where guests assemble just before it is time to enter the function room.

Premium brand

Indicates that the product is of high quality. It is more expensive than a call brand and much more expensive than a well brand.

Premium well brand

A well brand that is higher quality than the typical well brand poured by most bars. It is usually a call brand that is poured instead of a generic brand of liquor.

Pre-set service

Some food or beverage items are already on the table when guests arrive. The rest of the items are served with another type of service, such as plated (American) service.

Property manager

Responsible for all outside areas. Normally supervises landscaping, snow removal, pool and spa maintenance, and parking lot and sidewalk maintenance.

Proposal

Communication sent by a facility to a potential client detailing the facility's offerings and asking prices.

Proprietary brand

Another term for house brand or well brand.

Psychographics

Information about people's lifestyles and the way in which they perceive themselves.

Purchasing agent

Person whose primary responsibilities are to prepare product specifications for all foods, beverages, and supplies; select appropriate vendors; maintain adequate inventories; obtain the best possible purchase values; and ensure that product quality meets the property's standards.

Quarter-moon table

Quarter-round table. It is generally used as part of a buffet line.

Radial tablecloth drape

A cloth that drapes over a rectangular table and falls to just above the ground, and is not fitted, similar to that of a round tablecloth that falls to just above the ground on a round table.

Range pricing method

Pricing procedure. The caterer sets different prices for the same function, depending on the number of guests. Per-person prices will decrease as guest count increases. Similar to quantity discounts given by suppliers when purchasing agents buy a huge amount of product.

Reasonable pricing method

Pricing procedure. When setting a price, the caterer ponders, "If I were a customer, what would I be willing to pay for this meal?"

Reception

Stand-up social function at which beverages and light foods are served. Foods may be presented on small buffet tables or passed by servers. May precede a meal function.

Rechaud

A portable cooking stove.

Refresh

To clean a function room after a meeting, or during a meeting's break periods. Usually includes refilling water pitchers, removing soiled articles, changing glassware, and performing other housekeeping chores.

Refreshment break

Break time between meeting sessions. May include coffee, soft drinks, and some foods. Some breaks may be planned around a theme.

Rehearsal set

Amount of time needed to test the room setup to ensure that it will be adequate for the planned function. For instance, a keynote speaker may want to test the sound system and projection equipment after the room setup has been completed; if necessary, changes will be made at that time.

Request for proposal (RFP)

Used by clients who shop around for the best possible deals. It is a list of food, beverage, and services needed for a catered event and their specifications, given to potential caterers who are then asked to quote, or bid, the prices they would charge for them. Sometimes referred to as a request for quote (RFQ).

Resume

Summary of function room uses and other details of a convention or meeting. It is normally used whenever a meeting planner books two or more catered events to be held consecutively. Sometimes referred to as a convention resume.

REVPAR

Acronym for "revenue per available room." A way of measuring a hotel's financial performance.

Riser

Platform section used to build a stage or stairs.

Roll-in

Foods or beverages pre-set on rolling tables or carts and moved into a function room at a designated time.

Room service manager

In large hotels, room service typically handles hospitality functions that are held in a hotel suite. The client works with the room service manager to plan the service for this type of function. Generally the catering department is involved only when selling the event or when the hospitality suite is held in a public area.

Room turnover

Amount of time needed to tear down and reset a function room.

Round of 8

A 60-inch (5-foot) round table. It is usually used to seat 8 people, though it can seat 6 to 10 people. Sometimes referred to as an 8-top.

Round of 10

A 72-inch (6-foot) round table. It is usually used to seat 10 people, though it can seat 8 to 12 people. Sometimes referred to as a 10-top.

Round table, 66-inch

Dining table designed to take the place of the 60-inch and the 72-inch round. It can seat 8 to 10 people.

Russian service

Foods are cooked tableside on a rechaud that is on a gueridon. Servers place the food on platters (usually silver), then pass the platters at tableside. Guests help themselves from the platters.

SCAMPER

Acronym for a creative process that helps you think of major or minor adjustments you can make to an existing product or service or to create a fresh, original version. It is a brainstorming method that was created by Bob Eberle. The letters stand for "substitute, combine, adapt, modify/minimize/magnify, put to other purposes, eliminate, rearrange/reverse."

Scheduler

Enters bookings into the master log; oversees the timing of all functions and provides adequate turnover time; responsible for scheduling meeting rooms, reception areas, exhibit space, meal functions, beverage functions, and equipment requirements; keeps appropriate records to ensure against overbooking and double booking; responsible for communicating this information to all relevant departments. Sometimes referred to as a diary clerk.

Schoolroom table

Similar to the 6-foot and 8-foot banquet tables. It can be 18 or 24 inches wide and 6 or 8 feet long. Also referred to as a classroom table.

Security

Primarily responsible for crowd control and guest/employee safety. May also provide additional services, such as personal bodyguard for an event's high-profile speaker.

Seminar

A group receiving instruction and direction from an expert in a particular subject.

Serpentine table

S-shaped table typically used to add curves to a buffet line.

Server

There are various types. The most common ones are food servers, cocktail servers, and baristas. Food servers deliver foods, wine, nonalcoholic beverages, and utensils to tables; clear tables; and attend to guest needs. Cocktail servers perform similar duties but concentrate on serving alcoholic beverages, usually at receptions. Baristas prepare various coffee and tea drinks to order, then hand them off to other servers or serve them to guests personally.

Server parade

White-gloved servers march into the room and parade around the perimeter carrying food on trays, often to attention-getting music and dramatic lighting. When the entire room is circled, the music stops and service starts.

Service bar

Bar located outside a function room or a restaurant's public area. It is located in an area not visible to guests.

Service charge

A separate charge for labor.

Service contractor

Outside company used by clients or caterers to provide specific products or services, such as portable dance floors or flags.

Service ratios

Refers to the number of service personnel needed to handle a given number of guests.

Set-by time

The time that all the food, beverage, and service staff should be ready to go. It is usually about fifteen minutes before the function is scheduled to begin.

Set-over-guarantee

Another term for overset.

Set plate

Another term for base plate.

Shallow market

Portion of a market segment characterized by low-budget functions. These groups have limited resources and are very cost-conscious.

Show plate

Decorative plate pre-set at each place setting and removed before service begins.

Signature item

Product or service for which a facility is well known. The facility specializes in providing this item.

Silver service

Another term for Russian service.

Single-service contractor

Outside supplier that can provide only one service to the client. This contractor is usually a specialty supplier, such as a florist.

Skirting

Pleated or ruffled table draping used on buffet, reception, and head tables. Attaches to the side of the table and falls to just above the floor.

SMERF market

Acronym for "social, military, education, religious, and fraternal" market.

Sommelier

Wine steward; usually used only at upscale events.

Special event

A function that is more than just a standard meal or cocktail reception. There is another purpose for the event, such as a major fund-raiser, an awards banquet, or a fashion rollout.

Speed rail brand

Another term for well brand.

Spirits

Category of alcoholic beverage. Includes distilled beverages as well as many blends.

Split entree

Another term for dual entree.

Sponsored bar

Another term for open bar.

Station

A server's assigned area. Also refers to the individual buffet tables located throughout a function room or reception area, with each table offering one food item or representing one theme.

Steady

A server employed full-time by a facility.

Steward

Person whose major responsibilities include supervising kitchen sanitation and supervising the china, glass, and silver stockroom. Also referred to as an executive steward.

Stockout

Running out of a product; not having it available for guests who want it.

Swag

1) Term used to describe a cheap little trinket given to attendees so that they have something tangible to take with them after an event. Also referred to as a tchotchke. 2) Cloth streamers hung from a ceiling for decor.

Table drape

Table linen designed to cover the top of a table as well as extend covering down to the floor on all sides. Typically used for display tables at events and trade show booths.

Tent

Portable shelter. Usually used to house outdoor functions, but may also be used as a storage facility during an off-premise event.

Theme party

Party at which all foods, beverages, decorations, and entertainment relate to a single topic or idea.

Thirds method

Pricing procedure. Involves calculating a per-person price that will cover three things equally: (1) the cost of food, beverage, and other supplies (such as linen, dance floor, etc.); (2) the cost of labor needed to handle the function, plus overhead expenses needed to open the room (such as turning on the air-conditioning units, etc.); and (3) profit.

Ticket exchange

Banquet-control procedure whereby guests exchange event coupons for entry into the function room and, if appropriate, their seat assignments.

Ticket taker

Responsible for collecting tickets from guests before they are allowed to enter a function.

Tip

Voluntary gift. Usually given by clients in addition to a gratuity for extra service and/or superlative service.

Trade-out

Another term for barter. Instead of paying with cash, you may be able to trade something else.

Trial-and-error pricing method

Pricing procedure. The caterer relies on experience and intuition to set the price. If a price doesn't work, another one is tried. Amounts to educated guessing.

Truss

Framework suspended from the ceiling to hold lighting, draping, or decor.

Umami

A meaty, savory taste.

Underliner

Plate used under a bowl, a glass, condiment containers, and so forth.

Union call

Additional servers obtained from a union labor source shared by several catering facilities and foodservice operations. Servers and bartenders are hired as needed from this common labor source to work individual functions.

Upgrade

Something added to a catered function that is not part of the normal package; for example, extra servers for a wedding reception. The caterer will charge extra for this.

Upsell

Encouraging clients to purchase upgrades or more products and services than they initially planned.

U-shape setup

Tables are arranged to create a horseshoe pattern, surrounding a great deal of empty floor space. Usually used when attendees want to hold a meeting and meal function in the same room at the same tables. Attendees can conduct their meeting and, when it is time to eat, roll-ins can be placed in the room to allow self-service.

Value-driven pricing method

Another term for volume-driven pricing method.

Volume-driven pricing method

Pricing procedure a company will use to maintain a high level of activity in order to protect and increase its customer base and market share, even though at times it may necessitate lower prices in order to fill the room.

Walk-and-talk

A reception held during standard dinner hours. Intended to take the place of dinner.

Water station

Table or side stand with pitchers or other containers of water and glassware. May also include other types of soft drinks. Usually intended to be a self-service station.

Wave

A service method in which servers are not assigned workstations or tables. All servers start at one end of the room and work straight across to the other end for both service and plate removal.

Well brand

Refers to a spirit that customers order by type of liquor and not by brand name. *See also* Call brand; Premium brand.

White collar

Consumer market consisting of professional people or those whose jobs are clerical in nature.

Notes

Chapter 5:   Beverage Functions

1. http://www.foodnavigator.com/Financial-Industry/Wild-identifies-key
   -threebeverage-trends
2. http://entertaining.about.com/cs/recipesandmenus/a/beveragetrends.htm

Appendix

ACTION STATIONS

Pasta Station
Penne Pasta and Spinach Tortellini Filled with Ricotta Cheese
Alfredo, Creamy Pesto and Fresh Marinara Sauces
Medley of Fresh Italian Vegetables
Displayed with Warm Garlic Bread Sticks and
Freshly Grated Romano and Parmesan Cheeses
$ 11.50 per person

Asian Stir-Fry Station
Choice of Boneless Breast of Chicken or Shrimp
Stir Fried with Diced Asian Vegetables,
Bamboo Shoots, and Water Chestnuts
Steamed Jasmine Rice
Fortune Cookies and Chopsticks
$ 12.50 per person

Carving Station

Whole Roasted Tenderloin of Angus Beef to serve 30 guests ....$ 370.00
Roasted Turkey to serve 50 guests...$ 325.00
Honey Glazed Ham to serve 50 guests.... $ 295.00

Each station requires an attendant at $100.00 each
for a two-hour function.
Add $35.00 for each additional hour.
All food and beverage prices are subject to a 19 percent
service charge and applicable sales tax.
Prices will be quoted inclusive of the service
charge and tax upon request.

CATERING FUNCTION CHECKLIST

The following list shows important items that should be discussed with or explained to the client:

A. GENERAL INFORMATION

          1. Name of Client/Group _____

              Type of Function _____

              Address_____

              Date of Function _____

              Person in Charge _____

              Phone Number _____

              Fax Number _____

              E-Mail Address _____

  _____   2. Person(s) authorized to sign the check

  _____   3. How and where will meeting be posted?

  _____   4. Billing address. If different from confirmation address

  _____   5. Attendance (explain guarantee and overset policy)

  _____   6. Will registration or course materials be delivered to the facility?

  _____   7. How are messages to be handled?

  _____   8. Ticket control (Do servers pick up tickets? does this include the head table?)

  _____   9. Will there be an invocation? anthem? opening remarks?

  _____   10. Starting and ending times (be specific for all functions)

  _____   11. Review labor and service charges with client

B. ROOM SETUP

  _____   12. Type of setup–seating arrangements (rounds, u-shaped, classroom, etc.)

  _____   13. Head table size (number to be seated, elevated on a platform, etc.)

  _____   14. Staging requirements (get specific height, width, and length)

  _____   15. Will a display table be needed?

  _____   16. Will a registration table be needed?

  _____   17. Legal pads and pens/pencils–upsell

_____ 18. Bottled water–upsell

_____ 19. Candy–upsell

_____ 20. Will banners need to be hung?

_____ 21. Lighting requirements

_____ 22. Special linen requirements

_____ 23. All functions over 299 people to have a floor plan

_____ 24. American or state flag needed?

_____ 25. Piano?

C. AUDIOVISUAL REQUIREMENTS

_____ 26. Number of podium(s) needed. Table top or floor?

_____ 27. Amplification and number of microphones

_____ 28. Number of easels

_____ 29. Blackboards

_____ 30. Electrical requirements

_____ 31. Specific AV needs (e.g., electric pointer, LCD projector, DVD player, size of screen, Wi-Fi, etc.)

D. DECORATIONS AND MUSIC

_____ 32. Upsell music requirements (background dinner music, pianist, harp, flute, strolling strings, dance band, music for theme coffee breaks, etc.)

_____ 33. Upsell table centerpieces (e.g., fresh arrangement, silk flowers, candles, etc.)

_____ 34. Upsell decorations (theme props, trees, backdrops, etc.)

_____ 35. Upsell special table settings

_____ 36. Upsell special printed menus

_____ 37. Upsell special lighting

E. BREAKFAST

_____ 38. Upsell virtues of a group breakfast versus premeeting coffee break

_____ 39. Upsell new menu ideas

_____ 40. Upsell upgraded buffets or brunch

_____ 41. Upsell champagne or "eye-openers" (mimosas, screwdrivers, bloody Marys, etc.)

F. REFRESHMENT BREAKS

_____   42. Upsell a premeeting continental breakfast if a full group breakfast is not planned

_____   43. Upsell distinctive (theme) midmorning and midafternoon breaks

_____   44. Upsell flavored coffees

G. LUNCHEON

_____   45. Upsell an appetizer selection

_____   46. Upsell upgraded salad (Caesar, Nicoise, specialty dressing, etc.)

_____   47. Upsell new entrée ideas

_____   48. Upsell premium vegetable sides (artichokes, snow peas, etc.)

_____   49. Upsell specialty desserts (crepes, peach Melba, Haagen Daz ice cream, etc.)

_____   50. What type of wine would the client prefer? (Upsell a champagne toast for awards or retirement luncheons)

_____   51. Offer a selection of ethnic menus for variety

H. RECEPTIONS

_____   52. Bar arrangements (host or cash)

_____   53. Explain bartender charge

_____   54. Upsell theme menus

_____   55. Upsell action stations (pasta, gyros, etc.)

_____   56. Upsell in-room carving and/or action stations

_____   57. Upsell passed hors d'oeuvres

_____   58. Upsell an additional reception to follow dinner

I. DINNER

_____   59. Upsell upgraded appetizer (shrimp cocktail, crab legs, etc.)

_____   60. Upsell soup course (French onion, clam chowder, etc.)

_____   61. Upsell upgraded salad (Caesar tossed tableside or individual salads dressed by servers)

_____   62. Upsell champagne, dessert wine, or cordials

_____   63. Upsell special blend or flavored coffees and liqueur station

_____   64. Upsell specialty dessert (waiter parade of baked Alaska or flaming cherries jubilee prepared tableside, etc.)

Appetizer: _____

Soup: _____

Salad: _____

Intermezzo: _____

Entrée: _____

Dessert: _____

Wines: _____

Floral Requirements

Tables: Number _____ Size _____ Type _____

Buffets: Type _____ Quantity _____

               Type _____ Quantity _____

Bride: _____

Groom: _____

Bridesmaids: _____

Wedding Party: _____

Best Man: _____

Cake: _____

Photographer: Name _____ Phone _____

                      Time of Attendance _____

Videographer: Name _____ Phone _____

                      Time of Shooting _____

Cake: Bakery _____ Phone _____

          Type _____ Spec. Requirements _____

          Delivery Time: _____ Refrigerate: ____ Yes   No ____

Cake Knife and Server: _____

Bride and Groom Glasses: _____

Cocktail Napkins: Color _____ Quantity _____

       Inscription _____

       Printer _____ Phone _____

       Date Promised _____

Floor Plan: _____

POST EVENT EVALUATION

Event Name: _____

Event Date(s): _____

Client profile: _____

Attendee profile: _____

Profitability: _____

Challenges in sales process, execution, or planning: _____

Overall success (client, attendees): _____

Food and beverage (special diets, special products, unusual setups, theme parties, etc.):_____

What portion of the budget was spent on décor? _____

Room rental charge? _____

Was anything provided as complimentary? At a discounted price? If so, what? _____

_____

Feasibility of repeat bookings? _____

Additional comments, recommendations: _____

_____

_____

   (signed)   (title)   (date)

EVENT RECAP FORM

Show: _____   Date: _____

Date(s): _____   Department: _____

Dept. Head/Manager:_____

Sales Executive: _____

Event Coordinator: _____

Overview:

A. Staffing (Concerns, Problems–Service Problems, Delays, etc.–Comments)

_____

_____

_____

_____

_____

_____

_____

B. Culinary/Bakery _____

_____

_____

_____

C. Stewarding (Equipment, Follow-Up, etc.) _____

_____

_____

_____

D. Catering Sales_____

_____

_____

_____

_____

_____

E. Commissary _____

_____

_____

F. Operations (Set-Up, Housekeeping, Engineering, etc.) _____

_____

_____

_____

_____

SPECIAL MEAL REQUEST FORM

Following this form are the menus for the entire conference. As caterers, we realize that not all guests are able to consume the same foods. Some individuals have specific dietetic requirements, and some have specific dislikes (such as seafood, game meats, etc.). Please take a moment to look over the menus. If a menu features an entrée that you cannot eat, fill out the following information and return it to the Registration Desk. Please make sure that your Special Meal Requests are turned in by 10:30 A.M. on Saturday morning to allow time for the kitchen to accommodate the request.

Name _____

Meal Function Requiring Change _____

_____

Meal Requested _____

Name _____

Meal Function Requiring Change _____

_____

Meal Requested _____

Name _____

Meal Function Requiring Change _____

_____

Meal Requested _____

Name _____

Meal Function Requiring Change _____

_____

Meal Requested _____

Name _____

Meal Function Requiring Change _____

_____

Meal Requested _____

Index